WE DON'T WANT
NOBODY
NOBODY SENT

MILTON L. RAKOVE

We Don't Want Nobody Nobody Sent

AN ORAL HISTORY OF THE DALEY YEARS

INDIANA UNIVERSITY PRESS · BLOOMINGTON & LONDON

Manufactured in the United States of America

Library of Congress Cataloging in Publication Data

Rakove, Milton L
    We don't want nobody nobody sent.

    1. Chicago—Politics and government—1950–2. Daley, Richard J.,
1902–1976. I. Title. F548.52.R35   320.9'773'1104   79–5024
ISBN 0–253–17915–7
1 2 3 4 5 83 82 81 80 79

In memory of
Jacob and Rose Rakove
and Louis and Nellie Bloom

CONTENTS

FOREWORD BY
RICHARD M. DALEY   *The eldest son of the late Mayor Richard J. Daley. About thirty-six years old. Is a state senator and succeeded his father as Democratic ward committeeman of the 11th ward. Is also an attorney.*

I have no fear of how history will judge my father as a public official and a politician. My father was honored to be called a politician. The phrase that he used to express his governmental life was, "Good government is good politics and good politics is good government." To some it was a cliché, but to him it was the essence of his life. He believed that there must be a party responsibility as well as an individual responsibility with people. He believed in using his political structure as a way of assuring the accountability of government to its citizens. He was always proud, when he placed his name on a ballot, to be elected by its citizens rather than be appointed or anointed. The elected official responds more favorably to the citizens than the twentieth-century bureaucrat. During the 1950s and 1960s, during the great suburban expansion, my father, as mayor, believed in positive programs, in order to benefit not only the city of Chicago but also the suburban and county areas. A healthy city makes a healthy suburban area. My father was acknowledged as a fiscal expert and administrative genius. He gave full support to Chicago's commercial, cultural, educational, and labor communities. He became a symbol of our city's strength and determination, and the cherished values of the church, the home, and the neighborhood. More important for me, he was a great father. Learning directly from him was an education in itself, an experience that taught me to respect every person's opinion and realize the important quality that each person has in the political system with his cherished vote. Every time my father saw a child hungry or an older person isolated in society, he dedicated himself, personally, to that person or individual. He left our city better than when he came to office—a city able to face the future with confidence and determination and with an "I Will" spirit for each and every one of us.

Excerpted from remarks made by Senator Daley at a conference sponsored by the University of Illinois, Chicago Circle, at the Chicago Historical Society on October 14, 1977.

PREFACE

This book is about the Daley years in Chicago, about the politics of those years, and about people who were involved in politics in Chicago during those years.

I began the research on this book three years ago, a few months before Richard J. Daley died on December 20, 1976. Daley was then seventy-four years old and was in his sixth term as mayor of Chicago. It was clear that an era in Chicago's history was coming to an end, a period of almost a quarter of a century in which one man, Richard J. Daley, had dominated the city. No one had ever done so before, nor was it likely anyone would ever do so again.

Those years were the most important in the long and turbulent history of Chicago politics. They were also one of the most significant periods in American urban history, because they were the years when Chicago's Democratic political machine, under Daley's leadership, was at the apex of its power.

Contemporary observers have traditionally referred to the Chicago machine as "the Daley machine." But the machine was there long before Daley came to power and has survived Daley's passing, because it was, and still is, rooted in the character of the city, reflective of its polyglot population, and representative of the aspirations and drives of the constituent elements of the community.

Chicago, in the Daley era, was a microcosm of the nationwide urban revolutionary changes that swept over America's cities after World War II—the great migration of blacks and Latins into our cities; the flight of the white middle class to the suburbs; the transition from a big-city industrial society to an urbanized metropolitan society; and the concomitant cultural, social, economic, and political problems that were engendered by all of these changes. But Chicago differed from other cities in clinging to something most urban historians have regarded as archaic and obsolete in American life—the machine politics that had characterized the rapid growth of our cities in the earlier years of the twentieth century.

Mayor Daley was the most important cog in the Chicago machine, but he alone did not represent the political processes and political history of his era in Chicago. The Chicago machine was a complex structure, encompassing many elements of the community, and layered through the county, city, ward, and precinct levels. It was highly decentralized, feudalistically structured, and loosely tied together by a network of relationships among its constituent parts. There was authority at the top, but highly decentralized responsibility at the various levels of the system.

In order to understand the political dynamics of the Daley years in Chicago one must go beyond the late mayor's life and career, reach down into the infrastructure of the machine, and understand the aspirations, motivations, and actions of a broad range of people who were active participants in the political arena in that period.

That is what this book attempts to do—to present a portrait, not a photo, of the Daley years in Chicago through the spoken words of some of those participants. I learned years ago, as a student of Professor Hans J. Morgenthau at the University of Chicago, that for the political historian there is a difference between a photograph and a painted portrait. According to Morgenthau, "The photograph shows everything that can be seen by the naked eye; the painted portrait does not show everything that can be seen by the naked eye, but it shows, or at least seeks to show, one thing that the naked eye cannot see: the human essence of the person portrayed."

This book, then, is a portrait of the human essence of the politics of the Daley years in Chicago, as that essence was experienced and understood by some of the figures on the canvas of that scene. It focuses, not on Daley, but on the "why" and "how" of the behavior of Chicago politicians, and describes the "who" and "what" of the city's politics, using the tape-recorded interview as a research tool.

There were significant problems in utilizing this research technique. One was, for me, a major technical problem—I had never before used a tape recorder. There were problems of what questions could be safely asked of politicians, of reducing a two-hour interview and thirty pages of typewritten material to a few meaningful pages of text, of whom to interview, and then of which interviews to use. And there was always the problem, inherent in any work of this kind, of people presenting themselves, their motives, and their actions in the best possible light, and glossing over their inadequacies, errors, and failings. I have tried to take that into account in editing the tapes.

I decided at the beginning that I would only ask questions about the political side of politics, and would ignore the economic side, since no politician would talk about such matters on a tape recorder. As Alderman Tom Keane, the number-two man in the machine during the Daley years, said when he was approached to write a book about his political life and experiences, "What do they want me to do, put everybody in the penitentiary?" And, once, when asked by a close friend of mine, Father Joseph Small of Loyola University, whether he would be willing, for research purposes, to discuss a certain situation in Chicago in which he had played a major role, Keane responded in a gravel-voiced whisper, "I'll tell you about that in the confessional, Father."

I also decided early in the interviewing process that I would limit the book to people who were active participants in Chicago politics at various levels, and who represented a variety of backgrounds, viewpoints, and experiences, drawn from the rich, unmelted melting pot of Chicago's population, using ethnicity, race, religion, age, and geography as criteria for selection.

The book begins, in Chapter I, Prologue, with a look at the pre-Daley era in Chicago. Chapters II, III, and IV—The Old Guard, The Foot Soldiers, and The Young Turks—draw on the experiences of the key minions in the machine: the old-line ward committeemen, the precinct captains, and the rising young ward committeemen who were latecomers to the Daley era. Chapters V, VI, and VII offer viewpoints from special interest groups within the machine—blacks, women, and suburban township committeemen. Chapter VIII, The Losers, gives the reader some exposure to the six men who ran against Daley for the mayoralty of Chicago. Chapter IX, Some Dissidents, deals with Democrats who, once loosely or tightly allied to the machine, broke with it and suffered the consequences. And Chapter X, The Loyal Opposition, offers criticism and analysis of the machine and of Daley from a perspective outside of the machine.

Except for those in Chapter III, The Foot Soldiers, the interviewees are drawn from a broad geographic base. In the case of Chapter III I decided to limit the interviews to precinct captains from Alderman Vito Marzullo's West Side 25th ward, feeling that the reader would get a much better picture of precinct-level machine politics if I concentrated on a single typical, machine-run ward that mirrored the great cultural changes which had occurred in the Daley years. The 25th ward fulfilled these criteria.

I had hoped to include a chapter on people who worked closely with Daley. But nobody who had been close to Daley, with the exception of Mayor Jane Byrne, would consent to be interviewed on a tape recorder. I was not surprised. Daley would not have done it either. In fact, I asked him to give me an interview in the summer of 1976, when I first began to work on this book. Great politician that he was, he said, "Call me after the election in November." I did call and ask for an appointment on the day he died. But it would not have made any difference. He would not have given me or anyone else such an interview while he was in office. There were also some other key political figures in the Daley era with whom I was unable to arrange an interview, and some who were unwilling to do so.

I am grateful to all of those who did share some of their experiences, thoughts, recollections, and analyses with me on a tape recorder for this book, and ask their tolerance for whatever shortcomings emerge in the manuscript from the need to edit the tapes, sometimes severely, in order to put together a readable book. The tapes, including some I could not use for various reasons, will be available for reference for students, scholars, and interested citizens at the Chicago Public Library, the Chicago Historical Society, and the University of Illinois at Chicago Circle.

The *Chicago Sun-Times'* Herman Kogan, a Chicago historian in his own right, is responsible for the title of this book. It was he who came up with it, after I had told him about some of the incidents recounted by the politicians I had interviewed.

I owe an unmeasurable debt to Henry Walli, Manager of Campus Audiovisual Services, Office of Instructional Resource Development, at the University of Illinois at Chicago Circle, and to his excellent staff, particularly Richard Bieniek. They were at all times patient, helpful, and efficient in providing assistance and guidance to a neophyte trying to master the mechanics of using a tape recorder effectively.

My family has contributed in a number of ways to this book. My son, Jack, helped give me an historical framework and guidelines for organizing the material for this book. My daughter-in-law, Helen, counseled me on the legal problems of an oral history. My daughter, Roberta, and my son-in-law, Michael Plumpton, compiled the glossary and shared their insights into Chicago political life with me. My wife, Shirley, labored over this manuscript at least as much as I did. In a very real sense she is the co-author of this work. Finally, our grandson, Robert Benjamin Rakove, contributed by arriving on June 28, 1977, and enriching our lives for the past two years.

Chicago   Milton L. Rakove
June, 1979

ONE

Prologue: Background of the Daley Era

JACOB M. ARVEY / RALPH BERKOWITZ /
BUNNIE EAST / EDISON LOVE

JACOB M. ARVEY *Jewish. Long-time Democratic power-house. Alderman and ward committeeman of the West Side's 24th ward, called by President Franklin D. Roosevelt "the banner Democratic ward in the United States." Arvey was also Democratic Cook County Chairman 1946–1950, was a major force in the Democratic Party, and was close to President Harry Truman. Died in 1977 at the age of eighty-two.*

My father came here in 1892 from Poland, what was then Russia. He then sent for my mother and my four older brothers. She came here in 1894. He had a milk store on Pacific Avenue, now called LaSalle Street, between Harrison and Polk. On November 3, 1895 (not that it is an historic day), I was the first child born to them in America. This made me, in my father's eyes, a symbol of what he had striven for all the years, to come to America and find opportunity here for his children. My father died when I was thirteen. We then moved to what is now the 24th ward. I went to Crane Technical High School for the better part of a year. There was need for me to work. I worked all day and went to night school five nights a week, for six years, from the time I was fifteen until I was twenty-one, made up my high school credits, then went to law school. In November 1916, when I had become twenty-one years old, I took the bar examination and passed it.

In 1914, my law professor, a man named William J. Lindsey, ran as an independent candidate for judge and I volunteered to help him in a precinct in the 24th ward. I knew nothing about canvassing a precinct, but I took my job seriously, and got a great many votes for him against the machine. What I did attracted the attention of the political powers in the 24th ward (at that time it was the 34th ward), and both the head of the Roger Sullivan organization and the Carter Harrison organization tried to enlist me to participate in the 1915 election. I went with the Sullivan faction and I campaigned for Robert M. Schweitzer for mayor in 1915, even though I could not vote myself.

I learned about registration and all the other things that have to do with bringing the voters out to vote—literature and that sort of thing. In 1922, I was very active in the campaign of Mike Rosenberg, who was our committeeman and sanitary district trustee. All this time I'd been very active in B'nai B'rith, Young Men's Hebrew Association, and civic affairs. In 1923, when I was twenty-seven years old, there was a place open for alderman in the newly redistricted 24th ward, and I was lucky enough to be elected. I became the Democratic committeeman of the 24th ward in 1934, with the death of Moe Rosenberg. The precinct captains elected me unanimously, by the way.

I am more proud of my tenure as committeeman than I am of my stewardship as chairman of the party. I'll tell you why. I'm an intense Jew. This was a Jewish ward and I was able, by the grace of God and the power which He put in my hands, to make our ward organization an instrument of good. I demanded that any man who was a precinct captain of mine had to belong to a church—Catholic, Protestant, or Jewish. He had to belong to some organization—Elks, B'nai B'rith, Knights of Columbus, Masons, something. Now, there are some who said, "Sure, very astute, I wanted to extend my influence, I wanted people in all these things." They did help me politically. I admit that. There's no question about it. But, in the process, I made them charity-minded, civic-minded, culture-minded, and sensitive to the needs of other people. Sure, I was looking for votes. But, when I'd make a speech I'd say, "Ladies and gentlemen, you know what we've been doing in this ward. You know that no man goes hungry in this ward. You know we try to help whenever we can. We're able to do that because we have power, we have influence. And when you give me a mandate by your vote, I can go downtown to the leaders of our party and I can *demand* things, not ask for them, because they know that when I speak, I speak for you. I speak for a 25,000-vote majority." I am very candid about it. I never spoke for the people of my ward exclusively, but for the Jewish people.

And I didn't turn that vote out. My precinct captains turned it out. In the election of 1936, President Roosevelt called our ward the best Democratic ward in the country. The vote was about 29,000 for Roosevelt to about 700 for Landon. Every time we rolled up a majority like that, they would say, "Vote fraud." I pleaded with the newspapers, the election commissioners, and the state's attorney's office to come into my ward. They did, time and time again. And there were some discrepancies. But when you win by 25,000, you don't need any fraud. I would stir them up (maybe it's my fault), I would get them to compete with each other. And each precinct captain

wanted to be the premier precinct captain of the ward. He wanted
to be number one. And some of them went to illegal means to do it.
I know it. I regret it very much, but they were inconsequential in
relation to the ultimate result.

Let me tell you a story. There was an Italian family who moved
into a precinct of one of my precinct captains. There were six in the
family—man and wife and two daughters married to men with a
different name than the head of the house, but they all lived together. The head of the house was related to one of the most influential Republican politicians of Chicago. My precinct captain cultivated
them—six votes is an awful lot. He was not a drinking man but he had
to drink "Dago Red" every once in a while. In the mayoral campaign
of 1939, State's Attorney Tom Courtney ran against Ed Kelly for
mayor. My precinct captain, of course, was for Kelly, and was determined to make a good showing. He went to this man and asked him
to vote in the Democratic primary for Kelly. The man said, "I can't
do that! My cousin is a Republican committeeman. How would it be
if I voted in the Democratic primary?" My man kept after him for
one month and finally succeeded in working out this compromise—
that the two who bore the name of the cousin would vote Republican
so that it wouldn't reflect upon the cousin, and the other four, with
other names, would vote Democratic. That's the extent to which
they went to get votes.

I'll tell you about another incident to show you what some of our
precinct captains did. The 24th ward was fundamentally Jewish, but
we had two Catholic churches and a Lutheran church in the ward.
Saint Finbar's Church was in one of the precincts of our ward. Sam
Koppel was the precinct captain. He was very active in the church's
affairs. He was Jewish, he belonged to a synagogue, but he was very
friendly with Father McKinney, and they had a bazaar every year.
Sam Koppel would enlist the aid of many Jewish people in the precinct to help run the bazaar. One of them happened to be an old
Jewish man with a white beard who spoke broken English. I brought
Mayor Kelly, who was a Roman Catholic, out to the bazaar. We were
walking through, and this old Jew with the white beard was in charge
of a booth and needed some change. So he ran after Father McKinney yelling, "Father! Father! I need some change." Mayor Kelly
turned to me and he said, "Now that's real brotherhood."

I'll tell you how we ran our ward organization. We didn't start
working a month or two before election. We worked all year 'round.

We had weekly amateur prizefights, picnics, marathon runs, track meets. I would always try to get some literature to have our precinct captains bring in the homes from the B'nai B'rith Lodge, American Jewish Congress, or some political news about the New Deal or Roosevelt. I would always try to find ways of making my precinct captains more convenient to and more intimately associated with their voters. If I ever found a voter who wasn't seen at least two or three times a year by a precinct captain, I'd raise hell. This became a family affair—one man told another. You were kind enough to ask about Pauline [Arvey's long-time ward secretary]. She was at the headquarters every single day. The precinct captains would send people to her. We talk about patronage. During the Depression we had more jobs for people in our ward in private industry than we had in political offices.

We did a lot of things for business people. They were my friends. George Eisenberg was my cousin. Ninety percent of his employees were from the 24th ward. We got into Sears Roebuck. We were very enterprising because we were hungry for jobs, for the opportunities to do favors for people. This is hard for some people to believe! They think that in politics you go to a man, you send him literature, or you have a meeting, and you try to get his vote. Let me put it this way. You certainly don't vote by slogans and you don't vote one way because a precinct captain comes and sees you. But, on election day, there may be twenty men running for county commissioner. You don't know any of them, and the precinct captain who's been able to be of service to you comes to you and he says, "Mr. Rakove, Jack Arvey's running for county commissioner, he's a fine man, he's a friend of mine, and it'd help me an awful lot if you'd vote for him." And you'd do it, unless you had some interest in the man running against me, unless it were a candidate running for governor, or there were some issues involved, some reason for you to think the other man or I was no good. But, knowing nothing about it, it's just an act of friendship, an act of gratitude. "Sure. You want Jack Arvey? Okay, I'll vote for him." But people don't understand that. It's a matter of friendship.

It boils down to work. Let me put it in a crude way—put people under obligation to you. Make them your friends. You don't like to hurt a friend. In positions of power in the party, I had to rule against my friends—my close friends. But, barring that, I would certainly help a friend. And that's politics—put a man under obligation. I don't mean obligation in the sense that you

owe me something, but I like the story of the Italian family. He
became his friend. How could he vote against his friend? He
wasn't voting for Kelly against Courtney—he was voting for Elrod
against Courtney, don't you see?

*Is that also true of national politics, where people vote for
offices like president?*

No, that's altogether different. Our ward in 1922 went big for the
local ticket, but in 1924 the ward voted for a Republican president.
People know more about national candidates. The same with a
mayor or a governor. They hear more about it, they read more about
it, and they make up their own minds as to whether the Republican
or Democratic candidate for governor is the better man. But voting
for county commissioner or judges of the municipal court (you vote
for a lot of men, vote against a lot of men), you don't know them. With
the ballot the way it is, a man would have to take a two-month course
to learn about all the candidates. Which, by the way, is one of the
evils of our system. I believe in election rather than appointment, but
you can't do the right thing. If you could elect men at the top who'd
be honest, intelligent, and dedicated to public good, then let them
appoint the other men. But you can't always get that. I believe in the
elective system because of that.

But a ward committeeman, in terms of patronage, would pay more
attention to a local candidate than he would a candidate for president. If you're dealing with issues, with a matter of principle, if you
have certain ideas about government, you'd be more interested in
the president. Look, I had a tough time in 1972 voting for McGovern.
I had to do it only for one reason. I felt that Nixon was a crook. I
remember him in 1946 and '48 and '50 against Helen Gahagan
Douglas, my good friend. I couldn't vote for him. And there was one
time when it looked like a certain Democrat would be nominated for
president. I wouldn't have voted. I'd have gone to Israel so I'd have
an excuse not to vote. And I remember a time when Carter Harrison
was Democratic candidate for mayor. I voted for him, but I held my
finger to my nose.

Did you know Mayor Big Bill Thompson?

Very well. He was inept. They say he was corrupt, but I don't
know. I do know that he was very sick in the last few years of his term.
I had occasion to go to him, together with Alderman Oscar Nelson,
his floor leader, and Alderman John S. Clark, our Democratic leader

at that time, in 1928 or 1929, on an ordinance. I was chairman of the committee on utilities and I tried to explain the telephone ordinance to him and what it meant to the city in terms of revenue, and I'm sorry to say that when we finished, this conversation revealed that he hadn't understood the first thing that we were saying to him. He rode a wave, at a time when people, during Prohibition, wanted liberty of expression, liberty of action, and Big Bill the Builder said, "I'll fire any policeman who closes your saloon on a Sunday!" He was not the least of the demagogues that we have had. He was a product of his times.

What was politics like in Chicago in those days?

Well, it was a submission to "What can you get?" I don't mean bribes and stuff, but bookies ran wide open. Saloons didn't run wide open but there were speakeasies. Nobody bothered them. Prohibition was an unpopular law. Anti-gambling was unpopular. People would meet men that they knew were bookies, they treated them like they do in London, England, as first-class citizens. They weren't degraded at all. They weren't demeaned by the fact that they were doing an illegal act. I knew some men who were bookies in the old days who were well respected—real estate operators, capitalists, and very acceptable in high society. This was the aftermath of Prohibition and our attempt to regulate the lives of our citizens. Just let me give you an example. What would happen to these movie theatres of today if they tried to operate in the '20's? They would close 'em up. But this was a different sense of morality. This was against their Bible, their religion, their sense of morality. Whereas gambling and drinking were not.

What was Mayor Tony Cermak like?

Cermak was one of the most intelligent non-educated men I ever knew in my life. He would have submitted to him a report by engineers in technical language which he didn't understand when he read it. But, after he asked ten or fifteen questions, he knew as much about it as the men who prepared the report. He went to fourth grade in grammar school, but was a very practical man, and a very able man. Now, what kind of a mayor he would have made, I can't tell. He only served from 1931 to 1933, a year and a half. He installed me as his floor leader.

Some people say Pat Nash and Ed Kelly built what is called the

Daley machine, but it was Cermak who built it. In 1928 he stole a march on the old-line Democrats by making an alliance with Governor Dineen and submitting a good government ticket of judges. He elected them, and in 1930 he became leader and we elected our ticket, and in 1931 he was elected mayor.

When Cermak was killed in 1933, how did Ed Kelly become mayor?

Under state law, the city council was limited in its choice to a member of the council. Pat Nash at that time became the leader of the party and he was Irish. He was my loyal good friend and he wanted me. There was some suggestion that I would be the successor. Nash thought, and I agreed with him and other Jews (Henry Horner had just been elected governor after a bitter primary fight with Mike Igoe) that to have a governor of Illinois Jewish, and a mayor of Chicago Jewish, at that time would have been rubbing it in to the Irish. Under state law the city council was limited in its choice to a member of the council. So, with the aid of Governor Horner, we had the legislature pass a law removing that limitation. It was then that we selected Ed Kelly, who was then chief engineer of the sanitary district. He was a colorful figure, very active in politics, had never sought office, and Pat Nash wanted him. There were other potential candidates. I was one. Jim Bowler was one. John Clark was one. As a matter of fact, we had a fight in the council to select Corr as acting mayor. Frank Corr became the acting mayor until the legislature could pass the law removing the limitation.

What kind of a man was Pat Nash?

Everyone knew that he was a loyal man—a man of his word and very direct. Never said anything he didn't mean. I loved him like a father. We disagreed once in a while. He was a patriarch. He was paternalistic. He had this little Irish smile, very seldom lost his head —which, unfortunately, many Irish politicians do. But everyone knew that he didn't want anything for himself. We all followed him implicitly, faithfully. I did. Even if I disagreed with him, I would bow to his judgment in the end. When Nash died, Mayor Kelly succeeded him as county chairman. I was in the army already in 1941. Kelly succeeded him, I think, in 1943. In 1946, I came back and I succeeded Kelly. Then Joe Gill succeeded me, and Dick Daley succeeded Joe Gill.

When you came back from the army, did you come back to the city council?

Oh, no. I made up my mind I wasn't going to be in politics. Mayor Kelly caught me in a weak moment. He wanted to appoint me a member of the park board. I'd worked, during the time I had gone to school, as a busboy and a waiter, in a restaurant of the Chicago Park District. We used to play ball at Douglas Park, play tennis there. It appealed to me and I took the job. Then some of the leaders of our party, together with Kelly, asked me if I would take over the chairmanship. When I left in 1941, I resigned as chairman of the finance committee, as an alderman, and as a committeeman. I had no job whatsoever. When I came back in 1946, Arthur Elrod resigned as committeeman and I was elected committeeman of the 24th ward, which made me eligible to be chairman. But I did nothing in the ward whatsoever. I just held the title.

I was chosen county chairman because at that time there was a great deal of friction in the party between Kelly on one hand and a lot of Irish on the other side. When they came to me, I said I would accept it. All the factions agreed upon me—the Tom Nash faction, the Joe Gill faction, Al Horan, Ed Kelly, John Clark—all of them agreed upon me. I was elected by a unanimous vote. I wouldn't take it any other way. They were all striving for power. I had been away. I had not been involved in the intraparty maneuvers. I was fresh from the army and the papers had been very kind to me in their assessment of my contributions. It was easy for them to vote for me.

Were you responsible for picking Paul Douglas and Adlai Stevenson in 1948 for the Senate and the governorship?

I sponsored them to the county committee. I asked each of them to run. Stevenson did not want to run for governor. I had to go out to his house and convince his wife that he should run for governor. He was receptive to the nomination for senator, but not for governor. Stevenson was not the first man that I had in mind for governor. I wanted someone of his type. I wanted a Democrat who had not been involved in what you call machine politics, but with the organization. In 1947, I sponsored Otto Kerner for U.S. attorney. Why? I wanted a man not associated with the organization. He had just come back from army service, an ideal man. I say that despite what happened to him. He was a man of integrity, and if he were convicted of anything, it should be ineptness and stupidity to let himself be drawn into a thing like he did. This was a man I would swear was incorrupti-

ble. At any rate, I knew we had a tough fight and I looked around
for people to bring in to add to the organization, to enhance the
image of the organization. I found there was nobody that could
question Douglas' open-mindedness, his lack of subservience to the
organization, his independence, his integrity. And the same with
Stevenson. I hardly knew Stevenson, but I knew of him. I knew what
he stood for. Stevenson won by 570,000 votes. Just look at 1948.
People talk about picking Stevenson for governor. They say, "Well,
everybody voted for him because they thought he was a sure loser."
That helped me put him across. There's no question about it, I took
advantage of it. The same with Douglas. They figured it's a losing
year. But I had my way because of it. If they thought we were going
to win, my God! Courtney was a candidate, and others were candidates. Do you understand?

*Are you saying, Colonel, that the other powerful men in the county
committee would not have picked these two candidates if they
thought there was a chance to win?*
They may not have. I had to do a selling job. I admit quite candidly
that the very circumstance of it being a year when many of our men
thought we were going to lose helped me in getting an almost unanimous vote for Stevenson. I got a unanimous vote on Douglas. One
man voted against Stevenson.

*Why didn't you want Douglas slated for the governorship and
Stevenson for the Senate?*
I'll be very, very frank with you. I served in the city council with
Douglas. I loved him. We exchanged affectionate greetings. I had
every confidence in him. There was no man I knew of who had a
higher sense of integrity, but he was not a practical man. In the
council he was not open to compromise. He was an advocate more
than he was an administrator. He had an academic background
which was marvelous. He was intelligent, knowledgeable. I would
have run him for any office. But, having the two men, I thought
Stevenson, being a lawyer, being involved in agreements and com-
promises, would be a better administrator than Douglas. I worked
with Douglas as an alderman where at times he would turn to me and
say, "Does the chairman of the finance committee assure me that this
contract is in the best interests of the city?" Invariably, when I gave
him my word, "This is the best we can do," he would do it. But
Douglas was an advocate. He'd take a position and he'd hold to it

tenaciously, stubbornly. Sometimes he was hard to move. I always told him, "You ought to be a lawyer, Paul. You couldn't be a judge. You couldn't compromise." I'm very happy that it worked out that way because Stevenson made a great governor. Maybe Douglas would have too, but Douglas became known as the conscience of the Senate. I'd have to be pardoned if I took pride in that fact.

Can you tell me how Martin Kennelly was picked to run for mayor in 1947 over the incumbent, Ed Kelly?

Kelly wanted to run. I came to him, together with two other members of the party. I told him that, in my opinion, if he ran, he might win, but it would be by a scant margin as a result of what he had done when he took a stand on that Morgan Park open housing controversy, where he said, "As long as I am mayor any person will be allowed to live where they want to and can afford to live." That was laudable, but we took a poll after the 1946 election and we lost the 1946 election partly because of the resentment toward Mayor Kelly. The Irish and the Poles and Bohemians were all against him, and I told him so. I said, "Ed, you're being hurt by something that I believe in, and I believe you were right in. And if you want to run, Joe Gill, Al Horan, and I will be for you. But I think we owe it to you and we owe it to the party to disclose to you what our straw poll indicates." And we showed it to him. He didn't believe it. But when I told him who conducted the poll, then he believed it, because it was his closest friend. He suggested Kennelly.

I had met Kennelly at social functions, but I didn't know him very well. During the process, Kelly had a change of heart. He asked me to come to his home with a mutual friend, a judge, and asked me to reconsider. I said, "I can't; I've burned my bridges; I've gone to the newspapers. I can't do that." I said, "If you want to run, I'll vote for you, but I'll have to resign as chairman of the county committee because I've given my word and I have to keep it." He agreed with me. He was a good Democrat.

Let me tell you something about Mayor Kelly. There are many stories printed about him, many allusions to his getting rich at the sanitary district. I was chairman of the finance committee during the time he was mayor, and if he was corrupt, if he took money, then he's a better actor than John Barrymore. Because I saw him on at least one occasion that I know of, and another one that I vaguely remember, where he took a contract away from a high bidder because there were some politicians involved in it. It was the Midway Airport investment contract. He gave it to Marshall Field for less money because, he said, "No one will question Marshall Field."

After Kennelly became mayor, Kelly came to me and I tried to help him get a position. He disclosed his financial affairs to me. People thought he was a multimillionaire. He barely had enough assets to live, the income of which could support him in a modest way. And this is an unfortunate part of public life, that people get such exaggerated opinions about a man. You remember there was talk about him having hundreds of thousands of dollars in a vault and all that sort of thing. His widow said that there was a lot of cash missing. It hurts me because I don't want to mention the incident but he came to me and asked me to go to a certain official and plead for a job so he could earn $25,000 a year to augment his income.

Then, Kelly was not corrupt as mayor?

He wasn't, when he was mayor. I can't speak for what happened before. He had a very good record as mayor. He was not as knowledgeable as Daley, not as efficient as Daley, but much warmer. He could generate among his friends and supporters a greater affection than Daley had. Daley does it by sheer power. Kelly did it by affection, warmth.

Why was Kennelly picked as Kelly's successor?

Well, that was another mistake. I'm guilty of many of them. Kennelly was head of the Red Cross, very prominent and active in civic affairs, unblemished reputation, a man of high integrity, no question about it. Unfortunately, he was inept. The council ran him. Where Kelly and Daley were strong enough to dominate the council, the council ran Kennelly. It hurts me to say this. He was a good man but was not an efficient mayor.

You need a strong mayor, the kind of a man you would pick to run your business. If you were the major stockholder in a corporation, you'd want a man, not for his good looks, not for his popularity at golf clubs, but a man who's a good administrator and who runs the business. I've seen a lot of them and I've got to admit that Daley is that kind of a man.

Could you evaluate Daley both as a mayor and a politician in terms of both his strengths and his weaknesses?

His weaknesses are as a human being. He's short-tempered, very suspicious, chauvinistic (which is not a detriment—I'm for that), but inclined to be clannish. But he started as a clerk in City Hall. He's had experience in every facet of governmental life. And he's equipped to be mayor. He's knowledgeable. A department head can't come to him with a budget and fake the figures. Daley knows more than this guy knows about it. I've got to admit he's the strongest mayor that I've had any association with, and I knew Dever, Thompson, Cermak, Kelly, Kennelly, and Daley. And I say that despite the fact that I have reasons to think that he's been derelict in certain things. He's a very suspicious man. He has an idea, I think, that in order to be undisputed leader, he must divest everybody else of any vestige of leadership. He doesn't want competition. He wants people to be close to him, to have power, but always mindful of the fact that that power is subordinate to his power. But he's a very successful, efficient leader politically, and in a governmental capacity.

He plays it for all it's worth. He breathes and talks politics twenty-four hours a day, and his position as mayor helps him politically. His position as boss of the party helps him as mayor. Do you know why? I've always said that this could never work. In Daley's case it has worked because he's an honest man. He *knows* he's honest, and the people around him know that he's honest. So that when he asks someone or orders someone to do something, they know it's good for the party or good for the city—that he thinks so, at least. And that's why they subscribe to his leadership. And one more thing about Daley. You see people around him who have been indicted and all that, but everybody close to Daley who ever makes a misstep will be out the window and he knows it. Unfortunately, a lot of men around him have gotten in trouble. I think I know Dick Daley pretty well, and I bet they hurt him as much as though they had indicted him because he feels they have betrayed *him.* He's loyal to people who work for him. And he has a very warm spot for the widows of the people who were his friends, sometimes to a fault. He invites them to every function, caters to every want of theirs, every whim. But it shows a compassionate side of him which he doesn't always show to people working for him.

The Irish are very compassionate people. I've dealt with them all my life. Pat Nash, Ed Kelly, Dick Daley—they have a very compassionate side, but sometimes they fail to be compassionate because they think it's a sign of weakness. They never want to show weakness. And that's what Daley's fault is, always worried that people will think that he's weak. In other words, if he doesn't show strength, people will interpret it as a sign of weakness. Let me put it this way. When

I was chairman, I had to sponsor judges, make recommendations. I had to go against personal friends of mine. I had a judge come to me one day who had a promise from President Truman that he would appoint him a federal judge. All he needed was my okay. I couldn't give it to him. Today he's one of the most eminent judges in Washington because, three months later, another thing opened up where I *could* give him my support. I said, "I'm not a boss. I've got to consult Senator Douglas, Senator Scott Lucas, Mayor Kennelly, Ed Kelly, who was then national committeeman. I represent the organization and I must do what the organization deems best." For every big job that I had some voice in the filling of, there were three, four, five, sometimes six applicants. In order to give it to one, you had to disappoint five. It's not a nice system, but you've got to be made of stern stuff, and Daley can do it. In 1960, I knew of at least five men who thought Daley was going to pick them for governor. And Daley finally picked Kerner.

You have to have a quality which I don't have. You've got to forsake compassion. You've got to be insensitive to the feelings of others. I'll be very frank with you—those are two things that I could not do as a leader. That's why I got out as quickly as I could. I should have gotten out in 1948, when I wanted to, after the presidential election, but Al Horan and Joe Gill pleaded with me to stay. I'm speaking as a man who's going to be eighty-one years old—nothing to look forward to. It's a quality, but you've got to have it, the same as General MacArthur had it. He was a great military leader. Why? He didn't give a good damn about anybody. He wanted a thing done and it had to be done that way, and in the time that he allotted to it. He would sacrifice his best friend in order to attain it.

I don't know whether you have to be ruthless, but you have to be unmindful of everything except the ultimate goal. This is what we must attain. If anybody stands in the way, out with them! Look, I took definite stands. I went before the executive committee of the party in 1950 and I asked them to withhold all privileges, patronage, and everything else from a ward committeeman who lied to me and double-crossed the organization, supported another candidate when he'd given his word to support the organization candidate. That doesn't mean that you shouldn't stand firm for those things in which you believe. But it's a rough, tough game.

I'll tell you what politics is, the satisfaction one *can* get from it, and if he doesn't have this satisfaction, it's not worthwhile. Then he's either in it for money, or because he's an egotist and wants to have power. I used to tell my precinct captains, "You are responsible for social security. You are responsible for health care. You are responsible for WPA. If you and precinct captains around the country hadn't elected Roosevelt in 1932, you wouldn't have these things. So you ought to have the satisfaction of knowing that through politics you provide a government which takes care of the people who need government the most." This is the satisfaction one gets out of politics. I'm not trying to tell you that politics hasn't been good to me. It's helped me in my law business, it's enabled me to take care of my family and all that. But maybe I could have done as well in law. There are some people who said that I'd have made one of the great lawyers in Chicago if I'd have stuck to the law business. I disagree with that. But a man can get the satisfaction of feeling—not knowing, no one knows—that by being involved in politics he helps provide for good government.

To me politics is opportunity. When I first started, I was an un-known and was given an opportunity to run for alderman. My God! Who was I? A nobody! Nobody knew of Jacob M. Arvey. Yet I was elected alderman, I was able to vote, I came to the attention of people. When I got up and spoke before a civic group, a charitable group, a religious group, I had a position in back of me to sustain me in what I said, to bolster my argument. I was not just a man off the street. Sure, politics has been good to me, and I wouldn't undo it for anything in the world.

I have no regrets. Let me tell you something as a Jew. I've talked to you about the general satisfaction which comes to a man engaged in politics which I think ought to motivate him. But let me tell you about my greatest satisfaction. I come from poor, immigrant parents. My greatest satisfaction out of politics is that I was able, by reason of the influence and power which fate put in my hands through politics, to be of service to my people. I wouldn't be human if my heart didn't respond in gratitude to statements made about my part in the recog-nition of Israel, and in helping the American Jewish community in general. I've been honored many times in universities. I was just honored by the Hebrew University in Israel, the Jewish Theological Seminary, others. And the fact that I was able to be of some service to the people from whom I spring is the greatest satisfaction to me. It sounds corny. I know it does. But, from the bottom of my heart, that's the way I feel. When I talk about my Jewishness, I think if a man is a good Jew, he believes in the brotherhood of man. He couldn't be true to the Talmud and to the God he worships unless he believed in the rights of all people.

What is it that makes Chicago a great city?

It's my hometown, so I love it. It's a thriving city. I think it's the best-governed big city in the United States. We've had our problems. We went through the Capone days, the days of permissiveness, lawlessness. But, on the whole, I like to think that Carl Sandburg was right. This is a city with "big shoulders." We've tried to do big things. Looking back, I wish we had torn down the El tracks many years ago. I was for it forty years ago. I remember Midway Airport. We had an opportunity to condemn all the railroad tracks at Midway and extend it by three miles. The trouble is we don't see far enough ahead. When we built the Kennedy Expressway, people thought we were spending too much money. Eight lanes! My God! Within two years it was inadequate. And Midway Airport. Two incorruptible aldermen, marvelous aldermen, both good friends of mine, said, "Oh my God, we're squandering money!" And Dorsey Crowe, a former aviator of World War I, said, "Gentlemen, before Midway Airport is built, it'll be antiquated." We don't think far enough ahead. One thing about Daley (and I've got to pat him on the back), when he has a major project, he doesn't care how much money he spends—overtime, doubletime, tripletime—but he's got to get it done. Why? He says, "If you save two weeks for the motorists, it's an incalculable good for the city." If you think only in terms of dollars and cents, you won't grow. You've got to think ahead.

What role have you played in national politics in this country?

With Roosevelt I played an inconspicuous role as a leader of a ward organization, although he called our ward the best ward in the country. We gave him a *tremendous* majority. He's not the president for whom I have the greatest affection. But in terms of greatness, I must rate him number one, and that's partly due to the fact that he came at a time when greatness was needed. He came at a time when people were jumping out of windows, going into bankruptcy, abandoning families, when there was not only unrest but also uncertainty, despair, despondency. He gave faith and courage and trust to the American people. He gave them courage to carry on. I wonder what would have happened had he not done this. We might have become communistic or socialistic. We might have had riots like they've had in European countries. So I would have to rate him as the greatest president in my time. The most human president, for whom I have affection like that for my father, is Harry Truman. If I were asked to name, as a Jew, a typical American, loyal to his country, loyal to his

fellow man, dedicated to human kindness, I would have to say Harry
Truman, and the plainest one of them all.

I thought Harry Truman was a great president! Why? Because of
the dismissal of MacArthur. That was the greatest thing that happened to this country during his term. It established, once and for all,
that the military cannot rule, cannot countermand the civilian authority, cannot take the law in its own hands. And I was a member
of the 33rd Division which was supposed to make the invasion of
Japan. They had our plans—we might have been annihilated—his
dropping of the bomb averted that. How history will view that, I
don't know. But he had no alternative. The picture presented to him,
whether rightfully or wrongfully, whether it was accurate or not, we
stood to lose 300,000 men in an invasion, if it was not successful. And
he chose to drop the bomb. Doris Fleeson, a columnist who hated
Truman because he had made some uncomplimentary remarks
about her (one thing about him, he said what was on his mind), told
Governor David Lawrence and me one day, at a Democratic National Committee meeting, "I hate the little son of a bitch. But I've
got to admit that every big decision he's made has been right."
Which is the truth—NATO, Marshall Plan, everything else.

*You were one of the prime movers, weren't you, in trying to draft
Dwight Eisenhower for the Democratic Party?*
Yes, in 1947. That's right. I, Jimmy Roosevelt, and the mayor of
New York. We were certain that Truman could not win, which the
facts would have permitted us to say a month before he was elected
in 1948. Certain publishers and other people came to me saying that
what this country needed was a person, either Democratic or Republican, who could unite the country and heal the wounds of the world,
and reestablish the supremacy of our country in world affairs. Dwight
Eisenhower was that kind of a man. He was not a Democrat. He was
not a Republican. He was a world war hero. Phil Murray of the CIO
brought me speeches he had made by which he tried to prove that
Eisenhower had liberal tendencies. But we made the move, regardless of why, and he was very much interested. He was president of
Columbia University at the time. At the last minute he said no. There
were some people in our party who wanted to be for Justice William
O. Douglas, some who wanted to be for Senator Claude Pepper. I
determined upon Truman. I went to Mayor William O'Dwyer and he
authorized me to issue a statement for both of us, declaring for

Truman. Mr. Truman called me the next day and we had a talk, and from that time on he and I were close friends. If there was any bitterness in his heart about what I had done for Eisenhower, he certainly never showed it. On the contrary, he showed just the opposite. I'm prouder of his friendship for me than I am of any political associations I have had.

RALPH BERKOWITZ *Jewish. Active in local politics for fifty years. One of the best Republican campaign organizers; an analyst of the Chicago political scene for many years. Was also an attorney. Died April 8, 1978, at the age of seventy-five.*

When I got into politics fifty years ago in Chicago, the machine was a Republican organization run by Big Bill Thompson. Roger Brennan was the Democratic boss. The Republican Party was pretty solid, but it didn't take very long for it to splinter up into factions. You had the Dineen faction and the Brundage faction. The *Tribune* was violently anti-Thompson. He faced trouble in 1923 and he didn't run. Dever was elected, but Dever was too honest for the Democratic organization. So, when Thompson ran again in 1927, the old Democratic alliance with Thompson was renewed. Thompson had as many Democrats in his organization as he had Republicans, even though he was a Republican. They knew where their bread was buttered. And Thompson was very kind to the boys.

I knew Hinky Dink Kenna and Bathhouse John Coughlin. I was involved in the settling of Hinky Dink's will. Bathhouse John was a very pleasant, open-faced kind of a guy with not too much on the ball. He was a perfect attendant at a bathhouse or he could have made a hell of a good bartender. The Hink was bright and he was close-mouthed. He was the brains. Hinky Dink in his later years was taken over by the mob, but he was already senile. The mob moved in and took over the 1st ward, although the Hink was nominally the head of the ward. The mob was very powerful. They took over Dennis Cooney, they took over prostitution. It was always said that the Hink wouldn't go for it, that that was one thing he drew the line on. I'm not sure that that's true. But the fact was that Dennis Cooney didn't move in until the Hink was under their control and had become absolutely senile.

There was a scandal connected with Thompson's administration. The assessor and the tax board of appeals were corrupt. There was a board of local improvements which was responsible for the widening of streets and condemnations of all kinds. There were any number of people who got very rich as a result of that. When Tony Cermak (an extremely clever man) became president of the county board in 1930, he would always appoint a silk-stocking, blue-ribbon committee to investigate him and they would return a silk-stocking, blue-ribbon whitewash of anything they were investigating. Cermak defeated Thompson in an election in 1931 in which there was a surprisingly large vote cast. Thompson actually got more votes when he was defeated than he had gotten [in] the election before when he was elected.

Cermak was a very cunning Bohemian who made a lot of money through politics. He had a saloon and was connected with an association of brewers or saloonkeepers. He was an alderman, got himself elected president of the county board, and used that as a springboard for the mayoralty. When he was elected, he was smart enough to know that a Bohemian could not hold the Irish in line. He went to a very shrewd Irishman, Pat Nash. What is known as the Daley machine originally was the Nash-Cermak machine. They put it in motion. You know how well they were organized? The precinct captains were given bronze buttons to wear on their lapels so that when they walked into a courtroom or a public office they were recognized as precinct captains and there was an understanding that "God is here and you've got to take care of our boys." And God help you if you didn't take care of our boys. It was a well-knit organization. The ward committeeman remained king as long as he treated his precinct captains fairly. Nash was county chairman. The ward committeemen could undo any elected official. Nash was one of the West Side Irish from the 28th ward. He was a very cunning politician and really practical. He had organizational genius. He knew exactly what to do to whip 'em into line.

How did Ed Kelly become mayor?
For that you can thank a guy by the name of Colonel Robert R. McCormick. The law would have made Kelly ineligible. Kelly and McCormick were old friends. Under the law at that time you could only fill a vacancy for mayor from among the aldermen. A fellow by the name of Frank Corr was named to succeed Cermak as mayor. Corr understood that he was not going to remain as mayor and that his reward would be that he would be put on the bench. Actually, the

man who had the votes to become mayor was a guy by the name of Oscar Nelson. The Republican votes were there. There were two Republican aldermen in the City Council—Masson of the 48th ward and George Williston of the 49th ward. Those two aldermen were the keys. Kelly had met McCormick while Kelly was working at the sanitary district as a laborer. A foreman and he got into a fight and Kelly beat the hell out of the foreman. Kelly was fired. The word got to McCormick and McCormick wanted to meet Kelly. He liked the idea of someone standing up and not taking it. He met Kelly, who was a very handsome and articulate kind of a guy in his own rough way, and took a fancy to him. Instead of firing him, he promoted him and actually gave him a title, and he became an engineer at the sanitary district. McCormick at that time was not married and Kelly was good at fixing him up, so they went out together. They became very good friends. Now in order to make it possible for Kelly to be named mayor in view of what the law was, McCormick got his reporter down in Springfield to get to the legislature and the legislature passed an act which enabled the city council to fill the vacancy for mayor outside of their own ranks. Corr resigned and was put on the ticket for judge. Then Masson and Williston sold out. They were Dineen people. McCormick got Dineen to get Williston and Masson to vote for Kelly, plus the Democratic votes that they had, and Kelly became mayor.

Kelly had the advantage of guidance by Pat Nash. As mayor, he had a guy like Clarence Wagner, the chairman of the finance committee, and a guy like [Colonel Jack] Arvey. They sort of ran the show for him. The city council was much more independent in those days because Kelly was not the boss. The boss was Nash. When it came time for Kelly to run in 1947, he was dumped because the *Daily News* and the *Sun* said that if they didn't dump Kelly, they would go against him. By that time, in 1947, Arvey was county chairman. I remember (I can almost see it) the picture in the paper of Arvey and Kelly and the announcement that Kelly decided he wouldn't be a candidate for reelection, and he had tears in his eyes.

Arvey was very clever and very able, but he was unlike the old type politician. He was willing to go along with new ideas. The old-timers would say, "Screw the polls. This is our guy, we're for him and they're gonna vote for him, we're gonna elect him and they're gonna like it." Arvey was a more enlightened guy. He saw a poll and he decided the guy didn't have a chance. But that doesn't make

Arvey lily-pure. There were a lot of things connected with the operation of the city and the advantages that he had from politics that were bruited about. But he was more modern in his concept, more intellectual. He read books and he was a more modern thinker. The others weren't. Arvey was Jewish. He came out of the ghetto, the 24th ward, and the roughest kind of operation, but he was more enlightened. He began to think of himself as a statesman. And, as a statesman, you read. He probably read and knew more and was much better equipped, intellectually, than his predecessors. An old-fashioned Irishman would never have dumped Mayor Ed Kelly in 1947. He'd have gone down with the ship.

In 1947, Martin Kennelly was picked by Arvey and several other powerful committeemen to replace Kelly as the Democratic candidate for mayor. Kennelly was a fringe politician who dabbled in politics by being a blue-stocking contributor. When he became mayor, he was as naive as you could be. He knew very little about politics, but he was an honest man. And, being an honest man, a lot of things were not allowed. For example, Bill Dawson was being hampered. The cops couldn't operate as freely as they did before. And Kennelly was bright enough to know all that was going on. He was enough of a nuisance to these fellows so that at the end of his four years, Dawson said, "Nothing doing. I won't go for the guy!" Dawson wanted him dumped because Dawson was being interfered with, and Dawson was a tremendous power.

Joe Gill and Arvey changed places. Gill came in as county chairman during the second term of Kennelly in 1950, and then later came Daley. Kennelly was so anxious to be reslated that he went to Dawson and apologized! And Dawson reluctantly went along and he was slated again. But Kennelly didn't have that opportunity in 1955 when Daley was around, because Daley wanted the mayor's spot for himself. A guy like Tom Keane couldn't freewheel under Kennelly as he did later. Kennelly hampered him. He was an honorable guy. He was not a brilliant guy, but he did a hell of a lot of good for the city. Most of the original improvements that the city had during the first and a good part of the second term of Daley were improvements that were sponsored under Kennelly. They brag about the new street lights and paved streets and all that business—they were all Kennelly bond issues. He did a lot of good in this city.

He was dumped because Daley wanted the job, and the county organization went along with it because Daley became county chairman in 1953. By that time Gill was getting old and wanted to step down. He was only interim and Daley was picked by his fellow committeemen.

Daley was responsible in 1955 for dumping Kennelly. Daley was drafted, but Daley was drafted the way a lot of other people were drafted. It was a draft which he had maneuvered. Kennelly was a very stupid politician. He had the power of his office, but he had Tom Drennan as his publicity man who directed his campaign, and it was a typically Drennan-stupid campaign.

How would you evaluate Daley as a mayor and a politician?

You've got to divide Daley up into two parts. First, there was Daley, the politician and mayor prior to the time he became a living legend. Up to that point he was a target for every charge possible. He was criticized publicly. He was the most lonesome-looking man in the world when you saw him walk into a meeting. He'd practically sneak into his own meetings. He was not a cheerleader. He had an inferiority complex. But after he was elected to his third term, he changed completely and became a very dominant force. He had entrenched himself pretty well. By this time he had such complete control of the patronage of every single office as county chairman that nobody could say him no. And the quality of committeemen was fading. The real Dawson guys that could put up a fight were going along fine under him. Keane had nothing to complain about. Keane could have led a revolt, but he was waxing rich. In your book you quoted Keane as saying, "Daley wanted power and he [Keane] wanted to make money, and we both succeeded." And it's true—that's exactly what it was. So that Keane who could overthrow it, Dawson who could overthrow it, had nothing to complain about. And there was no new opposition. You've got to have men in the organization to say, "To hell with you," and take you on and attract people who will stand up and fight. But you couldn't mount a fight against Daley unless you had the manpower. They didn't love Daley. Daley delivered for them. That was their affection for Daley. Daley was elected, he had jobs, he let them make money, and that was it.

After his third-term election Daley was received by the press as a sort of conquering hero. He became a maker of presidents. Until 1962, he had an opposition Republican Party. There were county chairmen who would speak out and candidates would call him names. I was public relations director and I had something to say about Daley almost daily. Any move he made, he was criticized and

charges were made. Then, in 1962, Hayes Robertson came in as
Republican county chairman, and that was the beginning of the end
of the Republican Party as a voice, because from then on they were
completely silent about Daley. You'd hear criticism only during elections and during campaigns. In between there was nothing. When
John Kennedy was elected and put his arms around him, invited him
to the White House, and at the Inaugural Ball Daley sat in Kennedy's
box and all that kind of business, that seemed to have a very significant psychological effect on the guy. And somehow or other, the guy
who was the local ward boss (even though he was mayor of Chicago)
became a national figure. And, becoming a national figure, he began
to live the part. And the newspapers began to accept him as a sort
of a legend. I don't know how far it goes back, the idea of the man
who "makes the city work." I think it only goes back about seven or
eight years. When you live long enough, you become a legend, and
he became a legend.

Daley's strength was the fact that he kept things pretty much to
himself, he confided in no one. He had a very clever knack of listening and letting everybody think he was for them, and then the word
got around that the old man on the fifth floor was for that. And if you
were not informed, you didn't know the man, know about him, the
rumor spread and was repeated, and a lot of people thought, "He's
on my side." You'd think that those who were left out would get mad.
But he never tipped his mitt until the very end. He was hard to figure
out.

His weakness was that he could have done a great deal more good
with his power. When you have muscle, when you have a club as he
had, you don't have to be terribly smart or clever as a politician. You
win by clout. The miracle is that a Republican won at any time with
that power that they've got. When you knocked him over, somebody
was running a smarter campaign than he was running. Daley was not
as resourceful as you gave him credit for, but when he was beaten,
he knew the reasons why he got beat. The next time he didn't repeat
that mistake. In 1953, he got beat because judicial reform was the
issue and it was a winning issue. In the next election he stole judicial
reform. He stole it because the damn Republicans weren't smart
enough to recognize that this wasn't just a one-time business. He took
it away from us!

He had very deep prejudices and those prejudices were expressed
in many different ways in his attitude toward progress for the city.
This is a great city. He loved the city, but there are an awful lot of

us who love the city. I've lived here pretty nearly all my life. I came
here in 1910 when I was eight years old. This city is the hub of the
United States. It has the lake. It was the railroad center of the world.
A train couldn't go through Chicago. It had to make up in Chicago
in either direction. And the planes, too. That's why O'Hare is the
largest and busiest airport in the world. And Chicago has a business
community that inherited by osmosis the spirit of a Marshall Field,
of a Potter Palmer, and the others, that "I Will" spirit. It isn't merely
a slogan. There's an aggressiveness about the people in this community, the way they speak, and a cockiness. Just like New York is
known as the city where everybody is impolite and everybody snarls
at you, this is a city of "I Will."

And Daley served the businessmen's purposes. They knuckled
under. They figured that that's the way, and they accepted it. For
example, State Street became restive because they figured that
Daley was not looking after their best interests. He was interested in
moving south and north of the Loop. If you talked to some of these
people, they'd tell you confidentially. But the mayor's always had the
Loop. The Loop businessmen supported the mayor, no matter who
he was. They supported Thompson, Dever, Cermak. And they used
to buy their insurance from whomever was the guy. The Hink and
Bathhouse John got the insurance, then John D'Arco. They take care
of these boys because they play ball. That's downtown. The rest of
the community are like everybody else—they fall for propaganda.
Most of the business interests do not live in Chicago proper anymore,
and they haven't for some time. So they'd say, "Hooray for Daley, he
makes the city run."

*What did people like Kelly, Cermak, Thompson, and Daley do for
the business community?*

There's such a thing as a permit, parking privileges, zoning—all
sorts of things that a mayor can do for you. If State Street wants an
especially heavy police patrol up and down State Street, or if they
wanted a subway that led into Marshall Field's, those are things that
you can get from the mayor and he's your guy. And you don't borrow
trouble. I only know of one business (I don't want to make any
charges that others aren't doing it), that paid 100 percent personal
property tax in Chicago in the old days, and that was Sears Roebuck
under Julius Rosenwald. That was the only outfit. The rest of them
didn't pay. There are other advantages. Tax breaks. There's a million
things that the mayor can do for you. If you're in business and you

don't like this tax or that tax, you get him to shift the tax to something else. The head tax business was causing them a great deal of grief. Daley almost got the county to adopt the head tax and take him off the hook, but it was unconstitutional.

If Daley did that well with business, why was he so successful with labor?

Labor was his natural pal, they're of the same ilk, they come from the same neighborhoods. He could speak to them in what is known as *mama-loschen.* * They understood each other and he cultivated them. Don't forget that labor is involved with the city. The labor unions that deal with city employees get tremendous advantage from the mayor. There was no such thing as an effective strike. He'd step in at the last minute, negotiate, and the labor union won the strike. He was not supposed to have any control over the board of education, but he walked in at the last minute and got the board to agree to a budget that they couldn't legally support. And then the schools closed early.

There are an awful lot of things that you've got to understand about the average human being. Let me tell you a story. There was a fellow who's now dead who was executive vice-president of the Harris Trust and Savings Bank. He was one of the major reformers, head of the Crime Commission, the Citizens of Greater Chicago. He wanted me to manage a political campaign in 1954. A fellow by the name of Austin Wyman was the candidate. I knew Austin and was very fond of him, and he wanted him to run for the United States Senate. This fellow called me and said, "Ralph, you're the fellow that can get Wyman nominated." I said, "Will he have organization support, because without organization support, forget it. This is a primary. Either that or a lot of money." He said, "How much is a lot of money?" I said (in those days $150,000 was a lot of money), "Oh $100–$150,000." He said, "Oh, don't worry about it. I'll tell you something, he's gonna have organization support. The governor, Billy Stratton, and I are like this. I can pick up the telephone and get right to the governor and say, 'Hello, Billy.' " I hated to tell him I've been saying, "Hello, Billy" for a long time. But there is something, even in these fellows who are the blue bloods of our community, the shakers of our community. They get a vicarious thrill at rubbing shoulders with mayors, governors, senators, congressmen. And the

*A Yiddish expression which means, "Let's cut out the double talk."

idea that they could talk to the mayor and call him Dick, that's
something! There's a psychological reason for it. I wish I knew what
it was. I have a title and I call up and say, "This is the first assistant
state's attorney calling," "Oh Ralph," they say. Suddenly, they know
me by my first name. The guy never met me in his life! And this was
one of the major people in the business community. "Ralph," he says,
"I've been wanting to call you and get to meet you and have lunch
with you," and stuff like that, see? It's public position that seemed to
somehow draw them to Daley, so that he had a head start with the
business people. If the mayor calls up (I don't care who) and says, "I
would like to have you come down and I would like to talk with you,"
you're flattered as hell. You come a-running. And if the guy puts you
on some meaningless commission, there you are!

*You've been in politics all your life. What is politics to a profes-
sional like you?*

To me, politics is a craft. It's not a profession. I consider myself a
craftsman. Politics is a craft that has many practitioners and few
craftsmen. I like it because it gives me an opportunity to play an
important part in my government. It's exciting. It makes my adrenal-
in rise. I'm very proud of the fact that in all the years I've been in
politics, where I've been closely identified with a candidate, it's always been a candidate I didn't have to apologize for. I think that I
have rendered a service to my community that has made my son
proud, my grandchildren proud, and I hope to die with my boots on
in this business. The present job I have is first assistant state's attorney. I needed it like I need a hole in my head. I was comfortably
involved in the practice of law. I had a consultant relationship with
the attorney general that paid me substantially more than I am
making today. In those days I'd come down if I wanted at 10 or 10:30
A.M., or not come down at all. I could make my own hours. I could
go home whenever I darn pleased. I could decide in advance
whether I was going to be in court, draw up a contract, or talk to a
client. I could take it easy. Now I work on an average of ten to twelve
hours a day at a steady pace. I come home and my telephone is
constantly ringing and I'm really exhausted before the day is over.
But I do it and it's exciting. There are two reasons why. One is the
fact that retirement is a serious mistake for any man unless you have
hobbies that can absorb you. I've never had those kinds of hobbies.
I think I would vegetate. Too many of my friends are getting old and
they're younger than I am. I look at myself in the mirror and say, "My

God, am I older than this fellow?" And I don't believe it, because of the excitement I have in life, in living. The other reason is not quite that selfish. I like this job because I feel I'm contributing in a very trying time in our history to improving the criminal justice system in our community. And the record that's being made in this office, I take great pride in because I have been one of those who contributed to it. And if they put anything on my tombstone, that would be the thing they ought to put on it.

JOHN LEONARD (BUNNIE) EAST *Long-time Republican ward committeeman; eighty-six years old, and an intimate of both Democratic and Republican politicians and public figures in Chicago and Illinois for over fifty years.*

I was born in Illinois in St. Clair County, in a small community known as Lensburg. In 1911 I came to Chicago. I've lived in Hyde Park ever since.

It was a natural thing for me to be in politics. My father was a precinct committeeman in Randolph County in a little town called Colterville. He was also mayor of the city. I was attracted to politics because of his interest in it. When you ask why I'm a Republican, my people were one of the founders of the Republican Party in 1856. The first president they voted for was Fremont. There wasn't a single Democrat in that town because they were all old soldiers or sons and daughters of soldiers that served in the Civil War. They all used to gather in my grandfather's drugstore every afternoon. I fought every battle of that war listening to them talk of their experiences.

When I came to Chicago, I was associated with one of the great figures of the past, Senator William E. Lorimer. I learned a lot from Lorimer. I rode to Springfield with him during the sessions of the legislature every week, back and forth, and we had plenty of time to talk, beginning in 1926. His office was always full of old Jewish people. One day I said to him, "What are all these Jewish people in to see you about?" "Oh, they like to come in and visit with me," he said. "They gave me my start." He was a conductor and he drove a horsecar on the horsecar line and they were all peddlers on Halsted Street. He said, "We weren't required to pick them up. Car after car would pass them up. I always picked them up. Later, they got to be good friends of mine and when I ran for office they elected me." He would see anybody that wanted to see him. The old man carried his own precinct polling book in his pocket, to the day of his death. Lorimer was a great man, didn't drink, didn't smoke, didn't swear, but made one great mistake, he made an enemy of the *Tribune*. They were out to get him and they did. He's the fellow that taught William Hale Thompson everything he ever knew about politics.

Thompson had the most fertile brain of any politician I ever knew. I'm one of the few politicians that ever attended him to his grave. He happens to be buried in the same cemetery as my folks, and when I go by there, I always lift my hat and stop and think of William Hale Thompson. I respected him, but I didn't get along with him because he had one failing. His word was no good. But I still think he was one of the great mayors we've had. If you look around Chicago, any place, you'll find something that Thompson did. When you drive along Wacker Drive, Thompson built that. Thompson built the Michigan Avenue bridge. The arrangement he made with the Illinois Central Railroad allowed us to have our beautiful front yard, Grant Park. He had a bad reputation and he did have a lot of associates that I didn't approve of, but nevertheless, I always gave him credit for what he did. He was a person that was known as being a great sportsman. He used to drive an old Packard convertible down Michigan Avenue in the coldest weather with that top down, with a cowboy hat on. He was no more of a cowboy than I am, but he assumed that garment, I suppose, to publicize himself. He was a good man at publicizing himself. And he became very popular with the ethnic groups. He paid a lot of attention to them.

When Tony Cermak came along, he improved on Thompson. Cermak was really the father of the ethnic groups' being all in one party. I knew Cermak well. He came to Chicago from Braidwood, Illinois, and originally was a wood peddler from the days when they had wood stoves. I don't think he had much education, but he was a smart man. He didn't drink to excess. He liked money, but he was a very pleasant man to associate with and knew what makes politics click. He knew *every* employee that was employed by the city government.

Cermak built the Democratic Party with the ethnic groups. He was a Bohemian, but he had the Polish vote. He gave them a lot of representation. The Irish, of course, he took care of because he had to and because they were already in office. He had the ethnic groups pretty well wrapped up, with two exceptions. The Scandinavians and the Jews were all Republican in those days. He didn't make much inroad on them. The Jews became Democrats because of Henry Horner more than anything else, and they had a right to be proud of Horner because he was a great man. I knew him well.

I'll tell you how Cermak, not Roosevelt, made the Negroes Democrats. The Negroes loved to play whist, they loved to gamble a little (not to any great extent). Cermak put the police department to work. On Friday and Saturday nights, the police stations were crowded with Negroes that had been arrested in gambling raids. And when the aldermen would try to intercede for them, they would be told, "The minute you people find out there's something besides the Republican Party, come back and talk to us." That was one way to make them Democrats, and he did. Then Roosevelt, of course, improved on it, but Cermak was the man that made them.

Did you know William L. Dawson?

I brought Dawson into politics. I knew Dawson when he was a student at the University of Chicago. He was hustling baggage for the old Chicago Beach Hotel. My folks and my wife's folks used to come to see me from southern Illinois and I used to be down at the IC Station at 53rd Street quite often, and here was this young fellow, he used to sit on those trucks. He impressed me then as being a pretty bright boy. Then, in 1928, he decided to run as an independent candidate for Congress. Madden was our candidate and I handled Madden's campaign successfully. After the campaign, I went over to see Dawson and asked him to come in and join the organization, which he did. Dawson developed into being one of the great politicians of the age, one of the best ward committeemen that I ever knew.

When I left the 2nd ward and went back home (I'd always lived in the 5th), I agreed to run Dawson for committeeman of the 2nd ward and Billy King for the Senate, if the two of them would get together. We had a fellow that was the alderman and committeeman that I didn't approve of, and neither did they. They wanted to eliminate him and I knew they could together, and did. Dawson then became alderman also. He and King fell out, some say over a woman. The Republican authorities at that time turned it over to King. Dawson came out to see me and told me he was going to switch to the Democrats and I said, "Well, under the circumstances, I can't blame you, Bill. If my party doesn't want you, I don't blame you for being a Democrat." He said, "Well, I made a good deal with Kelly, and while I was about it, I made a good deal for you, too. He's very anxious to have you and I want you to go down and see Mayor Kelly." I said, "Bill, I don't blame you for being mad at them, but I've been a Republican all my life. I don't believe I can change as readily as you. I don't have as much reason to be as mad as you are." But we

remained friends until the day of his death. I was one of the very few
white people that was at Dawson's funeral, Republican or Democrat.
I always admired him. He was a very forceful man. He had a booming
voice, and if he whispered, you could hear him in the next county.

Dawson was the original Democrat in that South Side area. He
brought in Ralph Metcalfe and all the rest of them. He had two big
thick books in his office of his patronage jobs. He had an awful lot of
patronage. I said to him once, "Bill, how do you get along with these
southern congressmen?" He said, "I get along good with them.
They're the head of every committee there is down here. If I don't
get along with them, I don't get anything for my people." And he was
right.

Kelly agreed to support him for committeeman and for alderman.
He went from alderman to being congressman. I guess he went to
Congress after Mitchell and Oscar DePriest, who was an accident
politically. Old man Lorimer was in power at the time and Dan
Jackson, Republican committeeman of the 2nd ward, and Lorimer
were great friends. Jackson visited him once in Washington, and
Lorimer said, "You know, I think we ought to run a black for county
commissioner this time." First he offered it to Jackson, but Jackson
said, "No, I don't want any public office." So Lorimer said, "Find me
a good black and we'll name him." Jackson came back and got off the
New York Central train where it used to stop at 47th, and walking
across there, he ran across a fellow that was dressed in painters'
overalls with a ladder over his back and a paint bucket in his hand.
It was Oscar DePriest. He stopped Oscar and asked him if he'd like
to be a candidate for the county board. Of course DePriest was
tickled to death at the opportunity. That's why I say he was an
accident. He just happened to be on the proper street at the proper
time.

Did you know Pat Nash and Ed Kelly?
I knew them both well. Pat Nash was a kind old man. Nash's word
was good. He'd tell you the truth. Nash and Kelly inherited the
machine that Cermak built. They improved on it. They had more to
work with. They had more jobs, more money, and they had a Democratic president at that time that was very kind to them as far as
government jobs and government contracts were concerned.

Kelly was an extraordinary man in the sense that any place you go
here, there's two mayors that you'll find did something for this town
—Thompson and Kelly. I'm not including Daley because that's re-

cent. Everybody knows what Daley has done, and he's done a good job.

But Kelly did a lot for this town. I don't know of any corruption. All I know is that he did pay the government something like $375,000 back taxes and he never had a job in his life that paid more than $18,000 a year. He was a very smart politician. I got a call once and the lady says, "Mayor Kelly wants to talk to you." The mayor got on the phone and asked me if I'd meet him downtown at a hideaway he had. I came down and Kelly said, "Boy, I'll tell you what I want to talk to you about. I'm in trouble out there in the 5th ward. I've got two fellows out there—one's a liar and one's a thief." I said, "Mr. Mayor, you're all wrong. They're *both* liars and *both* thieves." "Well," he said, "that's my reason for sending for you. I'd like to have you take that over for the Democratic Party." I said, "Why, Mr. Mayor, I've been a Republican all my life. I don't see how I could do that." He said, "I'll make it worth your while. I know how close you are to Governor Green" (and I was). He said, "I'll guarantee you I'll make you more money than Green'll make you." I said, "That's easy because I don't make any with Green either. I'd like to help you, Mr. Mayor, but I'm sorry, I couldn't take it." He was very much disappointed but he still told me, "If there's anything in my administration you ever need, you let me know."

Why was Kelly dumped in 1947?
The story is that they were in real trouble with Kelly. He'd recently had that government suit for the back taxes that he'd settled, and Arvey was looking for a candidate. Arvey didn't find Kennelly. I found Kennelly first. I knew Kennelly very, very well and I proposed his name to the Republican committee as a candidate for mayor in 1943, four years previous to Arvey's taking him, and Kennelly would have been glad to run on the Republican ticket, even though he was a Democrat. But I couldn't sell him to my party.

Kennelly was probably the most honest man I ever knew. I think he ran a thoroughly honest administration, but he did nothing (I'm talking about my best friend now). I once said to him, after he became mayor, "Marty, let me ask you a question. How the hell is it that Thompson and Kelly are both noted or talked about as being such thieves, and did so much for this town? And here you are. I know how honest you are, and you haven't been able to do anything. If anybody came here from Cedar Rapids that I wanted to show them something the mayor had accomplished, there isn't any place I could take them and show them. And you've got twice the tax rate now than it was during the terms of Kelly and Thompson."

Arvey took Kennelly and sold him to the committee in 1947. Jack Arvey was a very resourceful man, and, as far as any dealings I ever had with him, absolutely forthright and honest. You always knew where Arvey stood. I was chairman of the Republican Party from 1946 to 1950 and we used to have a coalition of judges. The Democrats didn't want to have a fight so they'd give us a few and they'd take the majority. They'd have got them with an election, probably all of them as they do today, with an election.

You and Arvey worked out a deal on the judges?

I was chairman before Arvey was. Before that time, the judges always paid assessments to be slated, and the Democrats always got all the assessments of the Republican judges as well. So Arvey called me one day and asked, "Don't you think we ought to sit down and talk about the possibility of coalition?" I said, "Yeah, be glad to." So I sat down with him and I said, "Jack, I'm willing to be for coalition, provided we name the Republican candidates." Before that, the Democrats always named the Republicans, too. He looked at me in astonishment and he said, "Why, of course you ought to." We agreed on a number. I said, "And so far as the assessments are concerned, that ought to come to the Republican Party." "Why," he said, "of course it should! Why do you say that?" I said, "Because you fellows always took it all!" He said, "I didn't know that." After that they paid their assessments to us.

Why has the Republican Party been so unsuccessful for the last forty-five years?

In the first place, we've lost the old personnel we used to have. The dedicated people are all gone now, including our precinct workers. A precinct captain is an underrated individual. He performs a great service for the people. The average Joe Blow doesn't care whether he's registered or not, he doesn't know when election day is, he unfortunately doesn't have a chance to see the candidates much of the time. An effective precinct captain is one that keeps his people registered and informed on primaries and elections, and carries the Republican message, the same as the Democrats do. For that kind of work, he deserves some kind of compensation. Volunteers won't do it and you can't blame them. They don't have the time. They have to make a living. Here and there you'll find one that is good. But we don't have the jobs to give to them, and you just can't get good ones anymore unless you can compensate them. And you've had a great change in the thinking of people, whether they're right or they're wrong, over the last twenty-five years.

If you were asked by a young man or woman how to have a career in politics, what would you advise him or her?

I would advise him to see his committeeman, to take the precinct where he lives and make himself the best precinct captain of that ward, and if he was, he'd sure get recognition right away. I wouldn't let anybody be a committeeman until he's been a precinct captain first, because, being a precinct captain, you've got the real touch with the people. You see them individually. A precinct captain's not supposed to get you a thousand votes; he's supposed to get you *a* vote. Politics is a retail business, not a wholesale business. You get them one at a time.

I would tell him not to get in unnecessary arguments. It's fine to make friends, but the care you have to take is to make no enemies, because your friend will give you a little bit of assistance on election day, but an enemy will work like hell to beat you! Yes, he will! Another thing I always taught my precinct captains was, don't ever let an enemy occur in your precinct on your account. Everybody won't like you, and if they don't like you, make it his fault, not yours. Don't do anything to aggravate him. I taught my precinct captains how to dress—never overdress. Never dress like a slob. When you knock at a door and the lady answers, she'll say, "Who is it?" and you announce yourself, who you are. And if she opens that door, don't step forward, step back and have some books in your arms that shows her that you're not prepared for any form of attack. Get her confidence and she'll finally let you in to talk to her. And see the people. What is politics, but people?

EDISON LOVE *Black. One of William L. Dawson's top precinct captains for many years on Chicago's South Side. Seventy years old.*

I was born in New Orleans on January 12, 1909. I was brought to Chicago at a very early age in 1917 or 1918 by my mother. We lived in the 2nd ward. I graduated from high school and because of the Depression, there was no way of going to college for me and others like me, unless you were part of a black group in Chicago that were well founded, had some stability, like the professionals or near-professionals. The only thing that was open was dishwashing jobs for seven or eight dollars a week. That was one of the most terrible experiences that a young person could go through in that period. I went from one job to another, and sometimes I went for months without a job.

How did you get into politics?

Quite by accident. I was living with a family in 1932 and the lady across the alley was a Republican precinct captain and she was looking for a Republican precinct judge for the primary election. They were paying $15 for service as a judge, and I looked upon this as an opportunity to pick up some money. I served as a Republican judge of elections in the 1932 primary. We had the long Australian ballots (it looked to be longer than my arm), and we struggled through from 5 o'clock the morning of the election till noon the next day before we could get out of the polling place.

At that time, in my area, it was hard to get Democratic representatives on the board, or Democratic workers. When there were 650 to 700 people registered in the precinct, it was an unknown thing to get more than 35 to 40 Democratic votes out. I learned many things during that day. People coming in to vote had no perception about what they were doing and what they were doing it for. We had a steady influx of Republicans, and the Democratic precinct captain had been asked by the ward committeeman to bring in at least 100

Democratic votes. He would turn over hell and high water to do what the ward committeeman asked him to do. That was a superhuman task to ask this Democratic precinct captain to get 100 votes in that precinct. But, at the close of the election, he had 100 Democratic votes. The Republicans had 450. But this Democratic precinct captain, because of his diligence, had complied with the request of his boss, the Democratic ward committeeman. As the ballots came out and were unfolded and inspected, I noticed that each candidate that was endorsed by the regular Democratic organization had been given a vote, and that the X in the square opposite that endorsed candidate was almost in the exact place right down the ballot. And I knew that this was what I had read about as a chain ballot. I am not saying these people were dishonest. They weren't. These people were good, God-fearing folks.

I then became a Democratic assistant precinct captain in the 29th precinct of the 2nd ward, under a white precinct captain. At that time whites were moving out of an area that was being integrated by blacks. Most of the Democratic captains were Republicans who had become disenchanted with the promises of the Republican Party.

I met William L. Dawson politically when Dawson came over to the Democratic organization in 1935 during his two-year stint in the city council (at that time the aldermen were elected for a two-year period). Dawson had endeared himself to Mayor Ed Kelly because of the aid he had given Kelly in the council. Dawson had been elected as a Republican alderman without the backing of the regular Republican organization. He was more or less a freelance man, an independent. I think it was to the interest of both Dawson and Kelly to sort of complement each other. Dawson had a vote in the council to help Kelly put his programs over for the city of Chicago. Being a new mayor, Kelly definitely needed that, because at that time the council was more evenly divided than it is today. And Kelly had ideas with reference to expanding the vote of the Democratic Party in the black areas, in cementing some ties with Dawson who was admittedly a leader in his own right. Dawson had run for Congress in 1928 and some say he won it, but was counted out. The man was an established leader and was recognized among black people as being a person that they could trust.

What made Dawson a leader?
First of all, the man was a good army man. He was a first lieu-

tenant of infantry in 1917. After coming back from the army he
went to Northwestern University, got his law degree, and then he
became deeply immersed in the problems of his people here in
the 2nd ward. He was fighting the problems of his people and he
was always available to people to talk to. He had that milk of
human kindness. He was considerate. He would give you the shirt
off his back. There are stories about the man losing everything he
had, even mortgaging his property to help people, to keep his organization together. He ate with them. He broke bread with
them. Many times I heard the story about how they gave 25¢
each, or 30¢, whatever small money they had, he and his followers got together, made up a pot, and sent out and got food, and
they ate. This is the making of a leader. This is what Dawson had.
He had an understanding and he had humility that made him be
able to sit down with kings, but, at the same time, he had the
great understanding of what the problems of the downtrodden
could be, and would do what he could do to help them solve
those problems. He became the leader through hard work,
through helping people by understanding their problems, by always being willing to do things that would bring people to him.

Being a military man and having the understanding of delegating
authority to people, and having a keen insight into human nature and
characteristics, he was very keen in being able to select people that
he would make precinct captains. Dawson had that second sense of
people. The man was a genius, a genius at leadership, a genius at
being able to sit down with people whoever they were, and getting
from them those things that would satisfy him as to whether or not
they could be an integral part of his organization, for the purposes
which he desired. There were many people who came to him who
would not fit in the mold of precinct captains, and those people he
would use in other avenues.

Throughout my life with him (and I was with him until he passed
away in 1970), I never knew him to turn away anyone who came to
the office to see him. All they had to do (they didn't need an appointment) was to come in and say that they wanted to see Bill Dawson.
Or, "I want to see the chief," or "the boss." He didn't like anyone
calling him "boss." We refrained from that. We would call him
"chief," "the old man," "the congressman," or "the committeeman."
If there was a man, in my judgment, who had all the prerequisites
of a leader, particularly in such sensitive spots as ward committeeman, alderman, congressman, and a person who could mold a group

of people by careful selection into an organization that would move as a unit, this man had it.

I think one of the motivating objectives of his change from a Republican to a Democrat was that he realized that he had gone as far as he possibly could go in the Republican Party, and that they were not ready to make any changes in their philosophy and in their advancement of black people. He felt that, using his talents within the Democratic Party, he could do a great deal more for black people that he couldn't in the Republican Party.

Mayor Kelly recognized the type of job that Dawson could do, and the leadership ability and the talent that this man had. Kelly thought that it would be a good thing, since the 2nd ward was looking for leadership, to ask Dawson to take his forces into the Democratic organization. Kelly had to beat down opposition in the Democratic Party, primarily Pat Nash. When Dawson first entered the Democratic Party, it was because of the friendship that had been built up between Kelly and Dawson. There was a split in the leadership of the Democratic Party. Pat Nash was the county chairman and Ed Kelly was the mayor, but he did not run the county central committee. And, therefore, although Dawson was a leader in his own right, and had won the respect and admiration of Ed Kelly, selling Dawson to Pat Nash proved quite a job for Kelly. Pat Nash did not want any part of Bill Dawson. Not that he hated him. He recognized his qualifications and all that, but the man was a Republican, had given the Democratic organization hell out here, maybe from 1926 on, and he almost took the congressman's job from the incumbent back in 1928. I don't know just what was in Pat Nash's mind, but it was hard for Dawson to overcome some obstacles in entering the Democratic Party.

When Dawson was in Washington as a congressman, how did he maintain control of the organization back in Chicago?

Because he had men such as Alderman Harvey; Fred Smith, who was a state senator; Corneal Davis, who was a state representative. He had office help; he had a wonderful staff; he had people who were committed, loyal troops, and who understood the man's program. We understood what he was fighting for. He gave us a sense of importance that we were playing a vital role in the advancement of blacks in the Democratic Party. And he also could analyze and give to us, in a clear, concise, understandable manner, what would happen as a result of our helping him to lead our people in great numbers into the organization and change the whole complexion of what had

gone before. That is—changing the prejudice of our people against
the Democratic Party, and giving to the Democratic Party votes that
we had given for so long to the Republican Party. There was a
deep-seated emotional hangup about the Republican Party, mostly
because of the way the blacks were treated in the South and the
lynchings that had been going on. Abraham Lincoln played a great
part in their voting behavior. We were Republicans because Lincoln,
our great benefactor, had broken the shackles that bound us in servi-
tude.

*What role did Dawson play when Ed Kelly was dumped and
Martin Kennelly was picked for mayor in 1947?*

Dawson was always a party man. He was accepted by the leaders
of the Democratic Party after having been elected ward committeeman in 1940. So, in 1947, Dawson realized that these men in the
party had been there longer, had more experience, and had won
recognition. I think the chief architect of this small group who made
dumping Kelly possible was the premier ward committeeman and
leader of the Democratic Party at that time, Jake Arvey.

Why did Dawson oppose reslating Kennelly in 1951?

In 1951, Kennelly had disappointed not only Dawson but a number of strong ward committeemen within the city central committee
over patronage and other commitments that they had expected Kennelly to honor. As I recall, the organization had not been really
whipped up as an aggregation to go out and do a job for the candidate
for the mayor for reelection. The signs weren't there and we as
troops knew there was something wrong at the top. We could feel
it. In any good organization its members can just about get the
temperament or the feel of there being something rotten in Den-
mark, or wrong someplace. We were just dragging our feet. We had
nothing coming from the high command. As I get it, the word came
through from Washington. It might have been Jim Farley who said,
"Go and give that man a second term." You had important federal
elections coming up in 1952. Immediately there was a meeting called
at the church, and from that point on, we got the order to go out and
do the job. And we did the job.

*What was Dawson's role in the 1955 primary between Daley, Ken-
nelly, and Ben Adamowski?*

At that time, Dawson had five South Side wards which all acted as a unit. Naturally, he would be a power within the structure, and if there was going to be any type of insurrection within the party, they would want this powerful black leader who was responsible for five black wards. So Dawson was an integral part of that combination of people within the structure of the Democratic Party who wanted to displace Kennelly and make Richard J. Daley the mayor of Chicago. Dawson did a helluva lot for Daley that Daley couldn't do for himself. In this fight in 1955, you had another important factor in the primary. You had Ben Adamowski. We had three people in there of real importance. You had Daley, Kennelly, and Adamowski who was a recognized Polish leader, and who, perhaps, had the backing of a segment of not only his people, but people within the Democratic Party. Daley represented the ward committeemen, but certainly the votes that Adamowski got (I think it was about 100,000), had they gone to Kennelly, then Daley would not have been the candidate. But Ben was not able to do it because Dawson was such a dynamic person. The newspapers made a racial fight out of it. They came out hitting Daley day after day, that here was a black man who probably ruled Chicago, or at least had a great deal of influence with the regular organization candidate [Daley]. They did it to such an extent that they got everything they could get, but there were certain things that they needed for victory that they didn't get, and they cemented the black ties out here in those five wards which the old man was responsible for. And we gave Daley the margin of victory in the primary that he needed to overcome Adamowski and Kennelly.

Did Daley, in return, give Dawson the prerogatives due him as a leader in the party?

What else? When it comes down to nuts and bolts, when a man has proven that he has supplied that ingredient of victory or margin of victory for the party in making the boss, what else? Sure. And he was entitled to the prerogatives that a man in his position received.

Why was Daley selected as the organization candidate?

First of all, the mayor had been down in Springfield, he had been a state representative, and a state senator. He had run for sheriff, and he also was the county clerk. Within the structure, when they began to search for a likely candidate to oppose Kennelly, the party was going to make this person the mayor of Chicago. They had to control it, naturally. And when they decided on Daley, they tell me that

Daley was a bit reticent, that he backed off of it, and there was a lot of urging and pushing to get Daley to accept the backing of his party bigwigs. And the discussion went on for days, maybe over a period of a week or two. And, finally, Daley accepted.

You must remember that Daley had no great experience in my book as being a person who could assume the responsibilities of the job as mayor of Chicago. I don't think that his background experience was such that you could say, "Here's a man that's going to do it. He's going to immediately set the city on fire." He did not have that stature among the rank and file. Within the party structure there were a number of powerful men who formed a clique of the inner circle, who were plotting this course, who had become thoroughly disgusted with the non-leadership of Kennelly, who decided we need a man, and who finally decided that Daley was the man.

How did Daley change in his years in office?
I think that Daley was a man who grew. He had that great capacity and was thrown in with men such as the leaders of the party who were counselling with him, pointing out pitfalls, things of that nature. Now, I'm talking about Daley as a politician. I think that the man became one of the most astute political leaders that you could find any place in America. But the credit goes to men like Dawson and Jake Arvey, and some of the Polish and Italian leaders of that time. The Democratic Party is made up of ethnic groups, and within the Democratic Party there were leaders who were recognized and respected and were powerful because of what they represented within the ethnic groups. These men were respected at the high command because they represented these forces and these powers. Therefore, with these people talking and counselling, and Daley being able to take advantage of their experiences, he developed. He had the potential and he had become one of the greatest political figures and leaders of a great party in Chicago's history, and surely, if you try to compare him to others, Daley will probably stand head and shoulders above other political leaders in other sections of this country.

What did Dawson's death mean to black politics in Chicago?
Dawson's death was the end of an era. You could see that things began to change about six years prior to Dawson's death. I feel that those who represent the black people now are not like those stalwarts, the ward committeemen of former years—Dawson; Christopher C. Wimbish, the senator from the 3rd senatorial district; Colo-

nel Kenneth E. Campbell of the 20th ward; and, in the 4th ward, there was Claude W. B. Holman. I haven't seen anyone who approximates Dawson during the past thirty-five years. And it is doubtful, from what I see today, whether there is one who will do so in the next ten years.

Another thing that sort of eroded the strength of black politics on the South Side among the blacks that I am familiar with was a loosening of or change in attitude. One of the things that I think had a great deal to do with that was the Shakman Law, where you could not demand from those that were responsible for the nuts and bolts of politics at the precinct level, that they carry the ball.* If the person on the football field realizes that the coach has no power for taking him out of the game, or maybe benching him for two or three games, where do you get the enthusiasm? Where do you get that dedication and devotion? So I think that there were people who wanted to break up the power of the machine. Let's call it a machine, albeit a damn good machine, when it was run by men who had the right type of vision. A Cadillac is a damn good machine if you keep it oiled, if you keep it greased, keep it washed, keep it simonized. It may get old, but if you keep the mechanic there, keep things in working order, keep the body up, and keep the interior fine, it's a good machine. It gets you to where you want to go. That's the same thing. I have no qualms about saying, "I was a part of the Democratic machine." There are good machines and there are bad machines, and I just feel that the machine that I came along with was a part and parcel of a great machine, and accomplished a helluva lot for the people of Chicago, and certainly my people, people who were downtrodden, people who did not have much expectation of ever doing anything.

Isn't there another factor, though? In days like these, when you have approximately 1,300,000 blacks out of a population of 3,100,000 in the city, a powerful black political leader like Dawson could become the most powerful politician in the city, couldn't he? In other words, is it possible that the white ethnic politicians in the city, including Mayor Daley, have been unwilling to anoint any black leader like Dawson, because that man would be too powerful?

When you say "anoint," I'm one of those who believe that Dawson

---

*The Shakman ruling is a federal court order prohibiting the requirement of political work as a prerequisite to getting or keeping a government job in Chicago and Cook County.

wasn't anointed by Kelly or Daley. I can't cotton to that. Dawson was a leader in his own right. He had paid the price of leadership, prior to seeking Kelly's friendship, back in 1926, 1927, 1928, when he had his fights within the Republican Party with all those old recognized and wise black leaders—Ed Wright, William E. King, and Oscar DePriest. Those men were bellwethers, but they were in another party. Because he had that experience of having been with them, and disagreed with them, and could see a larger horizon that had some definite things that he wanted to accomplish, he paid the price back then of making himself accepted as a leader among his people. So when Dawson marched before Kelly or anybody else and said, "I'm Bill Dawson," if they knew politics, and if they could analyze a man, they knew immediately that there is a man, or there is *the* man, or someone who could become *the* man. All they had to do was to welcome him as a part of the in-group. This is the way I analyze it.

In the future, black politics in Chicago will have to follow a dynamic leadership. I feel that there is one man on the scene today, if he wanted to restrict himself to city politics, or to an area of politics, he could enunciate and also articulate a program for black voters. He could be that cohesive force, if he could win the confidence of the people. I think that Jesse Jackson (many people would disagree with me) does have the leadership capabilities and qualifications to be a top-grade politician. If our people could involve such a man, I think there again would evolve an era such as the one Dawson came out of. I am not saying that he should not reach for greater horizons and heights, etc. What I am saying is that you build a brick at a time, that he or any other person who hopes to be a powerful political leader, whether it is in a black group, a Polish group, a Jewish group, or an Italian group, must start among his people and build a brick at a time. He must have people come to him and swear by him, and become a part and parcel of his organization who are going to follow orders and take commands. I don't see anybody else. I am not saying that he is *the* man. I am saying that he has the potentialities. I think he has the vision. I think that he can enunciate it. I think he is respected by other groups. Unfortunately, he may not be the politician that he needs to be.

You are saying, then, Mr. Love, that the leadership would have to be professional political leadership, not the reform types.

Reform? What is reform? What are they going to reform?

TWO

The Old Guard

VITO MARZULLO / BERNARD
NEISTEIN / MARSHALL KORSHAK
GEORGE DUNNE

VITO MARZULLO *Italian. Eighty years old. Was a precinct captain, ward superintendent, and state representative, and has been alderman and ward committeeman for twenty-five years. Dean of the Chicago city council, leader of the Italian bloc, and a long-time political powerhouse boss of the West Side's 25th ward.*

I was born in Italy. I was twelve and a half years old when I came here. I've always lived in the same neighborhood. I went to school as far as the fourth grade, and after one year in grammar school I went to work for about four dollars a week. I saw the machines in these factories and I like to be a machinist, but I couldn't read, write, or speak English, so I started going to Lewis Institute on Madison and Damen two nights a week for about six years and I became a machinist.

I started in politics fifty-seven years ago. I was a young fellow. They couldn't get a Democratic precinct captain out my way. They were all Republicans. So they got the little greenhorn to sit in. The bug bit me and I stayed in. They beat the heck out of me the first couple of elections, but after a couple elections I made a Democratic precinct out of it. The first political job I had it was in the county treasurer's office—a clerk at $150 a month. From there I went as a deputy bailiff for the municipal court. I was made civil service ward superintendent of streets and sanitation December, 1939. In 1940, my organization put me up to run for state representative.

Why were you picked to run for the legislature?
I was always active. I was like eager beaver. Jim Bowler was the ward committeeman and the alderman, and he always used to make speeches in the organization. "You want to get somewhere in politics, watch how Vito Marzullo raise his family, watch how Vito Marzullo take his job, watch how Vito Marzullo take care of his precinct." I ran seven times for the legislature with no opposition. Nobody filed against me.

In 1953, Bowler ran for congressman and he call me in. He says,

"You gotta take my place as an alderman." I say, "You're crazy. I can't afford it." That job, the alderman, was $5,000 a year and $1,800 expenses. I was getting $6,000 a year as a ward superintendent and $5,000 a year in the legislature—$11,000 a year. He said, "Vito, you gotta take the ward over because after you're elected, I'm gonna resign as a ward committeeman. And if you run for alderman, nobody run against you." He was the boss. I had to do what he told me. After I was elected alderman he resign as ward committeeman. I was appointed and then in 1956 I ran for election. I ran seven times for the legislature, seven times for alderman, six times for ward committeeman, and I only had opposition once. Nineteen time nobody filed against me, even for public nuisance! One time I had opposition in 1967 for alderman. I defeated my opponent 15,000 to 1,000.

I'm like a midwife. I'm always on call, no matter where I go—weddings, wakes, social affairs, civic affair, religious affair, black, white, Mexican, and Poles. I'm always on the go. I never stop. I always like to pay my respect to everybody. I always say, like the Winston cigarette slogan, "You may not like my grammar very much, but you're gonna like my taste."

I always speak the truth. For a politician, it's not very good to speak the truth. But, at the long run, pays dividend. You get through talking to your people and they know you speak from the heart. I never manufacture any speeches or write anything.

I take care of my people like I take care of my own family. That's my philosophy in public life. My home is open twenty-four hours a day. Anybody can call me, day or night. If I'm not home, Mrs. Marzullo will take the message and I'll call back. An alderman and ward committeeman has to be everything from street cleaner to psychiatrist. They call me for everything under the sun. If I can help 'em, I will; if I can't, I tell 'em, "I can't help you." You gotta treat other people like you want to be treated yourself. Service and communication of all kind. You find that some people are elected because they say, "I'm an Italian, I'm a Jew, I'm a Pole, I'm Irish, I'm German." It isn't so. When a man elected to public office, you must try to understand everybody's problem. Not that you understand 'em all, but what you don't understand, you inquire and you find out, and you give the people service. I'm happier than they are when I can help 'em. If I can't, I'll tell them the reason why. I don't run away from them.

Whatever I got, I got it through the good grace of the people of America. That's why I wear this flag all the time. This is the country

made me what I am, not Italy. I'm proud I was born in Italy, but when
I came here, I came one thought in mind, to learn the American way
of life.

You can't have the cake and eat it too. Anything you do in life, you
gotta make sacrifice. And you make sacrifice, you make progress. To
make progress, you gotta be active, you gotta keep going. When
you're active and you keep going, you're aggressive, you make mistakes. And when you make mistakes, you don't make the second time.
The only one who don't make mistake are people not doing anything,
people dead from the toenail up. They not doing anything, they don't
make mistakes. Nobody's perfect. The best ballplayer in the country,
is he score a hundred percent? 'Course not. You score 75, 80 percent,
you're a good player. So it's same thing in politics. In politics, you gotta
say, "This is my life." You gotta love people, otherwise, as Truman
said, "You can't stand the heat, get out of the kitchen." And I can take
the heat. When people come in with requests, I like it better. But
when they come in with demands, they come in with a chip on their
shoulder, I warn 'em, "Don't come and see me with a chip on your
shoulder. You can't bluff this alderman because I happen to be a pretty
good poker player and I call all the bluffs."

One time twenty fellows come in—ten Black Panthers, ten Mexican, an Irish white priest from Precious Blood Church, with a 15- or
16-year-old girl. One black man come in with a bundle of paper in
his hand, and they come in like a bunch of animals. "Alderman, we
got certain demands to make of you!" You know, just that way. I took
one look at 'em all around. I say, "Look, sir, before you go any further,
I want you to know you don't make no goddam demands of this
alderman, you understand? Who's your precinct captain?" So the
priest says to me, "We represent 2,000 people in Precious Blood
parish." I say, "Who died and elected you boss? I'm the elected boss
in this ward." The priest says, "Alderman, that the way you talk to
us? After all, you're our alderman." I say, "You shut up! You're not
only disgrace my religion, you're a disgrace all religion." I say, "What
are you doing down here with all these animals in the first place? Get
outta here, never come back here again!" He says, "We'll see you're
never elected alderman again!" I say, "I'll be alderman when you're
dead and buried."

You talk that way to a priest?
I even talk that way to Jesus Christ if he don't come in like human
being.

I represent the most cosmopolitan ward in Chicago. You name the nationality, race, religion—I got 'em all. The majority, it's about 30 percent black. I got quite a few Mexicans, but a lot of them are not citizen, and I got Poles, Slovenians, Lithuanians, Italians (only 5 percent), a few Jews, and a few Irish. And I got businessmen, churches (I got about thirty-five churches in the ward), Protestant, Catholic, black churches. Every one get a Christmas contribution. Every affair they have, they get a donation. I got Mothers Clubs, Fathers Clubs, and social clubs. One election day, I come into the precinct polling place in the basement of St. Roman's Church, and the priest is passing out coffee and doughnuts. "What are you doing?" I asked. "What the hell do you think I'm doing?" he says. "I'm trying to get some Democratic votes."

How do you get precinct captains in your organization and what do you expect of them?
A precinct captain has gotta have something on the ball to deal with the general public. A precinct captain represent four or five hundred votes in the precinct, goes to church with the people, or go to wakes, go to weddings. He goes to local affairs, social affairs, become acquainted, and knows the people. I was precinct captain for thirty-three years. I was one of the best Democratic precinct captains in Chicago before I gave it up. A precinct captain is community leader that people go to, their neighbors wanted something. You know, when you represent a ward, 65,000 to 70,000 people, that's a city by itself! And not everyone in the ward knows the alderman personally. But through the precinct captain, through these social affairs, civic affairs, church affair and all that, they get acquainted with the precinct captain. I go to these affairs, they introduce me, I make a little talk, and that's how the progress is.

But the precinct captain—some of them good, some of them bad. You talk about crooks. Listen, professor, you find crooks in any walk of life—in business, industry, welfare, plenty of them, churches and cemetery. So what do you do if you catch a crook in the bank, a cashier that's stealing money? Are you gonna close the bank? Or are you gonna fire the cashier or send him to jail? What do you do if a priest goes wrong in the church? Are you gonna close the church or are you gonna close the religion? What do you do if a nun get caught fool around in the church, don't perform her duty?

In business, I remember when I was working in the factory, it's a lot of things going on right along. So what about when you operate a corporation like the City of Chicago, when you got 50,000 to 60,000 employees of all walk of life—professional people, mechanical trades-men, laborers, truckdrivers, clerks, stenographers, doctors? Certainly you find something goes wrong every day, big and small. Let the chips fall where they belong. Don't condemn the whole branch of a government! If this branch of government of Chicago was corrupt as some of the news media are trying to say it is, if this branch of a government of Chicago is just nothing but politician or a machine, then can anyone tell me why this great Mayor Daley been elected, reelected, six consecutive terms with bigger and bigger majority? You know, Abraham Lincoln says you can fool some of the people some of the time, but you can't fool all the people all the time. Can they tell me why I was elected, reelected twenty time for office, and nineteen time with no opposition? Can I been fooling the people, rob the people? I'm a crook all these years, and they still go out and elect, reelect me, just because I got precinct captain? It isn't so! There are no shakedown artists in the 25th ward.

What if a captain doesn't carry his precinct? Will he get fired?
If he don't carry intentionally, or neglect his duties, his work, naturally, I don't want no deadbeats around me. I'm looking for a live wire. Another thing, a lotta these politicians, they're allergic to people who are a little bit aggressive. They afraid of them. "You gotta watch this fella." I don't watch anyone! I want people around me to be aggressive. If they're not aggressive for themselves, how the heck they gonna be aggressive for me? It's ridiculous! So if a precinct captain don't function, he just don't want to do anything, or he's a shakedown artist, I'd get rid of him. Wouldn't you, if you had a business, somebody don't carry on your policy? Whether you're right or wrong, you're responsible. I'm responsible. I gotta give an account to the people of my act in public office. So any of my precinct captains or any of my employees of my committee don't carry on my policy, I don't want them.

I got pride in what I'm doing. I like to have a good ward. Before every primary and every election I have to give the county chairman an accurate count in my ward. I call in my precinct captains to give me an estimate. Lots of precincts, I give them the count. I haven't been in this game for fifty-seven years for nothing. I can come within 500 votes in any election, maybe 1 or 2 percent off. If a captain doesn't get the results he gave me, I can tell he's not in touch with the people. I usually come in number two or three in the city.

They talk about political machine! I like to ask anybody, including yourself, professor, can any education institution operate without the head of it? Can any industry operate, can any business operate? Even in a grocery store, where you got three, four people working, you got one man running. Same thing in politics. It's not machine! It's an organization that functions. You must have an organization in anything you do in life. Otherwise you'll go bankrupt. That's why the Republican Party are bankrupt. They're groundhogs, they're bankrupt. They come up once a year like the groundhog. They want run for office, they want build new schools, they want build new city. If you give them ten-dollar bill, they can't even get a dog outta dog pound for you! How they gonna take a place of a man like Daley, who comes from the very bottom—train, screen, and double screen judges and county officials, city official, ward committeemen. They call a machine the ward committeemen. Every ward elect a Democratic and Republican committeeman. They don't get no salary. These ward committeemen are simply to run the party policies and run the party's campaign. So I can't understand why they want to call a machine.

How do you provide services for your people?

In the 25th ward, we have a voice in every branch of government —city council, county board, state legislature. We have me as alderman, Matt Ropa as county commissioner, and Marco Domico as state representative. We got judges. We got lawyers give legal advice. All free. We got a nice congresswoman who always at our beck and call. She answers all our requests.

When you been in the office all these years from the bottom up, you get to see everybody who comes up, like the sheriff, the county clerk, the county treasurer, the president of the county board, the mayor, the governor. Naturally, you get things done more than the average fellow does. I have friends and they give me service. You know, not everybody was born and raised with a silver spoon in their mouth. Not everybody got a lawyer on their beck and call like corporation. I get calls. I call different people this morning, and they want this done; they ask for information, how to go about it. It don't cost them a dime. They come over here, they know they got a public servant here. Then, two nights a week, I got headquarter. Two nights a week over at the headquarter, they come over there on Tuesday and Thursday, and I interview an average of 13, 15, 20, 30 people every Tuesday and Thursday night.

What do you expect them to do for you in return?

When they come and ask me for service, I don't care who they are. I do it for everybody. I don't ask their politics. They ask me, "Alderman, what can we do for you?" Some offer money. I say, "No. You're talking to the wrong alderman, sir." They say, "What can we do for you in return?" I say, "When election day come, let your conscience be your guide." I got memorandum of all these things and I give it to the precinct captain when election day come, and the precinct captain goes over, and says, "The alderman send me over. Can you go along with our program?" And they say, "Certainly we do. Be glad to."

You say you do all these things for the people. Doesn't it take a lot of money to run a ward organization? How do you raise money, if you don't take any money from anybody?

The Democratic Party of the 25th ward run a dinner dance every year. You been to them. We got an ad book. We sell tickets. On the dinner tickets we don't make much money. On the ad book we make an average of $50,000 to $60,000 a year. With that money, we give campaign contribution to candidates, we help the community, whatever churches, social affairs, civic affair, whatever I'm invited to, go to different dinner, different outing. Otherwise, as I say, if I had to get it on my own, I never make that kind of money.

I get a check every year for $2,500 from an Italian magazine publisher in New York. I never met the man. He read about me in the paper. He said I remind him of his father. I got a check for $500 the other day from a company in my ward. Mt. Sinai Hospital buys a $250 table every year for our dinner dance and sends us back the tickets. They made me Man of the Year a couple of years ago.

Nobody pay any dues. Nobody is compulsory that you gotta take so many tickets, you gotta bring so many head. I call one meeting, and the precinct captains and the workers, they all get going. They know what they gotta do and they do it.

Did you have any ambitions for higher office?

I wanna stay home with my family and my people. I feel better at home. I could have gone to Congress in 1964. I didn't go. I got my ward and my people. I was in the state legislature for fourteen years, but I came back to be an alderman in the city council. I even feel better in the city council than the legislature. You must understand, here I end up to be the dean of the city council. That's quite an honor for an Italian boy came in this country when he was twelve years old. You don't get this any part of the world outside America. That's how great this country is. That's why I always like to stay at home with my people. I like to communicate with my people. I enjoy life that way.

One time Mayor Daley called me in and say, "Vito, how would you like to go on the county board?" I say, "No." Next year, he call me in again and say, "Vito, how would you like to be clerk of the probate court?" I say, "No." He says, "Everybody wants to move up. How come you don't want to move up?" I say, "I'm satisfied. I just want to stay where I am as an alderman and committeeman, where I can help my friends and shaft my enemies." And that really broke him up. He laughed so hard.

What did you think of Mayor Daley?

There's one answer to it, professor. The man come from the very bottom, from a community of working people, religious people, and he still live in the same community—never run away from his people. A great family man, which I'm a great believer. Great religious man, which I'm a great believer of any kind religion as long as the people believe in God. A great professional person. As public official, he start as a sergeant-at-arms in the city council, work in the county clerk, became deputy county clerk, he serve in the state senate for ten years, he serve as Director of Revenue for two years under Stevenson. He became a ward committeeman, he was elected Chairman of the Democratic County Central Committee, and he finally hold the mayor's office. He's like me—he never want run for no other office. He had the best rule in the world, "In this world, no one walks alone." One time, when I was gonna give him $10,000 for his campaign from my ward, he said he didn't want the money. I told him, "You run the city, but I run my goddam ward. You take the money." He love Chicago. He love his people.

I love Chicago, too, 'cause from the first day I come over here, Chicago and America has been nice to me. I would never have this opportunity in Italy. It's too bad that 95 to 99 percent of those who got the opportunity in this country better than I ever had, and many thousands of more like me, don't take advantage of the opportunity that this country's given 'em.

That's what's wrong with the so-called Independents in the city council. They contribute nothing, absolutely nothing. They're what you call publicity crazy. They get on television, newspapers. Someday they gonna be sent to Hollywood, or, when they get through, they be a bum. They have to get out and stay out because they can't face the people too much. I've seen so many from the president of the United States down, in all my years in politics. Four years, eight years, twelve years, they either quit, or they get defeated. They quit because they can't stand the gaff. They can't do what the people ask them to do and the people catch up with them. They figure, "I might as well get out." They're just, on my book, a dupe of obstructionist.

I'm gonna be honest about it. I got two sons. I wouldn't advise neither one of my sons to run for public office because, unless you're trained from the very bottom up, you can't stand the gaff, you can't take the abuse, especial in this day and age when you got so many animals marching 'round, destroying life and property, defying law and order—demonstrators and all that. This country better wake up or we won't have no country left some day.

BERNARD NEISTEIN *Jewish. Sixty years old. Was ward committeeman of the all-black 29th ward on Chicago's West Side, which always came in with phenomenal vote results (e.g., 27,000 Democrats to 500 Republicans). Formerly a precinct captain and state senator. Is also a successful attorney and a concert violinist.*

As a little boy, my father used to take me to political meetings at Guyon's Paradise Ballroom. I remember him taking me to one meeting where a white-haired fellow, Paul McNutt of Indiana, spoke, and one time Otto Kerner, Sr., spoke. He'd talk about "the sovereign state of Eelinois." Well, I was impressed, and as a little boy, I felt then I wanted to be a lawyer and I wanted to be in politics. I was eight or nine years old.

I started law school at seventeen, in 1934. I took extra subjects in high school to finish in three years. I graduated grammar school at twelve, high school at fifteen, law school at nineteen. I had to wait two years to take the bar exam. Law school was the easiest, academically, for me of all the years of education. My father had a cleaning store and I'd press clothes, and while I'd be pressing clothes, I'd have the law book on the machine and read cases. That's how I studied.

I was number one at law school. I won a dictionary. I came home and my father wasn't impressed at all. He said, "Is this what they give you for being a good student?" He thought I'd come home with ten thousand dollars or something. But it was Depression years then.

When I was seventeen, I also got active in precinct work in the 29th ward. We had the only cleaning shop from Madison Street to Roosevelt Road on Crawford Avenue. I knew all the people. I used to deliver the orders and go in their homes. So it was nothing to knock on a door and say I was the Democratic assistant and I was interested in Milton Rakove, or whoever, and the people liked me (in all modesty), and they used to go along. That's how I started.

The neighborhood was predominantly Jewish, some Irish, and partly Italian. Al Horan was the committeeman. A precinct captain by the name of Jockey Meyers recruited me to help in the precinct.

He was on the lazy side and he wasn't ambitious. He would say, "We'll do all right," but I'd go by myself and talk to people, make sure, and do anything additional to guarantee that they'd come out. During those years I didn't miss a thing at the synagogues, the churches, the wakes, bar mitzvahs, weddings. I'd act in the synagogue plays, the men's club, and all the other activities, while he never showed his face.

The essence of good precinct work is service to the people. It didn't hurt that I was a lawyer because, during all the times that I was active in politics, if anyone needed me or had any problems, I was there before the problem started. You know the old cliché, "I used to find cars before they were stolen." (They used to say that about robbers.) I was there at all times and they never had to pay me law fees. I'd help them. When it came election time, the people would go along. If I said I'm interested in John Smith, they'd vote for John Smith. They can't go to the candidate, but they can go to me. And they felt by making me strong, or big, that they'd have an entree to whatever they needed.

I was number one as a precinct captain, too. For example, in a primary fight when Daley ran against Kennelly, I had 603 votes for Daley to 3 for Kennelly. All through the years, the nonpartisan watchers used to come in with Republican buttons on, and, at the end of the day, after seeing the votes and counting them (and they could do the counting, it didn't bother me, the vote was there), they'd say, "Disgusting. If we didn't see it, we wouldn't know how it could happen." Had the vote been 600 for a Republican and 3 for a Democrat, they wouldn't have said it was disgusting. Another time, when I was a precinct captain, the vote was something like 300 to zero. There wasn't a single vote for the opposition. It looked too good to be true. We had wall-to-wall watchers from Sears Roebuck and Chicago Title and Trust, and they had notebooks about what to look for. At the end of the day they'd count the votes. They'd stand there with the judges and they'd say, "If we didn't see it, we couldn't believe it." They'd say, "Look how ignorant the people are. They all voted Democratic." But, on the North Shore, where they came from, if they voted 300 Republican, that was intelligent, that was all right.

Were you interested more in the local or the national ticket?
The local ticket was always number one. Local touched closer to home. Local, I could talk to whoever the candidate was. Nationally, I couldn't walk into the White House or any other spot to talk or

present problems. In a national election people had their minds
made up. You couldn't sway them much. Yet, wanting to be number
one, I wouldn't stop, whether it was local or national. I wanted to get
all the results that I could.

How did you get to be the ward committeeman?

I was a precinct captain for twenty-seven years. Al Horan was the
committeeman. He was an astute man. He knew politics inside out.
He didn't have the formal education, but, politically, he was one of
the smartest men around. From my experiences, the Irish, politics is
their field. If you read the book about Mayor Curley, he says in
Boston you give the Jews a few judgeships, you give the Italians a
statue of Garibaldi or Columbus, and that satisfied them. The Irish
know how to manipulate.

Horan died and there was a vacancy for ward committeeman. The
ward was predominantly run by Irish. At that time, there were more
Jews than Irish, and more Italians than Irish. Pete Callan was the
state representative, I was the state senator, and Tom Burke was the
alderman. The church stepped in all the time. They said the Irish
Catholics should be running the ward. I didn't make any overt moves
to be ward committeeman. The opposition wanted Jimmy Spangler,
who was a member of the board of tax appeals. While they thought
I was seeking it, I wasn't. Al Horan had schooled me, never lead with
your right, lead with your left, and while they thought they're knocking me down, I didn't care, because all I wanted to be was state
senator. I wanted Pete Callan to be ward committeeman. I got him
in the house one day and said, "Pete, you're going to be the one." He
turned white. He said, "I can't handle it. You've got to be the committeeman." He was my one ally in the whole fight. All the rest of
them lined up all against me and they were saying, "We're not going
to let any young whippersnapper be the committeeman," and, "It's
gotta be an Irish Catholic."

I didn't make a move. The precinct captains knew who they
wanted. For years I was carrying on for Horan, anyway. While Horan
was sick for two years before he died, I delivered better results than
he ever did. So Mayor Daley was receptive to me. You play politics
with the head, not the heart. Whether I was the acceptable one or
not, by performance, I was the one that *he* wanted. We had a meeting in Daley's office, and he said to Jimmy Spangler, "Bernie would
make a good ward committeeman." Spangler said, "Yes." So Daley
said, "I'm going to take your suggestion. I'll be in favor of Bernie."

The captains, of course, are the last word and they backed me all the way. That's how I was made committeeman.

To be a ward committeeman during the sixteen years that I was ward committeeman was a thankless job. You've got to keep an organization together. You've got to be handy at the beck and call of all the captains and all the people. I wanted to be responsive and to have a good ward, so I was diligent in trying to help with whatever problems arose. If there's sanitation problems, they come to you, although it's really the alderman's job, or the ward superintendent. If there's philanthropic or religious affairs, you've got to be active and be in the forefront. There's ever so many duties involved. People, especially in our era that came from Europe, or were the first generation, or maybe, at most, the second, never knew government that way, and could see it operate where they could go right to somebody and have their complaints heard. I was a witness for citizenship cases many, many times. It meant that somebody had to take a day off from work and go downtown and be a witness. I'd volunteer to be that witness and people appreciated it. And, of course, I could swear that for five years, or eight years, or whatever the length of time, that I knew them. A lot of them were immigrants from the old country. And people knew that government was a maze of bureaucracies and regulations that lost the common touch or the human touch. Everything's computerized, and people don't like that.

There are unlimited hours. You can't say one hour, two hours. I had a law office all through the years, and the people could find me downtown if they couldn't find me at the headquarters. Horan had a home in Florida, so he'd be down there six months; then he had a home in Wisconsin, so he'd be there six months. So, when they wanted something and they couldn't find him, they'd come to me when I was working under him. I'd assume the burdens and try to solve whatever problems, and that's where I got my start acting as committeeman. I was pretty popular. I knew most of the department heads and public officials, and if anything was legal or within reason, I'd get things done. And that's all that the people would be interested in.

How do you recruit precinct captains, and what do you expect of them?

There were a certain percentage of people that came in unannounced who were interested in politics and wanted to become precinct captains. I would interview them and see what I thought of them, personally, and I would give them a chance. That didn't mean that I would give them a job. "Patronage" is a dirty word, but if they worked out in the precinct, I'd try to get them employment.

I'd also go into the neighborhood to churches, synagogues, or find someone who was outstanding in community affairs, to see if they wanted to get involved in politics. I found that those who related to people and were sincere in trying to help their neighbors in the community turned out to be the best captains. If you were there with the people every day, when they had sadness or when they had pleasure, the people remember that. Sometimes outsiders would try to come in and influence their vote and they wouldn't stop at anything. The people would say, "No, we don't want to help you. We're in with so and so." You couldn't buy or swing over people that you have been with every day. But, if the results weren't good, I'd know the captain was falling down somewhere.

We got great results in the ward. When Johnson ran against Goldwater, I think it was 27,000 to 500; when Kerner ran against Percy, it was close to the same figure; Kennedy and Nixon, 25,000 to 500. And we got those percentages all through the years. In all humility, I'd say it shows good leadership.

In the years that you were committeeman, your ward changed from Irish/Italian/Jewish to black. What was politics like in the ward during that period?

During the time that it was changing, I remember the first black that moved into the neighborhood. When he moved in, I went over to see him and brought him a gift for the housewarming. He never forgot it. He was my best ally in all the years. You couldn't say a word about the grey boy (that's what he called me), to him. And the same with all the others that came there, black, white, green, or yellow. They're still people and if you treat them with respect and try to help them, they all appreciate it. But certain things happened during those times. When the ward was white there weren't many removals. People stayed where they lived and we didn't have a transition. When the ward eventually became all black, twenty to thirty percent move every year. You don't have the same voters year after year. You have a high degree of removal. So it's really hard to take root with the people, relate to them, and establish a real firm base with them. Before that, when the people saw and knew you, and you just didn't come around on election day, they were yours. Human nature is human nature. I don't care if they're white, black, green, or blue. If you're friendly with the people and you're there when they want you, they have the same feeling of respect and responsibility as any other group.

What about the charges of "plantation politics"?

I'll tell you about that. That's planted by do-gooders from Evanston and Glencoe who live in all-white neighborhoods and preach about integration. But the ones that live in the ward, when I'd tell them I wanted to quit, I'd have two hundred at my doorstep saying, "If you quit, we move out of the neighborhood." I've never had people in my area through the years come to me and say, "We want you out." As a matter of fact, they all used that speech about, "You play the Star Spangled Banner with white and black keys, you don't just play it on all white or all black."

The numbers have fallen off tremendously in wards like the 29th ward. Can you tell me why?

Number one, they put through the Congress Street Expressway, and that decimated the ward. After that, people would abandon buildings, break windows, cause damage, and move out in the middle of the night. We had a number of buildings that were torn down by the city because they became public nuisances. And we had a certain percentage that wouldn't register. The captains couldn't get them to register. Some of them had a record, and they didn't want to disclose that they were convicted and couldn't come in and vote. They didn't have their civil rights restored. Other groups were fearful because the creditors were always hounding them and chasing them, and could get a good line on them if they were on a poll sheet. They refused to register. Another percentage wouldn't register, because with public aid recipients who were on aid to dependent children, the father is responsible, and the mother of the children could say that their father ran away and abandoned the children and they're destitute. And a lot of them were living there. If they registered, the public aid office could get a line immediately that Mr. Jones is living there with Mrs. Jones and the family. So they wouldn't dare to bare their name, their situation, or their location. This is what we ran into. As for the argument that they are apathetic or disillusioned because of the political machine, I don't think that they are any more disillusioned or apathetic than people in any other area. I don't think that's it at all.

In the transition period, Bernie, did you keep the white captains, or recruit black captains?

Well, the white captains remained at first, and we had a real good voter turnout because the white captains knew, even though they moved out, that they had to be there. They would come there, day after day, and they'd say, "I'm as close as your telephone," and they'd give them a card. The white captains, little by little, became situated in the wards and townships they moved to, and were replaced by black captains. I didn't give any jobs to whites any more; I was giving them to blacks. The black captains, while they lived there and went to the people, were fine. But we had a different problem in our ward. A lot of black captains moved out of the ward. A few captains remained in the ward, but a higher percentage moved out. The only time they showed up was on election time and the voters resented it. The relationship to the voter wasn't there, and the response by the voter wasn't there. Their complaint was, "We can't find the captain." It happened in a lot of the transitional wards. While everything was deteriorating, the quality of political work was also deteriorating. If the captains hadn't moved out, the neighborhood might not have deteriorated either, because, while they were living there, they'd make sure that an abandoned car was picked up, that a hole in the street was fixed, that a building violation was corrected, but if they weren't around to know about it, there was no one around to turn to.

The whole thing was that the people used to say to a captain, "I don't know Mr. Jones, or I don't know Mr. Smith (whoever is running for whatever office), but I know you and you've been decent to me, so I'm voting for you." And after the transition, the people didn't really know the captains.

Another thing, in the old days, if you gave a captain $200 to take care of the precinct on election day, he would hire four or five workers to help in the precinct. But these new captains—if you gave them $200, they'd keep the $200 and nobody was working in the precinct on election day.

What is good politics to you, Bernie?

For me, politics has always been a great profession, an honorable profession. A lot of people say one of the attributes of a politician is that you have got to be a hypocrite, and many of them are. All through the years, what rubbed me wrong and made me wild down in Springfield, was the hypocrisy. I'd get despondent listening to the hypocrites.

Who are some good politicians in Chicago?

Vito Marzullo is the kind that practices politics every hour of the day, every day of the year. George Dunne has the same kind of pattern. Just take the good committeemen, and you'll find out. Mayor Daley eats and sleeps politics, and is responsive to people's needs. He is criticized a lot, but if anyone has a complaint, they can get through to him, and get into the office and he'll contact them, and something will be done with their problem. He's with the people. He loves the city and he revels in any success of one particular area of the city. It's like he's having that success, or going through whatever they're going through. He's like a big father and these are his children. This is a big, big strength. He's got warmth and a feeling for people. It's like in my field (I say "my field" because I love music)—I just read an article by Nathan Milstein and he says, "You can get ten violinists to play a selection, and they'll play it. But if they haven't got the heart, it sounds lousy, it stinks" (those are his words). And one out of ten, or maybe less, have the feeling, and that's so necessary in being an artist or a politician.

I know you are a violinist, Bernie, as well as being a politician and a lawyer.

Yes. When I was a little boy, I took violin lessons. Like any Jewish family, the boys took violin and the girls took piano. I took lessons when I was eight years old until I was about nine-and-a-half, and (in all humility) I was darn good. My teacher had thirty students. I wasn't number one. Number one was a fellow by the name of Ptashne. He's now the concertmaster of the Minneapolis Symphony. I was number two or three—there were two of us that were next, and I don't know who was better. We were both on a par. The other fellow, Joe Stepansky, was a concertmaster for WGN Symphony, and now he is in California and played with Percy Faith. He just sent me a record where he recorded a quartet with Jascha Heifetz. The teacher thought a lot of me, but, to my regret, I couldn't go to Hebrew school and public school and do other things, so I gave it up.

About forty-six years later, when I was in Springfield as a state senator, the sergeant-at-arms of the senate was an old retired vaudevillian named Joe Mack. He told me he had a violin that he wanted to sell. He said, "Will you give me $1,500?" I gave him the $1,500. I went to a wedding or a bar mitzvah with Dave Mall and I said that I had this violin. He said, "I'll give you $2,500 without looking at it." I said, "No, I don't want to sell it." He said, "Why don't you go to a

friend of mine and let him see it?" The following Saturday we met
with this fellow by the name of Bob Kagan on Wabash and Jackson.
Kagan opened the violin case, closed it and said, "That violin isn't
worth $10!" Well, I got my money back when I went back to Spring-
field! But that's not the point of the story. Kagan showed us a bro-
chure from Sotheby's auction house in London that described a
Guarnarius del Jesu violin (which in my opinion is even better than
a Stradivarius). There were like ten Guarnarius brothers, fathers,
uncles (they're all good violins), but the Guarnarius del Jesu is the
best. It was to be auctioned for $102,000.

Well, my eyes opened, and he said, "I have another one in the safe
here." I said, "Oh, can I play it?" I didn't come right out, I wasn't
brazen, but my eyes said that. So he turned to Dave Mall and said,
"Is he a player?" Dave Mall said, "No, he's just a fellow I know." I
got enough courage and said, "Can I see that violin?" He gave it to
me and I started playing it. He said, "Wait a minute." He dialed a
number and said, "I want you to hear somebody. When can you hear
him?" The fellow said, "Thursday." So Thursday, at 10 o'clock, I went
to this fellow that he had sent me to. It was George Perlman, a lawyer
(never practiced), who was a concert violinist and now he is a
teacher. His pupils were Albert Einstein, Jack Benny, Mischa Elman,
among many others. I played for him, and he was impressed. What
he said was what Kagan said, "In fifty years that I had people under
my tutelage, you're the second one with natural ability. That doesn't
mean you can play the violin, but you're a natural. I'd like to teach
you." So I'm saying to myself, "If these two fellows are so enthused,
I'm enthused too!"

I started taking lessons about three years ago. Since then, I think
I have progressed. I gave a concert playing the Vivaldi concerto at
Northwestern's Thorne Hall. I play with Milton Preves of the Chicago Symphony. He's our conductor with the Gold Coast Chamber
Orchestra. We've given four concerts and we're supposed to give a
concert in December at Orchestra Hall—Handel's *Messiah*. I love
music and always have. Any money that I had accumulated during
the Depression, I would buy symphonic records and deprive myself
of something else.

*Bernie, you have a reputation around Chicago as a ward boss and
a tough guy. How does this jibe with playing the violin?*

I wouldn't say I'm tough. I'd have to have others say it for me. I'm
a devout coward, but I was in the paratroops and won a battlefield

commission. I do run a tough ward and demand an awful lot from people. It's predominantly black, but I've never had any problems in all the years I've been there. I've threatened to throw a few from the window, from the twentieth floor here in my office, but aside from that, it's been very quiet.

MARSHALL KORSHAK

Jewish. Sixty-six years old. Long-time ward committeeman of the 5th ward on the South Side, which contains the University of Chicago and is a long-time liberal, reform ward. He has been a state senator, sanitary district trustee, city collector, and a candidate for county treasurer.

I was born in Lawndale here in Chicago. When my parents became a little affluent we moved to Douglas Blvd. I went to Lawson and Herzl grammar schools, to John Marshall High School, and then to the University of Wisconsin. Then came the Great Depression. I came back here and went to night law school at Central Y College. Then I went to DePaul and graduated from Kent College of Law in the middle of the Depression. I saw the vets selling pencils and apples. I became enamoured of Franklin Delano Roosevelt and became active in Democratic politics. Even then I recognized the Republican Party as being the party of the status quo, and the Democratic Party as being the party that was trying to do the most good for the greatest number of people.

At law school I met a guy by the name of George Duggan. He lived in Hyde Park, and he was a precinct captain for Judge Mike Igoe. George said to me in 1933, "C'mon out and help me in my precinct in the 5th ward. That ward is going to be a Jewish ward someday, and you'll be the committeeman." And that's the God's truth, Milt.

When I did become the 5th ward committeeman, there wasn't any captain who could kid me or misrepresent something because of the great experience I had myself. I was the best precinct captain in the city of Chicago because I was dedicated and I knew my people. I knew the wives, and the children, and the relatives. I got to know them like I was a member of their family, and they a member of my family. I was hungry. I worked hard. You don't get the same sense of dedication from precinct captains today. You lived through the Great Depression. I was fighting hard for a job to make good. And all the other captains were.

The precinct captain is the unsung and unheralded hero of our democracy. Because even if you didn't vote the way he told you to vote, at least he was letting you know there was an election. In my experience as a ward committeeman, there were elections that only 20 percent of our people turned out to vote. You had to get them registered. Mayor Daley always said that the registration was most important. And the primary was very important. It gave you an indication of what was going to happen. If they don't register, Milt, then they can never vote. That's very simple. Especially when you look out there after the registration is over and there's 75 Democratic votes, hopefully, that you could have gotten, but they're not registered, and so the game is over. You can't vote them. It's like the clock running out on a football game or a basketball game. Your team is going red hot in the last two minutes but time runs out. The primary is an indication that the person votes for you and votes Democratic. You can almost get an indemnity bond from Continental Insurance Company that they'll vote Democratic in the general election.

How did you become the ward committeeman?

I was the greatest volunteer in the world. That's why I'm so active in civic affairs. Someone would say, "We have to do this," and I would raise my hand and I would do it. As a precinct captain I was available, like the comic strip, Available Jones. Any captain that had to get a doctor or a coat for his wife, a pediatrician for his child, buy a car, or get a piece of jewelry, anything. I can't tell you why, but my chemistry was such that they would gravitate toward me. As a result, I was the closest man to the precinct captains. I celebrated with them on their joyous occasions, and I was with them in the moments of bereavement. I was available, always available. Without being critical, and without mentioning any names, ward committeemen are not necessarily always available, and I was. I was the closest man to everybody involved and it finally reached a point where the precinct captains were extremely unhappy with the then ward committeeman, and they asked me to take over the ward, and I did, in 1956.

You want to know about that election? The mayor had gotten word what was happening in the ward and the ward committeeman was going in to see Daley all the time. Daley called a meeting. I was there and the ward committeeman was there, and he said to the mayor, "Korshak is friendly with all the saloon keepers." I looked at the

mayor and I said, "I plead guilty." In our ward, the 5th ward, the
Dohertys and the McCarthys, all fine people who raised big families,
just happened to be wonderful, important, nice, law-abiding saloon
keepers, who went to church and were pillars of the community.
(We're not talking about Rush Street today, and some of the terrible
places.) I said, "Yes, I'm friendly with them. They're all good friends
of mine." I knew that Daley would love it, especially when I'm
talking about people who were pillars of the Irish Catholic community. Well, the ward committeeman, like Captain Queeg in *The
Caine Mutiny,* every time he opened his mouth, he put his foot into
it. And so, at the conclusion of this conversation, the committeeman
said to the mayor, "Well, what are you going to do about it?" And the
mayor said, "I don't know what you're going to do, but I'm going
home to have dinner." And that ended that! I was overwhelmingly
elected by the precinct captains. I'll go back to what I told you. I was
available. I was in their homes. They were in my home and their
children knew me, but no one knew him.

How do you run an independent, liberal ward like the 5th ward?
    When I inherited the ward, I inherited sixty-four precinct captains.
I made some changes. It was very difficult to get dedicated, conscientious precinct captains. I would tell them to be active, not be a
follower, but to attempt to be a leader. To be a volunteer, as I was.
Volunteer to do everything. When someone would come in and say,
"What do I have to do?" I would give him my blue plate special. I
would say, "Get to know all the religious leaders in the ward, get to
know the businessmen. I will supply the headquarters and coffee and
meeting place for you. Get to know the people. Talk to them about
their problems, and always be sure to tell them that there are some
things we can help them with and many, many, that we can't. Show
them that we are interested in their welfare." When someone would
come in and wanted a position of leadership, they'd say to me, "What
do you want me to do?" I'd always say to them, "I don't want you to
do a damn thing," because that's the person I didn't want. Too many
people were interested in instant politics. Politics isn't like instant tea
or coffee. It is something that has to be developed and nurtured and
worked with.
    When you talk about political jobs, it's disgraceful. I used to get jobs
for married men with two or three children and their jobs would pay
$400 a month, and the public would be very critical of the payroller.
Well, I want to tell you that these precinct captains and payrollers

(and there is some corruption) put in a full day's work for a full day's pay. I used to tell them to go to Westinghouse Electric, General Motors, U.S. Steel. "Go somewhere where you can build something," I said. "Use politics as a hobby, but make yourself self-sustaining and self-sufficient, because they will break your heart someday."

Politics is exciting, exhilarating, and just falls short of physical combat. But in terms of remuneration or wealth, it's very unrewarding financially. I'll bump into a guy that I worked with in the county treasurer's office a hundred years ago and he's still working there; he's raised a large family and he's sent them to school. That poor soul might now be making $900 a month. The pay is very poor for jobholders, outside of the key jobs.

Why do they do it, then?
I would say there is a certain amount of glamour to it. I'd say that they are lazy. They take the line of least resistance. You give a fellow a job in the park district, picking up papers, a married man with children. You give him a job parking cars. All kinds of jobs where the pay is absolutely shameful, a disgrace.

I always prided myself on the fact that I couldn't take blood money. I was one of the few ward committeemen in Chicago that never required a precinct captain or worker to buy tickets, or sell tickets, or sell ads. Never! I just happened to be in a position of having a lot of good friends, and I was a lawyer myself, and I would say to you, if I met you on the street, "Milt, the ward is in trouble and I could use $100," and you would give it to me and make it payable to the 5th Ward Regular Democratic Organization. I could name you some of the most responsible people in the city of Chicago who were friends of mine, and I would call them and I would say that this is the time, could I have a check for $250 for the 5th Ward Regular Democratic Organization, and to their credit, and to my satisfaction, they gave it to me.

What did you have to do for them?
Not a goddam thing. What could I do for the head of a large industrial firm? I, myself, have been a very successful lawyer (not to say that I didn't go through some terrible periods with Edith). When we got married in 1934, my wife made $16 a week and I was a lawyer. My mother-in-law always thought that when you became a lawyer, the government gave you some kind of subsidy, and she said you can't get married until you become a lawyer. I worked for $90

a month in the ward, and it passed through my mind at that time (I was frightened to death), "Oh, boy, if they will only make me civil service here." At $90 a month! I was going to law school and sold programs at Soldier Field. I got pneumonia at the Michigan–Northwestern game. I got to work up to $260 a month in the county treasurer's office where I worked with these very men that I talked to you about a few minutes ago, who stayed on and on. I got a job in the state's attorney's office, on a temporary payroll. My salary was $295 a month. I had lots of fear and frustration for many years. But then, in 1947, I resigned from the state's attorney's office and went into the private practice of law, and since that time my earnings have gone up and up, and I will admit to you that I am not poor anymore.

At the same time, I think I have held more political offices than many in the history of local Democratic politics. I was a state senator, director of revenue for the state of Illinois, director of revenue for the city of Chicago, city treasurer, a trustee of the metropolitan sanitary district, and city collector. You name it.

Have you had any major political ambitions that have been unfulfilled?

Yes, I have. I worked real hard and I had dreams. I always dreamed and hoped that the time would come when I could be a United States senator or governor. My resignation last year as director of revenue, the last cord that I cut with politics, so to speak, was a very traumatic experience, because I still had my dreams and I still had my hopes. Now, when fellas meet me on the street and say, "Oh, well, you'll run for office again," I say, "No, never!" I'm sixty-six years old and the ball game is over politically, as far as I'm concerned. Now I can sit back and reflect and be helpful. But you have to talk to yourself, Milt, in order to overcome the unhappiness, and what could have been but didn't happen.

You try to keep your hand in. People come to me by the scores for help, and I've made up for the missing of the political thing. I have accentuated my civic responsibilities and my fund raising, which keeps me busy. But you have to talk to yourself in order to fight off the terrible feelings of depression that set in. I go to meetings and look at fellas who apparently are very successful politically and (not to be unkind) they couldn't even carry my tennis shoes, but there they are, and I wish them well. And then I get to feeling sorry for myself, but I soon am able to cope with it and dismiss it from my mind. I think good thoughts, like the Christian Scientists tell you to do.

I am still active in Little Flower and Loyola University's Stritch School of Medicine. I still raise large sums. I am still extremely active in Israel bonds and the Jewish National Fund. It was almost like the last hurrah when I resigned. I was honored by the Weizmann Institute which created a chair in plant genetics in perpetuity in my name, and they had 2,300 people at the dinner. You were there. It was a testimonial that I will never forget. Dick Ogilvie was chairman. I never regarded my friends as Democrats or Republicans. When I was in the State Senate, I was always able to go to the Republican side of the aisle and get a vote for Chicago. I never looked at a man or cared anything about his politics as long as he was friendly with me. I was forthright. I wasn't partisan. I didn't wear my political heart on my sleeve, and I exhibited friendship and warmth and empathy for their problems as they did for mine. Now, that has nothing to do with election day where you go out and try to get every Democratic vote that you can get. And they understand that and they try to get every Republican vote they can get. I never regarded Republicans as enemies and I never regarded Democrats I couldn't get along with as enemies.

Why weren't you slated for higher office by the party?
It's like winning a ticket in the Irish Sweepstakes. When I was at the height of my political stature, along came Adlai Stevenson. When Governor Kerner resigned, there was Sam Shapiro (a delightful guy, and so was Adlai), and those are the breaks. And I had received some notoriety and attention in the newspapers with regard to stock that I had bought. I don't think that did me any good either. People aren't easy to forgive and forget. Also, I never was inhibited because I was Jewish, but I will say if there is a highly competent Christian and an equally highly competent person of the Jewish faith, and both aspiring to it, I think it is practical politics that the Christian will get it. It's unfortunate that living in perhaps the most enlightened period in the history of civilization, there is a great deal of prejudice. We have made the atom bomb and we landed on the moon, but in man's relationship to man, we still have a long way to go.

Tell me about the mayor.
I'll tell you a story, Milt. When I was through as city treasurer, I

decided to resign from politics. Daley saw me at a Democratic dinner and said, "I thought I told you to come over and see me." I said, "I know you've been busy." He said, "I'm not too busy." When Mayor Daley feels that he is indebted to you, or he owes you something, or you deserve something, he actually can't rest until he rewards you and repays that debt, even if you don't even know that a debt exists. So he said, "Forget about that. You come and see me." When I went up there on a Monday morning, he made a great statement to me. He said, "Marshall, I don't mean to demean you, but why don't you come back and be city collector?" And he used the words, "I don't mean to demean you." He knew that I would have liked to have been a United States senator or governor. So I said, "Well, the fact that you put it that way, Mr. Mayor, is reward enough for me." "No, no!" he said, "I want you to do it." I said, "I don't know that I want to come back." And he said, in what is almost, in our faith, a Talmudic statement, "Marshall, you can't live out there!" He meant that I couldn't live except within the confines of City Hall or the political apparatus.

What about Daley? People don't recognize that Mayor Daley can't breathe or live outside of the atmosphere of politics, or the proximity of City Hall. Can't breathe. It's a compulsion with him. I know his shortcomings and his low boiling point, but he is the most competent public official I have ever met. He knows more about each and every department than the department heads know themselves. And I was head of a department. He works (possibly a slight exaggeration) twenty hours a day at his job. And he is available. He has a press conference every day. He has a conference with the heads of all his departments so that he is on top of everything.

When anyone asks who is close to Mayor Daley, I say, "Nobody, except Mrs. Daley—Sis—and his children." I am a pretty good student of Mayor Daley and I know that there is no one that thinks for him. Anytime anyone will tell you that they are close to Mayor Daley, you tell them to go fly a kite, because he has lots of friends, but no one is really close to him. Don't let anyone ever tell you or interpret for you how Mayor Daley feels about you.

When he was ill, it looked as if he was never coming back, but he finally did. So when he had recovered and was coming down, I was at the Drake Hotel for breakfast. I called the city revenue department and Marge Sullivan mentioned that Mayor Daley was back. I wanted to say, in our expression, "Mazeltov, I'm happy he's back." I went up to the fifth floor and asked Kay Spear if I could see the mayor, and then went in. My God, Milt, he got off his chair and he put his arms around me and he was kissing my right cheek and I was kissing his left cheek, and he was crying and I was crying. I can respect a man who can shed tears, and I can shed tears, and the warmth in his embrace and mine was very, very great. It was one of the most unforgettable memories for me. It was just the most traumatic experience I have ever had.

GEORGE DUNNE *Irish. Sixty-five years old. Succeeded Daley as county central committee chairman. Is president of the Cook County board of commissioners. Long-time ward committeeman of the 42nd ward on Chicago's Near North Side. Was a precinct captain, park district supervisor, state representative, and state senator.*

I have been active politically since I was about fourteen years old, working in the precincts. I was a precinct captain for at least three or four years before I could cast a vote. I grew up here in the 42nd ward where I still live. I went to DeLaSalle High School, to Academy in Prairie du Chien, Wisconsin, and then to Northwestern University for a year. My father was the sexton of Holy Name Cathedral for thirty-three years. He passed away when I was twelve years old. We had a little bit of a problem financially at home, so I went to work for the then Lincoln Park District. I was the manager of the Lake Shore playground, a playground that I grew up in, became area supervisor, and subsequently became the assistant general superintendent of the park district.

I was a precinct captain all those years. Then a vacancy occurred in the state legislature, in the House, and I was selected to fill that slot from our district by State Senator William Connors, the 42nd ward Democratic committeeman. My father used to say that the Lord never closed one door that He didn't open another. And when He took my father from me I kind of think that He gave me Senator Connors, because we were very close and I looked upon him with a great deal of affection. I was in the legislature for eight years and became Democratic floor leader. Then I was selected to fill a vacancy on the county board. President John Duffy had passed away and the central committee had the responsibility of filling that vacancy on the board, and I was chosen.

I didn't want to go on the county board. I was perfectly happy with the park district and in the legislature. I was on the executive committee of the central committee. We had a luncheon meeting and Matt Danaher, who was then a kind of a secretary around the central committee, said to me, "George, the mayor wants you to go in as a possible candidate." I said, "Matt, I'm not interested in getting on the county board." He said, "The mayor thinks you ought to present yourself, George."

So I appeared before the committee and gave a brief résumé and in conclusion I said, "I want you to know if you don't get around to my name, there'll be no sour grapes as far as I'm concerned." I went back to the office and Mayor Daley called me and told me he wanted to let me know what the committee had done. I said, "You don't have to call me and tell me. I know they did what was right." He said, "Just hear me out. We selected Seymour Simon to be the president of the county board and we've selected you to be the chairman of the finance committee."

I was sick. I said, "I don't want to be on the board, let alone be chairman of the finance committee." "Well," he said, "come on over and talk to the committee." So I came over and there was considerable persuasion. The fellows were saying, "Come on, George, you know you have the capability and you'll do the kind of a job that's necessary. Don't let us down here. We all have to serve, we're all soldiers." So I said, "Okay, let's go" (reluctantly). I have been on the county board since 1962, and president of the board since 1969. I became ward committeeman of the 42nd ward on the occasion of Senator Connors' death in 1961.

I wasn't particularly interested in being a ward committeeman, either. The senator died in June and I just took a couple of weeks off. I felt quite bad about his demise. When I came back, I went in to see the mayor. I was the floor leader in the House and I wanted to bring him up to date on some of the things that had taken place during the session. He asked me about the committeemanship. I told him that I didn't have any particular desires or ambitions, and I said there were several people there. He said, "Well, George, wouldn't you consider that job? Let's be a little practical here. You know Bill, himself, would be a practical fellow. The people who are seeking it are really up in years, and one happens to be a pretty sick man. Now, would you think we should turn over that role, where it requires leadership, to people with this physical condition?" I said, "I realize it wouldn't be good for them or for the party." He said, "That's right. I think, George, you really ought to present yourself to the precinct captains." So I did, and I was elected ward committeeman and I've been serving in that capacity ever since.

What kinds of things does a ward committeeman have to do in a ward like yours?

The things you have to do in a ward like ours is the same thing that a committeeman has to do in every ward. He has to carry the candidates of his party. He has a slate-making role, where he has something to say about the kind of candidates who are chosen. He designates someone for each precinct to exercise leadership, to pass the message around to all of the voters, and to get out the vote on election day. Many people will come and volunteer. Other people you'll seek out. You know them and you know of their gregarious character and their knowledge in the community, their association and affiliation with various civic groups. So you seek them out, ask them, appoint them, and then you have to educate them how to do this task. You have to make yourself available to all of the people of the community so that they know that you're there and if they have problems they can come to you and you will assist them. This service aspect is really the only product that you have. You have meetings at the headquarters where rallies are held. You bring in the candidates, and the people, having seen the candidates, have a better idea of who they're voting for on election day. These are the kinds of things that you do. In the summer time you may have block parties, or you have hot dogs and beer and soft drinks, and some footraces for the children, different contests with prizes, and so forth.

The paramount thing is that you are available and people know that if they have a problem that they can contact you any hour of the day or night. And, then, you have to be responsive to them. What they come to you with is really the problem that they have and it may seem trivial to some, but to that person it's a very important thing. If you treat it in that light, they'll appreciate it and, come election day, they'll say, "These people here are all right, they're on the ball." And that is the philosophy that we hope we can inculcate in our precinct captains. Many captains get a sense of satisfaction that comes only from doing something for somebody else. We have many precinct captains who are volunteers. We have many attorneys who work a precinct, are on deck to serve, and get satisfaction out of the fact that they've helped their neighbor and that they've also played a role in electing people that they know personally will do the kind of a job that will enhance and enrich the democratic process. And there are many that have a political job.

If you have to exercise leadership on a compulsion basis, if you have to resort to that, your worker is not going to be a good worker.

You have to instill in your people a desire to do it willingly. A willing worker does a much better job. If somebody gets the impression that you're standing over them with a knife to cut away their employment (as a matter of fact, you can't do that now anyway under the law, but I never treated people like that), I don't think that you get the best or the most out of people. They have to be motivated at a higher level than compulsory scare tactics.

Could you describe Mayor Daley's modus operandi?
I suppose one could say that he is a man of many facets. I have watched him in one day where he would play more than one role. In the morning I happened to attend the city council where he was the presiding officer, where he was a parliamentarian and exercising those responsibilities, recognizing people, checkmating the different things that were going on in the council. Later that day I attended a county central committee meeting where he put on his hat as chairman of the county central committee, and he encouraged the committeemen to get on their feet and voice their opinion and their ideas relative to the subject matter at hand. He would call on them without them asking for recognition, encouraging them to come up and speak their piece so that people could get the benefit of the thinking of many people. He would make sure that almost everybody there would say something. Then I saw him again a little time after that where we were selecting candidates, one after another, coming in, relating their qualifications and so forth. Then there would be a discussion of the candidates. During the give and take of the evaluating sessions he would talk about qualifications, integrity, dedication to the public service. Then the selection process would take place. He displayed compassion and consideration for those who had not been chosen. He would talk about the fact that it was regrettable that there weren't more opportunities, because they were qualified, too, and that they should not feel downhearted because they were not chosen.

Naturally, he was laudatory to the person who was selected. He wanted to make certain that everybody who participated in the process would understand that it wasn't because of anything that was wrong with the others, but that one was a little more "electable," shall we say, than perhaps the others.

After the candidates were selected, we had another meeting late that day in which he talked to the candidates regarding their campaign techniques and tactics. Now he was showing his capability as a teacher. He said, for example, "When you start your campaign and you're going out to make your speeches, bear in mind the fact that there will be many other speakers and the audience, of course, grows tired. What you should do is prepare about a five-minute talk directed toward the most important facets of the office that you're seeking, giving your story as to what you will do in these particular areas. And be on time. And if, perchance, you're one of those fellows who has a drink before dinner, if you have that drink, then call up and tell them you won't be there. Don't go out to a meeting place with liquor on your breath, because you're insulting the audience. And certainly you have enough sense not to tell any off-color stories." Now, in this particular span of ten hours, you see this man in different roles. That's why I say he's a man of many-faceted capabilities.

Another facet is his progressive thinking with regard to the city of Chicago and its needs, and his burning dedication to the city. I think that we're very fortunate in having this man as mayor of the city of Chicago, particularly for the God-given period of time that we've had him.

The only weaknesses the Mayor has is on those few occasions when he hasn't agreed with me. But he's human. I talk about him here in such laudatory terms that you could get the impression that I look upon this man as a god. That's not the case. He may talk to twenty or thirty people on a particular subject, and he's formulating his own opinions. He's not telling you what he's going to do. He wants to know what your thoughts are, he picks your brains. And after he's done this to a number of people, he makes up his mind. He's not attempting to please anyone of the people he consulted. He has one question in his mind, "Is this good for Chicago?" If it is, that's it!

And he doesn't hesitate to ask you to do things. He calls upon people to serve in varying capacities. He is a taskmaster. He wants it done right and he wants it done thorough. And you'll know when you've displeased him. There isn't any question about that.

What do you do as county board president?
I generally get into the office at 8:30 and I'm here until 5:00. My practice has been to take Friday off and come in on Sunday. If I can't get away on Friday, I come in on Sunday anyway. I can pick up the loose ends on Sunday without the phone ringing, without interruptions, and I can accomplish a great deal. I don't know when I've had a vacation. I think I had four days off the first part of July, when my daughter came in with her children. But I like the job. I find it

challenging. There's many days when you go home and you're shaking your head, wondering what you like about it, why you wanted it.
But you do get a great sense of satisfaction when you see that you've
achieved something and rendered service to the people, brought
about a reduction in the cost of government, and improved its efficiency. That's the name of the game.

On a board meeting day, you go over the agenda. You communicate with the various departments. If there's any particular ordinance or resolution that's coming up, you want to be familiar with
that. You might go along for a period of time when things are routine.
But, in the main, you're constantly fighting the budget. You're either
passing it or attempting to generate revenues to sustain the subsequent budget, and first thing you know, you're going through the
new requests, the new year is here. It's just a never-ending thing with
your budgetary process. The president of the county board has a role
in relationship to other elected officials. He has to establish his own
priorities and then submit his executive budget and people can see
what his priorities are. In the budget of 1976, we received requests
from the elected officials for a total of over nine hundred jobs and we
approved five hundred of them. I'm talking about *additional* jobs. Of
the five hundred, all but seventeen went into the criminal justice
system. Fourteen of the seventeen are in the election board and this
is an election year. Next year those fourteen will not be approved,
so this gives you an idea of the priorities that we have established.
You have highway problems, speed limits, things of that kind. I wear
another hat as president of the forest preserve board of commissioners and there are problems there. So you have a pretty busy day and
people are coming in to see you on matters, and you try to see
everyone.

County government is really a peculiar type of government. A lot
of people know what a city or a village is; they know they have a
mayor, a city treasurer, a city clerk and the aldermanic body, or
village board. They assume that county government is just like city
government. It's not. County government is an agent of the state. All
of the activities that go on in county government are requirements
imposed upon us by the constitution or by the state legislature. We
do not create programs of our own. We must provide services as
called for by law. A lot of people don't understand this. If we fail to
do this, we could be held in contempt of court or the law, and actually
go to jail. Our government is subjected to forces over which we have
no control. The county board has no control over what the constitu-

tion says, over what the legislative statutes say, what the judiciary says, or what the people say.

Let me give you an example of what I mean in each instance. The constitution of Illinois took away from us the commissions that we used to receive on the collection of taxes. We used to get 2 percent. That loss of revenue of some sixteen to eighteen million dollars is a sizeable amount of money, and they didn't replace it. We have to get that money someplace.

The legislature imposes responsibilities upon us and we must comply with whatever they say. I can recall one time where they stated that automobiles used in the commission of a crime will be impounded by the county sheriff until adjudication of the trial is over, and the county can auction off that automobile and be reimbursed for the storage charges. Well, the legislature didn't quite realize that most of these cars have liens on them. So if we didn't get the money, it's an added cost to us. The legislature imposes requirements upon us. Quite frequently they will state that the salaries of certain of our employees will be such and such, and we have to generate that kind of revenue to make that salary. But they don't tell us where we'll do it, and of course the constitution prohibits us from certain areas of revenue generation.

The judiciary imposes responsibilities upon us without telling us where to get the revenue. For example, not too long ago, the courts decided that the county government should pay for the hospital expenses incurred by prisoners who were taken to the hospital by the police at the time they were arrested. The court ruled that it goes back for over five years. So we're in the throes of generating revenue to pay off these bills. We've no control over this, but the court says we will do it. If we don't do it, we could be held in contempt of court and go to jail.

The people voted to eliminate the coroner's office and to have a medical examiner system. This is going to cost more money than the coroner system, but the voters decided. We have to do it.

These are just examples of the position we're in. When we go out to generate the revenue to pay for these things, a lot of people who don't understand the role that we have to play blame us for everything, when all we're doing is complying with the law and upholding the oath of office we took. We do everything that we possibly can to keep down the cost of government. When you came in here today you saw some of the lights out in the hall. They're out because we're trying to save money. Over a year ago we got to thinking that there was entirely too much light in the juvenile temporary detention facility in the juvenile court. So we issued an order to cut back on some of the bulbs. I saw a report this morning that in this year we have saved over $100,000 in the cost of our light bill. We're trying to manage the affairs of your government in concert with the law, as economically and efficiently as possible, and being as responsive and as courteous to the people as possible.

But do most people believe that?

I would say that they not only don't believe it, but they don't know of it. People are amazed when I tell them that over seventy cents of every dollar that we spend goes for the criminal justice system. It amazes them, just imagine! The other day one of my colleagues came in with a resolution that was politically motivated. He wanted a task force appointed to study the tax structure and revenues. (You were on the commission, you went through all of this.) I said, "We shouldn't have a tax program. We should have a program to reduce the cost of government, to reduce taxes." And how many years I've been literally crying about what would bring down the cost of government—mainly self-discipline among the constituencies. If they behaved themselves we could reduce the cost of government.

Do you think the press is publicizing this? Do you think the media are getting this across? No! They don't even try. The press and the media have an affinity toward discord, toward crises, toward confrontation. This is the kind of thing they feed on. They sell their papers, get viewers to watch their programs. They don't get them when somebody is talking about motherhood and so forth. I think the day will dawn when the cost of government is going to reach such a peak that there's going to be a great tax strike and it's going to imperil the future existence of our democracy. That's when the press and the media will suddenly wake up as to their own existence. Then perhaps they'll pick up this thing called self-discipline.

There are times when it is very tough. I'll get letters and I'll try to answer them, and they'll answer back, and if I send them a form letter they'll criticize that and say, "Well, there must have been a lot of other people who objected, too." I don't have a public relations man. The press ought to tell the people what's going on. Why should I use maybe $50,000 of the taxpayers' money to tell the people what's going on? I know that there's a lot of office holders that have a public relations staff. I can recognize the necessity of it for the mayor of Chicago, the governor of Illinois, and the president of the United

States. But I don't think it's needed in any of the other offices that I've seen and I think it's a waste of the taxpayers' money. But I can't seem to penetrate that to the other officials.

We can stand a search, as they say. We have this responsibility and we should meet it. But many of my elected colleagues are kind of down on me because of the fact that I turn down a lot of things. I just can't help it, but somebody's got to say no.

You've been in public service all your life. Could you tell me what the rewards of this kind of career are, and what the bad things about it are?

Perhaps the greatest reward lies in the confidence that your neighbors and the people in the community have in you. I think it's a high compliment when people will say, "Here, you take my most priceless possession, my government, and you manage it for me." That's a tremendous compliment that people pay to somebody in public life. When you conduct the office that you're in in response to that, you derive a sense of satisfaction. You feel that, well, I've fulfilled my pledge and I have kept my faith and trust with the people. That's a reward unto itself.

I think it would be wonderful, just wonderful, if every citizen could, at some point in their lives, serve in a capacity of an elected official. I think they'd have a much greater respect for their government and a much greater regard for this thing called democracy. They'd have a fuller appreciation of the trials and tribulations that one goes through. Let me tell you, when you impose a tax on people, it is really a trial and a tribulation, one of the most distasteful things a man has to do. But in this position you just have to generate the revenue in order to run government. Four years ago, we pledged that we would not increase the county property tax rate. We've kept that pledge. We went in other directions but we had to in order to get money. We did not just easily say, "We'll increase the property tax," and let it go at that. I think property is already taxed almost on a confiscatory basis. Being exposed to government (and perhaps this might be a little cynical, Milton), but you've heard me say, as Tom Paine once said, "Society is a blessing and government is a necessary evil." I believe that. I marvel at the fact that we're two hundred years old as a democracy. Let me tell you why. Because it is an instrumentality that's run by and for human beings. When we think in terms of the frailty of the human being, the selfishness, the ego, the *laissez-faire* attitude that all of us have within our makeup, and we think in terms of two hundred years, many varying cities and states across the fifty states of this nation, and the varying plateaus and changes of administration from one to another, but we constantly manage (not necessarily on all occasions) to be run by human beings who have these human frailties. The human ego. Ambition is a laudable characteristic, but when that ambition consumes someone and you can't control it, then I say that you might very well be devoured in its flames. The thing is that when a person is elected to an office and they have their eyes on another one, their ego is uncontrollable. What happens to the office that they're in is tragic, absolutely tragic. And, boy, when I've seen this, and we're still a democracy, I say God certainly must love us and I hope He continues to love us.

THREE

The Foot Soldiers

MARCO DOMICO / EMIL
EVANGELISTI / JOHN DOMAGALA
EDWARD PRZISLICKI / THEODORE
CLARK / BEN MARTINEZ

MARCO DOMICO *Italian. About sixty years old. Precinct captain in Marzullo's 25th ward. Patronage worker in department of streets and sanitation for twenty-five years. Is now a state representative.*

I was born in Chicago. My dad came here from Italy. My mother was born here and went to the Dante School. I went to the same school. I graduated from Jackson Junior High School, and went to McKinley High. I lived on Taylor Street all my life and have been living in the 25th ward for thirty-eight years. Prior to that I lived in the 1st ward and in the 27th ward.

I started off in politics in 1939 under the Kelly–Courtney fight through some friends of mine who knew the late State Senator Sam Romano. In them days, in the late 1930s, we used to have social clubs. I was the president of the Taylor Club and the West Side Inter-Club Council, which we had over twenty clubs in the neighborhood. This was in 1937–38. When the time came for the 1939 Kelly–Courtney fight, Sam Romano and other fellows who were in politics asked if I would help out. In them days they were for Kelly, and this friend of mine, Marco Constantino, was a top-notch precinct captain in the 27th ward. He broke away from the Touhy–Sain organization. They took twelve Italian precincts. We had our headquarters on Polk and Marshfield. So, by me being the president of this organization (we had fifty-five members), it was to their benefit to ask us. All twelve precincts carried very big for Mayor Kelly.

Alderman Vito Marzullo, at that time, was the ward superintendent of the 29th ward and affiliated with the 25th ward. In 1940, he was running for state representative for the first time. Sam Romano brought Vito Marzullo's name up. His name was very, very much popular in them days on the West Side and the East Side. Again we brought our forces together, all the clubs and everything, for Vito Marzullo and also for Jimmy Ryan who was very popular. This is how the name of Vito Marzullo came to my attention in them days, through Romano. He was a precinct captain, and him and Vito Marzullo were very close. That's how I started in politics, and I got to like it and stayed in.

I did not have a political job until 1947. I didn't ask for anything. They came up to me and asked me if I would like a political job, and I says, "No, I'm not interested in a political job." At the time I had a nice job as a candy maker at E. J. Brach Candy Company. I became an assistant supervisor. But in 1947, I was a little disappointed. My foreman passed away and everyone was congratulating me that I would be the next foreman. If you think that politics is big in Chicago, in city government, when you work for a private company, you see that politics is played in companies. They took a fellow from out of the office, probably an accountant, and made him a foreman. He did not know much about the candy business. I got very disturbed about it. I went to Sam Romano and I said, "I'd like to be in politics, and, if I can get a political job, I would appreciate it." So I got a political job from the Republican ward committeeman, Andrew J. Flando (that's the chairman of our Democratic ward organization today). Flando gave me my first political job in the department of revenue. I was a sales tax investigator under Governor Green. Then I became a factory inspector. I stayed there until 1952. I became a deputy sheriff, and then I went back to the department of revenue under Governor Stratton in 1953.

Why did you decide to become a Republican? Did you believe in the Republican Party?

No, no. I did not follow the Republicans. But I wasn't associated with Vito Marzullo at the time. I became associated with Vito Marzullo afterwards. Got to know who he was. A fine gentleman, a tremendous precinct captain, and a terrific legislator. I just joined because most of the fellows that I knew when I moved in the 25th ward, fellows who used to bowl together, gentlemen like the late George Barbusse, the late Rocky Piscento, were in our bowling league and they asked if I would go into politics with them as a Republican.

I became a Republican precinct captain with Flando. In them days, Republican precinct captains were very, very scarce, especially in the 25th ward. I was fortunate. We had a beautiful relationship with Senator Romano and Vito Marzullo. Many times I would go to them. They were Democrats, but they never turned me down.

In 1954, Alderman Marzullo asked if I would like to be with him. I enjoyed his friendship very much. In fact, in 1953, I asked him if

I could circulate his petitions for alderman in my precinct, and I was a Republican. He said, "You would do that for me?" I said, "I certainly would!" He gave me two petitions. I asked for four. The gentleman would never ask you if you were a Democrat or a Republican, if you asked him for a favor. He was fantastic as an alderman, as a representative. In the latter part of 1954, I changed, when Mayor Daley was running.

I went to Vito Marzullo and I switched over to him. The precinct at that time was the 22nd precinct. Vito Sessa was the precinct captain, and we took the precinct for Mayor Daley in the primary, 484 to 6. Combined the forces.

That same evening, Alderman Marzullo said to me, "You are now going into the 43rd precinct," which I had five weeks. "Where's the 43rd precinct?" I asked. Sam Romano said, "That's where you live at." That's the first time I moved away from Taylor Street. I lived on Lexington and California for a short few years. Much to my amazement, I says, "How many votes did they get there for you?" He said, "They got 31 votes for Daley." I said, "Why do this to me?" He said, "You're taking the 43rd precinct. You are the precinct captain there and if anybody doesn't want to work along with you, you just get rid of them. But I want that precinct brought up by the April 20th election." In five weeks' time, from 31 votes for Daley, I got 450 for Daley to 25 for Merriam. I changed that precinct.

Marco, how do you convert a precinct like that?
What I did, I knew quite a bit of people around that neck of the woods. I went ahead and found what is it that they are disgruntled about. I found the precinct captains. They told me that there was a fellow there by the name of William Serritella. "If you can get him, he is a helluva good man." I knew the Republican captain there, Vito Cascio. He said he would help me because he did not have any political job at the time. The Republicans had nothing, no jobs. The Democrats took over everything in 1954, and many people in the sheriff's office who were Republicans switched over to the Democrats. Ten precinct captains who were top-notch Republicans went over to Vito Marzullo. Vito Marzullo just took them and put his arms around them. We switched over and became Democrats in 1955 for Mayor Daley's election, and we stayed with Alderman Marzullo.

Most of the people in the 43rd precinct were probably neglected. That was my virgin territory. Alderman Marzullo, at that time, just became the alderman and ward committeeman. The people there knew that Marzullo was the state representative. They got to find out that when he made some promises and everything, he kept them. At that time they wanted the lights on Sacramento and Lexington, because some young lad, I believe, was killed there by an automobile. Somehow or other, they did not get their lights, and they were showing their wrath, the way they felt, and they went against the organization. (Marzullo did not know why the people were mad, because if the precinct captain doesn't convey this message to him, why the people are disgruntled, the favors are not being done, he does not know.)

When I found out all this here, I had meetings and everything in the church hall. Alderman Marzullo came there, wanted to know what was wrong, what's it all about, why were they disgruntled, why were they against the Democratic Party, and why were they against the 25th ward alderman? At that time, Vito Marzullo was not the ward committeeman, but he was the acting committeeman, and he made a promise. He said, "You will have lights there." And, by golly, Alderman Marzullo had it done before the election in April, and a few other things there that people were being neglected. We done it and the folks came out. I got all the Republican leaders in the precinct and the Democrats like William Serritella, and a few good other friends in the neighborhood there. This is how we got 450 to 25.

Is that the essence of good precinct work in Chicago?

Yes, communication, and service that you give to the people in your precinct. This is what counts. People look forward to their precinct captain. How else are they going to get to see their alderman? How are they going to see their state representatives? When they come to our headquarters, they come in and say, "I want to see the alderman." Everytime you go into a headquarters, you cannot come in and say, "I want to see the alderman." Of course he'll see everybody. But most of the time, before he serves you, he would like to know your party politics, who's your precinct captain. Many of them come in, "I don't know my precinct captain. I lived there two or three years. Nobody has ever approached me." But, under Alderman Marzullo, that does not happen. When we have registration day, by golly, the captain had better be out there registering people. Don't let Marzullo hear that people come to his office and say to him, "I never seen my precinct captain." First thing he'll do, he'll call the precinct captain and say, "Come over here." I'd hate to be in that precinct captain's shoes, because Marzullo's success in politics is to give service, do not lie to the people, tell the truth. This is what he tells the precinct captains. "Do not make any promises you cannot fulfill."

We are public relations men. We go in there, we have to talk about the Democratic Party, what it does for the people, and we have to be there to do little favors here and there. You know, on the West Side, many lads get into little problems, go to the juvenile home or something. Well, we're there to help them. We help these parents out. We go to courts. We have to help get them people serviced, to try to see what we can do for the youth of our neighborhood. We give them legal service. We have attorneys in our organization Tuesdays and Thursdays, giving legal advice. We do not charge them. If you have to have anything notarized, there's a notary there, free of charge. This is the function of the 25th ward organization, and this is the way Alderman Vito Marzullo functions. By him doing these favors for us, this is why people vote, because they have confidence in the precinct captains.

We have precinct captains that are very, very good, because you can tell that they are in their precincts on registration day. They always come in with a remarkable tally of new registered voters and changes of addresses. We know that the precinct captain is working when he comes in with that good registration. Registration, that's your election, the most important thing of all. When you register your new voters, you have many, many people. You can tell them the polling place is open from 8:00 A.M. until 9:00 P.M. that day, but they couldn't care less. Especially if you have registration day in the wintertime. You know, a man comes home at five or six o'clock, and once he takes his shoes off, forget about it, he's not going to leave the house. And once a woman, after three o'clock or four o'clock, and the children come home, and she has to start cooking and everything, and she has to leave the house, forget it! It is up to the precinct captain to work all day long. You actually have to beg them to register. They're doing you a favor. You're not doing them a favor. Them people that don't register, they're the first ones to complain, to scream and holler, "What's going on?" Those are the people that are doing all the complaining after the election is over, the people that do not vote. They're the biggest complainers.

Why is the registration so important, Marco?
When you have so many people move out (if you have 25,000

people registered in a ward), if you don't register them at that particular time, every six months or so, you might have 500 to 1,000 move out, probably more. In our ward, we have them move out so fast. It's transient. We usually register 2,000 people. But when you register 2,000, you probably lose 3,000. Now, if you don't register in that year, six months later, that ward may be down from 25,000 to 18,000 and there will be seven thousand people there that have not been registered. You got to keep that registration up. You have to have that voting power there. If you don't register these people, the vote goes down every year.

If you have to do something for your voters in your precinct, do you take them to see the alderman, or do you make contacts yourself in the city government?

The precinct captains come down with their people to see the alderman. The people in Chicago, they only know one thing. They do not know much about their legislators, or their congressmen, or their county commissioners. They know their aldermen! Their alderman is their doctor, their lawyer, their janitor. He takes all of this in stride. He is the man that the people know in the ward. They do not know what committeeman means, that he's the patronage boss. They want to see their alderman. That's why an alderman should be a ward committeeman also. Because he does not have to go to the ward committeeman and say, "Listen, I have to get a job for so and so." He can make his decision right there and then. He says to you that I will do this favor for you. He does not have to consult with anybody else. He is the supreme commander. And believe me, nothing can go on without the alderman knowing about it. If you want parking signs, if you want a permit for driveways, he has to sign all that stuff. This is why, to the people of Chicago, their alderman is the most important man in city government, if he is the committeeman. It makes it much easier if an alderman is a ward committeeman. There's a conflict of personalities there, sometimes, if you have a different ward committeeman and alderman.

I'm in the office every Tuesday and Thursday when I am not in session in the legislature. County Commissioner Matt Ropa is there. They don't ask to see us. Even if I say, "Can I help you?" they still want to see the alderman. We try to alleviate all this burden on Alderman Marzullo, the commissioner and I, the secretary, John Domagala. We try to take some of their problems, but they still want to see their alderman. I told the alderman, "Sometimes you ought to let us handle this, but they still want to see you. Even if it is a garbage can, or they need a sign somewhere, they want to talk to you." He's the guy. He's the one. Our alderman—one thing about him. He sees everybody. He is the most devoted public official that I have had the honor to serve with for the last twenty-two years.

What if a voter comes in to see him without the captain?
Many of them do come in. We talk to them, ask them for their name, and say, "What's your problem?" They say, "I want to see the alderman." I say, "Listen, I would suggest to you to see your precinct captain because he will ask you the same question I am asking you now, 'Who's your precinct captain?' If you have problems, he'll want to know why you're not seeing your precinct captain." The alderman wants to know if the precinct captain is doing his job or not. If they don't know who their precinct captain is, well, then, we'll find out where they live at and we'll certainly ask the precinct captain, "Why don't you know these people? Why aren't you talking to them?" And I tell them, for their benefit, to make sure, before they go in to see the alderman, not to lie to him. Tell the truth. The alderman will talk to them. He'll also want to know why the precinct captain isn't here, which is no more than right, because many a time the precinct captain says to him, "They're Republicans!" The alderman says, "What difference does that make? You bring them down here, if they're Republicans or not, or Democrats. Leave that up to me. I will do the talking afterwards." This is his policy. He does not care what politics you are. He is a very, very persuasive and convincing man.

Marco, what do you expect in return from a voter if you take him in and do him a favor?
The only thing I would ask him, when the time comes when we have our election for our officials for our city government, state government, federal government, if you would consider voting for the party of our choice. I never tell anybody how to vote. In my own family, my sisters, my brothers, I never use the words, "You have to." They do me a favor. I say, "I would appreciate it very much if you would come out to vote for the Democratic ticket, and if you have anybody that you do not like on the ticket, explain to me why." My job is to try to sell the Democratic ticket and the Democratic candidates.

They read the paper about this candidate and what he has done. I tell them that only these candidates are good for the Democratic Party. It's good for the alderman of our ward, or the ward committeeman, because you cannot go to the governor, the mayor, or the state's attorney and ask him for a favor. But you can go to the alderman of the 25th ward, your leader of that ward, for a favor. But the more votes we get out for the Democratic ticket, the more favors in return we can do for the people in our ward. That's how we get out votes.

A precinct captain is like a salesman, professor. He's the fellow that goes in there. He sells himself first. Fifty percent of the battle is won when he sells himself. Like selling a vacuum cleaner. The minute you can get into that home and sell that person interested in that vacuum cleaner, you have sold him. The minute you knock on that door, you have to listen for the tone of the man's voice, when he talks, "Who's there?" Or the woman, she may have been cranky, or just had an argument. You have to say, "Excuse me, I'll be back later." In this game you really have to know your people. When the precinct captain walks in there, he has to know if they are mad. He has to know what time of day or evening to go there. With a lot of people you have to go on Saturdays. Do not go there when the woman is cleaning her home and she is looking at her worst. You are in politics. I have been studying people many years and listening to them many times. I tell the precinct captains, "Do not go in their homes during the daytime. When you go, go on a Saturday."

During the daytime, first place, the man of the house is not there. He is working. This is the psychology of it. I start my canvassing after 5 o'clock in the evening. Of course, if the precinct captain knows his voters, maybe the husband works nights. Then, he goes there during the daytime. If he works days, he goes in the evenings. But you never go to a man's home while he's working. It's not proper, and many a time, them neighbors, they see you. I don't believe you would like it if someone comes to your home while you weren't there, discussing politics to your wife. You would rather have him there to discuss it with you, as the man of the house. Sure, the woman has the right to her opinion, but you discuss this politics while the man is home and the wife is there. This is the way I taught my assistants, and three or four of those assistants are top-notch precinct captains today. Go there in the evenings, or go there on Sunday afternoon, or meet them in church, or at social affairs, fathers' clubs, all that stuff. You have your wife have coffee klatches with the women and spread this little good word around. My sons used to do the same thing. It was so nice and easy when my boys were younger. I'd walk into their home and they would say, "That's Paul's father, there's Butchie's father." It was much easier to get into their homes in them days. But always remember one thing—never go into a man's home while he is at work.

How much time does it take to man a precinct?

"My job as a precinct captain, in the last twenty years, I devoted 365 days a year to politics. My telephone number is given to every-body in the precinct, and I told them, "No matter what time of the day or night, you call me if you need me." On Saturdays, my assis-tants and I would walk throughout the precinct, during the summer time especially. You get to see many people on their doorsteps. I never like to hear anybody say, "Gee, we only see you on election day." Because that's the remarks you will hear, "We only see you on election day." There are 365 days and you got 600 people in the precinct. How in God's name can I come to see you today and see somebody else tomorrow? You can't! We like to have a little time to ourselves. I have devoted many, many days to the precinct to be a successful precinct captain and a good precinct captain. You have to know your people. You have to be there for their wants and needs. Communication and service is the success of a precinct captain.

Does the alderman require you, before an election, to come in and discuss your precinct?

What Alderman Marzullo does, on registration day, the precinct captains, we bring in how many people we have brought in for the new registrants and he wants to know how many people are to be removed. Two days before the election, he calls every precinct cap-tain in, and wants to know how many votes they are going to bring out. If he doesn't like what you are telling him, you step outside and come back. He wants a true estimate. He doesn't want you to lie or exaggerate, or be below. You have a month or six weeks to do your canvassing and if you do not know how many votes you are going to get out, an estimate, by the time he talks to you, you haven't done your job. The county chairman will call in the ward committeemen to give their estimate how many votes their wards are going to bring in. They have to get the figures first from their precinct captains. Alderman Marzullo, this last election, was one percentage point off on his estimate to the mayor.

What kinds of changes have taken place in the neighborhood since you started working in politics?

It was predominately Italians and Jewish people, which you know, professor. You were a part of that era. Today, we have the most cosmopolitan ward in the city of Chicago. We have 30 percent black, and the rest Latinos, Italians, Poles, Slovenians, Lithuanians. You name 'em, we got 'em. It has changed considerably. On the north end of the ward, east of Ashland Avenue, it is all the Circle Campus. West of Ashland, there is the Medical Center. Most of the Italians and the Jewish people have moved out of the West Side to the North and Northwest Side.

It's different than twenty years ago. There are many people on welfare. You can't help them on welfare. That's all federal. We have a poor, poor ward. We haven't got the people that we used to have years back. We are likely to have the Latinos, many are on welfare. But you have good people. Many of them are hard-working people. They're proud people. They do have problems. But we have problems all over the country, all over the world, all over the city. Who hasn't got the problems we have?

They talk about people who move to the suburbs for better living. The suburbs are worse than Chicago. We have better police protection than they have in the suburbs. We have the best lighting system, street lights, sewers, service for sanitation, pick up, everything. People in the suburbs have to pay extra for everything, for all this. They have many problems in the suburbs today. The crime rate in the suburbs went up twice as much as in Chicago. During the riot, we weren't scared to walk in the neighborhood there. Alderman Marzullo went there to see what he could do to help the people, and was never threatened. We have beautiful, wonderful people in our ward. Not all of them are good, but we don't have the problems that other wards have. You are acquainted with our ward. You've seen our problems. We function. You've been to many of our meetings, and you've seen people from all walks of life attend our meetings. Proud people, and working people.

Let me ask you about your political career, Marco. Did you move up in the organization on the basis of how well you did in your precinct?

Oh, yes! You are rewarded by your performance in the precinct, the time you put in, the vote you get out. When you are a top-notch precinct captain you are rewarded with a good job, a better paying job. If you are not a good captain, if you are a laborer, you are going to stay a laborer. If you don't have any ambition, if you want to stay as a foreman, that's your job. If that's as far as you want to go, fine.

But I've climbed up the ladder. The alderman slated me in 1970 for state central committeeman. When he seen the opportunity for state representative, because of the death of the late Senator Sam Romano, I was picked by the senatorial committee of the 20th district, all the ward committeemen, to replace John D'Arco, Jr., as the state representative. They elevated him to state senator.

Before you were slated for state representative, Marco, what other jobs did you hold?

I held a job as assistant superintendent of the street and sanitation department, curb and gutter division. Before that I was a general foreman of the division. I was in the same department for seventeen years. I have only had two jobs with the city. Five years I was with Alderman Marzullo. I was an investigator on judicial legislation. My chairman was Alderman Nick Bohling.

I started as state representative March 3, 1976. When I went to the House of Representatives, I was always under the impression that them downstaters were shit-kickers. But, much to my amazement, in the first month or so, I found out differently. I spoke to many legislators (there are 176 of them plus myself, 177), downstate Republicans, downstate Democrats. Much to my amazement, ninety-five percent of them are attorneys, pharmacists, presidents of banks, real estate operators, and they are so educated that they make us look like we are the shit-kickers. This is the truth. I have changed my mind about the way I think about them. They are very shrewd, competent legislators. They eat and sleep politics downstate. They fight for their constituents. Downstate, they try to get everything they possibly can for their people. Just like the Cook County Democrats. We fight for everything, just like they do, to see what we can get for the people of Chicago and the county. But when we are down there and it comes to voting as a body, we do not vote geography. We are voting and putting our laws in for all the people in the state of Illinois and the welfare of the people. That's when we combine together and vote for the good of the people of the state.

When you vote in the legislature, Marco, does the party leadership tell you how to vote?

No. They recommend what is good for the party, what's good for Chicago. We have to really fight for everything we get for Chicago because you have them downstaters. They're rough. (It seems as if Chicago looks like it is a different state, like we don't even belong to the state of Illinois, sometimes, when you listen to them downstaters talk.) You do have to have some sort of leadership to propose this legislation, and we vote for it. But if we don't like it, we let them know about it. But most of our legislation that is proposed in Chicago and Cook County has been very, very good legislation.

Marco, do you have any higher political ambitions?

No. I am so happy right now. I am fifty-nine years old, professor, and I have no ambition to become anything else. I know my limitations. I only went to high school. I also took up one semester for public speaking four years ago. That gave me some help in the legislature for public speaking. And I passed with good marks. I love being in the legislature very much. It's a dream come true that I am one of the 177 men to make the laws of this state. I am proud to be an American. I am proud to be born in this country. I'm so proud of being one of the lawmakers of this state. I am ever so happy that this dream came true, and will always be beholden to Alderman Marzullo, who made my dream come true. I love him very, very much for this. My family is so proud. Most of all, my two sons and my wife, they are so proud that they know, after thirty-six years of politics, our Good Lord has been nice to me, that my dream has come true.

EMIL EVANGELISTI   *Italian; seventy years old. Has been a precinct captain in the 25th ward for forty-seven years.*

I was born in 1909, in Franklin Mine, Michigan, a copper mining town. My father didn't want us to work in the copper mines so we came to Chicago in 1922. We moved to 2414 W. 25th Street on the Southwest Side in the 25th ward. It was and still is an Italian neighborhood, but it's changing now. I graduated from the Picker Grammar School, and went two years to high school. We were a family of six children and didn't have much money. My father earned $20 a week. There were eight of us living off that. My father suggested that I get a job when I was sixteen years old. I went to Crane Evening School and finished my high school education. I used to walk six miles up and back. On my first job, the salary was so small that I used to hitch hike up and back, catching trucks. I didn't have money for carfare. This was during the Depression.

I started in politics in 1932. My daddy was given a job working with the asphalt crew for the city, through a Republican politician, filling in potholes. My daddy said to me, "Emil, the man who got me this job wants me to work as a precinct captain." My father wasn't speaking English too well, so I became the Republican precinct captain, and stayed as a Republican until 1947. My precinct was a mixed precinct—Polish, Lithuanian, and Italian. The Poles lived on 25th Street, the Lithuanians on 23rd Place, and the Italians were all on 24th Street. But I didn't have a political job. I was just working the precinct.

How did you become a Democratic precinct captain?

I quit the Republicans in 1947. The Republicans hadn't done a thing for me for the last ten years. Joseph Ropa was the alderman of the 21st ward and Jim Bowler was the committeeman in the "bloody 20th ward." In that ward, every election, ballot boxes were taken out of the polling places. People got injured. They took people out to Niagara Falls, so they couldn't get back for election day. The "bloody

20th ward" and the 21st ward were two of the smallest wards at that particular time, and they were combined as the new 25th ward in 1951, with Bowler as the alderman and committeeman. Bowler was a strict Democrat, Irish, and on the stern side. If he said, "I want 450 votes," and you brought in 260, he'd say, "What did you do here?" I'd say, "That's all that I could get out." He'd say, "The next time you do something like this, you're not going to be working here no more." He was rather tough.

Emil, what does a good precinct captain do?

What does a good precinct captain do? If somebody wants a job, we try to get him a job in politics or in private industry. I search for jobs in private industry, to see if we could get somebody off our alderman's back. I have fifteen or twenty people that own factories and they tell me, "Emil, if you have somebody that qualifies for a position, I will gladly hire them for you." That's one of the things we do, find jobs for people.

If people need something removed that's piled up in their alleys, I call the bulk truck and have the bulk truck pick that thing up, whatever it is—a mattress, a desk, a couch, old tires—we pick up everything. If somebody has a car parked in front of their door, and nobody comes in and out for a ten-day period, I turn it into the auto pound. They take the car away.

I look in the *West Side Times* every week—it says, "So and so is naturalized." I see if there is anybody from my precinct. If there aren't, when I'm canvassing the precinct for the election, I knock on the door and the lady says, "Who's there?" I say, "Emil, the Democratic precinct captain. I represent the 25th ward, Alderman Vito Marzullo. Are there any new voters here, upstairs, downstairs, throughout the building?" She says, "There's a man downstairs that just come from Italy." So I go down and knock on his door and find out if he wants to become a citizen. I fill out all his applications that he gets to be a citizen, and then I go downtown with him as a witness when he gets his papers.

In case somebody asks me for a garbage can on election day, I fill in my poll sheet, "One garbage can, 2315 West 23rd Street; another garbage can, 2318 Oakley." I call the Democratic headquarters in our ward and they deliver the garbage cans. It's free of charge. I give garbage cans to whoever needs them.

If somebody comes and says, "Emil, my daughter is eighteen years old and we just bought a car. Can you help me with the questions and answers at the driver's test?" I say, "Sure I can. I have the questions and answers right here. There's twenty-one questions and twenty-one answers. Study them before you go to pass this automobile test."

You don't take them down and try to fix the license?
No. I just give them the paper and tell them to study these questions.

If somebody needs legal help, the 25th ward has lawyers at the headquarters every night, in case someone has a puzzle or something that they can't clear up by themselves. We have lawyers and they're free. No charge for anything they want, within a reasonable doubt.

If someone says, "How come my street hasn't been swept?" I will immediately get on the telephone and call the ward yard where they keep the sweepers. John Lascola is in charge of the sweepers. I say, "Johnny, will you please sweep 23rd Place? Tomorrow there's going to be a wedding at the Lithuanian Church, Our Lady of Vilna. Is it possible to get that street swept?" He says, "Yes sir, Emil."

If the nuns want to go to Whiting, Indiana, on Saturday, I say, "What time do you want me to pick you up?" I drive them to Whiting, Indiana, and drop them at a convent there and they say, "Be back here at 5 o'clock." I don't bother coming back home. I go to Gary, have lunch, and go to a park and watch the birds fly around. Then at 5 o'clock, I go back and bring them home.

When election comes along, I have a polling place that is clean, and has heat and light. Most polling places don't have what I just got through mentioning. The girls that work for me appreciate working for me. Some of the Republican clerks and judges even say, "Emil, we're all with you in the 25th ward." The Republicans won't do anything to hurt me. A Republican said to me the other day, "Emil, I need a drum [a garbage can]. I asked Stearney [the Republican ward committeeman] months ago for a drum. Can you get me one, Emil?" She's a Republican election clerk. I said, "Sure I can." A few days later she called me and said, "Emil, I want to thank you for the drum."

Six months ago there was a delegation of three or four men that live over on 23rd Street. They said that there has been three or four accidents on 23rd Street and Oakley Avenue. I said, "I suggest that you should get a petition, get 200 people to sign it, and see if we can get a stop sign because the children are going by 23rd Street to go to St. Michael's and Our Lady of Vilna Schools." So they got a petition with 200 names on it. I took it and I brought it to the alderman. The city sent a survey truck and took a survey of the street, and, believe it or not, the city put a stop sign at 23rd and Oakley, six months ago.

I come along the street and I say, "Hey, what happened to that tree you used to have in front of the yard here?" The lady says, "The kids knocked it over." I say, "You want a new one? I'll get you a new tree, if you want one." She says, "Will you do me a special favor? See that one down on the parkway? There's no leaves on it. How about getting that one removed and bringing me a new one?" I say, "Give me a couple of weeks and I'll get you a new one, and I'll get the old one taken out of there." I know a person that works for the tree removal at the conservatory in Humboldt Park, and they give trees out like giving out glasses of water.

People say, "Did you know Vito Puccini was in the hospital?" I say, "I don't. What hospital is he in?" I go home and send him a get-well card. When he comes home, I make it my duty to stop and see how Vito is feeling. He and his family votes for me.

We bend over backwards to take care of the churches in the ward, any need that they may have. They need a lot of drums, they need trees, grass, seeds, they need everything. And we do our best.

When Marzullo's secretary calls and says, "Emil, there's a wake tonight at Galewood Funeral Home. Such and such a person died," I make it my duty to attend the wake, not only by myself, but with two or three of my constituents that help me in the precinct. When someone invites me to a wedding in the precinct, I try to attend their wedding. If I'm out of town, I make a donation.

A lady down the block has five children, her husband is sick and doesn't work. I say to my wife and daughters, "Don't throw any clothes away. If they're presentable, I want to bring them over to that lady."

We fix curbs, we repair sidewalks. We don't hesitate to take care of anybody's needs within a reasonable demand. I've taken care of a lot of people over the years.

I have three or four men that help me in the precinct and they are out of this world. Before I hire them as assistants, I have an application that I have them fill out—"Do you smoke? Do you drink, excessive? Do you get along with people easily? Are you scared in the dark?" That's when you have to go out in the precinct, in the dark, to chase and register people. All my canvassing is done at night or on Saturdays. I don't want anybody around me that's intoxicated.

When Nixon ran against McGovern, and Alderman Marzullo was for Nixon, we had sample voting machines that we took around to show the voters how to pull the lever for Nixon and for Ogilvie against Walker. In 1977, I got 250 Democrats to 11 Republicans in the mayoral election. Another time, I got 336 Democrats to 4 Republicans.

I have never, ever, stolen a glass of water. I have never, ever, paid anybody to vote. I sell myself, the 25th ward, and Vito Marzullo.

I work from 8:30 to 4:30 on my job at the Bureau of Equipment Services. I've been here twenty-nine years. I've been promoted. I came from a $354-a-month job to $18,000 a year. My title went from clerk to administrative assistant. Alderman Marzullo controls my position. If something should happen to me tomorrow, he'd have another man here to replace me, not doing the same thing necessarily, but this job belongs to the ward.

I had three girls in school, two in college and one in business school. It was tough but we did it.

Alderman Marzullo is a wonderful man. He always brings out these proverbs—"If it gets too hot in the kitchen, leave the kitchen." And "No man walks alone." That's what I tell the men helping me. We are part of an organization, the 25th ward Regular Democratic Organization.

JOHN DOMAGALA   *Polish. Sixty-seven years old. Long-time precinct captain in the 25th ward. Also was Marzullo's ward secretary for a number of years.*

I have been in politics since 1957. Prior to that I had worked for Advanced Aluminum Casting Corporation Foundry in the production of armaments and cookware for twenty-nine years. I started there as an ordinary laborer in 1928 after I got out of grammar school, and became a production manager. In 1957, when the company went out of business, I knew the ward secretary to Congressman Bowler, who had also been alderman and ward committeeman of our ward prior to Alderman Vito Marzullo. I asked this gentleman that I bowled with about a job. I told him the company is folding, so he came back with word that he had talked with the alderman. Of course, me being in the neighborhood all my life, knowing the people, being active with the church (I am, incidentally, a Roman Catholic), president of the church choir, president of the Holy Name, president of the Marshall Square Homeowners Organization, meant that I came in contact with people every day, even though I only had an eighth grade education. When I went to see Alderman Marzullo, of course, like a man in politics, he knew that knowing people is the main thing. As long as you came in contact with people every day, you figure, this man can be of some benefit.

The following Monday I was told to come in and he put me to work with the committee on finance upstairs, just an ordinary clerk at a very mediocre salary, but I was glad to start working because I didn't have a job at the foundry, and half a loaf was better than none.

I immediately got a precinct of 615 voters in the same parish where I lived, so I knew most of the people. I got the job on a Monday. Monday evening, after I got home from work, right after supper, I started to go out, block by block, house by house. I got myself a poll sheet of the registered voters, and who I didn't know, I got to know by knocking on their door. Alderman Marzullo printed some cards that I was a representative of that ward, and with those,

I went around and got acquainted with the folks. We had a judicial election six weeks after I got the job, and out of 615 voters, I brought out 400 for the party. It was a good return.

How do you handle a precinct?

If you live in a neighborhood, you know people, and you walk down the street and chat with them. You don't have to have elections just to talk to people. You meet people every day, and you don't run away from them. Many of these folks, if you were a drinking fellow, you really could get yourself real drunk, but I am not a drinking man to that point. You don't even have to visit them. If you meet them in front of the house, they are nice enough that they want to call you inside, and you don't want to hurt nobody's feelings.

As a precinct captain you find a lot of people who follow candidates and their records. So you better be prepared for a half-way decent debate with them, or at least, reason with those you know. You don't get up there to try to harrass them and argue with them, because you'll get no place. Sometimes you learn by association with these people.

You never argue with one of your voters. When you canvass your precinct you can tell pretty much just by talking to someone whether he is a Democrat or a Republican. You know darned well if they don't come out in the primary, you haven't sold them at all. If he is going to be a good Democrat, he'll come out and vote in the primary. He's your friend. But if he comes out in the general election, you don't know how he is going to vote. And there's no way you are going to find out either.

You tell them you are a Democratic representative and present them with a card. "If at any time I can be of any help to you, don't hesitate to call me. I am at a particular address on the card, the telephone is there. You can always get ahold of me. And, if not, my wife will take a message. When I get home, I'll return you a visit or call, whichever way you want it." I try to walk through the neighborhood and see people as often as possible, if they are outside at all. Chat with them. You don't even have to discuss politics. Just things in general. Today it's a little tougher because we have many of the Spanish element and I don't speak it. But since I have been in politics for as long as I have, I've got a Latino assistant who goes along and helps me in that respect.

Primarily what you sell is yourself. I don't care whatever party a man was from. If he was a decent guy with me, I say, "I'll help you anytime." I don't say that only about Democratic candidates. There's many good candidates on both sides. You win friendship with a man. I had a Lutheran minister at the church in my precinct, Reverend Ross. He never used to vote in any primary. He always used to tell me, "Mr. Domagala, we're Republicans—just as our religion, you know." I said, "Look, Reverend, don't come out to vote at all. Do whatever you like." But then it came to the general election. Him and his two sons and his wife used to sit down at the long table in his living room, and he used to spread it out and say, "Which one of these candidates can I really help you with? I think that you are a nice guy." And I thought that was an accomplishment.

Are you required, before an election or a primary, to give the alderman an estimate of the votes in your precinct?

Yes, we are, and it better be very close. A fellow who knows his precinct is always quite close. Maybe ten votes one way or the other, which I don't think is too bad.

What kinds of things do you do for people in your precinct?

The very first thing I do each morning, I get my car out of the garage and I take a ride through the alleys. Many of the people, the Latinos and some of these nonresident landlords, they have a piece of furniture to throw out in the alley, or a mattress, and I'm afraid that punks will set a match to it and set a garage on fire. I make a list. I stop at the ward yard at 20th and Damen and give it to the superintendent, and ask them if they have a bulk truck, because I know garbage men don't pick that up. If not today, possibly tomorrow. And they'll pick it up. I also see when a man needs a garbage can. I have access to garbage cans in my yard, always a dozen on hand for my precinct. If a fella really needs one, I'll tell him, "Look, when you get home from work, come over and pick one up." They're happy to get them. Also, the Latinos ask questions or explanations of some of the papers they get. Many times, if they have a traffic violation, we have a lawyer in the organization who goes and represents these lads in court for no fee to them. That's a free service that the organization provides if a fella gets a ticket. But there is no such thing, like some guys say, "Fix it!"

We don't like to bother with kids in jail. If a fellow comes to the house and he says, "Could you recommend an attorney?" I don't like to recommend an attorney for nobody in any case of that kind, because, if the result isn't what they wanted, they'll blame me that it was my attorney. Or, if this fella took this lawyer that I said, and he might have gotten three or four hundred dollars for a fee, and if things didn't work out, maybe he would have thought that I got a hundred dollars out of it. I don't want no part of that. I always tell the fella, "Look, take a telephone book and look under lawyers, and select yourself a lawyer unless some friend of yours has one."

We help fill out their forms in citizenship cases. I take them over to the Immigration Service when they get called for their two witnesses to come in with them. I explain the formality. We have printed matter, answers, in English and Spanish.

We have County Commissioner Matt Ropa who has a girl working with the office of public aid. If there is any way possible we help them. Maybe their payment has been cut for some reason. We look into the whole matter to find out what the story is.

If somebody is looking for a job in my precinct, like this one lad that I have now, and if he can be of some help to me, the alderman was kind enough to put him to work. He is a helper in my precinct with me, because the neighborhood has changed where me being the only one able to speak my language, the American language. I'm Polish.

Do you always bring him to see the alderman?
Yes, I do. I wouldn't lie to him to tell him I'm not going to do it. If I thought he was of some good to me, I naturally would bring him in. But sometimes I could see the fella wouldn't be of any help to me. I've even helped fellas in the neighborhood get jobs in industry.

We have a company in the neighborhood, the Handy Button Company, Spiegels, for the ladies. I've met them since my association with the organization. Also, like I say, I'm president of Homeowners. They know who I am and they call me for a thing here and there, so, in return, when the woman wants a job, I'll stop there and I see Mr. Pearlman of Handy Button. There's three or four women in my precinct that work there.

Are you available to them for services, in return, if they need it?
That's correct. Let's say that around their plant is an accumulation of a lot of litter from employees. They sit at the curbs and throw beer cans or stuff at the curbs. So they'll say, "When are we going to get the street cleaned?" I stop at the ward yard and make some arrangements within the next three or four days. Of course, that's a service that should be given people anyway. It's cleanliness for the ward and for the city.

Are you required, as a precinct captain, John, to sell tickets to people in these industries or in your precinct?

Never. Never as long as I have been in this ward. We have a yearly ad book, I guess, as everybody knows that sees the book of the 25th ward. You go out and get a certain amount of ads in whatever amount you can possibly get. I do my darndest to get whatever share I can. Nobody forces me. I don't force anybody in the ward. This Handy Button Company, they are there every year with an ad. I don't have to worry about it. I just walk in and leave the contract, and, when they get ready, they'll mail it to the organization.

Do you only service people in your precinct who are good Democratic voters?

No, I wouldn't say that. Well, let's be honest about it. It would help. Of course, I let it be known to the guy that I am a Democratic precinct captain. Let's say that he's a new guy coming in. I usually watch for somebody that might be moving in today. Tomorrow, at the latest, I'll try to make my introduction to him and let him know who I am. Like just recently, a fellow moved in and he outright told me, "I'm a Republican." I said, "Let's not get mad at one another. You'll still be my neighbor." So, kiddingly, I said to him, "Someday, you'll see the light, but I am a Democratic precinct captain." What am I gonna tell him? Can't start off on the wrong foot. In fact, this one individual I'm talking about, only yesterday he came out of the house for the first time and met my wife. I said, "I want you to meet my wife," because he sees her more during the day because he's a security man and he is home during the day. If you didn't do things for Republicans, too, you would just get yourself in bad with the neighborhood.

I've always been a Democrat. My parents were Democrats, and all the people I knew throughout the area as I grew up in the neighborhood. I was born at the address I'm at now. I've been there over fifty years, so I didn't know of anybody else but a Democratic precinct captain. Never saw a Republican precinct captain in my neighborhood. Never had one knock on my door, and don't have opposition in my precinct. The ward used to be heavily Polish and Bohemian. Many of the lads in my area have moved out to the 23rd ward, around 57th and Malvina, and throughout that area. Some south of Berwyn.

What kinds of returns do you get in your precinct in elections?

It could sometimes be a little better. I wish I had more registered

voters now, because the area has changed. It used to be a precinct
of 600 voters. I have only about 320 now. In a primary, most Republicans I ever got was five. Then, in a general election, there would be
forty-five to fifty Republicans, and about 75–80 percent (about 500–
550) Democrats. But the people are not there any more.

Mexicans are moving in and many are noncitizens. Some of them,
when I walk around with forms and ask them to file the papers to
become citizens, say, "Next week, next week, next week." A lot of
transients. They don't stay. I'm happy when I see a guy buy a house.
At least I know he's going to be there. I do my utmost to try to help
them. Just recently I helped a young lad (in fact my wife was a
witness) because we knew the young boy. Right after he became a
citizen he took off and got married. He's not even here for the
coming election. So the work that you've done is lost, but I'm sure,
wherever he moves in Chicago, he's going to be a Democrat anyway.
He always sounded like a real clean-cut, loyal lad.

What kinds of jobs have you had since you started in politics?

I was a clerk up in the committee on finance. After that I was a
water rate taker in a water distribution plant on Chicago and Michigan Avenues. Then I was an inspector on paving of alleys with the
board of local improvements. And I've been Marzullo's secretary
for a good many years now. I follow up matters that he is too busy
to follow. He'll ask me to go here and ask me to go there in any
department. Somebody requests something, and the following day
I follow all these matters as close as I possibly can, unless I definitely need his help, and then I call him. After being in this business for as many years as I have, I've learned the department
heads. For sewers, you know you have to go to Quigley. I carry a
little black book that has all the various department heads, plus
rodent control and all that.

Then you let people know of the service that was done. If a block
has bad curbs and you go to the curb department and have the curbs
fixed, you let them know that it was done through the efforts of the
25th ward. You let them know that the organization did do it. Because they certainly wouldn't have done it on their own.

*Have you any political ambitions of your own, John, beyond your
present job?*

No, I really don't. I'm sixty-seven years old. I'm not thinking of
running for anything. I only hope that the alderman and I can stick

together for as many years as the good Lord allows us. I'm happy at what I'm doing.

I like the people where I'm at and I live within my income. I couldn't afford a home right now in one of these other areas. At least, where I live now, I have an income piece of property. I have a Spanish family in one apartment, and I have a three-story building which has a rent that anyone can pay, and there is just my wife and I that are left. My kids are all on their own. They each have their own home and they're all doing well. I did something with my wife for our youngsters that I never had an opportunity. My son got his doctorate in education just recently. Lives in Champaign. My other daughter is quite an accomplished pianist. Another daughter has a musical background. She teaches music education at Gage Park High School. So I think we have done our share.

EDWARD PRZISLICKI   *Polish. Fifty years old. Democratic precinct captain in Alderman Vito Marzullo's 25th ward. Former truck driver, then a security guard; is now a bridge tender.*

I was born and raised in the neighborhood. I attended St. Pius Grammar School and Harrison High School. I quit school when I was sixteen years old. We were a family of six and we needed money, so I had to go to work. I worked for Bell Oil Company as a helper on a truck, then got to be a truck driver.

I got involved in politics when I was thirty years old. I was a member of the Marshall Square Homeowners Association with John Domagala. He was a precinct captain and asked me if I wanted to take a walk around with him, and I did. I liked it, I liked going around, I liked being with people. I went around with John for three or four years, and then I took my own precinct, which I had for seven years. Then Alderman Marzullo asked me to take the precinct I have now. I've been in this precinct for about nine years. I've been a captain for about fourteen years, and with the alderman for about nineteen years.

At that time, I had no ambition of getting a job in politics. I had a job. But we had slow seasons in the heating business, so Alderman Marzullo called me in in April 1960 and offered me a job at the county hospital as a security officer. It was on the late shift, which would work in very well with my business during the day. I took the job.

I was seven years at the county hospital. When I first started in 1960, I was paid $264 a month. When I left there, they were paying $363 a month. From there, I went to the Port of Chicago, which has now merged with the Department of Public Works, bridge operations. I am a bridge tender. It's about a $15,000-a-year job. But truck drivers are making $20,000–$22,000 a year. And I work a precinct on the side.

What do you do as a precinct captain?

A precinct captain is everything. He's a person's confessor, he's their flunky, he's almost anything. He's got to be versed in many fields. Whoever calls from my precinct, I'm always there. There are so many questions we'll be asked by people. "What's wrong with my electricity?" "What's wrong with my plumbing?" "Is it the city's obligation to fix the sewer that's plugged up?" You have to know which department to call, what's their obligation, how much work the city will do for people. The water is leaking in somebody's parkway. That's the city's obligation. If it's by the house, naturally, it's the homeowner's obligation. I got called one time to take a constituent to the hospital with a fish bone in his throat. People want their license plates and vehicle stickers picked up. People want me to take them down for a driver's license. When we take them down for a driver's license, people think we have it fixed for them. There's no fixing. Nine times out of ten, they can pass the test themselves, but they need that last support, somebody to be with them and assure them, "Don't worry, you're going to make it." They're nervous and if they don't have somebody with them they just draw a blank when they go for the test. One of the big things we have to do is get garbage cans. We make a connection with somebody who is going to discard some 55-gallon drums. We'll cut off the tops and use them as garbage cans. Garbage cans are very expensive today, six or seven dollars each. I give out at least two hundred garbage cans a year in my precinct. Republicans can't get garbage cans.

When someone asks me to do something for them, I never put myself over a barrel. I'll tell them I'll look into it, and I'll see what I can do, and I'll get back in touch with them, or follow it to its conclusion. I am not going to make a promise I can't keep.

If a captain is active and is conscientious, he'll do anything he can for his people in the precinct. I got a call today from Mrs. Guererro at 3031 South Troy. Her husband passed away. She wants to sell the house and she needs me to help get her affairs in order. Now her husband can't vote anymore. He's dead. So maybe another precinct captain would say, "Look, I don't know nothing about that kind of stuff. You have to get a lawyer." I told her to get her house papers in order. I'll contact the bank, I'll find out if her payments are current, if they are late on any other payments, what they owe on the house, and then I would direct her to a real estate agent. Johnny Witunski, a friend of mine in our organization, has a real estate business. I'll take her to him. He can appraise the house and can handle the matter. In fact, I have a man in my precinct who may even be interested in buying the house. I may be able to save her the commission, because her husband didn't leave her well off. She has no people here, no relatives, very few friends, and I feel honored that she would call me, her precinct captain, that she has enough faith in me, enough trust in me, to help her out in these matters. Before her husband passed away, he told her that if anything happened she should get in touch with me. He was sure that I would help her. Joe (her husband) has always been good to me, always came out and supported me, always voted for the candidate I suggested to him. I'm glad that he thought enough of me to tell her to contact me and I'm glad to help her out. I'll do anything I can. I'll follow it to its conclusion.

How did you build up this network of people to help you?

It's not something you learn overnight. When you're in politics, you do make friends with people that work in all the departments of the City of Chicago. These departments are in operation for the people. This is what they're paying their taxes for. All a good precinct captain does is direct them to the right department. People call with a problem with rodents. I call rodent control, I say, "My name is Ed Przislicki. I'm calling from Alderman Marzullo's 25th ward, and I have these alleys in my precinct that need baiting." They come out and bait the alleys. The street lights are out. You call the Department of Electricity, and tell them to put the switch back on. It takes years to make these contacts in all these departments.

We have John Domagala, the secretary to the alderman, downtown. He's always at our beck and call for any information or if we need help. We have people in the Secretary of State's office, the Department of Sewers, in Water Distribution, etc. We have representatives in every branch of government—Commissioner Ropa with the Cook County Board, State Representative Marco Domico, State Senator John D'Arco, Jr., Alderman Marzullo in the City Council, and Judge Kogut, Judge Janczy, Judge Novoselsky, and Congresswoman Collins. I have had correspondence with her on behalf of my voters. She's been very wonderful. There is always instant response, and she'll follow things to the conclusion. If she can do it, she'll do it, and if she can't, she'll write a nice letter explaining why it can't be done. It took eighteen years to know what I know about politics, how organizations run, how the city, the county, the state, the federal government run, how to go to different departments—it comes with experience.

These services are not favoritism. The Mirage scandal that was in the *Sun-Times* gives every city department a black eye.* It happens in private industry, too. People will steal materials that they are loading on trucks. People that work at Western Electric wrap copper around their waist and sell it. People will take money. That doesn't mean that everyone that works for Western Electric is no good, that they're all thieves. In all walks of life you're going to find people that will take money. I have yet to take my first dime from anybody that I have ever done anything for. The only thing I tell them is, "Support me on election day. I'll be around 364 days a year. On the 365th day, election day, you come out and support me."

I wouldn't give a person ten cents to vote. I may give elderly people in my precinct a couple of dollars, but this is not to buy a vote. They live on food stamps, on pensions. If you have a neighbor living next door to you, and they can't buy a loaf of bread, you're going to slip them a few bucks, "Here, go buy a loaf of bread and some lunch meat." The money comes out of my own pocket. That doesn't mean you're buying a vote. I'm just being a good neighbor. It's a privilege to go out and exercise your right to vote. I wouldn't buy anybody's vote.

There are times when Alderman Marzullo gives money from the ward treasury to precinct captains at election time to hire workers to ask the people to come out. You get people who are pensioned, who can't work, give them $15 or $20 for the day, and ask them to cover this block and come back to the polling place every once in a while to give you a list of the people that haven't voted yet, and remind them to come out.

If Mickey Mouse was running, I would try to get every vote out of the precinct that I could. This is what makes a good precinct captain. If he takes any pride in being a precinct captain, he wants to bring out as many votes as he can, he wants to be close to the count that he brings to the boss. In one election, I told Vito I would come in with 155 and I came in with 152. When Nixon ran, I called the vote in my precinct right on the button. In the primary election in March 1978, I had a total of about 230 votes in my precinct. I cast 152 votes—149 Democrats, 3 Republicans. There were two Republican judges, and one other Republican vote. That was probably a mistake. He must have asked for the wrong ballot.

*In 1978, the *Chicago Sun-Times* did a series exposing corruption among city inspectors dealing with a tavern the paper had purchased named The Mirage.

In the 1977 mayoral primary, I got 194 Democrats. There were two Republicans. In the general election, I carried for Bilandic over Block 173 to 21. I go for the whole ticket. Black candidates do as well as white ethnic candidates in my precinct, and I only have one black family in the precinct. I'm an organization person. If you believe in the organization, you don't care what color skin a man has or what nationality a man is. If you're supporting the Democratic Party, you're supporting the regular Democratic candidates, whether they're black, green, white, purple, or whatever. If they're endorsed by the Democratic Party, then they're my candidate.

Republicans don't come out in a primary, but, then, some of them come out in a general election. They want to use you for favors, and they'll come out and vote Democratic in the primary, but then in the general election they go back to their party and vote for what they want. But they support you (the precinct captain) because they know that all year long you're at their beck and call and you do favors for them. There used to be a Republican precinct captain, but when I took over the precinct I had a nice talk with him and he was no longer active in the Republican Party after that. If I can do a favor for a Republican in my precinct, I'll do it, because I may get him to come over to my side and vote my way. If he's a hard-core Republican, I might just ask him to give me three candidates on the ticket that I really want, and he can vote for the rest of the Republicans on the ticket. Many times, I will get him to do that.

People vote for the precinct captain. I tell my people, when I'm canvassing, "There's no way that you are going to see any of these people that are seeking public office after the election. The only people you'll see is me, or the alderman, or the state representative. Anything you want you're going to come to me or the alderman."

When it comes to jobs, I can't get people jobs. That's up to Vito. He's the boss. He's got to give them a letter of recommendation. I can recommend somebody to him. If I sent him downtown with a letter of recommendation to Tom Donovan, Donovan would laugh.* But the alderman wouldn't do anything about anyone from my precinct without a recommendation from me. If a person came into the headquarters and asked for a job, the first thing the alderman would ask is, "Where's your precinct captain?" Vito clears everything

*Tom Donovan was administrative assistant to Mayor Richard J. Daley and Mayor Michael Bilandic, and was the chief patronage dispenser for the Democratic organization of Cook County.

through the precinct captain. And Vito doesn't argue with success. If you're doing a good job in the precinct, he's not going to pat you on the back and tell you what a perfect job you're doing. He doesn't care how you do it. If you bring in a good precinct on election day, this is all he wants.

Politics is stimulating. You find out that elected officials are on the same level as you are. You meet them at parties, dinner dances, and talk to them on your own level. I also enjoy being with my people in the precinct. After an election, I don't run away from my people. You cannot put yourself above your people. You're only as good as the lowest person in your precinct. If you look down at the people who voted for you, after an election, you're not going to get anyplace. You have to be interested in them, you have to support them, just like they supported you on election day.

If the phone wasn't ringing, I'd miss it. If people didn't call me and ask me for something, I'd wonder what's wrong. Why don't they call me? Who are they going to? I always feel good when I can help someone out. It gives you a sense of importance, too. I'm not just a run-of-the-mill dummy. I can accomplish something for people.

THEODORE CLARK
Black. Fifty-three years old. Precinct captain in Alderman Vito Marzullo's 25th ward, and section foreman in the department of streets and sanitation 25th ward yard.

I was born in New Orleans in 1926. I went to the eighth grade in school. I came to Chicago in 1947 to try to find a job and lived with my sister on the South Side. I got a job at Hokin Steel Company at $1.25 an hour. I was there for eleven years, and, at the end of that time, I had gotten an 85¢ raise. I had gotten married and had a family. I was barely making it. I wanted to better my conditions, with five kids, living in four rooms, paying $110 a month. I moved to the West Side in 1961, to 2857 Flournoy, where I still live. I was the first black that moved in the 2800 block on Flournoy. I didn't have any problems. In the seventeen years that I have lived there, the area has changed from white to black.

How did you get into politics, Ted?
I was cleaning the catch basin at the place I bought on Flournoy. Marco Domico was the precinct captain. He introduced himself, asked me what kind of work I was doing, and asked me if I had ever been involved in politics. I told him, "No." He said, "How would you like to go around with me? I can show you what it's all about." I said, "I don't have anything to lose." He carried me with him for maybe a year, off and on. Everytime he was getting ready to go out canvassing, he'd come and get me. The area was turning black and he needed a black worker.

I went with him for two or three years as a volunteer. He showed me how it was done, and I likes people. This was very educational to me. I had never been involved in politics, and with me, the more I do, the more I want to do. It's like money—the more you get, the more you want. The more votes I could get to come out, the more I wanted to get out. After about a year, Alderman Marzullo gave me a job as a laborer on the back of a garbage truck. I don't remember the salary, but it was twice as much as I was making at the steel company. I guess I proved myself to the alderman.

Everyone I could get, I got them to come out. People that are there in the precinct, they're not too much concerned about the candidate. The captain is the name of the whole thing. They come out mainly for the captain. They come out for me. I have it understood at all times that I'm the underdog, that I need them. I do need them. I guess that's why I am as successful as I am.

They're exercising their rights. So many of our black people seem to forget that in the South, people lost their lives in order to get the privilege to register to vote. This was one of my main things with those people. Marco taught me. I learned them what I learned from Marco about politics. Everything I know, it come from Marco. I'm not bragging, but I will go into any precinct there is in the ward (in the black precincts, I don't mean the white precincts), and, give me at least one election, enough time to work with them, and I will persuade them.

It costs. I might go to John's house this weekend, I might spend maybe thirty dollars buying drinks. And we sit there and talk and laugh, and then the word gets around, "Ted's all right." I go to the next guy's house the next couple of weeks and do the same thing. And this happens quite often, when I was drinking. I don't hardly drink now, but I still buy it for them. I was in the precinct yesterday. It cost me twelve dollars just for ones that really need something. I only had about twenty-eight dollars in my pocket. I ran into this lady yesterday, she didn't have milk for her kids. She said her check didn't come. I can understand that. I was thinking at the same time, "She's already in my corner, but this will make her come to the polls if she's sick." It's the little things that mean a lot.

I might run into someone that's a hard-nose. I haven't got him to go directly for me yet. I will talk to him about maybe anything, just to get him for me. The only thing you can sell is yourself. A lot of them, they believe in this black and white, but I believe in anyone that the organization slates. And I have it understood, that there's not just one, whether white, purple, black or what have you, but anyone that the organization slates.

You remember when Hanrahan ran for state's attorney? The worst election that I had ever been through! It was after the Black Panthers got killed, not far from my precinct here. The alderman said we were going to carry Hanrahan. I said, "Jesus Christ, what am I going to do?" I never mentioned Hanrahan. I just went for the straight ticket.

And I carried him. I didn't like him, but I had to go along. I was called every name in the book on this election when we were going for Hanrahan. When I was working for Marco, we also carried the precinct for Nixon over McGovern in 1972, when the alderman went for Nixon.

I never start an argument with a voter. I never will win it. If I go along with him, I'll have a chance to come back to him later. You can tell when a person just wants to be arrogant and don't want to go along with nothing. This is the guy that I'll go to his house and buy him a few drinks, and we set down and talk. Then he'll be the first one at the polls the next time. This is the truth.

What about these allegations that in precincts like yours on the West Side, there is a lot of vote stealing, vote fraud, vote buying?

You don't have to buy no votes or steal no votes, if you canvass your precinct. If they're buying votes, that means the captains not doing their homework. I don't have to buy no votes. Let's say a man moves into the precinct. Right away I go and introduce myself. He'll remember me. Don't cost me nothing to go there. Right away, I tell him, "If there's anything I can do for you, I'm the precinct captain, you let me know." There's so many places he don't know where to go. He might have problems to need the Board of Health. He don't know how to get it, don't know what to do about it. I direct him on this. He might need garbage cans. The alderman tries to keep garbage cans at the ward yard. I dispatch a truck out there, let them get him a garbage can, and anything else that I can do.

We have a book of every department—sanitation, water, electric, or what have you. I give them the number or the address. They can call, and whatever their complaint is, they can tell it to them. They might have a street light out. They give it to me and I call the street light in. I do whatever I can do myself. But, on the building department, I don't want them to be the one to say that I called the building department on them. I might lose a vote. If anyone had problems, let them have problems, not me.

There's very few things I take to the alderman. I worry him as less as possible. He has enough problems. When it comes to something I can't handle, I come to him or Marco. I have mother-wit. I *mean* mother-wit. That means you brought this from home with you. You grew up with it as a kid. Common sense. How to deal with people. I have ran into every type of person there is. I could talk to you for just five or ten minutes, strictly talking business, and I'll tell what kind of person you are just through conversation. You might be lying and you might think I don't know, but I just go along. I've got common sense, that's all. That's the way I deal with the voters. Some of these voters have college degrees, but it don't mean nothing to me. I don't care *who* you are. I can *talk* to you. You understand what I say? Like the alderman says, "You might not like my grammar, but you're going to like my taste." That's the only thing that's really important to me, is you accepting me. I don't recall ever striking out.

I don't promise them nothing in the beginning. I say, "If I can," because I don't know what the alderman has, I don't know what's going to happen. You'd rather me to tell you the truth than to lie to you. If I can, I will. If I can't, I can't. I'm only going to do so much. I'm only going to give them so much. I have won them with a lousy half pint, a bottle of wine, a quart of beer, a six-pack of beer, what have you. It don't mean anything. I want them. And this will last until maybe the next time they see me. Who knows?

Do I pay for this out of my pocket? Yes. And I think nothing about it. I was brought up the hard way. I didn't have anything when I was a kid. I know what it's like to want milk, want bread. God has blessed me so I can have a few dollars in my pocket, and I was able to give to this lady. Whether I was looking for her vote in return or not, I would have gave it to her.

Some people will ask you stupid questions that they can take care of themselves. All kinds of things. Some of them want you to baby-sit. Mainly, they want jobs. That's the big thing. That has to go through the alderman. I might go to a construction job, or see people that have a factory, and I ask them if they need any men, to get in touch with me. A couple of places have got in touch with me, and I got people from the area jobs.

Can you give me some numbers in your precinct in the 1977 mayoral primary, when Bilandic ran, and there was a black candidate, Harold Washington?

Washington got either four or fourteen votes. Bilandic got about 280 votes. The vote wasn't for the candidate. It was for me. I've never been a racist, which I was born in the South. There's good and bad in all nationalities. I hates to even talk to anyone that tell me, "Well, he's black, or he's white, or anything," because that don't mean anything to me. But our young black people is a lot different from the old ones. They are much more harder to win over. It's changing fast.

What about in a general election?

We have three Republican judges. We get three Republican votes in a general election. We had two other Republicans, ten years ago. They were white people. They were diehard Republicans, but they moved out.

We have an *organization.* Together we will stand, but divided we going to fall. That's what keeps the organization together. And whether we was in politics or not (this goes for both of those men), I will always think highly of the alderman and Marco. This is the truth from my heart. They have done so much for me. They brought me out of working on a job for an 85¢ raise in eleven years. How much do you think I'd be making now? How could I make it? You understand me? Marco made my whole life for me. He put the foundation for me for my whole life, and I appreciate it.

BEN MARTINEZ   *Mexican. Fifty-four years old. Precinct captain in the 25th ward and secretary to Alderman Vito Marzullo.*

I was born in Chicago in the Back-of-the-Yards area in 1925. I went to grammar school and high school. I dropped out of high school when I was seventeen years old. In them days, crew cut haircuts were popular. Not being one to go against the craze of the time, I went for my crew cut. The barber gave me a crew cut that was more like a bald head, and I just didn't have the nerve to go back to school.

I went into the service for three years and came back in 1947. We moved to the West Side in the vicinity of Taylor and Ashland Avenues. I went to work when I came home, took some menial jobs, worked in a couple of factories, and then I drove a truck for about eighteen or nineteen years.

During that time when I was driving a truck, I had gotten into the tavern business and came into contact with a man by the name of Eddie Ragan. Eddie Ragan became a very close and dear friend of mine. He was a precinct captain with the old 21st ward, which later became the 25th ward. During the years that I was in business, I bought ads from Eddie. There were many occasions when I needed his political expertise, and he never failed me. The area was mixed —Polish, Bohemian, Croatian, all types of European cultures. At that time there was very few Mexicans. They were just starting to come in there.

I got out of trucking and out of the liquor business. I had an occasion, one time, when a man pointed a gun at me, pulled the trigger, but the gun jammed. My nephew, David Vega, quite poetically put it—"You can see the writing on the wall. It's time to get out." So I got out, and, after almost twenty years of driving a truck, my physical condition, I couldn't take that any more. I talked to my friend, Eddie Ragan, and he said, "Well, you know how you get into politics—volunteering, helping with the people, getting them to

come out and vote. So I did, and that's when I got to meet Alderman
Marzullo. The alderman was just as he is right now. Somewhat reluc-
tant, he said, "Well, work out there and come back and see me."
That's exactly what I did. He started taking notice of my work and
Eddie was very generous in his praise for me.

I was assistant precinct captain under Eddie Ragan for about eight
or nine years. I was very helpful to him, canvassing the precinct and
getting ads for the ward ad book. I gave him some myself and then
I talked to some of my friends. The alderman is a shrewd man. He
knew all along what I was doing. When I got out of the truckdriving
and tavern business, I asked for a job. My first job was with the sign
division for about a year. I was a clerk at not a very good salary. If
I was a watchman, I would have been listed as a laborer [at prevailing
union wage rates] and I would probably have still been there. From
there I went to the sheriff's department for a couple of years. I was
a bailiff. I had some trying experiences. I was over at the juvenile
home. Boy, is that a place to work! That's worse than working in the
big court room. Those kids are something else! Some of them are
giants. From there I went to work on the alderman's committee on
local transportation for a couple of years. Then, I learned that somebody had started at the building department and lasted one day,
when they put him out in the southeast area. He stayed one day and
he quit. I heard about that opening and asked the alderman about
it and he said, "Okay." I was sent up there and worked there about
a year and a half as a building inspector. My district encompassed a
big part of the black area and some of the Spanish-speaking area on
the Southeast Side.

There is no way in the world that you can get used to that area.
You never know when you're going to come back. I came to find out
that there's no such thing as a made-to-order job. You come up with
some situations there that are very touchy, that you walk into inad-
vertently, and there you are, you're making your report, and you
can't get out of there fast enough. Some of them buildings have thirty
or forty units, different hallways. You have to live through it to know
what it is. You don't know which hallway you're going to get pulled
over. Fortunately, it never did happen to me. But it worked on me.
I had talked to the alderman about possibly getting out of the area
and getting someplace else.

The first of the year, the city council voted to give the aldermen
a secretary. Alderman Marzullo didn't have anybody, so he started
mentioning it to me. And, with him, when he starts mentioning

something, it's usually going to come about. So I was hired as his personal secretary.

Do you think it was because the ward was becoming Mexican?

Possibly that might have had something to do with it. It might have had some small significance, but I would like to think it was based on merit. At this time there was only one Mexican precinct captain. I replaced him. Since I've become the alderman's secretary, I have been instrumental in having two more Mexicans being made precinct captains. I have also been sent by the alderman or his representative, on occasions, where something has come up in the Mexican community. He'll usually say, "Ben, I want you to go and see these people, and then report back to me."

What's the makeup of your precinct?

I have only been a precinct captain for a short time. But, during the years I worked with Ragan, I watched the makeup of that precinct change steadily. In the short time I've been in charge of the 39th precinct, there has been a dramatic change. Where, during a precinct canvass, there were European voters, the next time you come around, there were legal as well as illegal Mexicans residing. This, of course, cuts down our voting population. And I'm sure the alderman is concerned that, from one election to another, our voting numbers are on the decline.

There has been, in the past few years, a terribly big influx of persons from Mexico into the Chicago area. For the most part, these persons are legally documented aliens, who have come in legally and have green cards (immigration permits). But, most recently, there has been an alarming rise in the amount of undocumented illegals arriving and settling in our communities. What was once a cosmopolitan neighborhood has steadily changed into a Mexican one. Unfortunately, many of the documented aliens are not in the least bit interested in becoming United States citizens. Many of them complain of no Spanish elected officials or of Spanish representation in city government. But, at the same time, they do not make the effort of becoming citizens so that they could participate in the voting privileges that citizenship provides. They fail to realize what a power bloc they could be. What good does it do them, if there are a half million or even a million of them, if they do not have a say, simply because they are not citizens and cannot vote?

From a humanitarian standpoint, I have no objection to the migration of Mexican nationals into the United States. I realize that they are trying to escape a government that is completely insensitive to the needs of the working class. These people are simply coming over in an effort to make a living, something that has been impossible for them to achieve in their own country. The United States government should admit that it is impossible to stem the illegals and, at least, demand that these persons become a part of the country that is accepting them by becoming law-abiding citizens, that this be a condition by which they can enter and remain in this country. This is preferable to the present cat-and-mouse game the United States is playing with hordes of illegals entering the country on a daily basis.

From a political standpoint, I am alarmed by the daily arrivals of Mexican nationals. These persons number in big figures. They all manage to get jobs, save their money, and acquire property (another area in which the government has no objection). As the areas in which these aliens arrive get heavily populated, there begins an exodus of the persons of other ethnic backgrounds for two obvious reasons: first, the Europeans tend to follow others into neighborhoods predominated by their own nationalities, or go to the suburbs; second, the new arrivals, having worked a few years, accumulate the money needed to make down payments on their own homes (brought from the fleeing European ethnics). And so the change takes place. If these Mexican nationals have no interest in becoming citizens (largely because the government doesn't require them to do so, and this is the case quite often), then the political structure in the area suffers. The European ethnics who, at least, had become citizens and voted, now are gone, and in their place there are now legal or illegal Mexicans who have it in their minds that they are just here to work and make money, and don't feel it advantageous to become citizens.

I hear stories that there may be half a million illegal Mexicans in Chicago. Have you any idea, Ben, how many Mexicans there are in Chicago, and what types of people are coming here?

I don't know the numbers. This has been going on for years. Years ago, we were getting a type of Mexican immigrant coming from the bigger cities. Many of them were educated. But now we are getting an influx of people, not from the cities, but coming from the hinterlands, the countryside. They have their own way of living from way back, like Mexican Indians. When they come over here, they do not try to adapt. They come in with their set standards, and they try to live their own way. Back in Mexico, they're used to carrying guns and knives without the police to bother them.

The people that were coming ten, fifteen years ago, were more or less city folk. They dressed accordingly. You could hardly distinguish them from people who were born and raised here. You can distinguish the people from the countryside by their mode of dress. You'll see them with these hats, with the strings on their backs. There's not any fears of the laws of the country, because we have to protect their rights. The immigration authorities seem to be helpless, because they have to be careful not to violate their rights.

If we don't put a stopgap of this exodus from Mexico up here, the migration will continue. Europeans will be moving out, a bigger percentage of people living here will be Mexican aliens, and the politics of this city will be seriously affected.

I have a selfish motive. I am in politics, and I'm seeing our ward and our precinct overrun with these people. It has a detrimental affect on our election results. They don't vote. They have no aspirations to become citizens. There's a state of apathy that exists in the Mexican community. A lot of them have the conception that they are going to go back to Mexico. I argue with that. I tell them that if you've been here for fifteen years, why not become a citizen? The likelihood of them going back is very little. Why can't they get their papers, become citizens, and participate in politics while they're here?

We have two different factions in the Mexican community. We have people like me in the political field who want these people to become citizens so that they can vote. That's my selfish motive. The other people don't want to become citizens because they don't have to. The country doesn't obligate them. These businessmen over here would like to see even more people coming over because they'll get fat, they'll make a lot of money. There's a perpetual motion. I think we're the ones that are losing, the ones on the political end. I can't, for the life of me, understand why the government can't stop them, because there is no such thing as this government not being able to stop them.

Why doesn't the government want to do anything?
Let's look at it this way. Many of those people coming from over there, since they're breaking the law by entering illegally, they're not here under their right names. So in order to work, what do they have to do? Get a social security card, right? If that is not the right name, the money that is being collected for social security very well

could be staying with this country. Again, we're talking perpetual motion. (I hope I don't go to jail because of this.) But these are feelings that I have had.

How do you see your own future in the ward organization and in Chicago politics?

I don't think too much about that. I would like to think the alderman would go on forever, because we are in dire need of the type of leadership he provides. I think a good example is what happened to the city when Mayor Daley died. In general, I like public life. I'm not an elected official. I do the will of the people who are in office. I do my work to try to help the 25th ward and the Democratic organization. I am not actively seeking elective office, but if our organization wanted to put me up for a better position, I would be proud to serve. I am a loyalist—let's put it that way.

FOUR

The Young Turks

EDWARD VRDOLYAK / EDWARD M. BURKE / LOUIS VIVERITO

EDWARD VRDOLYAK
Croatian. Thirty-nine years old. Tough, brilliant, successful lawyer. Is alderman and committeeman of the 10th ward on the Southeast Side, and is one of the key figures in the machine and the city council.

I grew up here in South Chicago. My father had a tavern for fifty-one years. He was an immigrant from Dalmatia in Yugoslavia, the same place my mother came from. Some people in this neighborhood still think of me as Pete's boy. I went to a seminary the first three years of high school, but I just didn't have it as far as that particular vocation is concerned. I left and went to St. Joseph's College in Rensselaer, Indiana, and then to Law School at the University of Chicago.

After I graduated I got hold of one of the neighborhood lawyers, and worked out an arrangement where I would have my own practice, that I would do some things for him which would, in turn, pay for my rent because I was busted. That's how I started. We now have twenty-six people working full time, including ten lawyers.

I got into politics sitting at lunch one day with some friends of mine from the area in 1966. The aldermanic election was coming up about ten months away, in February 1967. They said, "You ought to run for alderman." I asked the standard question. "What is an alderman and what does he do?" Some of them were involved in politics, so they filled me in. I said, "Okay, who do I talk to?" They said, "You contact the committeeman." I contacted the committeeman and made three appointments. He never kept the appointments. I got mad and put a release in a local paper stating that I was going to be a candidate for alderman. The incumbent alderman, John Buchanan, called me and said that if I supported him for alderman, and was his campaign manager and raised some dough for him, he would support me for committeeman. I agreed. We ran and he won handily. Then he told me that everyone wanted him to run for committeeman, as well. I told him he could do whatever he wanted to do, that I was still going to run for committeeman. I ran for committeeman and defeated the incumbent by 497 votes out of 1,808 cast.

Isn't it hard to beat an incumbent committeeman in Chicago?
You can't beat an incumbent committeeman in the city of Chicago unless he lets you beat him. If he is doing his job, you can't beat him at all.

How did you get to be an alderman?
Serious personality problems between Buchanan and I developed. We reached a parting of the ways, and I ran and beat him.

Politics is a game of addition, not subtraction, and not exclusion. I had everybody. I had all the people we had from before. He had very few people left. When he ran for alderman the first time, he had a core of an organization, but they couldn't man every precinct of the ward. When we ran his organization, we manned every precinct in the ward, and we just grew from there until I ran for committee-man, and then we put both organizations together.

So you're an alderman, a committeeman, and a lawyer?
No, I'm a lawyer first, then a committeeman, and then an alder-man.

How do you run your ward organization?
When I beat the organization I didn't have any jobs. They had all the jobs. We were out there and took it away from them. Why? Because I told everybody they were going to get a job? I never told anybody they were going to get a job. Right now probably 25 percent of my captains aren't involved in any governmental position whatso-ever. These are friends. I think you have to show people that you like them and that you really want to do the right thing, and you can get a great deal from that. I never had a harsh word with anybody, except if someone lied to me. That's the only time I ever have an argument with anybody. If someone can't get the job done, I ask them to please let me send them some help or make a co-captain. Or, I'll go into the precinct myself. Before the election, I'll spot-check half the precincts in the ward myself. We're on the phones every night, calling people in every precinct. I call them myself, personally. "How many times has the captain been around? What did he say?" We also have a sign check. I want signs up in windows. That means people have been around and are committed. We get good results.

In 1976, when everybody dumped with Howlett, we carried him
60/40. With Carter, we carried him 2 to 1. We may have trouble,
time to time, with a given election, but, in the last election, 84
percent of the people voted. We have as high a black vote from our
black section in the ward as any other black vote in the city, if not
higher. Only because we work at it.

Some of the captains work in governmental positions, whether it
be the city or the county or the district. Some of them are not looking
for anything and just want to be involved in their own precinct, or
with people, or in their neighborhood. There are a lot of good solid
people like that. There are people who work for the city who make
$27,000 a year that I wouldn't want to ring a doorbell, because all
they would do is hurt you. I've got people who work at the back end
of a garbage truck who are some of the best captains you ever saw.
I have probably forty people waiting in line who want to be a captain.
They got to want to be a captain. They got to want to knock on doors.
They got to want to have a personal relationship with people. They
got to want to have a personal relationship with me because I call
them all myself, personally. They got to want to be proud of getting
things done on their block or in their precinct and to be the person
that people call when something goes wrong there. They have to
want to do those things, they got to want to be involved, and they
got to want to make their community a better community.

*In 1974, you challenged the organization and ran against Tom
Tully for Cook County assessor. Why did you do that?*

Because it was the right thing for me to do. There were some
things said, personal commitments were not kept, confidences were
not kept, and I made up my mind that even if I wasn't going to be
in politics any more, whether I won or lost for assessor, that no one
would ever treat me like that again. If you give your word you better
keep it, in business, or politics, or talking to your wife.

Good politics is really good government, like Mayor Daley did say,
and vice versa. I think if you do a workmanlike and effective job,
people know. If you like what you are doing and like people, people
know it. If you get things done, they know it. Look at results and look
at the numbers on election day, and you'll know who the good committeemen are. As far as the council is concerned, look at the people
that do most of the floor work.

Mayor Daley's strengths were his great love for Chicago and his
family roots, which came through. He loved being mayor of Chicago

more than anything else in the world. It wasn't his job, it was his life. He was a great administrator and his other strength was his great budgetary prowess. He was a great man of numbers. That's what kept the city budget on an even keel. Those were his strengths. He had the same weaknesses we all have. He had his likes and his dislikes. He had certain areas where he would see red, where he wouldn't budge.

He didn't necessarily like everything that I have done. I didn't like everything he did. But he was my friend and I considered myself his friend, and if he asked me to do anything in particular before I made a commitment, I would do it. And he would do the same for me. I told him what I was doing all the time in front. I told him I was going to run for assessor in front. He was the chairman of the party and I considered him a friend, and I went and told him what I was going to do.

A lot of people in Chicago call you "Fast Eddie." Where do you want to go from here?

People have been saying to me for three, four years, "You're going to be the next guy—you're going to do this, you're going to do that." Maybe I could. But, when you run for office, you have to know what the job entails. I have three sons, thirteen, twelve, and one going to be four. I've got a thriving business that is flourishing more and more every day that requires my attention, and I don't want to jeopardize my family, and the next time I'll see my boys, it will be at their college graduation because I have been, perhaps, in a major office, where it would require my full time and attention as many of the positions would. And the same thing with my business.

I know what a job entails and I wouldn't want to take a job unless I was going to do it the way it should be done. I think I could handle anything I want to. I don't lack for confidence. I never did that, rightly or wrongly. But that's the way I want to live my life. I want to be able to say to the wife this weekend, "Let's take the kids out of school Friday; we'll leave Thursday afternoon, go to Palm Springs for four days, come back for school Monday. Let's just do this. Let's just do that." I want to be with them. I think boys need that. About four years ago I made an evaluation that if I was going to stay in this business of politics, that I would not go out more than two nights a week. In the last four years, except at campaign time, I've kept that rule. If you want to reach me at night, I'm at home.

Do you have any national ambitions?

No. I like it here. I like people here. I like the action here. I like to be involved with people that I know and that have known me. I like to do things for people right here. Congress is great, but if my congressman wants to get something done in Chicago, he has to call me. I handle more requests in a week than he handles in a term of two years from people in my ward. Not that he doesn't do a good job. We're just at different levels. I'm at the nuts and bolts end of it, and he's flying on a plane back and forth to Washington. Even to Spring- field. Good God! Even if you're the governor, I just wouldn't want to do it. I don't want to live like that. I make six figures plus. I've got a big office. I've got a fine home. I've got a great family. I want to live.

If the party drafted you for an office like mayor, now or sometime in the future, would you seriously consider doing it?

Now, the answer is no. If things change in the future, say in ten, twelve years from now, I'd be fifty years old and my family would be relatively grown, then I might consider it.

What about the party chairmanship?

The only way I would want the party chairmanship, and the only way I would ever accept it, would be if I felt that the position is a position of leadership. I think it is a position which requires someone to devote more time and attention to it than has been devoted to it in the past. I think that it has to be one where people would respect your opinion, think that you are the best man for the job, and wouldn't worry about the fact that you have a bigger car than they do, that you make more dough than they do, all those petty little things that go on, silly, stupid things. There would have to be a sincere feeling among the committeemen that they really want to put this thing together and make the central committee just what my organization is (and I sincerely mean it), not just an organization, but a family. I think if we start treating one another like that, suburban/ city committeemen, altogether, we're going to have something. Until that time, we're going to nominate people from the city in the primaries and we're going to get beat in the general elections in the suburbs, which is the equivalent of playing with oneself. You're wast- ing time.

With Daley there, everybody, except for a few people, was just sitting there waiting for him to tell them what was going to be done. Now that he died, the first thing that happened, it wasn't so much,

"Let's get George Dunne elected or Eddie Kelly elected," but, "Jesus, we can't let that crazy guy, Vrdolyak, get in there." And the reason why stemmed from a feeling of pettiness or jealousy or what. It certainly can't be incompetency. I'll argue that to the death with anybody. But these feelings came out. It's a sin that you have to waste your life feeling about other people like that, rather than being on the go yourself and trying to do something yourself.

I said I wouldn't even consider letting my name be nominated or calling anyone to ask them for support for that position. Whether I could have gotten their support or not, I don't know, but I could have put on a damn good fight, and I don't think some people have stomachs for fighting. I said, "I don't want to do that. I don't want to fight to say that I'm the best man for the job." I said that we're professional enough to look around and say, "Hey, these people are the best men for the job. These people can probably help us raise more dough than anyone we ever had before. This guy would give us more time and attention. This guy would bring everybody in. Whether he likes you or not, he'll give you a square shake." Now if they can't figure that out about me or some other guys in the party, then I'm wasting my time. What do I want to be chairman of the party for, if the fellas are so bananas that they can't figure that I treat politics like a business? I would try to run it as efficiently as I can, and I know as a business you want everyone as happy as they can, as content as they can, then you know people aren't spinning their wheels, but that they are devoting full time and attention to the results. And that's the only thing that counts—the results.

EDWARD M. BURKE *Irish. About thirty-four years old. His father was alderman and committeeman of the South Side's 14th ward. Burke succeeded him and is regarded as one of the most able young men in the party. Is also a lawyer.*

I was born and raised in Visitation Parish on the South Side. (In Chicago, if you are Catholic, you identify with a parish—Nativity, Visitation, Little Flower, etc.). I went to Visitation Grammar School, Quigley Seminary, and undergraduate school and Law School at DePaul University. When I was going to law school, I was a policeman assigned to the states attorney's office.

My father, who had very little formal education, was a precinct captain in the 14th ward and got his first political job through Jim McDermott, as a laborer in the water pipe division, spent ten years as a deputy sheriff, and then McDermott asked him to become his personal bailiff, which was a pretty big slot for a young man. He was elected alderman in 1953, at the same time as Vito Marzullo, and served in the city council until he died in 1968. In 1965, he succeeded Don O'Brien as the committeeman for the 14th ward, so he was both committeeman and alderman.

I grew up in politics. The entire family structure revolved around politics. I can remember going to political meetings with my father when I was just a toddler.

I wasn't a precinct captain, but I knew everyone in the organization, attended all the meetings. In 1968, when I was a senior in law school, my father got sick in February, three months prior to the primary election. During that period of time when he was ill, I ran the ward organization on a day-to-day basis.

He died on May 11, 1968, and the remains had not even been cold when the political animals of our organization began plotting as to who would become the committeeman, and who would become the alderman. My most vivid recollections of the wake were the little clusters of men around the funeral parlor, discussing who would get what. It was almost like the Roman soldiers casting lots for the garment under the cross at the crucifixion. I was offended by this kind of conduct, and decided that I would not allow the successors to succeed to his dual roles without a fight. There was a fight but I won and was elected by the precinct captains. I was twenty-four years old at the time, the youngest man in Chicago's history to become a ward committeeman.

What does it mean to be a committeeman in Chicago these days?
Well, at one time, it was very important. Right now it is not as important. In the future it will again become important.*

Today politics is dominated principally by one man, Richard J. Daley. In the past, you would see powerful ward leaders like Tom Keane, Colonel Arvey, Joe Gill, and a variety of strong Democratic committeemen who were recognized leaders. You don't have that today, although there are strong personalities. No one has much power or much to say about what happens. For the last twenty-three years, politics has been centrally dominated by one individual. In the early years, some of those old ward leaders were still around, but they're all gone now and the only remaining one is Richard J. Daley.

Having been there for so long, he has been instrumental in the selection, election, or appointment of virtually every Democratic figure in local government affairs. But aside from that (and most people don't realize it), he controls, to a great extent, the organized labor movement in Chicago. Organized labor does not make a move without checking it out first with Richard J. Daley. In addition to that he has been able to couple his dominance in politics and labor with a very close working relationship with the business community and the principal business leaders, who control a great deal of public opinion of Chicago.

Daley is a remarkable man. He started from the very bottom, and all those people who knew him in his youth have a great deal of respect for him. He obviously was a very tenacious individual. He had some very good innate talents and abilities that I think a lot of people have ignored down through the years. He worked very hard and long to get his law degree. He became the director of revenue under Adlai Stevenson, and was, at the time of his service in the legislature, the man in the county clerk's office responsible for the duties of the comptroller. So he had a very broad base in

*This interview was taped on December 17, 1976, three days before Mayor Daley died.

budgetary and fiscal matters very early in his career.

Politically, he was able to pull off a coup d'état that hasn't been matched in American politics, let alone Chicago politics. In his first mayoral campaign he said that if elected mayor, he would step down as leader of the Democratic Party. But, of course, he knew, just as I knew when I became the committeeman of the 14th ward, that if I did not consolidate my position as both committeeman and alderman, I wouldn't be either one, next time around. He consolidated his position early in his career as mayor, and he continued to do so and build for the last twenty years, to the point, now, where I am of the opinion that he is absolutely invulnerable in both positions. There is no one, in my opinion, that I can identify now who could take him on in either role and win.

What do you think will happen to Chicago politics after Daley?
You'll see a reemergence of local ward leaders as being influential in policies and programs of the Democratic Party. You will see a return of the role of the city council to what it should be traditionally under the form of government we have. Chicago government is supposed to be a strong council/weak mayor form of government, but for the last twenty years we know it is not a strong council/weak mayor form of government. We virtually have abandoned the legislative branch of government in Chicago. It is government by executive fiat.

So you see a revival of the city council as a governmental agency, and a decline in the power of the mayor.
As you know, Milt, the succession to the office of mayor, should Mayor Daley die in office or resign, would be controlled by the city council. The next mayor must be a member of the city council. He must be selected by the members of the city council to serve out the term of office if it is less than one year. Otherwise, the council must meet and select a successor to serve on an interim basis, and then pass an ordinance setting up the machinery for a special election for mayor. Whomever gets elected as an interim mayor is going to be very reluctant to remove his derrière from that green chair on the fifth floor once he gets used to the comfortable surroundings of the office of the mayor.

I don't perceive that anyone will ever be able to again consolidate his power as both mayor and head of the Democratic Party. I don't think it is going to happen. Everything is contingent on the status of

Richard J. Daley at the time these changes are to take place. If Richard J. Daley today decided to give up the office of mayor and remain as county chairman, he could designate whomever he wished to be the mayor. However, if he is not on the scene, I don't think he could do it posthumously. He must be here to do it.

You are one of the key figures in this thing. How do you think the decision will be made about who is going to be party chairman and who is going to be mayor, if Daley is not on the scene?

I don't really know. I am hoping that most of us who are ward committeemen now could reach an accord as to who would be designated as the leader. It could ultimately be resolved in a triumvirate or quadrumvirate. I think that would be an interesting way of running the affairs of the Democratic Party in Cook County, despite the fact that there is no legislative sanction for that kind of arrangement (there is no legislative sanction for having a co-chairperson, but we have one, so I imagine the law is not all that important in terms of political structure).* Perhaps a quadrumvirate, or a triumvirate, with men or women representing a broad ethnic background, with an executive director who would handle day-to-day operations of the Democratic Party, might be an interesting solution to that kind of dilemma, a diffusion of power, so that power would not be placed in the hands of simply one man, so that everyone can have a piece of the action, or an opportunity to have his opinions heard and acted upon.

However, let me say this. I had lunch with the mayor two days ago and he looks as good as, if not better than, he has in the last ten years. I don't want to give you the impression that I am sending out to the local florist shop ordering any floral wreaths, because he looks real good, and as long as he is as healthy as he is today, he will continue to hold both those offices, in my opinion. His stamina and his zest for doing what he is doing is remarkable. He thrives on politics and on government, and, in my opinion, he will never leave the office of mayor voluntarily. He will continue to serve until the Grim Reaper takes his toll.

How do you see your role in the future in Chicago politics?

I would like to be around Chicago politics for a while. I'm thirty-two years old. I enjoy the excitement of politics. I don't

*Daley had appointed Jane Byrne to that position.

know if I am going to make a total commitment and make the
kinds of personal sacrifices necessary that one would need to be
the principal figure in Chicago politics. A fellow like Neil Hartigan, I think, is motivated along those lines. He seems to enjoy the
seven-nights-a-week campaign trail and circuit. I personally don't
like that kind of life. I like to spend a little time with my family.
But it's really impossible to speculate about one's future. I think
that in the years to come the city council will be a more exciting
place to be and I do like the freedom of the legislative branch of
government. It allows me to practice law, and do the kinds of
things that I want to do, without the total responsibility that one
finds in the executive branch of government.

I look at Daley and see a man who probably has watched his kids
grow from infanthood to adulthood without ever spending any time
with them. In his life he has probably been on the banquet circuit
every night of the week. He works eighteen-hour days, although he
personally seems to thrive on it. I don't know that my personality is
such that it would allow me to do that. It can be a very draining
experience. It takes a certain kind of individual to be successful in
that particular framework.

I suppose all politicians would like their constituents to believe
that they are totally unselfish in their attitudes toward their political service. But that is not totally true. One does get some degree
of satisfaction from serving in public office, but the satisfaction
one gets in terms of the kind of commitment one must make in
politics today does not bear out the commitment. The sacrifices
that one must make in terms of privacy, and the times he will be
held up to public ridicule and scorn in modern American politics,
deters many people from becoming involved in politics. I can see
it happening myself. I am not all that greatly interested in seeking higher public offices. One must be very highly motivated
today, willing to make an almost total commitment of his personal
and public life to the office he seeks, and I don't know that I am
willing to make that kind of sacrifice.

I would like people to think of me primarily as a lawyer. However,
I find most people don't think of me that way. They think of me as
an alderman or a committeeman, and sometimes it's not good for
business either.

I enjoy the city council and I enjoy politics, and I think I'm good
at it. In the last election I think our results bear that out. I think of
the so-called white wards in Chicago; the only two that carried for

all three of our candidates were Ed Vrdolyak and myself. Despite the public relations that is generated in the newspapers by some of our brother colleagues about their futures in Chicago politics, when it comes right down to it, it's a question of the bottom line. Either you win or you don't win. We win. A lot of the others that would like you to believe that they are the successors to the purple cape over there on the fifth floor don't deliver. They can deliver in an easy election. If they compare their figures from Richard J. Daley's last election with what happened in this last election, there is no comparison. Daley's election was an easy election. Daley against Singer was no contest. I keep telling my friend Bill Singer that a Jew will never be elected mayor of Chicago. There is a latent anti-Semitism in Chicago and a large population that will never vote for a Jew. They would vote for anybody before a Jew.

Let me ask you about the ethnic thing. Is there a South Side Irish Mafia running the city?

That kind of an attitude, to which I subscribe, that the Irish Mafia runs Chicago, does more to hurt me than help me. Now it is a disadvantage to be identified as an Irish Catholic, because the Poles, the Lithuanians, the Eastern European ethnic groups, are looking to be recognized in some way. Daley, although he has had a great talent for spreading around the opportunities for every ethnic, religious, and racial group in the past, has made a serious mistake with respect to the Poles and the Jews. Can anyone show me a highly visible, identifiable Jewish political leader? There doesn't seem to be one, and traditionally in Chicago, there has always been a highly recognizable, identifiable Jewish candidate, whether it was Jake Arvey, or Marshall Korshak, or someone else the Jewish community could look to as a political leader.

In the primary election, when the Poles were clamoring for a Polish candidate to replace Tom Kluczynski in the State Supreme Court, Daley chose not to follow the political course which I thought would have been wise, and selected Joe Power and Henry Dieringer. It turned out to be a debacle, a disaster.

You can look to the results of that election and pick out the so-called Polish wards and see the fall-off in votes there, which could have been the signal that we were in trouble. But we continue to go along and appoint Irish Catholics to high offices and select Irish Catholics to run. (I don't want to sound like I am knocking the Irish Catholics, but it's just a fact of life.) And it does appear, to my disadvantage, that there is a widely held opinion, not without a great deal of facts and figures to back it up. The Irish, in my opinion, have never worked together closely in Chicago politics. I think they have generally been fighting with one another. Jim McDermott and Daley never got along. Clarence Wagner and Daley never got along. Tom Nash and Daley never got along. It was the Poles and the blacks, ultimately, that really put Daley in as county chairman.

How do you see the future of the blacks politically in Chicago?
I don't think that we are anywhere close to seeing a black mayor in Chicago. I don't see it as a viable possibility in the near future. If there arises a highly qualified, attractive, black candidate, I think that he will have a tremendous opportunity in Democratic politics, but a black is never going to win a major statewide office in Illinois in the foreseeable future, just as I don't think a Catholic is going to win a major statewide office. Mike Howlett did win statewide for secretary of state, but that's a different kind of office.

There are an awful lot of people outside of Cook County in Illinois, and we are somewhat incestuous here in Chicago or Cook County because we grow up with this heavily Catholic kind of ethnic domination. But outside of Chicago and Cook County there are a lot of Protestants, and, to be very frank, there still remains a prejudice against Catholics, just as there still remains a prejudice against Jews. It may be latent, it may be the kind of prejudice that would not come to the surface in a business, professional, or personal relationship, but when that individual gets behind that curtain on election day, and he sees that name on the ballot, he has an opportunity to satisfy his latent biases or prejudices. Nobody else but himself knows about it, and that's when he does it.

It is true, then, that blacks, Catholics, and Jews in Chicago, recognizing this statewide situation, almost inevitably pursue and satisfy their political ambitions locally.
I would personally look at it in that way. I'm not about to become a sacrificial lamb for an office I don't think I can win. I would prefer to remain as the alderman and ward committeeman of the 14th ward where I think I enjoy a good reputation, where I think I have a rapport with my constituents, where I think I can contribute something to the overall commonweal of Chicago through representing my constituents in the legislative branch of government, as opposed

to running for an office just to be a candidate on the Democratic ticket.

I thought, at one time, that I wanted to go to Congress, that if I could get into the Congress at my age, I would be content to remain there for an extended period of time. I think that one, if he appreciates the role of the legislator, could get a great deal of self-satisfaction from serving in the U.S. Congress. I think that at the beginning it would be difficult, because of the seniority system, but, ultimately, if he can put five or six terms in, it would be at a point where he could really have something to say about government and the direction of our national policy.

Once again, we come to the Polish question. Jack Kluczynski died, and the mayor and I had a conversation right before the mayoral election in 1975. I told him I wanted to go to Congress, that Kluczynski came from the 14th ward, that the 14th ward had the bulk of the precincts in the congressional district, along with the 11th ward; that I thought I would be a good congressman, a good representative; that my wife had agreed, that although it would be a bit of a strain, if I wanted that, it would be all right with her. I thought that I had the blessings of the mayor until the Monday before the selection was made. Then he pulled the rug out from beneath me and told me that instead of me he was going to slate John Fary because he was Polish. At that time, Ed Hanrahan, who was running against Daley in the primary, was screaming about the Poles, and was saying "Kick the Irish out of the City Hall!" Hanrahan alienated the Irish, and didn't get any of the Poles anyway, so he didn't accomplish anything. But he may have contributed to my inability to get to Congress. Now, on reflection, I am just as happy it didn't go that way because I see my friends in Congress—Morgan Murphy, Dan Rostenkowski—operating on a treadmill, back and forth from Washington on planes like a fiddler's elbow. It's a real hassle and a real pressure kind of thing. In addition to which, now the opinion most Americans have of their congressmen probably would rate underneath that of a used car salesman.

Going back to the racial issue again, do you foresee a black/ white ethnic conflict within the organization or collaboration?

I think that, for everyone's benefit, there has to be collaboration. However, it is difficult to predict, and, when you look around at the black leaders, with the exception of Wilson Frost, who is my good friend and for whom I have a great deal of respect, and perhaps Tim Evans, I don't see any signs yet of a black leader who is going to emerge. I think it will take awhile before they can find somebody that they can really join behind. I think the ethnics will continue to dominate the city for some time.

LOUIS VIVERITO *Italian. Forty-five years old. Committeeman of southwest suburban Stickney Township, and is also
Township Supervisor. High school graduate who was a barber
before getting into politics. Is one of the best young suburban
committeemen.*

I grew up in the Bridgeport area in Chicago. I went to
McCall Grammar School, Tilden Tech High School, and then to the
Chicago Barber College. That was all of my educational background.
My mother is Croatian and my father is Italian. Both of them were
raised in Bridgeport. My mother is still a crossing guard at 30th and
Wallace. She bought a home in Oak Lawn, lived out there for two
years, but found that she wasn't happy in the suburbs and moved
back to Bridgeport.

I moved out here to Stickney over twenty years ago, when I was
twenty-five. This was an area that was for a newly married man like
myself and my wife. It was an area that was new and the house
offered more than other areas because it was more house, and it had
a low down payment and a cheaper price than most areas.

I had a small barber shop that I owned at 79th and Narragansett.
I had been in business there for almost sixteen years. The local com-
mitteeman at that time was a dentist by the name of Dr. Robert L.
Smith, who was also the township supervisor. He talked to me about
getting into politics. I was involved in the barber shop and did a lot
of the people in my area, so I was an ideal precinct captain. When
I would walk down the street or knock on the door, they'd say, "Oh,
Louis the barber is here." I had an avenue to get into the homes.

*Lou, how do you work a precinct in the suburbs, compared to the
city?*

It is much more difficult to work a precinct in the suburbs than in
the city. We don't give the garbage can concept. People aren't asking
for as much. You can't do as many favors. But local services are
extremely important to the voters. A lot of people want to be In-

dependents. They don't want to be Republican, maybe, but they don't want to say that they're Democrats either. But, because I cut a lot of their hair, they would come out and cast a Democratic Party vote in the primary for me.

I became a township officer in 1965. Then, in 1970, Smith decided to quit politics. He moved from the area and the party was up for grabs. I had been a precinct captain and the president of the township Democratic Party for five years. So I ran for committeeman and was elected.

It's very difficult to be a Democratic committeeman in the suburbs. You have to really get involved in the community as a public official. You don't get enough help. The county central committee feels that the Democratic Party ends at Cicero Avenue, and that there is a wall around us. We don't have any candidates from our area; we don't have a state representative; we don't have a state senator. We have never had a Democratic county board commissioner in the suburbs that I know of. All the representation is from Chicago. But the party has given me some jobs for my people which has been helpful, and has helped me with a lot of people that would be unemployed today if it weren't for them. Every one of my precincts is covered, and I have had good success with it. Some of the workers have patronage jobs, but about half of them are volunteers.

Mayor Daley never interfered in my township. He never dictated who should be the Democratic committeeman. He didn't even know who Lou Viverito was. He left the suburbs alone, although I think he was becoming more aware of the suburban areas in his last years. But the input into the county central committee from the suburbs has been minimal.

A real opportunity lies in the suburbs, if the Democratic Party will start looking toward the suburban leaders and letting them participate more. Chairman George Dunne is the kind of person that will be able to lead and develop the suburban area. He exemplifies the kind of person that can be sold in this area. I know exactly what every precinct has done since I have been a Democratic committeeman, and I don't like those fellows who say to me, "You guys in the suburbs don't know what the heck you are doing." There are too many committeemen in Chicago that are working with one alderman and will talk about how great he's doing in his ward. I have to work with three incorporated areas and three different mayors in Stickney Township. They're not Democrats and they're not Republicans, and dammit, you wouldn't be able to get most of them to say that they are one or the other. They want to appeal to the total populace within their areas. When you are a Democratic committeeman you have a certain amount of them against you, because a lot of people automatically are against the Democratic Party in the suburbs, and against Richard J. Daley. You don't have near the clout that committeemen in the city wards do. But if some of those so-called good committeemen wanted to come out in the suburbs, they would find out what politics really is.

How do you deal with municipal officials, as a Democratic committeeman?

I deal with them basically by, first of all, trying to find out if there is any way that I can possibly help them. We have legislators that have been helpful to us in getting bills passed, or getting monies into the area. I have tried to help any mayor when he couldn't help himself or didn't know an avenue to go to. I tried to cut some of the red tape, if at all possible. I have excellent cooperation from the three mayors in my township because I have tried to help them in any way I possibly could. I have been very helpful with backup services. We provide dog catcher services for the City of Burbank. Mayor Fitzgerald likes that and says that Lou Viverito is okay to work with.

We started a senior citizens program in the Village of Stickney. We've got all these senior citizens coming to us and George Fargo likes this. He knows that his people are happy. And George Wrench from the Village of Stickney says, "Gee, Lou is doing a pretty good job there. He's providing services for seniors." This is the kind of thing that the committeeman has to do. He has to work with the elected officials within his township, and without that help and cooperation he will never be successful. The recognition we are getting today from the Democratic Party is because of the fact that township government works here with the mayors in providing services.

Lou, are these people in Stickney ever going back to the city?

They don't want to go back to Chicago. They may go there to work, but when the people cross Cicero Avenue, they're in their own little suburban area and they are happy here. They think of it as small-town politics. Small-town politics is knowing that Lou Viverito used to cut their hair. They like that. I'm not a guy that they don't see, and I think that this is the reason they want to hold on to this identity.

There was a time that you had to be ashamed to say that you lived in Stickney Township. When I first moved here, I would say that I lived in Oak Lawn. I didn't live in Oak Lawn; I lived in Stickney. Somebody would say, "Where do you live in Oak Lawn?" I'd say that I lived at 85th and Mobile. "85th and Mobile?" they would say. "That's not Oak Lawn, it's Stickney!" They wouldn't even let me say that I lived in Oak Lawn. You know what I say to them today? I say that I live in Stickney Township in Burbank, and I'm proud of it. In our township today the people have a sense of pride, and a lot of it has come through the help that I've received from the Democratic Party, in implementing different programs here, and learning organizational ability. I'm getting good at that. You have to have a goal. You have to put good people around you, and you have to have an organization to achieve anything worthwhile. We have open meetings every month at Caesar's Inn, open to the public, and we encourage people to come in and participate in the Democratic Party. Our room is getting so crowded today, Milt, that there's barely a chair.

Do you have any further political ambitions?
No further than I am now. I don't have the academic background. I feel limited in that capacity sometimes. I know I can do well in what I am doing. I know that there has to be a lot of things done yet, and I think that my best place is right here. But I've got some young attorneys and very articulate people around me, and I'm trying to help to get them where they will be in a position of representation here. But not me. I want to be in Stickney what Daley was in Bridgeport.

I like politics, it costs me time, energy, and physical work, but the satisfaction comes from being able to participate within an organization, being able to meet exciting candidates, and being able to see different platforms being presented to the people. I like running for office, myself, I find it very exciting, knowing when you put your name on a ballot, having people saying they're going to vote for you. And, on the final day, finding out all the people that said they were going to vote didn't. Isn't that exciting? I love being involved and I like meeting people. I meet a lot of people that I wouldn't have met in my barber shop. Fortunately, my wife is an executive secretary with a law firm and she has given me expertise in the background. She likes politics too. She's helped me, and without her help, I couldn't do all the things I'm doing. My son is a senior at St. Xavier

College. Hopefully, he'll go on for a law degree and go on to a bigger position than I want. I wouldn't discourage him from going into politics because I think that I can give him a lot of insight, and I'll tell him the things to avoid. It's a worthwhile profession, if you enjoy people. But if you don't like people, you shouldn't get involved in politics.

FIVE

Dawson's Heirs

CECIL PARTEE / JAMES TAYLOR
JOHN STROGER / MADISON BROWN

CECIL PARTEE *Committeeman of the South Side 20th ward, a middle-class black ward. Was a state senator for twenty years and was elected president of the Illinois state senate, holding the highest office held by any black at the state level in this country. Was commissioner of Chicago's department of human services. Is also a successful lawyer and is one of the most powerful black politicians in Chicago at the present time. In 1979 was elected city clerk of Chicago.*

I was born in a small town in Arkansas, graduated from high school in 1938 at the top of my class, and graduated cum laude from Tennessee State University. I made application to the University of Arkansas Law School and was denied admission because they were not admitting blacks. They offered to pay my tuition at some other school. I laughed all the way to Chicago, because I had been accepted at the University of Chicago and Northwestern University. I went to Northwestern. They had an accelerated program and I was able to finish in two calendar years.

I began the practice of law and felt that I might become a precinct captain in order to know at least five hundred people by their first name, and vice-versa, as a way of building my practice. I went to Congressman Dawson and told him I wanted a precinct. He asked me what kind of a job I was looking for. I said, "I'm not looking for a job, I'm looking for a precinct." He called some fellows in and said, "I want you to see a strange animal. Most lawyers want jobs and no precinct, and here's a guy that wants a precinct and no job." He gave me a precinct and I got the chance to know some people. I kept my precinct from 1948 to 1970. When I went into that precinct in 1948, it was an all-black Republican precinct. I was able to carry that precinct for President Truman in 1948, and never had any problems after that. A year later they asked me if I would like to go into the state's attorney's office. I worked in various parts of the office and spent a number of years trying cases. In 1956, I was elected to the general assembly and served ten years. In 1965, I went to the state senate and served for ten years. I was elected president pro-tem and leader, and, in 1975, was elected president of the senate. In 1976, I ran for attorney general of Illinois and lost to Bill Scott. I was then appointed commissioner of human services for the city of Chicago.

Why did you run for attorney general, when you were holding the highest office any black man held in this country in state government, and no black man had ever been elected to a major statewide office in Illinois?

Twenty years is a long time in the legislature. It was a combination of circumstances. I wanted a new challenge. I wanted to open up the state ticket for a black candidate. There had never been a black candidate for a major state office. The other motivation was of family concern. My younger daughter (I have two daughters) was going away to college, and it was the first time in many years that my wife would be at home alone. If I won, I could be at home more, and if I didn't, I could certainly be at home. The other thing was, that after twenty years in the legislature, my pension was secure.

How well did you know Congressman Dawson?

I knew him very well. He was a very thorough organizer and he came along when politics for blacks in terms of participation was really burgeoning. He kept his word. And he helped people to help themselves. He had what we jokingly called "The Dawson College." His organization met every Friday night, and there you heard the history of blacks in politics in Chicago. The political organization served several purposes. Many of the social events were around the 2nd ward Democratic organization. They rented a club where they would have cocktails, and talk and debate problems. As the black population grew, Dawson was able to almost unilaterally select persons to serve as the committeemen of four or five wards that became predominately black. He had a liaison with those people that heightened and increased his own power because all of them were very loyal to him, a great deal more loyalty than exists today.

After Dawson died, the strongest men were Claude Holman, Kenneth Campbell, and Ralph Metcalfe, and there were times that they did not always see eye to eye on particular issues. There was a tendency to go their own way. Every particular committeeman was concerned about running his show, and all of them were sort of peers. None of them were very willing to let one of them become the over-all leader of the tribe.

What was the basis of their strength?

The Democratic Party had, at the national level, the kind of leadership that was very helpful. President Franklin Roosevelt brought blacks out of the Republican Party into the Democratic Party with social programs and programs of concern for little people. Roosevelt put together a strange coalition with some of the most liberal and most conservative people in the world. Then, Truman was really the first person that really made an assault on segregation, particularly in the armed forces. Hubert Humphrey, at the 1948 convention, had done some fabulous things in fighting a rather entrenched southern group. And, in 1948, we elected two liberal-minded, outstanding Democrats in Illinois, Stevenson and Douglas, and things began to move.

It really started to move about 1948. I came to Chicago in 1944, so I really don't have much in-depth knowledge of what happened before then. But blacks were not attracted until about 1948, because they only had two or three wards. They had the 2nd, 3rd and 4th wards. The 1948 election gave us the 20th ward, and thereafter the 6th, the 17th, and the 16th wards, and you know the rest of the story.

How did you get to be the committeeman after Campbell died?

I was the president of the ward organization for a number of years, and as a consequence it evolved on my shoulders. The organization made the selection and I then made the presentation downtown. Being a committeeman is a headache. A ward committeeman's job is a noncompensatory job. You have the obligation of trying to find employment for people, which we do in both the public and private sector. We made certain that there were essential city services delivered. If someone wants curbs repaired or trees down, or something like that, you call your ward office. We help churches, young people, senior citizens, you name it—we're there.

Colonel Campbell taught me that the only way to run an organization is to organize, deputize, and supervise, and you can't very well supervise or organize unless you've done it yourself. Having been there myself, I knew precisely what needed to be done in every precinct. We organized the precincts. We have a captain, assistant captain, and the other workers who are assigned to various parts of the precinct, so that the precinct captain has first to organize it, then he deputizes various people to do certain things. I have supervision over the captains, who in turn have supervision over the other people in that area. The captain is responsible to the committeeman.

And the other persons in that precinct are responsible to their supervisor just above them.

A lot of people have a real pleasure going from door to door, talking to people, talking to neighbors, and getting them out to vote. Many of them have jobs. But just the job alone, particularly at a time when there are a lot of jobs available, isn't enough of an incentive. You have to be a person who wants to help, who wants to be involved with other people, to be a successful precinct captain. Some of our captains now are people whose fathers before them were captains. They like to be around. They like to have a chance to meet the mayor, or the governor, or people who were running for public office. A lot of other people come in like I did, interested in the process for other reasons.

I remember that your ward went for Johnson over Goldwater in 1964 by a margin of 37,000 to 1,000. What about the allegations that in wards like yours there was a lot of vote stealing and vote buying?

I can only answer for my own ward, the 20th. There was no vote buying. We did things to stimulate interest and we spent a lot of time with people. We gave parties, helped the children, and ran social and cultural and athletic events. You can't carry a precinct or a ward by going out two weeks before an election and talking to people. It's a day-to-day activity where you are with people, where you help them from day to day. When a precinct captain does his job well, people vote for *him,* not the candidate. Sometimes people wouldn't care who the candidate was, as long as they felt they were going to continue to get good service.

You were in the legislature for twenty years. Could you tell me what the legislature is like?

The Illinois Senate is a body of fifty-nine people, fifty-eight prima donnas and myself. Elected officials sometimes feel that they have beaten everybody else in their districts and they have some appreciation of themselves and their ability. It is very difficult to meld the various philosophies, attitudes, and parochial kinds of views on many questions. When you lose you don't cry; when you win you don't gloat, and you don't lord it over anybody.

There has always been, as long as I have been down there, two divisions—upstate and downstate. The suburban part of the formula came into being after we had reapportionment, when a large number of people were elected from suburban areas. Up to that time the districts were quite disproportionate in size, and downstate had really the advantage of it, because they had more than we had with less population.

The fact that I was black was, of course, omnipresent. I think the fact that I had capability, political savvy, and the ability to articulate my thoughts sort of helped to counterbalance my ethnic origins. There were times when things would get a little sticky. I would always respond with a joke, or a clever remark, just to get things back on the track. I'll tell you a story that might be relevant to how I handled that situation. I guess I belong in the *Guinness Book of Records.* I spent the night in two southern governors' mansions. I spent the night in Arkansas with the then Governor Dale Bumpers, who is now a United States senator from Arkansas, and later, I spent the night in the mansion in Georgia in September 1974, when the governor was a man named Jimmy Carter. I called my mother from the mansion and told her that I was spending the night in Atlanta. She asked if I was staying at one of the hotels and I said no, I was staying at the governor's mansion. My mother, who was then eighty-three, said, "Now you behave yourself, you hear!"

You have known and dealt with Mayor Daley for a number of years. Could you evaluate Daley as a mayor and a politician?

He was a very well-organized man and a very good organizer. He had an almost phenomenal memory. I think he almost had total recall. In the years that I dealt closely with him, when matters arose, he could always remember some precedent or some other period in history when a similar matter arose, and he would give me the benefit of that history. And, unlike what most people think, he never gave me commands. I made my own judgments. Many a time we would talk about something, and he'd say that in 1948, such a thing happened. Then I could, on the basis of my own instincts and judgments, make a decision. Of course, there were times when you knew he was very interested in a particular program, and you would have to say it was a part of our program. He believed very strongly in trying to follow the Democratic platform. On one side of the column there were things promised, and on the other side of that ledger were things delivered, things accomplished. It was your job to try to convert the promises into accomplishments. And he was very loyal to his friends.

He believed very much in programs. On one occasion he could not understand a candidate who had won, when he talked with him the first time and asked, "What is your program?" He had no program and Daley just couldn't believe it! To run for public office without a program, without an agenda to be carried out! He was, in my judgment, a very astute man. I talked with him one on one, and there were areas that I really didn't think he would be knowledgeable, just because he had no need to be. When I came back from Israel, I talked to him about my trip. Some of the questions he asked me astounded me, because it reflected his intricate knowledge of the politics of Israel. He was a very knowledgeable man.

I don't know if there were any weaknesses. I think the school system sort of got away from him. But I don't think it was a personal weakness, as much as it was a weakness that sort of permeated the country.

How do you see the future of black politics evolving in Chicago?
When you say black politics, I am not really certain what that means. There is implicit in the phrase a feeling of homogeneity, that all blacks are going to be responsive to the same stimuli, and that all blacks are going to do a certain thing and vote a certain way. What people don't realize is that as this country has grown and developed, and as more and more blacks have moved into the main stream of life, that there are as many stratifications of thought and as many approaches to what is the quality of life among black people as there are among white people. We probably will not have a unanimous kind of thought process as to what is best for our group.

I think that all black people, as well as any other kinds of people, are interested in getting their fair share of whatever there is to be gotten out of government. All of them are concerned that government has some sensitivity to their needs, their wants, and their ambitions. But I don't think we are that homogeneous. This is a heterogeneous kind of a world. So far as a desire to be recognized, to be treated fairly, and have the constitution mean exactly what it says for all of us, is, of course, black politics in that context.

What about these allegations that Chicago is run only for the bankers and the real estate men, and that poor people, especially black poor people in Chicago, get shafted?
That is absolutely untrue. As a matter of fact, many of the federal programs in place today that have as their focus helping poor people originated in Chicago. The Model Cities package started here, and Daley was doing those kinds of things, in some instances, before the

federal government was. Some of the environmental concerns we now talk about a lot started in Chicago. Mike Bilandic is the guy who happened to draw them up. Chicago was ahead of many state programs as well as national programs, which had the over-all benefit of helping the little guy and the poor guy.

What about your role in Chicago in the future?

I'm really enjoying doing what I am doing here. It is a new challenge for me. It is really an extension of what I have been doing for twenty years, providing human services one way or another. As commissioner of human services for the city of Chicago, I have the job of supervising the delivery of those services, and that is, for me, about the same thing, except from another vantage point. As to the future, I'll let the future take care of itself.

JAMES TAYLOR *About forty-nine years old. Ward commit-*
teeman of the South Side's 16th ward. Has been a state repre-
sentative for ten years. Dropped out of high school in his first
year. Was a prize fighter and began his political career as a
precinct captain and laborer on a garbage truck. Is probably the
best black ward committeeman in Chicago today.

I was born in Crawfordsville, Arkansas in 1930. I went to
grade school in Memphis, Tennessee in between working in the
fields. I left high school after one year. My mother gave me $18 and
I came to Chicago, when I was fourteen years old, in 1945.

We in the South used to look at Chicago as a great, fantastic city,
and everybody in Chicago was rich. Every black that came here felt
that he was going to strike it rich right away, and, coming here, I had
the idea that this was the land that I could make it in. I worked as
a dishwasher and did odd jobs. I went into the army in 1951 and
spent two years there. I was a prize fighter in the service. I had 96
amateur fights—91 wins. I had 43 knockouts, and I fought in the
Golden Gloves, CYO in Chicago here, a light heavyweight at the
time. My blood pressure started fluctuating and I had to give it up.

When I came back home, my life really started. I drove a cab for
awhile. I opened up a tavern, and that didn't work. I opened up a
restaurant, and that didn't work. In 1960, John Kennedy came on the
scene, and I volunteered my help and worked hard for the man. I was
living in the 16th ward, but I was not a part of the organization. The
precinct captain was dragging his foot, always telling me he was
going to take me in and introduce me to the committeeman. I came
in to see the committeeman on my own. I sent him fifteen cards a
day that I typed out myself from the people in the precinct, telling
him that they wanted me to be the precinct captain. He gave me the
precinct, and in the election that year he told me, "If you bring in
75 Democratic votes I would be happy." I said, "What if I bring in
150?" He said, "I'll give you what you want." I brought in 211 Democrats to 3 Republicans.

How did you do that?

It was just talking to the people. Many of the persons who vote don't vote for the candidate that is running, because you don't know but one or two candidates. They vote for their local individual who is there with them on a daily basis, who is trying to help them with services that they rightfully deserve. I was there, I was talking to them about how much it would help me if they voted for our particular candidates. That was the thing that I was going to sell to them. "You help me and put me in a position where I will be able to help you." They came out and they voted well. I sold Jim Taylor and I do it today. That's what they want. They want to know that their local officials do care enough to give them that assistance.

I eventually became the best precinct captain in the ward. I had the number one precinct from the third election that I had up until the time that I became ward committeeman. In 1964, I had 558 people in my precinct in the Johnson election. I had 531 come to the polls; 495 voted for Johnson.

Paul Sheridan, who was running the ward, got me a job as a laborer on the garbage truck. The first job he offered me was at County Jail as a guard. I said that I could go to jail on my own, I don't need that. The next job was with the sewer department, but I felt that I should have a job that I could be respected on. I wanted the health department, building inspector, something of that sort. He said that all those jobs were civil service. I then asked for the sewer department job, and he said, "I don't have that one anymore. All I got is the garbage man." I said, "Well, give me that." I worked six months as a laborer on the garbage truck. Then I went to the State of Illinois as a truck driver. I worked for the motor pool as a heavy construction equipment operator. Then I was a foreman, when they were building the Stevenson Expressway.

In 1967, the man called me in and told me that he needed me here in the ward because they were having an awful lot of racial problems. I took over as ward superintendent, started talking to the people, trying to formulate programs, give them what they want with services, and let them know that we were trying to help them and do the best that we could.

The ward superintendent is the housekeeper for the ward. He takes care of the garbage, is in charge of all the refuse trucks, reports the holes in the street, abandoned buildings that need to come down, lights that are out, stop signs turned around going the wrong way (kids usually do that), getting vacant lots cleaned, seeing that they get the rodents out of here, the stray dogs problem. I don't know how we're ever going to deal with that. It's a real serious problem all over the city. Stray dogs run in packs, different hours of the morning. They're smarter than the dog catchers. That's why they can't catch them. I think when they get that truck close to them, they sort of sense that they are in the community and they disappear. It's those kinds of things that the people are concerned about which don't mean a lot to the people downtown or other places, but a little thing such as a dog in the morning does frighten some of the people. The ward superintendent is the guy that makes the alderman and the ward committeeman look good, because he is actually in the field there and sees all the problems.

When you were ward superintendent, how did the problems get to you and how would you deal with those things?

Some of them are brought to my attention by the laborers on the garbage trucks. Then, in my travels, in the car that I have now, I have a little place in there where I just write down things I see. I get back to my office and make the necessary calls. If there is a hole in the street, we want the asphalt men out there, or a place where the gutter is caving in. We call in these different types of things to make certain that we keep our ward in shape. We're not doing the best job in the world, but we're doing the best that we can. The area is old, but we're working at it. That's what we do on a daily basis.

The ward superintendent calls the various department heads. When he doesn't seem to be getting the type of help that he should get, he'll call the alderman, and if he don't get it there, he calls the committeeman. The committeeman is the guy who has the muscle to go in and make certain that people do what they are supposed to do. For instance, if you need a sewer repaired and Sewer Commissioner Ed Quigley is not doing it, I tell Quigley his payroll is going to come up next budget time, and the alderman is going to be there and is going to raise an awful lot of hell. He don't like to hear that. Rather than have me raise all that hell, he says, "I'm going to get along with this fellow and am going to do the job."

If a good precinct captain is out here doing a good job, I'm doing my darndest to make certain that he gets everything he wants. Downtown, in the upper echelon, they look at a ward that's really producing, then they are going to do it, because they don't want to lose that. The city really wants you to do that, and Mayor Daley did. He wanted you to service the people. That was his whole theory. If you were good for the people in your community, you were good for him. But if you were not good for the people in your community, you're no good to him. And he wanted to make certain that those people were being taken care of. You were doing the job for him.

How did you become a committeeman?

In 1965, the alderman died and I tried to get the aldermanic seat, but the organization said that Paul Sheridan, who was the son of the ex-alderman, should have the position. They offered me the job as secretary to the alderman. I told them, "I don't want to be a secretary. That's a flunky job. I am a boss man. I've got eighty men working for me on the Stevenson Expressway, and I'm not going to give that up to be a secretary." Dan Coman, the committeeman, then made me the ward superintendent. I worked a year as a ward superintendent and Coman nominated me to be the state representative from this district. When the legislative committee met, they did not select me. They selected my neighbor. He was the minister at the Shiloh Baptist Church, with a congregation of some three or four thousand people. I only had one little precinct. So he had more muscle than I had. He won the election and then he ran for reelection. He never lived to finish that term of office. He died on September 16, 1968. I was nominated and went to the state legislature.

The 16th ward was redistricted and had become more black. On November 11, 1970, Mayor Daley called me at my ward yard office. I felt good, knowing that they thought enough of me to be the guy that they talked to about who the committeeman was going to be. When I walked into the door, the mayor met me, and he told me I was going to be the committeeman of the 16th ward. I said, "I'm the committeeman?" He said, "Don't worry about it—just c'mon in." I walked into the room and the executive committee of the Democratic Party was there, and I never knew the mayor knew as much about me as he knew, until that day. He put my whole life story on the line, which really amazed me. He told me to get myself an aldermanic candidate, if I wasn't going to be the alderman.

People said Daley was a dictator. That's a lie. He was not a dictator. The mayor never told anyone to do any doggone thing. The guy always put you in a box where you wound up telling him what you were going to do. He never asked you to do anything. He always asked me how was I going to do, and I would tell him, and he would say, "Jim, you run a good ward." And that was it. He'd say, "Any help you need, let me know." He was a great mayor. Some people say that he was just taking care of the Loop. His whole heart was in the city.

When I came back to my ward, many of the white captains that was in this ward left, leaving me with people that was there for just passing out literature and had no ability or even no interest in knowing how to talk to people about what was going on. They didn't care. They were just looking for jobs. So I come into a situation where all I had was about ten first string captains, and fifty-six precincts. I didn't know exactly what to do.

We lost the aldermanic election to Anna Langford, and I knew we had to find people that could do the job. I started going to various church groups, block club meetings, civic meetings. We got the whole community involved, and I picked one up here, and one there, until I got the type of persons that I thought would make a fine organization. I looked for persons that were concerned, persons that had some interest in their community, a block captain, or some wide-mouth person in the back of the room who was talking loud, who had concern, who knew something about what was going on. A good precinct captain is a person who is concerned about their community. Many persons in many communities, they complain, they argue with one another, they never call the city agency or the alderman's office. They moan and groan to each other across the fence. But when you find one of those that moan and groan and you teach them how it should be done, then you get service and a better community.

My alderwoman was a judge of election. I went down to the polling place, saw how she was working there, and how she was trying to assist the people to make certain that they did not lose their vote. I was very impressed. I asked her, would she come into the organization, and she came in. I made her the ward committeewoman and when it came time to nominate a person to be the alderman, we nominated her.

What do precinct captains get out of this, besides jobs?
They get the self-respect of being someone in their community. They know that people need help. They enjoy being able to do that. They've done a little extra. Sure, if you can put him on a job, it's better than having him out there loose. You have some control over him. You need that. The captain is just like your children. They'll try you. And when they know that you are going to stop on a certain point, then you got them going. But you can't lie to them. You've got to do the things that you say you're going to do.

I try to allocate jobs on the question of needs. You look for people who really need help. Then I try to help them. But they're not always the type of person that should be the captain. I have a fellow who died here, we buried him a week ago. He was very sharp, a very smooth young fellow. He had a problem—he drank. And he was in a community where I needed someone. When I told him that I wanted him to be the precinct captain, he said, "Senator, I'm not the guy for the precinct captain. I'll tell you what. You give that precinct to my wife and you'll have a good precinct captain." I said, "Your wife is kind of mean." He said, "She has to be mean to get along with me." That was the theory. We made her precinct captain. She goes to church right there in the precinct. She knows everybody. He was right. She did know how to deal with it and made the precinct one of the better precincts we had in the ward. Then, lo and behold, she needed additional money. She had four children and she wanted a job. She is now working for the county as a bailiff, loves her job, loves being a precinct captain, loves the community she represents. It gives her some status in life. The good captains aren't people who just want a job. The good captains are really the ones who want to help.

Some people gonna say, "We got nice, intelligent precinct captains." I don't want a school teacher to be a precinct captain for me, because a school teacher is going to go out in the field, and she meets another school teacher, and they are going to debate on the issues. They're going to do so much arguing that they'll never get out of one house. But if you take a fella who has a limited amount of education—he goes there and talks to a school teacher, the first thing that he's going to tell her is that he needs her help. She's gonna look at him. She can't argue with this guy because she doesn't know, and she says, "Well, maybe I'm gonna help the poor slob out." But you get two brainy people and let them match wits, you haven't got a good precinct captain.

Being a ward committeeman is a very trying position. I want to do a good job. I put the time in and that's what it takes. My job is never done, seven days a week. I have people calling me at home in the middle of the night. They've got problems. I have had people call me when they move into the community, just wanting to know where the library is at. These are little things that we spend a lot of time with. Kids have problems with the police. One kid, one day, was going home. Policeman had stopped him while he was driving, had mistaken him for someone else, had taken his driving license, and was going to arrest him. The kid got frightened and ran. The police-

man fired a shot and missed him. He lives here at 66th and Emerald.
He was heading home; squad cars was all around his house. So he
went to Cabrini-Green and called his mother. His mother called one
of my precinct captains. Precinct captain called me. I asked him what
had he done? He hadn't done anything! I said, "Okay. Then I will go
and see the kid." I went to Cabrini-Green and met with the kid. He
told me that he was frightened and didn't know what to do. He didn't
want to go to the station because he thought they would kill him. I
asked him, "Would you trust me?" He said, "Yes." I brought him to
the 7th district police station and turned him in. Met his mother right
there at 61st street. The kid hadn't did anything, but he was frightened. Thank God the policeman didn't shoot him, but he did shoot
in the air.

   I have tried to stay out of police business here. I very seldom go
in and say anything until I talk to the commander. I don't like it to
come to the point where people like to pin it on me to do the things
in the jail, because I'm not going to do that. But there has been cases
come up that I thought that I had some input. I got a fellow out of
jail. In 1949 he was running from the policeman over here around
49th and LaFayette and the policeman was shooting at him, and I
guess he shot back. There were so many shots there, we don't know
who killed the policeman, but he went to jail. His father died. I tried
to get him out to come to the funeral. They wouldn't let him go. The
morning of the funeral, I finally got permission from the parole and
pardon board. I had enough policemen who volunteered their time
and services to make sure that we would get that boy back to jail. We
picked him up at the jail, brought him out to the funeral. When we
walked in to the casket, I told him that I knew his brother, and his
father and mother, and that I was taking a chance bringing him
home. "They told me that you were very vicious," I said. "But I want
you to know one thing. You see upstairs there, all around you I got
policemen, and they are going to shoot if you try anything." He said,
"Mr. Taylor, I understand. All I want to do is see my father." The guy
went back to jail, wrote me a letter, thanked me. He came out on the
work release program, and we finally got him interested in government. He is working on a job today. He's been out five years—no
problem, a good man. I give scholarship to students. Never realized
in the years gone by that we had the general assembly scholarships.
I make certain that kids in the community get them. There are so
many different things that you do to run a ward.

What are your responsibilities downtown in turning out the vote?
The county chairman will call us all in on the Saturday before
election. He wants to know what is going to happen in your area. I
require that precinct captains tell me what they think is going to
happen, and when I go downtown, I give my count, based on what
they have given me out here. If they are off a lot, I'll point that out,
and I know that they do not know what is going on in their precinct.
I don't miss by more than 10 percent of the vote in predicting an
election. I make it my business to study this very closely. I call my
precinct captains in and ask, "What's wrong? Why wasn't we able to
get these people in here? You got ten or twelve houses and you only
got four voters coming out here." I ask them, "What happened here,
at 1504? There is one vote in there. Did you talk to anyone?" I want
to know. I tell them, "If the name doesn't appear on this sheet as a
registered voter in this ward, don't come here looking for service, if
they lived here for any length of time." Every person should be in
a position to exercise his constitutional rights, whether you vote for
my candidates or not. I want them to vote. I insist on that.

You can tell from the hard cards when the captains are working
or not. I've got my hard cards going back for years and I read them
like some people read the Bible. The hard card is the precinct registration. The red here indicates the Democratic vote, the blue indicates the Republican vote. In this precinct here, there must be 400
voters and there's only three registered Republicans. It's an accurate
record. On Marquette Road, he's got twenty registered voters and
only four come out. When you have that type of problem, that where
I raise hell. I will check that particular area. I will go to those homes
and give them a dime, and tell them to call me when the precinct
captain gets to their house. People like to call into the office. This is
just a way of me checking to know that you got the service that you
are supposed to have.

How did you learn this procedure, Jim?
It was just something I developed. Sometimes I wonder about a lot
of things that I do. I had a very limited amount of education, but
when I got involved, and there was interesting people that were
working in politics, I just watched. Then I went back and said that
this won't work in my area like it will here. I said mine's got to be
different. And this is the way I've been doing it.

Being concerned, being there, is what makes good politicians. Oh,
sure, you can go out and get those fellas who got all the education

and make nice pretty speeches. They're not the best politicians. They're talking a lot of hot air. Good politicians means what he is going to do and say. He knows and he delivers. I won't never make a promise on anything that I don't know. When I tell you that I am going to do something, I'm going to do it. My word is all that I have. Persons come to me and ask me about certain things. I tell them, "I'll look into it, I'll see what I can do. Let me check it out." That way you never box me in that I said, "I'll do that." Because I won't say that I'll do that unless I have it in my hand. Then, if I tell you, you can rest assured that you are going to get it. That's good politics.

What about these allegations, Jim, that in wards like yours there is a lot of vote stealing and vote buying going on?
Oh, that's a lot of malarkey. We don't have to steal votes out here. In an area like mine, my people are basically Democrats. They're with me. Maybe someone don't know how to operate the machine the way they should; they don't know anything about those candidates. You got sixty names across that top line up there, and it would take them three minutes to find out one name, and that's all the time they are allowed in the machine. What happened is that you might have them asking for assistance from the judge to make certain that they will be able to cast a complete Democratic or Republican ticket. You can sit there in any polling place that we have and you'll find out that that is the way it is done. They don't have to steal. Those that's coming out, they gonna come out anyway.

If a precinct captain is worth his salt, he won't have any problems getting those people out. They want to vote. Believe me, they do. I make it my business to try to make certain that they are informed, and I try to make it my business to make certain that we won their respect by trying to give them the kind of services they need. But the IVI [Independent Voters of Illinois] and the Republican Party, any type of harrassment they can cause us will make it better for them on the other end. They know that they are not going to get many Republican votes in this area and they make as much confusions as they can cause. This has been a poor area. Most of these people are Democrats. The Democratic Party has been the type of party that takes care of the poor people since my being around, and that's what they want. They can't read, many of them; they can't write. They don't understand. They ask for assistance and we try to make certain that they get it. But you don't have to buy and you don't have to cheat. They're there.

What kinds of relationships do you have with other groups in the community, like churches and businesses?

I got good relationships with all of them. The churches support this organization. We does the things that they want. Services. That's all. Visitation Church called me a few weeks ago. There is a building next door to them that they wanted out of there. I was fighting with the judge, and let him know that this was causing some problems in our area. We speed him along. The bureaucracy is slow at times. But as a result of me going in and making a personal appeal, many times a judge is going to render a decision. We expedite things. That's all.

How do you raise money in your ward organization?

We have my annual dinner. Many of the businessmen came out there. They buy one ticket. I'm not like the average politician. I don't go in for that five dollar and ten dollar ticket, because you can't make any money out of it. You get a lot of people out there but, when you get through, you haven't made any money. The money has went to the caterer and the establishment there. So what I do, I charge a good buck for mine, because it's really for a donation to help us run the organization. We had a testimonial dinner on the 25th where we raised a few thousand dollars. Then we had a hundred dollar a plate dinner at the Conrad Hilton. We had four hundred people out. Ninety percent of them was from this community.

What do you use money from your ward organization for?

The secretary, rent, heat, light, utilities. Telephone bill here runs you two hundred and some odd dollars a month. We send God knows how many telegrams. I had a funeral yesterday; got another one next week. Had one last week and one the week before then. Just my flower bill alone is tremendous, keeping good contact. It's important on that day, when those persons are in trouble, that you make yourself known. I was at a funeral yesterday. The precinct captain of the 51st precinct, his son died, a boy 22 years old. Last week, this precinct captain, her husband died. On the 18th, my attorney died. When you do those types of things, then you keep the people together and that's important.

I had a lady who came in here. Her husband was an alcoholic and he was in bad shape, and she needed $50. I made a loan of $50 to her. Two weeks ago, she came in here and paid the $50 back. One of my precinct captains needed $300 to get his boiler fixed. One had a problem with a lady. Her roof caved in and she didn't have the

money. So we helped out. People need food. Christmas time, every
year, we give away baskets here. Every summer we give away a few
thousand dollars on a picnic. We give away things to kids. Oh, we do
a lot of things here.

What kinds of problems do you have in a black community like
Englewood?

It's working class here, more or less middle class, although this is
designated as a slum–ghetto area. You will find people have been
there twenty years. They own their homes and have a heck of a lot
of equity in there. And they're here to stay. The people that are here
are good, solid people. We don't have the problems we had years ago
in Englewood. I have a good, solid constituency here. There is not
a lot of transit going on at all, although you, from outside the community, think that who lives here is the worst. Englewood is a good area,
a proud area. We got proud people out here and they're working
hard to try to survive. It's tough, but we're trying hard.

In Englewood you will see an influx of people coming back. We are
fortunate in Englewood. We have the best transportation facilities in
the world. Everything is right here and we are not too far from the
Loop. I see Englewood as an area that is going to come back, whether
it is going to be black or white. I, for one, is going to stay here and
encourage my people not to do what we did in the past. We come
in, and what happened? Most of the whites have been pretty smart.
They come in, build these new homes, live here for twenty years, get
all the equity out of their property, and then, when things started to
happening, then they sell it to me. They get all their money back out.
I come along and take all of their headaches, and then go to rebuild
it, and that costs us too much money. I've been out trying to tell my
people, either we are going to stand here and develop this community or we are forever going to be in the shoes that we have been in
in the past. "Don't go out to Forest Park or those other places where
people been for years and think that you are going to find heaven.
You're going out there, the old place is ready to go, the roof is going,
the garage needs repainting, and this is the kind of stuff that you are
going to go buy?" What the whites did, they got all that money, that
free living, and we go and buy these homes at inflated prices, and
they come back here and live in the city in a nice luxury apartment,
and you got the headaches. I don't want anything like this to happen.
I believe in the concept that the Chinese have in Chinatown. You

build that up and everybody goes and sees what Chinatown is like. I believe I'll build Englewood. It will be just like you, you came out here to see what Jim Taylor is doing. That's been my theory, and you've been an answer to one of my dreams. I wanted you to come, because we're going to show you.

Do you have any further political ambitions?
I have gone further than I had ever anticipated going. When I got involved in politics, all I was looking for was a place that I could fit in. Each year I have done something different since I have been involved. I'm also deputy general superintendent of sanitation of Chicago. In 1977, I opened up a restaurant across the street. I'm a businessman now. I don't know where I'm going, or if there is any more, or have I reached the top.

In Arkansas, we learned how to work from sunup to sundown, and I have never had any problems with working. Nowadays kids are getting bad advice. People in government teach young people bad work habits and they live with it all their lives. Young kids, when they are going to school, they cut their first class and they get there late. They come out of school and they try to get jobs, and they can't miss that first hour. As a result of that, they got problems with themselves. These federal programs that you got today, where you are just giving kids a job and not giving them tools and equipment to work with, I don't like that. I don't believe in government just giving money for the sake of appeasing people. I went to the Urban Progress Center and argued with the people there, because of the habits that our kids were developing. They get a paper bag, walk around the street and play ball all day long, and tell them that they got jobs, and then, when they come and finally get out of school and going to where they can't practice that any more, they're not ready to accept this type of society that we live in. That's a mistake. I raise hell about it, because I believe they should work. Anyone that gets involved in politics, don't come in and think it's a bed of flowers. You've got to work. That's what you're judged by, the work that you do. That's what I'm judged by. I'm not smart. I work, though. You might out-think me, but you can't out-work me.

I'm ambitious. When you're not ambitious, you got no business in this business, because you got one place to go and that is downhill. I would like to be mayor, but I'm not the kind of guy they might want to support for that. I'm a little rough at times. Whether we will be able to get another black congressman, I don't know. Or to head one of the departments in the city, I really don't know. But whatever comes my way, there are other things that I will accept. I know one thing, I'm not through. I make aldermen, state representatives, judges, and sanitary district trustees. I enjoy being just what I am. That's a powerhouse, the ward committeeman.

JOHN STROGER *About forty-nine years old. Committee-man of South Side 8th ward. Is a lawyer and has a background in social work and criminal justice. Is also a Cook County commissioner and probable future candidate for major county office or Congress.*

I was born in Helena, Arkansas. My father never had any education. He could not read or write. He went away from home when he was nine years old and went to work in a bucket factory. When he was in his teens, he had learned to press men's clothes and do tailoring work, and he worked the rest of his life, mostly doing alterations and cleaning work.

My mother was a very intelligent person, very well read, very alert, a good person to talk with. She worked hard all of her days, doing work in the homes of families, and also worked in the fields. There were four children. All of us had the opportunity to go to high school. We never had, like a lot of kids on our street, to drop school and go to work in the fields. My father always wanted us to have an education and do some of the things that he wanted to do. I graduated from Xavier University in New Orleans, taught school one year in the South, and came up here.

When I was in Helena, Arkansas, I became fascinated with politics, selling people on the ideas of government, organizing them, and trying to get them to pay a poll tax to get out the vote. In 1948, Congressman William L. Dawson came down and gave a big speech urging black people to solidify efforts behind Harry S Truman. When I went to college that fall, Dawson came to New Orleans. I was fascinated by the whole political machinery, and when I came to Chicago I became an assistant precinct captain in 1953, in the 3rd ward, under Congressman Ralph Metcalfe.

People took much more pride in being a precinct captain in those days than they do now. They don't treat precinct captains now with the same reverence as they historically had done. They still appreciate the captains, but their horizons have been broadened politically and socially. Over the years, a social revolution brought on new organizations promoting different political ideas. As a result, the precinct captain is just one of the individuals they deal with as opposed to being *the* individual.

In the 1950s, most causes were promoted by the precinct captains or the ward committeemen. The precinct captain kept constant contact with his voters. It was a ritual to see them all the time, be with them, commiserate with them when they had problems, and celebrate with them when things were going good. Prior to the civil rights movement, the whole life of the community revolved around the church and the political establishment in the community. Sometimes they would be interwoven. Most of the social life of the black community was within the 2nd and 3rd wards. That was prior to people going downtown, like they do now. There were some who came downtown, but, back in those days, you would go out within the boundary of the community you lived in. Chicago is allegedly a northern city, but the doors to many places just weren't open in the manner in which they are now to all people. Now, when people think of going out, they think of going out of the community.

The civil rights movement in the 1950s and 1960s had a tremendous social and economic impact on the industrial North, and on Chicago in particular, just as it did on the South. There are many doors open economically for blacks, and when these doors open, the social life also opens up. Blacks became residents in and citizens of the city. But I don't think blacks were ever as residentially or provincially conscious as the ethnics who came over from Europe, because blacks who came to Chicago always considered themselves as Americans and had assimilated the same cultures that were allegedly American, whereas the other groups were coming in from other parts of the world, bringing their cultural backgrounds into the confines of where they lived. They could have a much more clannish group, because they could establish themselves around the cultures they had traditionally had in Europe. The setting was different for blacks. The culture that we had had been pretty well taken from us through slavery, and we had assimilated and adopted the culture of the people who brought us here. So we could always be considered citizens of the country, and wherever we went, we had no problem with that sort of thing.

In 1954, I became the president of the Young Democrats in the 3rd ward. When Ralph Metcalfe was going in as alderman for the first time, I promoted a lot of activity among young people and helped him. Sheriff Joe Lohman made me assistant to the warden at the

County Jail, in charge of personnel. By that time, I was married and had a couple of babies. I was thinking that I needed some more education. I was thirty-one. I had several jobs and was a precinct captain. I went to law school at night, graduated, and passed the bar.

I had moved from the 3rd ward out to 79th and Langley in the 8th ward, and took a precinct there, as well as the one I had in the 3rd ward. Joe McMahon had become committeeman and asked me to help him. When McMahon decided to step out, the captains elected me acting committeeman. Then I was elected 8th ward Democratic committeeman in 1968. Two years later, I was elected to the Cook County Board of Commissioners. I'm still on the board.

When I became committeeman, the 8th ward was about 40 percent white, and the ward organization was originally about 50 percent white and 50 percent black. The predominant group of precinct captains were black, and the Democratic Party felt that it would be in the interest of the party to have a black leader, although the decision to make me committeeman was a ward decision by the captains.

What's it like to be a ward committeeman in a middle-class, black South Side ward?

The problems in the ward are the same now that it is predominantly black as when it was white. People look for their political leadership to help them resolve problems that they don't know how to go about resolving themselves. They come in with complaints about services, or want information about how to contact agencies, or they want you to help them organize block clubs, or help them with youth activities. I have not found any dramatic shift in the needs of the people since the ward changed racially from white to black. People want the political system to work for them. It doesn't matter how educated they are, or how they express it, they are trying to get the most out of government for themselves. People are generally not concerned with issues of a broad-based appeal. They're concerned with "I," or "My basement flooded." You try to accept it, work with people, and deal with their complaints.

I spend tremendous hours, about seventy hours a week, being a ward committeeman. Practically most of my time, when I'm not doing anything here in the county building, is spent doing things related to the ward and my responsibility as a committeeman. I'm always going to parties and affairs, and getting all kinds of calls, usually complaints. The job of committeeman is non-paying, but if

you really want to work at it, it takes a lot of time. I get tired, but
I enjoy being able to do something for people. When I see that
something has been done, and it's productive and someone has benefited, I am happy. I get a great kick out of it and want to do things
better than other people. You have to deliver services. That's the
thing I do. When it's election time, we debate issues. After the people
have made a decision, I just get out there and start working until
another election comes along.

How do you see the evolution of black politics in Chicago?
I think that, eventually, all the segments, both black and white, will
come together—not everybody—but the majority that really counts,
to try to determine the future of the black community in Chicago.
You're going to find, as time goes on, that there is less division among
political people than you find now. You'll find more people from the
regular organization, the so-called civil rights movement, and the
business community, working together for a common cause. Just like
any other group that went through an evolutionary period on the
American political scene, you'll find, that as they grow and develop
and become educated, they learn to work with each other, even
though there are differences. You're going to find the same thing in
the black community. But I do think you are going to find blacks
being more responsive, not just to the black community. You are
going to find blacks who want to do things for people, and who will
feel that if they service the people right, that blacks, necessarily, will
be taken care of too. To ever be a real potent political force, you have
to have a base in every community, because that's important in
government. You can't govern a city or a nation unless you have
support from every area. That's where you get your consensus in
government.

There's going to be some black/white confrontations, because
wherever any group, whether it is black or white, is a dominant force
and in control of things, they're not going to just walk away without
some fight. Even the more reasonable people who are in the power
structure are not willing to give up what they have. Even if they want
to give up, there are people who are willing to fight under any
circumstances. So there's a possibility that there will be some confrontation between candidates who are vying for office, whether they be
black or white. But eventually, like they've done in other parts of the
country, we'll work out some solutions to those problems, where the
whites can get used to blacks in government. They did it in California.

John, would you comment on the role of the black community in the mayoral succession to Daley, and the candidacy of a black, like Alderman Wilson Frost.

Wilson Frost, when it came to counting the actual numbers (and this is a numbers game), didn't have the numbers. When he accepted a deal that allowed him to be chairman of the city council finance committee, when Bilandic was chosen as mayor by the council, I think the black constituency in Chicago fared very well. Wilson Frost is a very able person and the chairman of the finance committee is one of the most powerful people in city government. He is right next to the mayor in terms of actual day-to-day power. I think that he can and will use his vast new source of power for the betterment of all the people of Chicago, particularly the black community, because never before have we ever been in a position where someone can direct the expenditure of over a billion dollars in the city budget. As chairman of the finance committee he has to supervise approval of the budget and then also observe how it will be spent. When you can do that, you can always ask the question, "Why is something being spent in this community," or, "Why are you not going to spend any in that community?" And when these questions are not answered to your satisfaction, you can use your power of parliamentary maneuvering to bring it to the attention of the public, or even hold up legislation until something is worked out that is equitable for all the people in Chicago.

I think that Wilson Frost is in a position to do a great service for all the people in Chicago. From a political point of view, he had no other alternative, if he wanted to stay within the power structure. He could have turned down the offer and been defeated. He would have been a martyr. But the question is, would he have been able to deliver for black people? He could have been something that black people could have rallied around, but in terms of really accomplishing something, he would not have been in a position to deliver. What we need in our community is people who can deliver for our people, and Wilson has a good chance now to do that. He knows the importance of trying to see that we get our fair share of the patronage and the dollar.

I don't think anybody, black or white, can run and be elected mayor unless he or she has a broad base of support and is able to appeal to all people. It doesn't just have to be in the organization as we have known it, but it has to be broadly based in the major political organization in order to successfully wage a campaign.

Where would you like to go in life politically?

I would like to run for some other office where I could render greater public service than on the county board. I presented myself to the last Democratic slatemaking meeting to be a candidate for Cook County state's attorney. But, frankly, I don't think they believed that a black man could be elected countywide in Cook County.

I think a black man could win a countywide race in Cook County, because you are just incidentally black, and you run to sell yourself to the people on the basis of the services that you can render for the betterment of their lives. Massachusetts elected Senator Ed Brooke in a state where blacks are less than one percent of the population. I think that some people use color an an excuse. Cecil Partee ran as well as the major candidates on the statewide ticket in 1976, and the circumstances were against him because he was running against Attorney General Bill Scott, who had real name recognition. All the political analysts were surprised at how close Partee ran. That was the first time that a black had been exposed. The next time, I think you'll find a black winning.* Each time a black is exposed to the public, the public accepts the fact that he is a candidate, as opposed to being a black. It's the same thing as when the first Bohemian ran, or the first Irishman. The voters get used to the fact that these people are running and that they can do things once they're elected. And that's what people are looking for.

I wouldn't want to go to Springfield unless I was going down there as the governor. I wouldn't want to be a state representative or a state senator. My family is at the age at which I would not want to leave them and spend all that time in Springfield. When you are getting close to fifty, you want to spend your time with your family before they leave you. The Springfield route is mostly for younger men, or men whose families are already gone. I would like to go to Washington and would enjoy being a United States Congressman, if the occasion presented itself. I could move my family to Washington and have a stable life. And I think I could handle the job.

*A black man, Roland Burris, was elected state comptroller in 1978, after winning the Democratic primary against a white opponent.

Edison Love, with political trophies

Bunnie East, in the 1940s
(photo by Maurice Seymour)

Left to right: Israeli Prime Minister
Ben-Gurion, Al Meltzer, Jacob
Arvey

Ralph Berkowitz (standing) with
Candidate Adamowski

Alderman Marzullo and Mayor Bilandic

Left to right: County Board President George Dunne, President Carter, Mayor Bilandic, Lynn Williams

Bernard Neistein

Marshall Korshak, Comedian
Buddy Hackett

Emil Evangelisti in the 1960s

John Domagala with Alderman Marzullo

State Representative Marco
Domico *(photo by City of Chicago
Department of Streets and Sanitation)*

Mr. and Mrs. Edward Przislicki

Left to right: County Clerk Stanley Kusper, Commissioner
Madison Brown, Alderman Marzullo, Mayor Bilandic, Representative Marco Domico, Ben Martinez, Commissioner
Matt Ropa

Representative James Taylor, Alderman Eloise Barden

Commissioner Madison Brown, Mayor Daley *(photo by City of Chicago Department of Streets and Sanitation)*

Commissioner John Stroger with daughter Yonnie Lynn
Stroger and County Board President George Dunne

City Clerk Cecil Partee, with constituents

Lou Viverito

Mayor Daley and Alderman Edward M. Burke, 1974 St. Patrick's Day Parade

Alderman Edward Vrdolyak and Mayor Daley on the day of Daley's death

MADISON BROWN

Fifty-four years old. Long-time precinct captain in the West Side's 25th ward—one of the best precinct captains in the city. Was first deputy commissioner of the department of streets and sanitation. Earned a bachelor's degree in political science and a master's degree in public administration, going to school at night, and is working on a Ph.D. Currently is commissioner of rodent control.

I was born in Chicago in 1925 and grew up on the West Side. I was educated in the Chicago public schools, received a B.A. from Roosevelt University, attended John Marshall Law School, and returned to Roosevelt University and received a master's degree. I am presently a candidate for a Ph.D. at Nova University in Fort Lauderdale, Florida. My father was a chemist and my mother was a housewife. My grandmother was a Democratic precinct captain in Chicago.

When I was a little boy I used to make the stairs for my grandmother. I would climb up three-story walk-ups and knock on the door, so the person could holler out the window, and my grandmother downstairs would call up for them to go to the polls. I finished high school and went into the service. When I returned from service, I went to work for the post office for five or six years and saw myself going nowhere. We received a nickel an hour a year increase in salary. With that kind of progress, I thought I just couldn't make it. I got into the political arena in the 28th ward with George Kells, who was white, and was the alderman and ward committeeman of the ward. My grandmother was becoming less active and I took over the precinct.

I was one of the few fellas in the neighborhood who didn't work for the policy wheel. In the 28th ward, Big Jim Martin was the head of the policy wheel, and had full control over the blacks in the ward politically. He had charisma, and was, in the 28th ward, like William L. Dawson was in the 2nd ward.

The policy wheel was the old numbers game, where they had drawings two or three times a day. For a nickel or dime, you could

catch $100 if you had two or three numbers that came out, or
dreamed the right numbers, or got the right numbers from a fortune
teller, or combined the right numbers from some numbers you saw
on the back end of a truck, or some license plate number that you
decided that you wanted to play. Most of the kids in my day knew
what the numbers stood for—like Robert, James, Jesse, car, house,
street—the numbers represented all of those things. They knew
what the numbers represented before they knew what the ABCs
would tell them in terms of an object, a noun, a subject.

The policy wheel was an integral part of the culture. It wasn't until
one of the Jones brothers, who ran the policy wheel, went to jail that
the syndicate learned what policy was all about in the black community and pushed out most of the black policy figures.

The fellows who were working in politics operated the policy apparatus. They were runners, collectors, and turn-in men. They wrote
the gigs and the dreams up for the people. If a person didn't know
what a particular object stood for, they would interpret that object
for the person in terms of the number that should be played for it.
They were the link between the people in the community and the
policy wheel, and almost one person in every family in the black
community played policy. Policy was considered only a misde-
meanor in those days. No one paid any attention to it. It wasn't a
crime. The real crime was when other people got into it and made
it a syndicate operation, and then it became a felony. Playing the
numbers of that day was no different than playing the numbers that
you play for the state lottery today.

Most of the runners and writers were also connected with Jim
Martin, who was head of the policy wheel. They also worked in the
precincts in the areas where they made the collections or rode the
rounds in a district or their route. They were acquainted with everybody in the route. Black politics on the West Side was built around
relationships. Anybody who lived on the West Side knew everybody
else. People didn't bother locking their doors. The kids ran in and out
of our house from next door or the house down the street as much
as I did.

There was no basic ideology in black politics whatsoever until the
civil rights movement began to develop ideologies around politics.
Some of us who had the opportunity to attend college began to relate
to the real meaning of the political environment, with the advantages it gave to other ethnic groups. There began to develop an
ideological sense of responsibility, relative to the political arena in

terms of advancement for black people. That ideology developed out of the civil rights movement, not out of the political sense of what is right and what should be done. The idea was that if education, economics, and politics were advantageous for others, it should also be advantageous for blacks who had not really had an opportunity to use it as a mechanism or tool for progress and advancement. Whites could, by the color of their skin, merge into the mainstream of society, and you would never know whether they were affluent or non-affluent. If a black tried to merge into the mainstream of society, his skin first told you who he was. His identification was there. He had to have something going for him if he merged into the mainstream of society. In most instances, you will find that the children of the old-line West Siders are now among the major affluent sectors of Chicago. Most went to college. Those kids knew what it meant to acquire an education, to have a stable economic base in employment, and how to use their political strength to their advantage. They first learned how the system worked, which, many times, their parents didn't know, and after they found out how the system worked, they made the system work for them. Not on the radical end of the spectrum, but within the framework of the established rules of the game, within the party, within the political structure. Many went into private industry, but within the structure. They knew what the rules of the game were, and took the rules of the game and made the rules of the game work for them.

I left the 28th ward and bought a home at 2943 Jackson Blvd. The neighborhood was integrated, part black, part white, part Spanish, and was changing by the day. Blacks and Puerto Ricans were moving in, and whites were selling. Arthur Kris, an Irish Democratic precinct captain for more than forty years under Congressman James Bowler, came to see me, and said, "I understand that you used to be with the 28th ward. How would you like to work with me?" That was in 1954.

In 1955, Daley ran against Kennelly. Art Kris was with Daley, and therefore, I went with Daley. I had a pretty fair rapport with black people in the new community. They saw that I was someone who was concerned about what happened to the area. Kris could no longer climb up and down the stairs because he had had a heart attack previously. So I did most of the work, canvassing the precinct. On election day he had an attack, and I ran the precinct. We came out like 512 for Richard J. Daley and about 30 for Kennelly. Then Vito Marzullo made me the precinct captain. I am still a precinct captain. However, I have moved into a home at 2826 West Polk Street, and

I am carrying a precinct that I have now since 1963, from the day I moved into that particular community.

I am more proud of the Kennedy election than I am of any other election, other than for the mayor of Chicago. In 1960, I had three attorneys as watchers. They were not from the organization. They were from outside, from the suburbs. They were for good government. They were watching the polls on the West Side. They asked me, "What do you think you will get in this election?" We had about 570 voters registered in the precinct. I said that I expect we will get about 500 or so for the Democratic Party. They asked, "What will we get for the Republican Party?" I told them that that would be difficult to tell until I rechecked my sources again, but I expected they would get about fifteen. They said, "That's impossible!" I think the outcome was 540 for John F. Kennedy, and eight for Richard Nixon. When the machine was opened, they just couldn't believe their own eyes. They invited me out to their suburban towns. I guess they wanted to coopt me into the Republican Party to work a precinct in the suburbs.

How do you get those kinds of results?

Number one, you are available to the people. Two, you provide service to the people. Three, you make yourself on call twenty-four hours a day to the needs of the people that really need you. You're there to advise people. Many times, all they are looking for is a direction, where to go to get something done. They don't want you to do it. They just want to know where to go. How to go about getting it done.

But then, you have the more human side. You will get up at two o'clock in the morning and help take a mother and a baby to the hospital. That family is not going to forget that. You make a contribution to help bury somebody who didn't have any insurance. I just did, the other day, helped to bury a young twenty-seven-year-old lad, who, every election day for the last ten years, had helped me. When he was shot mysteriously in the back of the head by an assailant, his mother didn't have any money to bury him. She was on welfare herself. The burial was about $400. She arranged to have him buried in the afternoon (they didn't have to pay as much), and the workers in the precinct and myself helped to raise the difference from what she received from the welfare, so that he could have a fairly decent burial.

Issues are not what we discuss in terms of politics in our neighborhood. We will inform people of the candidates' merits. We talk with every person in our precinct before every election to try to get their views, to try to be sure they understand our views, and where we are coming from. We try to also make sure that they understand that we have a leadership that is unique in our area, in Alderman Vito Marzullo. Even though he is a white man, he has demonstrated to the black people of our area, the 25th ward, that he is truly concerned with their interests, and has demonstrated, time after time, that concern. You may find that he is the only white person in the middle of a black congregation at a church, or at an affair. And he relates his views, whether they are the views that they really agree with or that they disagree with. They respect him for that, because he lets them know where he stands, regardless of what the position is. But he also lets them know that he is there for their benefit, and that he is there to provide service for them when they need it. They don't have to wait to go downtown or go to the headquarters to see him. If necessary, they can see him in his home on Oakley Blvd.

What about these allegations that in precincts likes yours on the West Side, in black neighborhoods, votes are either stolen, bought, or coerced?

Let me say this: when you come in for one day, trying to run a precinct on the West Side of Chicago, and you only get eight or ten votes, it should be no surprise to you, when the captain that you are working against has been there 365 days a year and has worked directly with those people every day of the year. Then, when you try to explain why you only got eight or ten votes, the next thing that you can come up with is that they stole it from me. They don't have to steal it from you. The people come through. You have Democratic judges and you have Republican judges, and they are there to see that the election is carried on orderly and by law. You also have watchers, and the watchers come from everywhere under the sun. At one time I had watchers in my precinct from a different state. In addition, the federal people come in with their walkie-talkies, and they are talking to the federal building downtown, or the attorney general's office, or the state's attorney's office. They are always looking for something and they are always trying to imply something in most of those areas.

The essence of good politics in a city like Chicago, with people who have very little in areas like I am talking about, is service to the people. You service the people and they will respond to you. Informing the people, having good communication with them. You've done your job when you have informed the people. And you also sell yourself. You have to sell yourself, because if you do not sell yourself to the people, if they haven't developed a trust for you, you're not likely to get the kind of results that I have been describing to you here today.

The essence of being a good politician is to never make a promise that you do not already have a solution for. If you make a promise, people are looking for you to hold to your word. If you don't already have a solution for the promise, you may or may not be able to carry forth with your promise. I don't give my word, unless I know that I can deliver what it is that they are asking for. I will take the information, will follow up the information, and then, when I know I can deliver it, that's when they get my promise, and only then. If you know in advance that you cannot fulfill the promise, don't make it. People will respect you more if you say, "I can't do it, but if something occurs in the future that it can get done, I'll be more than willing to do it for you. But, at this time, I cannot do it." I have never made a promise that I've been unable to keep. I've never had to cross over on the other side of the street because a neighbor or a friend or a voter was coming down the same side of the street that I was on, because I did not keep a promise.

Tell me about your governmental career since you became a precinct captain.

I started out as a deputy clerk in the board of election commissioners at $390 a month, in 1956. I applied for the job and I took an examination. I also had a recommendation from Alderman Marzullo. I then became a special investigator for the board of elections. From there I went to the department of streets and sanitation as a street traffic patrolman, at a substantial increase, to a salary of $690 a month. I then became the assistant ward superintendent of the 25th ward, a position that placed me second in providing services for the ward. The 25th ward had two ward yards. The superintendent ran one of the ward yards, and I ran the other. I then became a coordinator and then administrator, for the West Side, for the Model Cities Program from 1968 to 1972. I had to resign as precinct captain because I was being paid by the federal government under the Hatch Act. My daughter, who was a college student, took over and ran my precinct. In 1970, I was elected to the Constitutional Convention from the 20th senatorial district, and I served on the local government committee to write the

new constitution for the state of Illinois. In 1972, the Chicago Home
Rule Commission selected me as principal research associate. I came
back to the department of streets and sanitation as assistant commissioner. In 1974, I was selected as commissioner of the Chicago board
of elections commission, where I had started as an investigator. We
supervised and administered the election machinery for the city of
Chicago and a couple of suburban areas. Then I was appointed by the
mayor to be the first deputy commissioner of the department of
streets and sanitation, second in charge of the department, an operation that spends something like close to $200,000,000 a year providing
services to the citizens of Chicago. In 1978, I was made a department
head, as commissioner of rodent control.

*Madison, you have really climbed the ladder from the bottom up
to a very substantial administrative position now with the city of
Chicago. Did your political affiliations have anything to do with this
at all?*

I'd have to say yes and no. The earlier aspect was certainly yes.
Political backing and political influence was necessary, and also the
experience that I gained in that process. But after you reach a certain
level, then primarily, it's your capability, your level of sophistication,
your educational background, and your experience. You deal with
people in politics as a precinct captain. You learn the nature of
people and how to discern behavior patterns of people. In that inter-
relation, that interfacing that you develop with people, you develop
kind of an insight that can only be obtained in that process that
occurs between you as a political figure and the people that you
serve. It does not occur as a salesman selling to a customer.

I also prepared myself by going to school. In 1955, I had about two
years of college. I had begun to go to college immediately after I
returned from the service, and then I completed my college at night.
It took eight years for my bachelor's degree at night, taking one or
two subjects each term. Sometimes I would take two subjects and be
out for a year. I was raising three children at the same time. I had
to make sure my priorities were in order. When it was a question of
whether I should spend the money for education or to spend the
money on the family, the family had to come first. So, many times,
I just didn't have the money to continue for the next semester. Then
I would accumulate enough to go the following semester, or the
following semester after that. It took two years to get the master's
degree going at night again.

*I want to take you to contemporary black politics and the future
of black politics in Chicago. How do you see that situation?*

There has been a great difference in black politics on the South
Side and the West Side. The black South Side had a cohesiveness
under the leadership of William L. Dawson, who wielded power
through his control of one unit of six or seven powerful wards. Dawson had great charisma. But many blacks, as they became more
affluent, began to view William L. Dawson in a different light than
the early people viewed him, because they just didn't know what the
man had really done for black politics in the city of Chicago. He used
political power to the advantage of blacks. No other black had ever
done that in Chicago. Dawson used power to gain jobs for his people.
He laid the groundwork for political influence and the benefits of
political influence within the Democratic machine.

On the West Side, for the most part, politics was controlled, except
for one ward, by those who were in power during the time of the
white ethnic majority who still maintained control over the black
wards. They controlled the political apparatus, had the connections
with the Democratic Party, and had the finances to carry on and still
produce a good Democratic vote for the party. The blacks felt quite
helpless until George Collins became the ward committeeman of the
24th ward, and, later, Ike Sims became the committeeman of the
28th ward. That gave some impetus to blacks on the West Side to
acquire some political power.

On the West Side, there has never been an amalgam of wards as
a power group, except when it was controlled by whites—the West
Side bloc—the 1st, 24th, 25th, 27th, 28th, 29th wards. It's a fragmented black political situation. For example, on the far West Side,
two independent blacks won races for seats in the state legislature.
I think, if the Democratic powers are not very careful, that the kind
of an amalgam that will develop will be one which they could find
it difficult to live with.

If you were to take the black population and combine it with the
Latin population, you would have a majority coalition. Most of the
blacks who are eligible are registered, but there are a great number
that are not. Many of the Latins who are eligible are registered, but
there are great numbers that are not. If those groups, together with
any other ethnic group, were to combine, they would be a formida-
ble force politically. But the present active black politicians of Chicago have got to become more ready to grasp the opportunity when
it presents itself. As long as they are factionalized, and as long as they

are in their own little segmented boxes and doing their own thing, it will be many more years before black leadership will emerge in Chicago as the basic unit of politics.

I think one day they are going to wake up and find that that is their only salvation in politics in Chicago. Los Angeles, Detroit, Cleveland, and Newark experienced it. Take Maynard Jackson of Atlanta, where the black population of Atlanta is really not the majority. It was that kind of coalition that Jackson was able to put together and the willingness of the white population to say that we can vote for the man, not his color. The blacks have been doing that for whites in Chicago all along. We have been voting for the white person who we have thought would be the better person to run government for us. I don't see any reason why the other ethnic groups cannot say that they can vote for the man, regardless of his color. Candidates should appeal to both black and white voters in terms of feeling that they have the capability, will be fair, and will be willing to share, which is something that is not exactly done today.

SIX

The Women

JANE BYRNE / MARILOU McCARTHY
HEDLUND / ELOISE BARDEN /
IRENE HERNANDEZ

JANE BYRNE *Irish. Forty-five years old. Was city commis-*
sioner of consumer sales. Close to Mayor Daley, and was ap-
pointed by him co-chairman of the Democratic county central
committee. After Daley's death, broke with his successor, Mayor
Michael Bilandic. Ran against Bilandic and was elected mayor
of Chicago April 3, 1979.

I grew up in Chicago, went to Barat College of the Sacred
Heart, did not major in anything like political science and government, and was totally immersed in science—biology and chemistry.
My sister Carol, who was more outgoing, was president of the Young
Democrats at Barat in 1959. That was the same year that my husband
was killed and I had come back home from North Carolina. She was
working in John Kennedy's campaign in 1960. She opened the Democratic headquarters in Chicago and was literally getting on my
nerves with all the Kennedy talk. I heard Kennedy on the radio
saying that there were as many young boys dying in the cold war as
there were in the hot shooting war. That seemed to strike me, and
I changed my mind about politics and decided that if I could help,
I would. It was a very, very personal commitment. So I went down
to the headquarters, and from that time on I have been involved.

A lot of people said later, when I would be traipsing on trains to
Springfield with the precinct captains, that I was working my way
down. People usually start out as precinct captains and work their
way up to the national campaign, but I went the other route. If you
wonder how that happened, I didn't get to know Mayor Daley very
much at all by working in the Kennedy campaign. He knew my
name, I would see him at the regular organization-sponsored events
for a candidate, but I was just a face to him. The Kennedys offered
me a job in Washington, or they said they would write a letter of
recommendation to Mayor Daley, if I wanted to continue in politics.
I had a baby, so I thought I would go back to school and get a master's
and teach. It was a great big bubble, a lot of fun, but it was over, the
man was in the White House, and that was what I was looking for.
Three weeks before Kennedy was killed, he was nice enough to

invite my daughter Kathy and me to sit in the president's box at the
Air Force–Army game, and we went. If you remember, that was the
day that the big coup took place in Vietnam, Madam Nhu and her
husband. Kennedy didn't come, but everyone else I had gotten to
know quite well—Kenny O'Donnell, John Riley, Pierre Salinger—
they all came. They all said that I should come out to Washington.
The mayor was also present and I chatted with him for a little while.
He asked me why he always saw me at these political functions but
that I wasn't really involved. He said, "Why don't you come to see
me?" So I did. We didn't start off well at all.

It was funny. I had heard only the Kennedy side of the Mayor
Daley legend at that time. I guess he was only in then for about five
years, as mayor. But they were close. We were told, "Never upset the
mayor!" It was quite a thing—right down to the parade routes that
would have to be changed if he didn't like the way the headquarters
did it. One time, Kennedy's plane was supposed to land at O'Hare
and the mayor decided it would be better to bring the president into
Meigs. The weather was going to be bad, and somebody made the
statement through his advance man, "We don't want to take the
plane in there. We have everything planned at O'Hare." The mayor
said, "Why don't you want to land at Meigs? I can get a bigger
crowd." They said, "It wouldn't be too safe." That's all they had to
say to him. "Meigs airport is the safest airport in the world," he said.
"My engineers tell me that there is no finer runway." They finally
called John Kennedy in the plane, asking where he wanted them to
land. "There's a crowd at O'Hare and a bigger crowd at Meigs." They
settled it, believe it or not, by landing at O'Hare to satisfy the little
crowd, and putting the presidential candidate in a helicopter and
flying him to Meigs. That would salve both sides. I saw those things,
and of course you could say, if you were smart, that there were no
more than three hundred people at O'Hare but there were ten
thousand at Meigs. That was the difference between our office and
the regular organization. And you could definitely see that.

Was that typical of the mayor?

Of everything, yes. He didn't even want the Kennedy headquarters in Chicago. He had to be convinced by John Kennedy personally
that we were doing it in every other city, so we would look bad if we
didn't do it here. He felt that there was a Chicago Democratic Party
and he didn't need a Kennedy headquarters. The local party was
sufficient.

It was his city, his party, and he could take care of it. Right?

Let me tell you—you have exactly quoted John Kennedy. His words were, "That's Mayor Daley's city. Give Mayor Daley what he wants." And that was how it was. It was a very strict commitment on the part of the Kennedys to be sure that the way the mayor wanted it was the way it was.

But, as I was saying, when I first walked in there to see the mayor three years later, I had some awe, because I had seen all this. In fact, I thought he was very nice, very cordial and everything. I thought it was going to be a nice meeting. I was trying to study him a little bit, which you know everybody always did, but didn't get too far. I was trying to draw my conclusions from his face. Finally, he very arrogantly said, "Why did you go to them?" I said, "To whom?" He said, "The Kennedys. Why did you go to them?" I said, "Well, I wanted to help out." He said, "Did you not know of the Democratic Party in Chicago?" I said, "Well, yes." He said, "Why didn't you come to us?" I said, "It wasn't that kind of thing. You don't understand. Nobody was beating my door down to get me. You weren't and they weren't, and I was glad I was able to get involved." He said, "Do you know that we have the finest speakers' bureau? Do you know that we have the finest organization?" He said, "You know, you wasted your time. You've lost two years." It was like boom, boom, boom. He said, "Besides that, what did you get out of it?"

Then I got mad. I said, "What do you mean what did I get out of it?" He said, "What did they do for you? We take care of our people. If somebody works hard for us, we're sure that they get something." I said, "I didn't want anything. Do you mean a job?" He said, "Yes." I said, "They offered me a job in Washington, but I didn't want to go. I have a baby. I didn't want to go that far away. She has been uprooted twice." He put his hand over his mouth and said, "Oh."

But now I was insulted, when someone says what did you get out of it? I picked my purse up off the floor, and I said, "I think I've come to the wrong place, and I am sorry that I took up your time and I really do think that I am leaving." He looked at me and said, "What do you mean?" I said, "I don't like what you asked me—what did I get out of it? Up until this moment with all the hurrah about this big bossism and you, I basically believed that I got the same thing out of it that you got out of it!" He said, "What was that?" I said, "I thought that what I got out of it was the first Catholic president of the United States. With all your political clout, I thought that deep down inside in your heart that was what you wanted. If you are going to sit here and talk to me about the spoils and who got what, then I really am not too interested in staying. And I want to say something else. You have been hitting that headquarters pretty much since I came in here. Why did I go there? What did they do? And they accomplished nothing? That was a very close vote in Illinois, and there was no doubt in anybody's mind that Cook County carried the presidency. But on such a small vote, maybe if we got five or six of those extra five thousand out there in the suburbs, maybe that was worth while. And that is really all I have to say, and thank you very much for your time."

He said, "Sit down!" I sat down. Then he pushed his chair back and I guess my closing sentence was, "I guess it really didn't matter too much anyway what either of us has got out of it, did it?" He said, "What does that mean?" I said, "Well, it means he's dead anyway." Well, at that, he said, "Excuse me a minute." His chair went back and he was down under his desk doing something, and I thought to myself, "What am I doing in this place?" Those were my actual thoughts. He said, "My shoelace is untied," and he is saying this down low, and all of a sudden he comes up and his face is soaked and he is crying. We established an understanding at that moment. I said, "I feel awful. I didn't mean to come in here and make you cry." Then he turned his head, which he was common to do, then turned back in a few minutes and said, "Well, do you want to work with us? Do you want to come to us?" I said, "Well, yes." He said, "What would you like?" I said, "I don't know. You invited me. That's a silly question to ask me, because you are the kingmaker. From what I hear you can look at somebody and decide if they got it or they haven't." He said, "Why don't you start coming here about once a month." Then we went into what I was doing and he said, "You've got to go and work for the ward organization. You've got to." I said, "I'll be happy to." He said, "Will you ring doorbells?" I said, "Sure." He said, "Will you put up signs?" I said, "Yes." He said, "Well, you go there, and you tell them that I suggested that you work there as a volunteer at the ward organization." Then he looked at me and he said, "I could give you anything I want to. I could name you to any post. I could put you on committees and your name would get known throughout, but if you don't help out, no matter what I try to do, they'll get you down below, so go and work for your ward organization."

So that's how I started. I kidded him about it later. The last time

he ran, I said to him, "I never got over the rudeness of you that day."
He said, "I took a look at you that day and I said to myself, 'You need
taking down.' And it didn't hurt you one bit."

*So the mayor was saying, Jane, that if you wanted to be active in
politics in the Democratic organization in Chicago, you had to be
active in your ward and precinct, too.*

That's right. I think people can say that there are a lot of problems
in our major cities. You can look at New York, you can look at Chicago, and I think that we do have some (and I think the city hurts
because of that), but I think that the precinct captains have a dual
role. They don't just get out the vote. The mayor was concerned
about getting out that vote, but if there was something going on in
the precincts, he wanted to know about it. That provided better grass
roots communication back to the establishment called government.
We don't have that today as well as we should. That's what we should
be doing, but I don't think we have that strong dedication today. We
do in some wards and in some precincts, but we don't have it
throughout the city.

Can you tell me how you moved up politically and in government?

Well, I think after we had that little tiff, or whatever you want to
call it, we had sort of a mutual understanding and respect. Maybe he
thought, "Boy, this is really a pushy one," hearing me say, "I'm
leaving, I didn't mean to come here, and you're not my kind." But
he knew that I would never let him down, that I would always tell
the truth, and I certainly knew that he would. So he then later on
assigned me to the poverty program, and he would have me come
over. He wanted other opinions coming in and I was one of those
opinions. And he grew to understand, I guess, that I was okay, as far
as thinking, and had some brains, and could be trusted. From there
I went on to become commissioner of consumer sales. I was active
in the 1967 campaign. From 1968 on there was a tremendous
amount of shifting sands on the national scene, with the assassination
of Robert Kennedy—even before he got killed. Well, I never gave up
those other friends and I would often times get some information out
there. Up until Bobby was killed, there was still the belief the Kennedys would come back, so we kept the foot soldiers we had in order,
so that whatever was going on, I would be able to tell him. That does
not mean in any way that he didn't have a direct line of communications right to Bobby. But the underlying stuff about who's with who,

what Mayor Tate might be going to do in Philadelphia, and who was with us here and there, I'd get from the others. That was a good way to hear. That helped him. And he liked those people.

He was very smart that way. I would walk in and his hands would go up, and he would say to me, "What are you picking up?" That would mean, "What do you hear out there?" There was one time that he was mad at them all, and he said to me, when I went in to ask him a question, "You can tell them I have no interest in the national scene." This was after 1968. So then six months went by and he was still calling me and talking to me, and we were getting ready for a new campaign, I think. All the rules and regulations, etc. One day, I was down there and he said, "So what are you hearing?" I said, "I'm not hearing anything." He said, "What do you mean?" I said, "You told me you're not interested in the national scene. They don't tell me anything." He said, "Did I say that?" and laughed. So then I went and made a few phone calls and got the answers shortly as to what he wanted to know. And that was a help to him.

What was the mayor's attitude about women in politics?

I think it was a dual thing. I don't think it was just women in politics. He had a sincere hope to get women in government as well. And I do not think that the mayor was acting as some people say because of my "in." It was started before my "in." There were maybe four others that were moving up. I had worked in the '67 campaign with Neil Hartigan, and then, in 1971, I worked out of the Bismarck with John Daley [the youngest son] and Mrs. Daley. And for her, it wasn't big parties at the Drake Hotel and the crowds. She said, "I don't care if it is ten or fifteen women in a room, I want little afternoon teas. I want to hear what the people are saying." And so Johnny and I scheduled those with no publicity. When she came back, she said, "Dick, you don't know what they're doing out there in some of those wards." She called me and said, "Janie, after this campaign is over, you and I are going to go to all the ward organizations and line up the women." (This was Mrs. Daley.) And she told him (I was there), she said, "Do you know what they're doing to the women in this area? They are not getting services. Furthermore, the women do not know what you are trying to do." So she was the one that convinced him, and that was before Miami. She was the one that planted that seed. And I think that the mayor also, as a good politician and an excellent mayor, did sense if they reach more people through the women's angle that there would be more hope left to save the neighborhoods.

Even when he had the stroke, he called and said he wanted to see if some of the women can become ward superintendents. Well, that never happened. The committeemen think that it is one of their plums. They didn't want that. But he felt that the women see that the garbage is picked up. That was the mayor's reasoning. They are there all day. They know what is going on in the neighborhoods. Their husbands are out to work. They see it—they live with it day in and day out. He thought that some of those people are very necessary to get involved as ward superintendents. But that went down the drain faster than other things.

Is there a lot of prejudice against women among a lot of people in the Democratic organization in Chicago?

Yes, I think so. They don't think they are incapable. It's a matter of not letting a new kid in. It's not only women. When the mayor said I should go to my ward—it takes a lot to even get accepted in the ward. They've got their own thing, they know how to do their thing, and it's, "Don't rain on my parade." I don't think it makes any difference if you are a woman or a very young, gung-ho, ambitious college graduate that wants to get in. There is a little fear that maybe they are better trained, the young college students coming out. Some of the precinct captains feel, "We have been in the street. That kid has gone to college." You hear that and it is a prejudice, but it's just a prejudice against anybody trying to get in and get involved and maybe upgrade it. It's got to be the way they want it, or it can't be.

It isn't easy to break into [a ward organization]. In fact, when I first went there, I was, my gosh, only twenty-six. And the mayor told me to go there and say that he sent me, and it was a good thing, to say that he sent me. I didn't get a tumble. I didn't hear from them for three months. Meanwhile, I was supposed to come back and report to him about what I was doing. I kept calling and calling. You know me. But they'd say to me, each time, "Well, didn't your precinct captain tell you it was going to be last night? It was last night." So I went to see the precinct captain, and I said, "Why didn't you tell me?" And then I saw it at its lowest form. The precinct captain in our neighborhood (we live in Sauganash and it is a wealthy neighborhood and you can't do much for the public) didn't want me there, and I knew him all my life. I knew him as a nice man and a neighbor. He'd say, "You don't have to come, it's just for precinct captains." I'd say, "I know, but I'm trying to learn." I would have to call to find out when the meeting was going to be, where it was going to be, to be sure that I could come. And that man didn't mean to hurt me. He didn't want me ringing doorbells, and he didn't want me on his turf. And that's what it is.

It works two ways. On another occasion we waited and waited to get our streets fixed. After I had worked for the city for awhile (everyone was getting their tires cut on our curb), I called the head of patronage, who was a friend of mine. Now, I'm working through the system. I said, "Gee Bob, we've been waiting for two years, and they say it still is eighteen months away. We're ruining all the tires." The very next day, in came the crews, and the curb was fixed. Well, that was very nice. I didn't feel powerful about it. I thought, "Gee that's nice." I didn't tell anybody about it. It was just done. My mother and father knew. Three days later, in comes a letter from our alderman and committeeman, "Your precinct captain is very much on his toes. He noticed your crumbling sidewalk and got it fixed." I thought, "What?" That's what I'm saying—they don't want any inter-ference—it's their system. I think it's wrong, but that's the way it is. But it's changing. People aren't accepting it anymore. It's going to get worse.

You look at all the strong wards. You'll find out that the 50th ward isn't doing well. The 49th ward. The 43rd ward is gone. The 44th ward. So where is the strength left? So I say that they have to wake up. They have to go back to the concept of letting people in and opening it up. The mayor was trying to do that.

Essentially what you are saying is that there is a kind of atrophy in the organization.

Not in all the wards. The 11th ward does well. It serves those people, and it gets out. Let me put it to you this way, and I am sure many people will challenge this, but it is the truth. Back in 1971, the mayor called me down one day, and I was now Democratic national committeewoman, and also chairman of the resolutions committee. I had moved along under his guidance. He called me down this one day, and it is proof of what I am saying, and how well he recognized it. He said to me, "You know, Janie, we have all these anti-groups taking over every ward, and for some reason, they're selling it to the people or the people wouldn't be joining, and there is somewhere in there that we are missing." He said (now you won't believe this, but there were people who can verify it), "What I want you to do is to set up an anti-organization in the wards." (Now, this is the truth. You know, I still have the charts and everything.) "I want you to start with the 50th and go all the way down, and you gotta get people that you trust in each ward, and you gotta get them to convince the others that they are independent." And he said, "I will help you do it financially. Number one, we've got to prove to those committeemen that there is a need out there that is not being met by other people joining us, and let them be the people that say they hate Daley. I don't care. Because the only reason we are going to get in there and build something again in those neighborhoods is this way." So, I contacted some people, trusted people that I knew lived in those wards. If it was something he thought would stimulate the Democratic Party again, as well as give the people an alternative, then they should have it. If it was his name or something they were turned off on, still the party should survive, and that was what he wanted.

How would you evaluate the mayor, Jane, as a politician and an administrator? You dealt with him at both levels.

I thought the mayor was an outstanding politician and I thought he was an even better mayor than he was a politician. I think he was a person who knew how people felt. Unless you know how to use power and you know how to pull the strings and votes, you shouldn't be one. It is something you have to grow into. I think that is why he was a superb mayor. He understood the hardships, and he understood the trials in the neighborhoods and how people felt. And he knew that there was enough strength in him that if there was a borderline thing, he would ultimately end up back to the people. He had close enough communication to what had been a very strong organization at that time, to know the need. It was the blending of the power. As an administrator, he never let me down. There would be committeemen who would come in and say, "She's creaming those stores in my neighborhood." He'd say to me, "What are you doing?" I would explain what we were doing to him, and he would tell me to go right on doing it.

As a politician he would always weigh both sides, but he wouldn't just jump. And then you could see him take in the interplays, maybe, of people's reactions, but in the long run he would go back to the fact that he was the mayor of Chicago. I think he didn't remain just an isolated committeeman. He ultimately had to relate that power to keeping the city viable. And he did.

I think as he got older, he became more and more a statesman and saw more and more of the fallacies, like saying, "We've got to reorganize the lakefront wards, every ward from the 50th on down." Now you hear people saying, "He didn't field a good ticket" or "He abandoned the suburbs," and that was blown completely out of proportion. He was talking about getting into the suburbs for six or seven years. His little output out there through those Democratic clubs, when he wanted those done, he said not to be divisive, to be inclusive, and since there's no room for regulars, it would be the same thing he was going to do in the wards.*

How did the mayor deal with department heads?
He always wanted facts. He always wanted answers immediately. If somebody came in and griped about something that was going on, and if he thought you were wrong, he would tell you. I think he treated everybody about the same way. There would be times that you would wish he would run them a little bit more, because you would be sitting there thinking, "How is this going to break?" And you would go down, just to be assured that what you were doing was right. He backed you up. And some of the decisions that he made in here that I know of were very hard to make. I knew from other pressures.

Jane, you worked with the mayor for a long time, and I know how you felt about him. Did he have any weaknesses as a mayor and a politician?
I could not find any in him as a mayor. I used to think sometimes from what he would say to me (and you have to understand that I was for a two-and-one-half-year period a co-chairperson of the county central committee and we would talk about things), I used to think sometimes maybe he was a little too soft on some of the committeemen. We would sit and discuss what some issue was, and let's say it was something about some individual, and he'd say, "Well, maybe I shouldn't have expected more." Or, "He let me down," and you could see that there was a hurtness in his face about it. At the same time I would think to myself, "You know, why don't you cut him a little bit? That would be my reaction." And he'd say, "Well, what can you do?" Every once in a while, of course, he would say things too, like, "Don't get mad, get even." Or "Forgive, but never forget." And,

*In 1976, Mayor Daley and Mrs. Byrne attempted to form Democratic clubs in some of Chicago's suburbs to supplement the Democratic township organizations, a move which met with considerable hostility and resistance from the Democratic township committeemen in those areas.

then, I think, after the stroke, he got even more kindly that way, because he'd say—and openly—to the press, "I'm lucky I'm here. I have none of that left in me. I don't want to hurt, whatever they do." The sting came out of him.

How do you see the future of politics evolving in Chicago, now that the mayor is gone?

I think it's going to be a much more fragmented Democratic Party. I don't think that the chairman is going to be the mayor, and I think, as we have seen, everything is for party unity, don't get upset about it, we have to stick together, but the commitments that are being made won't last. The main decisions are being reached, and we have to have it that way, but I think you will see more comers pushing a little harder.

You know, everybody wanted to cream him, after the last election, which really burned me up. But when you really look at the facts and who delivered the wards, the basis of the Democratic Party has always been the clerk of the circuit court, the patronage, and he carried that very well. There was certainly an absolute vendetta to get power on the part of many, and I didn't attribute that to Mayor Daley. He also thought, in retrospect, that he had perhaps slated weak candidates. He mentioned it to me. He asked me did I want to hold a Christmas breakfast for the Democratic women, which was very close to the time that he died. I said, "Are you going to hold one for the men?" He said, "No." I said, "You're not? Maybe you ought to." He said, "Well, I'll think about it." Then he said to me in the afternoon, "No, I thought that over, by the way. I'm not holding it." He said, "After all, Janie, you know, I didn't let them down. They let me down. You look at the returns of some of those wards. You go study them well." It's easy to say, "Yes, I think it is going to be fragmented because they didn't deliver the last time." I didn't blame that on the mayor. Everyone was supposed to do their job.

What impact do you think this change in the party structure will have on the city itself?

They better keep their act together. That's what I am also saying. I think the city will hurt. I think that the city can survive without them right now because the city has done that. I think that people are going to find out that the great pluralities came not always from the precinct captains. (I hope I can find a place to work after this is published.) I hope that people find out that want to go around saying in wards or precincts that are easily Democratic that there were two things here. One, the man himself, in the name of Daley, that the public either liked or backed individually in his own elections. And then I think there were Democrats and independents, but he had a role that carried many precinct captains, rather than precinct captains carrying him.

You're a life-long Chicagoan, Jane. Describe this city for me.

Well, we're doing better than most. That's about the best way to put it. I think that the people here have a pride in being Chicagoans. I think that right now we have a deeper concern than we had when the mayor was here, and I think that our neighborhoods need a lot of work. I think the belief in the city has to go back into many of the neighborhoods. I think that anybody who reads the census knows that the schools are down. There is an exodus to the suburbs. I don't know that those are all governmental problems. I think some of them are sociological as well as psychological problems. The trick will be who will be able to try to blend them together. That's the leader we will have to have. That will be the problem in the city.

Are you saying we will need another Daley in Chicago?

I don't think we will get another Daley, but you are going to have to get somebody who understands people's psyches as Mayor Daley did. And I think that is going to be hard to do. I always thought of the mayor exactly the same way (it's not corny) like Carl Sandburg said, "Show me another city with the tough shoulders." You can think of that and identify that with the mayor. Tough shoulders. And I think in that same gutsy thing that you had in all of Carl Sandburg's definitions of Chicago—you had that in Mayor Daley. If it was going to be a racial problem and it had to be settled, he would tackle it. If he went in there with any prejudices, and he talked to the ministers and he heard the other side, he would blend it. And I think if the city is to survive we have to have that.

MARILOU McCARTHY HEDLUND

Irish. Was first woman elected to the city council. Is a long-time community activist and organizer in the North Side 48th ward. Left the council after one term to do graduate work at the University of Chicago. Is a member of the zoning board of appeals and will surely be back on the political scene in the future.

I was born in Chicago, educated in Catholic schools in Chicago, and was graduated from Barat College in Lake Forest, in 1959. I worked for the *Chicago Tribune* for twelve years.

In 1971, I ran for alderman in the 48th ward. This ward was represented, we felt inadequately, by a Republican, so I challenged him in the aldermanic election. I called State Senator Bob Cherry, who was the only politician I knew. I found out from him who the Democratic ward committeeman was of the 48th ward, called the committeeman, Martin Tuchow, and said that I wanted to come in and talk to him. I wound up in an interview session with their slate-making committee which had twenty-seven or twenty-eight candidates, and was selected as their candidate. I think they had no hope of winning and felt that whoever they slated was going to lose. They wanted to find someone who wasn't going to put the organization into debt, and I probably looked like I would be more scrupulous about paying my bills than some of the other contenders. I had determined that there was no point in running an independent campaign here. This is not the kind of middle-class or upper-class area that attracts that sort of vote.

We organized our own campaign effort, because the Democratic organization was just too new to have any real strength or any real delivery capabilities. We had to raise our own money, between $15,000 and $17,000, but we raised the funds and didn't go into personal debt. We did everything. We wrote everybody we had ever gone to school with that we could find and asked if they would contribute $50. They, in turn, would send that letter on to six of their friends (the old chain letter appeal), and a number of those very wisely responded by sending in $300 checks and not bothering their friends.

We tapped every available source for workers. I asked neighbors and friends in the community, people in PTAs, and my husband, Reuben, asked people from his office. We had the nuns from Barat College licking envelopes and stamping them, and anybody, literally, whose name ever cropped up in any address was asked for at least one thing, and roughly two. Sometimes they'd bring their friends in. What was astonishing was that even people I didn't know would come in and help. Some did it out of anger, some did it just because they were curious, and others because they had time on their hands.

What was it like to run for office for the first time, in a ward like this, in a city like this?

It was educational. Frightening, at first, because, if you are the product of a Catholic women's educational process, you are not used to being aggressive or terribly assertive. It was a very audacious thing that I had done. I suddenly found myself giving speeches and appearing on radio and television talk shows which I had no background or preparation for. But I began to realize that I knew a lot more than some of the others who were saying that they knew everything. Now I can get up and give a speech anywhere.

An aldermanic campaign isn't filled with glamour. It's not an exciting effort. It was trying, at times. There was no way you could go easily into a half-way house filled with recently discharged mental patients, or nursing homes (Uptown being the kind of area it is). Sometimes it just tore your heart out. I thought I had seen everything because of my background at the newspapers, but there was an awful lot I hadn't seen, and a lot that makes you toughen your hide, not against, but in order to do anything about it. It was nice to see the shared concern on all economic levels. I learned that no matter if you are poor, middle, or upper class, what you want is safe neighborhoods for your children, good schools, and well-kept houses, apartments, and streets. Basic human needs for service are so simple.

It was tiring. It was a strain. The first time you do it is always the hardest because there aren't too many people who are used to getting up at 5:30 A.M. and go stand on a street corner. These were subzero days. There is a rhyme and reason, I guess, to having the aldermanic elections in February, but there would be a lot more voters if they were held in June, July, or August (which is why they are in February). A lot of it was fun, in a way. One of the most rewarding things was just seeing how people would respond when you asked them for their help. Our friends in advertising produced some of the most magnificent copy. People like you came in and gave us ideas for how to use issues. Everybody was really helpful. I don't think I was ever suspicious of my fellow human beings, but if I ever was, it allayed all those suspicions.

You were the first woman alderman elected in the history of the Chicago city council; you beat Anna Langford in by eight hours. What was it like when you first got to the city council, as a woman?

I was treated with great wariness. I was a new breed. The day after the election, Dave Stahl, who was then deputy mayor, called Reuben and said, "Reuben, I just want you to know the first two assignments I have on my desk this morning are to install a new bathroom in the city council chambers, and to order a sign that says, 'Women.' I don't know if I like this."

There is a period of time from the election in February until April, before you are sworn in. I used that period to go around and have meetings with each of the major department heads. In so doing I learned a great deal that I hadn't known when I was campaigning. Also, in that period, I met Tom Keane for the first time, who was the finance chairman of the city council and really the leader. Tom is a real student of government and of Chicago politics, and he certainly found a welcome listener in me. Tom was not in the least bit threatened by a woman, so he was intrigued at the possibilities. He sort of took me under his wing and he gave me lots of things to read to put me off. I came back and said, "I've read those. Now what?" So, we developed a friendship. He was one who took me around and introduced me to a number of aldermen, which made it a little easier.

I was treated differently by different ethnic groups. The Italians treated me with great suspicion. The Poles split. Some of them just stayed as far away as they could; others were quite friendly. The blacks were very welcoming. The independents—we came to battle right away. The Jews were fine. There really isn't a Jewish bloc. Seymour Simon is Jewish, but he certainly isn't anything close to Paul Wigoda or Bernie Stone, or Len Despres. Paul Wigoda was on my left, and I am eternally grateful for that, because in the city council you are seated in order of the numbers of the wards, and Paul represented the 49th ward and is a very bright, witty man. He provided a lot of comic relief, at times, with an absolutely straight face, and would have something over his mouth, and I would be rolling. He, too, was terribly helpful. I don't think there really is an Irish bloc either. Ed Burke was fine, Cullerton was shook up, Tom Keane was just the over-all leader. There was the Croatian bloc—Ed Vrdolyak and Mike Bilandic. Ed and I got along because he liked to spar in humor, but I was small potatoes in his dictionary.

How did Mayor Daley respond to having a young woman like you in the city council for the first time?

He was the most wary of all. When Marty Tuchow went to tell him whom he had endorsed for the aldermanic seat in the 48th ward, the mayor just put his head in his hands and shook his head a lot. He was not pleased. The mayor treated me at arm's length. I think Tom Keane at some point told him that he thought I was okay. Gradually, for a number of reasons, the mayor came to like me (I hope). I certainly came to like and respect him a great deal. One reason was that on my own initiative I took on the independent bloc over an issue of such momentous concern as dog waste, and none of his regulars had ever done that. I think that sort of tickled him. I showed that I could be poised under attack. Another time, I really stood up against him on something some very greedy people were advising, and I think he respected that. I never asked him for personal favors. I was always asking him for something for the neighborhood—parks, schools, etc.—never anything for myself or my family. And he truly did love the city and was very proud of it, and of his own neighborhood. He liked people who were proud of theirs, and he saw the city as depending on those who had a sincere concern for it, not a selfish interest.

If the mayor ever asked me to do anything, I was very flattered. I saw more and more of him, but I certainly was not one of his personal friends, nor one of those who saw him all the time. I continued with that long after I stopped being an alderman, and enjoyed and learned every time. I would just sit there and gulp up all the knowledge that he had, and what I learned was that he was an absolutely brilliant man. I have very few heroes, and they include Thomas Jefferson, Winston Churchill, and Mayor Daley. Thomas Jefferson was much more of an aristocrat, as was Churchill, who was much more articulate. But the mayor probably was the finest mayor that ever was. A comprehensive man.

How did the mayor and Keane run the council?

Vigorously. Effectively. The council is like a captive body, not a deliberative body, nor should it be. It is a forum for those who want to give vent to their spleen, or had causes that they want to popular-ize. It's a legislative necessity and it is essential. I don't mean to demean it in any way. If there comes a time when there are honest issues that have to be brought forth, that forum is absolutely essential. But the fact is that it meets every two weeks, and, of those meetings, maybe five a year are what I would consider essential, excluding those that are in the budgetary process. The others are pretty much pro forma. The work is essentially done by the executive branch. It has to be. Our city councils are different than national legislatures. Cities have to function hour by hour by hour, the vouchers have to be signed, the paychecks have to be signed, the money has to be deposited, streets have to be repaired, and all of that has to be done. We don't have the luxury of five years to debate.

So you don't believe that the council necessarily should be given more power in Chicago to run the city?

Oh, God, no! That once was the case. People forget that Mayor Daley was a reform mayor. When he came in in 1955, it was the era of the grey wolves, and the council in fact did run the city. What they did was to take the budget every year and divide it up between them. I don't think that the people were well served. One of the first things that Mayor Daley did was introduce an ex-ecutive budget, which is an absolute necessity. I don't think that the council should be given more power unless you are going to reduce it in size, make it a full-time job, and reward those who are in it with sufficient income to attract good people. Right now it is not a first class job.

Can you evaluate Alderman Keane for me, Marilou?

When I was in the council, Tom Keane was a very effective leader, and a man whom Reuben and I respect a great deal, a man with comprehensive knowledge about city government and local affairs. Tom treated me with great respect, with great courtesy. He was one of the very few in the council who was willing to debate an issue and argue, and who could be convinced he was wrong. He came into things with a pretty open mind, or, if he came in with an apparent mind set, he would listen. He just wasn't threatened the way lesser men are when you try to say, "Well, maybe that's not the best way." I testified to his character at his trial. Tom, I know, feels he is a political prisoner. I have absolutely no personal knowledge of any personal corruption on his part. I think Tom's mistake probably was that he stayed there too long. There comes a time when the Young Turks just insist on taking over, and he was an obvious target—he was an easier target than the mayor.

Were you successful in getting good services for your ward when you were an alderman?

I thought we were very successful. I had an administrative assistant, named Pearl Simon, who is going to have all of her glories delivered in her later life, if they are not now delivered. When I was first elected, I interviewed every department head, so I knew the parameters and what was reasonable and how they would rather be approached and things. Instead of going a circuitous route, I just went directly to the commissioners generally, and had very quick service. Our community, Uptown, because it is so diverse and has such a poverty population, such an old population, as well as the normal middle class and the low-income family population, has every problem. I think this area is much more demanding than many others.

I had an office in the ward. I would go there and handle what had to be handled, and those were a variety of things. The statute is about three paragraphs long, as far as what aldermanic responsibilities are. All they really are is to approve the city budget. However, traditionally, we aldermen have served as almost glorified ward superintendents, and while an alderman has absolutely no direct responsibility for schools, for example, that is who people call because the schools don't answer. So I spent an awful lot of time doing school business, which I loved doing. We spent a lot of time trying to get economic development here, senior citizen housing, low-income housing, that whole CHA question.

The state has dumped ninety percent of its mental hospital dischargees in this area. Most of them were ill-housed and were a community problem, more of the nuisance variety, but a terrible problem. This is a very compassionate community, but we were overloaded and something had to explode. So we had lots of marches and hearings, and finally the state revised it. We had been also inundated with the program development that HUD had directed toward us. Every sleazy and not so sleazy developer in town decided that it was a very beneficial tax shelter program which would work for them, but it would only work in Uptown because it was the last white area of poverty.

The main thing we did was to organize block clubs. When I took office there were maybe four or five very dormant block clubs, and, when I left, every corner was organized in some form. That's essential because people have to look after their own self-interest. I don't think an alderman should be driving up and down checking curbs for chips. I think the block club president should call the alderman's office once a month, or whatever, and say, "This is what we need," and then that gets done. That is the efficient way of doing it.

What did this do to your personal life?

It was rough at times, but I think it enriched it much more than it disrupted it. I think we all benefited. My children got to meet a lot of people whom they never would have seen before. Aldermen have a lot of night meetings, so our times were restructured frequently. It took a while to adjust to that. It was a whole different life style. It was so not like something from nine to five. When somebody calls you at two in the morning, or whatever, you don't know whether it is a serious call (and some of them were very serious), and, because of the mental patient load, some of those calls really had to be pursued with the police, the social department, and whatever. Occasionally, the person (usually whom you had helped the most), would come with a group to picket your house. At that time, you would grind your teeth, not use those words that first came to your mind, and you do learn a lot of tolerance. It was very different than leading a private life and you just have to keep repeating, "Grace under pressure, grace under pressure, grace under pressure."

It really was a quantum jump, an incredible jump, as far as our family was concerned. I can't imagine what our life would have been now, without that. At times, it was exhausting. You were just frantic, wrung out, nervous, cross, and, at times, exasperated. There were a couple of times when I came up very hard against regular political interests that were certainly below the mayor's interest. Those included the threatening phone calls, and all the rest of it. In hindsight, it's not that much, but at the time it was very harrowing. I am grateful now that I had the experience, because I am much stronger for it, and I don't have an ulcer.

Why did you quit, Marilou?

I think I had exhausted my own contributions to the job. If I had gone a second term, I just would have been repeating myself. All the things that I had said that I wanted to do as an alderman had been done, or were underway, or had been ruled out of the question, and a lot of other things were never going to be realized. I thought I could help my neighborhood in other ways. The other thing is that this kind of a neighborhood should replace its aldermen frequently. It should be a shared responsibility because an aldermanic seat is not a fiefdom. If you are going to have a strong city, people have got to care about it, be involved and know the process themselves. The only way to do that is to participate. If they don't vote, if they let George do it, George is going to do it for George's benefit, not for anyone else's. I think it is just terribly important that the job get a little more prestige than it has, and that people learn to rely and depend on an alderman as a conscientious figure. I don't think being an alderman is an honor, but I think it is one of those things that you just have to do.

Reelection would have been easy. Tom Keane didn't believe that I was not going to run again. He said, "You're going to be back." I found myself (I don't know what the first political function I returned to was) like an old racehorse at the starting gate. Sure, I will be back. I don't know enough to serve well yet. That is why I am back in school now, getting a greater economic and financial background.

Marilou, can you evaluate Mayor Daley for me?

I would not presume to know him that well. I think he was a man of great honor, great intelligence, and great love and compassion. That, unfortunately, did not come through. The 1968 convention must have been just horrible for him, and was antithetical to his real nature. But if you look at his family (a man is frequently what he leaves behind), his family is pretty impressive. I worked in the mayor's campaign last time, and his sons would come out to various coffees. I had never known them. I am a little bit wary of the children of well-known people, because frequently, they tend to have the arrogance that their parents never do. Those boys were all very responsive, humble, very modest and self-effacing, and were very qualified to answer and talk, when it was their turn. They were not the least bit overbearing. One of the nicest things I can think of is that he was able to raise a family like that. That's a silly measure, but I think the best people pay attention to everything in their lives, and his family obviously had a great deal of his and Mrs. Daley's personal attention. They cared very much about those kids and their family structure, and family was very important. The same kind of attention was given to his city. He had that same amount of caring. I am sure that he liked to get up every morning and go to work. Most people want to get rid of some of the chores, the dirty work and all the rest of it. He just wasn't a lazy man, and the older I get the more I am impressed with how rare a lack of laziness is. He was also just incredibly intelligent. His political analyses were mind-boggling. I would always have my chin on my chest saying, "Why didn't I think of that?" It became so obvious, as it was explained. Sometimes I disagreed with him. He would tolerate and welcome that kind of disagreement. He knew who had the final word. It was a game, but again, it was an educational game.

Did he have any weaknesses?

I didn't know him well enough to know about his weaknesses. I think the mayor had a very short fuse until his operation. I think he became a much finer person after that first surgery. I think, at some point there, he made his peace with his Maker. He just became a more serene person. I don't think after that operation he would have had the kind of confrontation we saw between Simpson and Mayor Daley.* He had an Irish temper, the Irish instincts. My maiden name was McCarthy, so I can understand it very well. At some point, all Irishmen abandon reason and dig in, and they are just going to fight back because you challenged them (I suppose Brendan Behan exemplifies it best at the intellectual level), and you can't change them. I think the police case was an example of that [the discrimination suit in the police department]. He was convinced that was pure politics and I spent hours and hours trying to convince him to do something different in that. He would track me to a point, but then it became difficult to move him.

Did you know Mrs. Daley?

No, I only saw her at the large dinners and meetings. She is a very elegant woman, very refined and reserved. I never saw her lose that reserve at any time. I know she is a very warm person, but I was just so far removed from that kind of socializing. I came to appreciate and learn that he listened to her more than to anybody. Once I wrote an article, after I was out of office, on residency requirements on "Why is it that everybody that is telling us what to do lives outside of the town?" The first call I got that morning was from Mayor Daley. He

---

*Mayor Daley once exploded in rage at Alderman Dick Simpson during a city council debate.

really liked the argument, saying, "That was well received at home, too." He was pleased, and I was flattered to death.

I'll tell you when I admired her most, and the family. At the Mayor's wake, Reuben and I went out there. The body was brought into the church at noon, and we were standing in line with everybody else. They had some special people who went in and the Cardinal had a short service. Then people started going in. I was standing outside (it was one of those bitter, bitter cold days), and I assumed that when they finally let the public in, that the family would have been gone. Well, no, the family was there when we got there, and that was tough. By that time, we had gotten to know the family much better and liked them very much. To see any friend grieve is difficult, and they were all obviously grieving deeply. The boys were dry-eyed, but their eyes were red-rimmed. The girls were absolutely bereft. Mrs. Daley was so strong, saying, "How kind of you to come," and sincere. She had her family in shape for that. Those boys stayed in that church until seven the next morning, through the night. Do you know what tough duty that is? That's a mother who is giving stiffness to the spines of her children. A mother never asks more than can be delivered, and she knew how much they could give. She asked it and they gave it, and I am sure, willingly. I don't think you could ask any human being to do that and be sure they would come through. I guess I am very impressed with her in that way. I suggested to Rich [Daley], who is now the ward committeeman, that his mother ought to be the alderman for the 11th ward. She would be terrific, because she is a very straight and honorable woman.

As long as we are on the subject of women, Marilou, how do you see the future role of women in the Democratic Party in Chicago?

Speaking from the truth of how I came in, I can say that nothing was easier than to break into the ranks of the Democratic Party in Chicago. The mayor was particularly interested in furthering women, and was very supportive of that. He really gave so much that he angered many of the ward committeemen, but it was within his domain to give, and he did. He named women to slate-making positions just arbitrarily, where men had been waiting and facing elections, and doing all the rest of it. I think that the party is open, but there aren't many women out there who want to stand up and run. That's the problem. There just aren't the women. Women are going to have to volunteer. There is no reason why a woman can't run and be a ward committeeman. But first they are going to have to say that they want the job. It's a very hard job. It's easy to be appointed. It's not easy to be elected. Women traditionally have chosen more appointive roles (at least my generation and older) because they were not trained to be the assertive way that you have to be in electoral politics. Little boys are taught team games from the time they are three. Women weren't, although I guess now they are. When I was in the city council, fifty percent of the aldermen there had served less than five years. I bet if you did a screening of ward committeemen, you would find seventy percent had been there less than five years. It's not a case of the same old faces all the time. Those faces change. Winning an election is a matter of orientation. Any woman who wants to organize can get herself elected.

How do you foresee the future of politics in Chicago, particularly the independent movement in Chicago?

Let me take the easy part first, which is the independents. They have fallen into so much bickering between themselves and they really have no mutual loyalties. There is an awful lot of individual star effort, and that is going to fail. They are going to have to learn to cooperate. Politics is the art of compromise. You have to learn that you cannot be selfish. You cannot be greedy. Or, there is the Dick Simpson experience, which is sort of an academic approach. I keep having the feeling that everything he does is a chapter for his next book.

In politics, I guess you have to get into what a city is. A city is a port of entry for the poor; a city is a collection of primarily poor people. It was that way in Rome, in Athens, in Paris, in London, and in every traditional city. People come to the city because there is cheaper lodging, unskilled jobs available, whatever. The first avenue people see as a way out, generally, and the first one that every minority group or poverty group tackles, is politics, because it is the easiest. There are written rules and you know how to proceed, and it is a question of votes. It is a lot easier for a Polish man to succeed in the political arena than it is to succeed within the corporate hierarchy of IBM. The same is true if you look at the politics of this city. I am sure, in great part, it's, "Where's mine?" That's the politics of the world. Everybody wants more of whatever it is, for them. And you somehow have to get a compromise out of that.

I guess that reflects on the independent movement. The independent movement is primarily white, it is really upper middle class, and it has an intellectual understanding, but it doesn't have too much real sympathy for what poverty means, or what not having any of it means. The best analogy I can give is busing, as far as racial integration in schools is concerned. That same liberal upper middle class is very supportive of busing. Their children go to private schools or they live in the suburbs, like the federal judge who handed down the busing decree in Boston. When asked, "Why is your child in private school?" he said, "When I am on the bench I am a judge, but when I am at home I am a father." That kind of dichotomy is a wonderful luxury of economic discretion. But, if you don't have that kind of discretion, you are going to react more violently and move with your feet.

I don't think "Where's mine" is necessarily bad, because what I find in the 48th ward (which has got a little bit of everything), "Where's mine?" meant you should hear from mothers, you should hear from parents, you should hear from people who have some real needs and problems. You don't have to hear from the zoning lawyers or the real estate appraisers. But, "Where's mine?" means (I don't care whether you are on welfare or on social security) a safe neighborhood, a physically attractive neighborhood, good schools, clean parks. The basic needs are the same, regardless of income. "Where's mine?" is okay if you translate it right, and if you can reassure people that everybody is getting a fair shake.

That's good politics. That's also Mayor Daley's legacy, if you look at the city as a whole. The mayor looked at the city as a whole and made sure that everybody did get some. The mayor is always regarded as having been a terrible provincial or segregationist or something like that. But I don't know of any single government executive who gave more to more minority groups. If you go through City Hall, there are more blacks working in City Hall than there are in any non-black-owned firm in private business. If you go through any of the departments you see that. There is a Latino movement—it's absorbed. More is given to whatever the population is. The blacks are just about through being the minority group. It is the Latino population, and it is going to be the same problem.

The mayor was not afraid to share, and that's very important. Politicians, generally, are paranoid and are reluctant because they have to count on votes, and they are so frequently afraid for such puny reasons. They are afraid to share because they think it will not do them any good. The mayor was very different. He really understood what love does—the more you give, the more you have to give. He was a very expansive man. As I listened to the priest who gave his eulogy at his funeral mass, the man's speech was on love, and it was absolutely accurate. That's a word most of us are loath to use, and I am uncomfortable with it, because I see myself as a rational person, not as an emotional person. Mayor Daley really did love people, and, as such, he shared whatever there was.

ELOISE BARDEN *Black. Elected to the city council from the South Side 16th ward as an organization candidate, beating the first black woman alderman elected as a reform candidate. Was a precinct captain for a number of years and a community activist before that.*

I was born in Georgia in 1927. I came to Chicago as a young girl, graduated from Englewood High School, took a course in business administration at Kennedy-King College, worked as a receptionist, married my husband in 1948, and raised three children. I have been a community worker for thirty-six years. I have never been out of Englewood.

I met Representative James Taylor when I was asking for food for the needy in this area in 1968. He was a precinct captain and he gave me some help. In the early 1970s, I was looking for a place to get Christmas baskets for the needy. Representative Taylor gave me a check for $500 for the needy. I began to work in the organization, was appointed a precinct captain, and went from a precinct captain to committeewoman for the 16th ward and president of the women's auxiliary. No pay was involved in these jobs.

I'm still a precinct captain, although I am an assistant to Eddie Torrence, who has taken my place. On election day you'll find me in my own polling place, talking to the voters that come in which are residents of my area. I have been a precinct captain for about seven years. My precinct has 629 voters, which is 100 percent total registered. In a general election, they come out something like 85 percent. In the last election, it was approximately 22 Republican votes and we had something like 425 for Carter.

How do you get results like that in a precinct?
You have to be an everyday person. I'm there with the people every day, and I talk with them. When I see some of the residents coming from the store and they are carrying a bag, I stop and pick them up. Whatever I can do that they need me, they don't fail to call me, even on Sunday mornings. I get calls when I am going to church.

I am always there to help my neighbor, and, in turn, when an election comes up, they are with me.

We see that their streets are clean and the trees are trimmed. I've had new curbs put in there. Whenever there is a death come in that block, we are there with a donation to that family, and that comes from my block. That goes for that entire precinct. Whenever a family has to go away, when something has happened out of town, we go in, get a small collection to help this family in the emergency that has happened. I think this brings a closer reality to being closer to your neighbor.

Why were you selected as an aldermanic candidate in 1975?
I think from the work that I had did in the community, and from being a Christian. I believe wholeheartedly in prayer and I think that played a great part with me being elected as an alderman. When Representative Taylor was talking about whom they were going to run as the next alderman of the 16th ward, I had no idea that it would be me. I knew that I had a close relation with the community, but I didn't have no ties with the political ideas. When I was nominated, I said to the precinct captains that nominated me that I couldn't accept it, but I would go home and talk it over with my husband, and I would let them know in a couple of days. Not only did I talk it over with my husband (he told me that whatever I wanted in life that I should go forward with it), I also talked it over with my pastor and several more ministers in this area. They told me that the churches was 100 percent with me, and that I could campaign and speak in their 11 o'clock morning services. I knew that I was taking a great step. I am a Capricorn and I want to be a winner. I didn't want to say that I would take this nomination and didn't know that I had the churches with me and the communities in the 16th ward. That's why I went to the ministers of the area. Then I come back to Representative Taylor and the precinct captains of the 16th ward, and told them that I would run.

You had to take on Alderman Anna Langford, who was the first independent black woman alderman ever elected to the city council of Chicago, and you beat her. Can you tell me about that campaign?
We were debating at various churches and schools on Sunday mornings. She would speak and I would speak at the same place. I just had a desire that I was going to win. I would speak from my heart, and I would try to relate to the people what I thought that I would

be able to do for this area. My opponent had had some trouble in the city council, as far as the late Mayor Richard J. Daley was concerned, and, in the city council, you must be closer with the department heads down there to get some of the things that you want. The former alderwoman hadn't been close with the department heads. I knew that if I won, I would go in there and try to work with the department heads to get some of the things that I wanted for the 16th ward, which she hadn't did in the four years. These were some of the campaign platforms that I was bringing to the people. I beat her two to one.

What is it like to be an alderwoman in the city council?
It is quite exciting to be a freshman alderman. My colleagues who had been there for years made me feel at home and directed me. When you are in there as a new alderman, you are lost. They let me know where all the committee rooms were, the washroom, where the various department heads were, who you would be seeing, and do whatever they could do to enlighten me as a freshman alderman. This was very inspiring because it is real terrible when you go in there, but being with friends helps you out quite a bit. The city council don't meet but twice a month, but we are on various committees that hold meetings every so often.

Chicago has a billion-dollar budget. You look it over, and a lot of times, it don't apply to your ward, the things that you are voting on. But you say to yourself, "Next time, maybe it will." So you vote for a lot of things that don't apply to your ward, and then when something do come up for your ward, you're glad that you are able to vote "yes" on it.

We hold meetings here quite often with the residents in this area, and we let them know what's coming up. Sometimes I get a feedback from them how I should vote in the city council. As, for one example, on the ERA, I didn't know which way I should vote. So I did a raffle-poll contest with the womens and I found out that in my area that a lot of the women wasn't for it, so I voted "no" because it would bring a lot of things into law that a lot of us womens wouldn't be able to accept. Going to jail, there would be no separation between womens and the men. In the washroom, you would remove the sign off the door and say, "Washroom"!

Mostly, I am on the conservative side. I don't believe in what we call "women's lib." I am not like the average element. I have never had to actually get out and work as some other women have, catching

the bus early in the morning. I have been fortunate that I didn't have
to work. I was at home and reared my children. Most of the women
are head of the household and they do have to get out and make a
living.

What kinds of demands are made on you by your constituents?
Getting rezoned, various areas in the 16th ward. Stop signs, stop
lights, debris, curbs, sewers cleaned, various violations that have
come upon some of the homes, and I don't think the qualification on
it is correct. I look into it and go before the zoning board of appeals
with my constituents to see that they get a right share of what they
are supposed to. On sewers and curbs, I work with the department
on that. I talk to the commissioners about what's going on in my
ward. Department heads work very closely with me to get some of
the things done. If you will walk through the 16th ward with me one
day, you would find that I don't have too many trees that are overlap-
ping in the street that haven't been taken care of. When I started as
alderman in 1975, I had 1,100 abandoned buildings. Today it is 942.
Slowly, but surely, we are getting them down.
Let me speak on one thing, about property here. If my people find
that there is a zoning being changed, or there is a McDonald coming
in the community, they will call me and ask me what is my thoughts
on it and how did I vote on it. I will ask my constituents how they
are involved in it, is it next door to their property, or what have you.
If it is next door to one of my voters, or several in the community that
they're against it, I don't vote for it. Englewood is a very poor community. But it is a very proud community. We don't have quite a bit
out here as other wards have, but the people out here has been here
for years and they are just proud of what they have. I am a part of
it and I could have moved away years ago, but I decided to stay here
with the people that I grew up with, and this is where I am today.
I am striving to see in Englewood what you call a multi-service
center to be built in the center of the 16th ward, a mini-City Hall that
the residents could come to and wouldn't have to go downtown to
pay a gas bill, or light bill, or pay your taxes, or what have you. I would
like to see new development, new housing. Counseling is one of the
things we need in Englewood. Go and shape the people's minds. We
need a parent and child center out here very bad. If they could help
us reach this goal, Englewood would be on the map again, because
as a girl, it was a beautiful community to me.

How do you see the future of black/white relationships in Chi-cago?

You are going to have to judge a person by the work he does. And you are not going to have to have that race thing there. You are going to have to work closer. Because on a huge basis, you are judged by whoever you are. You are going to have to forget this race thing and judge the person by what he can do. The only thing about that is understanding. Understanding, and, believe me, prayer.

I found Mayor Daley to be a Christian man, and he found me to be a Christian woman, because he would always hear me saying, "Amen," whenever we would have prayer in the city council. He would watch and look up at me and smile, and he would address me as "the church-going lady," because I never stood up to address the council without thanking God in some kind of way. I think that let him know what category I was in. He let me know that he was a Christian man. He said, "Alderman, believe me, it takes prayer all the time." I know, for myself, not only does it take prayer, it takes ingenuity and understanding, and hard work, along with prayer. You just can't pray and expect the thing to come to you, because it does-n't. But it takes all that to make up whatever you want to be in life.

Do you have any further political ambitions?

Maybe as congresswoman. You got to get more women in the Congress, and, if it is the Lord's will, and He worked everything else out for me, so who knows? I might go further. But right now, I'm just satisfied being an alderwoman of the 16th ward.

Politics is a job that you get involved in. It's helping the area you live in. I got into this job by being a community person. I think I am an alderwoman by being a community woman. That's the way I feel. I don't base my life on just a politician's life. I would say that it should be a person that is involved with what is coming in years to come. What you have now, you should always seek improvement for better. Represent the area that you have been elected to do for. The alder-man is called the housekeeper of the community. This is what I have been trying to do the two years that I have been in this seat, to be a housekeeper for the ward that I represent. I vote on various budg-ets and things that come through the city council and those are great things to do. But my most concern is getting things for the 16th ward.

I make $17,500 a year. Most of my money goes for helping the needy. I sit in here on a Friday night and people come in to see me —it's five dollars here, and ten dollars here out of my pocket, because when I interview some of the people, they say that they didn't have no money to get over here and that they have to borrow money to get back home. The unemployment compensation checks haven't arrived in time. I am just a softie for things like that. At Christmas-time, I spent over $600 for candy and nuts and small toys for the needy children. But I just thank God that He give it to me to give back to the constituents that love me so much that they went out and voted for me. It just makes me grateful.

I sit here behind this desk and I think about how I came about this job. I have the voters and the residents in the area coming in to see me, but I never make a promise that I can't fulfill. I'm not like the politician who sits behind the desk and says they're going to do this and they are going to do that, and don't end up getting anything did for the people, but make a promise. When I tell a constituent some-thing, if I have to wait six months, I'm going to get it fulfilled, because I promised that I would do that. I tell them, if they come in here and ask for something, I will look into that problem and I will relate back to them what happened. I don't think no one in life should promise a person something that they can't fulfill. And that's good politics.

IRENE HERNANDEZ   *Mexican. Holds the highest position any Latin holds in Chicago, as a Cook County Commissioner. Was a precinct captain, patronage employee, and community worker before that.*

I was born in Taylor, Texas and came to Chicago in 1927.
I got involved in politics in 1943, when I became a judge of elections.
I wasn't working. I was raising a family. I liked to talk to people, so
I helped the precinct captain. I was a judge of elections for ten years.
In 1954, we moved from Harrison and Morgan to where we live now
in Logan Square. My children were going to school when my husband's place of business folded up. I said to him that I have to go out
and help him. He said, "What are you going to do?" I said, "We help
our precinct captain. I am going to talk to him. Maybe I can get into
a government agency." (I used to be a Spanish/English stenographer
for export departments before I stopped working.) I went to work for
Sid Olsen, who was my committeeman, and was also the clerk of the
criminal court. Naturally, when I started to work, I started to do some
canvassing, and my committeeman appointed me as precinct captain. My husband had a job in real estate, and used to do all the work.
You know, when you are home for eighteen years, women have two
kinds of dresses, either the dress she wears to go out, or housedresses.
I started to buy clothes to wear to work and I liked it. I was only going
to work for one year (famous last words).

I went to work in the state's attorney's office from 1961 until 1967.
In 1964, I told my husband, "I'm going to quit this summer. I'm going
to buy myself a second-hand car with the money that I have in the
old age pension, and I am going to go out and visit my friends and
have lunch with them, which I haven't done for many years." I told
him that in January and in March 1964 I lost him. I had five children
in school (I have seven children, by the way), so, instead of quitting
work, I kept going. In 1967 I went to work for Judge David Cerda
as a personal bailiff.

Meanwhile, I started joining different organizations. I was active in all the Democratic campaigns. My children and I volunteered for every campaign that we could get into. In 1974, a dear friend of mine, Lillian Piotrowski, who was a county commissioner, passed away. A committee got together of Spanish-speaking people to see what the possibilities were of having a Spanish-speaking person to replace her. Lillian had two jobs. She was committeeman of the 22nd ward, and she was also county commissioner. The position of committeeman belonged to the 22nd ward. The position of commissioner did not belong to the 22nd ward. That could belong to anyone. They looked at the county board membership and they felt that all the other ethnic groups were represented on the board, but not the Spanish-speaking. They decided to back me. Eleven of us candidates went before the slatemaking committee and I was appointed to fill out her term.

The one that saw the need for the Spanish-speaking people to have representation was Mayor Daley. He also wanted to have women involved more. People will come out to vote, but the Spanish-speaking is just like every other vote. When Spanish-speaking people saw Hernandez there, a Valasquez there, this motivated them, because they could identify with someone there on the slate. And this means a lot.

Approximately how many Spanish-speaking people do you think there are in Chicago now?

As a guess, I would say about a million people, not registered votes, but about a million people. We have been trying to put four groups together. We have about 500,000 Mexican-Americans, and more or less the same amount of Puerto Ricans. We have quite a few Cubans and we have a lot of South Americans. We have our differences of opinion, but when the chips are down, we're all there. The Spanish-speaking people are becoming very sophisticated in the way of voting. They study the issues, listen to the radio, look at television, and read the newspapers.

What kind of problems have the Spanish-speaking immigrants encountered coming to this city and settling here?

The language barrier is a problem at the beginning, but then they encounter employment problems, education problems, housing problems. The majority of the people, outside of the Cubans, come here because of economic reasons, to find a better job. I can speak more for the Mexicans than I can for any other ethnic group because

these are the ones that I deal with. The majority of them come from
Mexico because they have no way of employment in Mexico. The
relatives come. They say, "Come to Chicago. Come to the United
States. You see gold all over."

How well has the city government dealt with the problems that the
Spanish-speaking encounter in a city like this?

It's been kind of slow, and I can't tell you the reason for it. The
public schools have helped. We have now the bilingual program. The
children that do not speak a word of English should be helped. I am
for everyone that comes to this country to learn the English language. But the Spanish-speaking are trying to adjust to this culture
and to our ways, and do not forget their culture, which I think is very
important. I would say that 75 percent come with the intention of
staying. Maybe the rest don't come with the intention of staying
because they have ties back in Mexico. But eventually they stay,
because they see the opportunity they have here, more so than back
home.

What about the problem of the illegals?

That's a very touchy subject. It is very important. Countless people
come here to my office with all sorts of problems not belonging to this
office. Being fortunate to have worked in different government agencies, we're able to guide them to the right place where they can help.
Our duty is to our citizens here, not to the illegals. But my heart goes
out to the illegal aliens because I know they would not come here
(and I am not talking only about Mexicans; I am talking about even
those who come from Europe), they would not leave their country
where they are born and raised and have family ties, if it wasn't for
economic conditions. This is why they come.

The Cuban people are different. They did not come for economic
reasons. They came because they were fighting communism. The
Cubans that have come here are professionals. Therefore, their battle has been won already, while the Mexicans were not the educated
kind, so they had a bigger battle to fight.

These illegal aliens have come here (and I am not for someone to
take a job away from someone that is here already), they find themselves a job. They're afraid that they are going to be caught, so they
behave themselves, they work, they stay home. Of course, there are
exceptions to the rule. But they contribute. It is a very important
question, and sometimes I say my heart doesn't go with my head

thinking, but I feel very sorry for them, and I also acknowledge the fact that their being here raises some tension. I know that problems have been created. But the majority are good people. They do not cause any problems. That doesn't mean that they have a license to stay here. I'm not saying that. But I hope, very sincerely, that we will be able to iron out that problem.

How do you see the future of the Latin political community in Chicago developing?

If you had asked me that two months ago, before December 20th, 1976, the day Mayor Daley died, I would have told you, "Very positive." I still see it positive. We have encouraged very many people to register. We have a young group of Spanish-speaking boys and girls who have really worked their heads off in registering people, and I believe that we are going to get to the point where we can say that we have 250,000 registered voters, Spanish-speaking people. The vote is the voice.

Spanish-speaking people have to really be organized, not only from the voting end of it, but the financial end of it. It takes money, it takes votes, and it takes organization. We're getting there, but it's going to take ourselves to do it. The rest of the groups, the Polish people, the Jewish people did it, and we have to do it ourselves.

Some people foresee a political coalition in Chicago between the Spanish-speaking and the blacks. How do you view that?

I don't see that. I don't mean that we're not going to work with the blacks, but I think that we are going to stand on our own two feet. I don't think that we have different interests. I think that we are all working toward the same goals. But the blacks and the Polish people went through that already. We want to get there on our own. We will cooperate with any group.

The majority of Spanish-speaking people are Democrats. My mother used to tell me that the Democratic Party is for the working people and we are working people. Sometimes we get a little frustrated in regard to a problem or a program. White and black, and where is the color brown? We come from a different mixture. My grandfather came from Spain, my grandmother was mostly Mexican–Indian, my great grandfather came from Germany. But we're waking up. I heard a newscaster discussing, when the mayor passed away, that the Spanish-speaking people did not have much political power. However, big corporations like Illinois Bell Telephone Company, and the Chicago Transit Authority, put their sign directions in Spanish and English. There is some power there, there is some recognition. We're not the largest, but we are the fastest growing community. We want to have our own identity. Not that we will not work with any other group. We will. Anytime that you could prove to me that you are working for the betterment of the community, I don't care what color you are, I'll work with you. Even if I don't agree completely with you or with the issues, I will try to meet you halfway. But we want to prove ourselves. You don't keep your own culture, but you don't forget where you came from. I'll never forget Mayor Daley. I've been to swearing-ins of different people, and he always used to tell them, "Never forget where you came from," and he meant here and there.

You've been in politics now much of your adult life, Irene. What is politics like for someone like you?

To me it means serving my community. That's exactly what it means. The bad thing that I find is the misunderstanding. Sometimes you do something to the best of your judgment, and they misunderstand and take it wrong. Politics is a very tough game. When you are in political life, you are a so-called leader. Maybe, because I am a woman, I have found it difficult with the Latino men. Latino men are still very much chauvinistic macho. The fact that I am a woman and that I happen to be the highest elective legislative official, Latino men resent that, not me personally, but because of the position I have. But if you work hard enough, the majority of the community will respect you, will recognize it. And I have no further ambition, except to work for my community.

SEVEN

The View from
the Suburbs

JAMES KIRIE / NICHOLAS BLASE /
LYNN WILLIAMS

JAMES KIRIE *Greek. About sixty-five years old. Committee-man of west suburban Leyden Township. Vice-president of sanitary district board of trustees. Is also a successful businessman. Has dealt in real estate and owns a restaurant. Is an organization supporter, but differs frequently with its policies.*

I was born here in River Grove. My mother and father were both Greek immigrants who came to this country and settled in River Grove. I graduated from the River Grove Grammar School and I also attended the Socrates Greek School. Between the confusion of the Greek and the English, it was almost a mental impossibility for me either to comprehend and understand what I was reading, English or Greek, so I became a dropout in high school, but I finally graduated from Leyden Community High School. I went to Central YMCA College, Elmhurst College, and John Marshall Law School. I was elected township clerk at the age of twenty, and had to wait until I was twenty-one to take office.

I was elected committeeman of Leyden township in 1961, and have held that position now for sixteen years. I was in the legislature for six years and later on came over here to the Metropolitan Sanitary District as a trustee.

I got into politics accidentally, because I needed a job to go to college. But when people go into politics, they get bitten with an ego bug, and the egotism completely encloses your life. I have tried to psychoanalyze myself to find out why I would put up with politics and with people, and I think it is egotism. You enjoy people coming to you and asking you for favors, and your being able to try to help them, like the priest or the rabbi. People come to you and they say, "Can you help me?" If you can, you feel that you fulfilled your job.

It takes a tremendous amount of your life away from you, your personal life with your family. You become extremely cautious of what you say to people, even with your own wife or children, because they might repeat it. This makes you a more secretive, cautious man, and it inhibits you because you cannot trust anyone in politics. Ninety percent of the people you are dealing with, you have to be very cautious with. They are going to use you, and, if you are a good politician, you will help all the people you possibly can, but expect nothing in return. This is humanity. The human being is so constructed that he can justify anything that he wants to as long as he finds justification to salve his conscience. You can help a man or a woman continuously, and all of a sudden, something better comes along, and he'll drop you. It has happened to me time and time again. You must not get bitter at these people, because, if you do, you are going to destroy yourself. And you cannot put the onus on people because they don't have the capacity to do what you want them to do.

I have stayed in politics to a complete detriment to myself financially. I enjoy being busy at it. I am down here at the sanitary district at 7 o'clock in the morning most of the time. I enjoy what I do, and I enjoy politics. I don't consider myself a public politician. I have been in business all my life—restaurants, home building, industrial building. When I went to the legislature, I lost $380,000 in six years, and it cost me my restaurant, as a public service, because I wasn't there to watch it. The help was carrying it out the back door and the front door as fast as it was brought in.

Most people figure that all politicians are crooks. The truth of the matter is that the people are crooks themselves. A workman is stealing tools, hammer, nails; an office girl is taking pencils, fountain pens, paper clips home, stealing on the boss by going for thirty-minute coffee breaks instead of taking her ten minutes. This is all stealing, and this is true of all people. The honest housewife who goes to the grocery store, the kleptomaniac; the honest bankers who will take your eye teeth out; the real estate men; the union agents. You name them. Newspaper people are notorious. If I had a boy, I would be very cautious about even letting him join the boy scouts, because of some of the characters who are boy scout leaders. And, still, everything is focused on the politician. But you can't condemn the entire world on account of it. You set your own standards. You take nothing from no one, because you have to have an accountability to yourself and your family.

What was it like, being in the legislature?
It was the greatest experience of my life. I went down there as a blue ribbon candidate. Ninety percent of the men who went there were the most unusual men that I have ever met anywhere in one room in my life. No corporation could have hired all these men and

paid them the salary they were worth. Ninety percent of these men were absolutely honest. Sure, there was the ten percent who weren't. That's a small minority. I sat on the appropriations committee. It was a great experience for me, listening to testimony from every walk of life—lobbyists, pressure groups, schoolteacher groups, nurses, unions, mental health groups, retarded children's groups, the Catholic Church, the Lutheran Church—all good people who were exploiting the state. All fine people, mind you, but they were all there with their hands in the pocketbook of the legislature, and you had to sit back and listen to it. But I had a choice of going broke or staying in the legislature, so I came back here and Mayor Daley slated me for the sanitary district. I was very much involved in pollution control in the legislature. I thought that I would like to get into something where I could make a contribution to our society and asked to be slated for this.

The sanitary district is a huge octopus, and it is frustrating because it's a bureaucracy personified. All civil service. If any corporation or business operated in the same vein that you do in civil service, it has to fail. Civil service is one of the greatest curses that has ever been perpetrated and sold to the public. I don't believe that people should be fired when a change in the administration has taken place, because you need people with knowledge to run the agency. But I think it should be based on merit and merit only, and if a man isn't doing his job, you should be able to remove him.

Is that generally true of most governmental agencies?
Yes. As soon as it gets so big, it's just untenable. There is no way that you can make it function properly. There aren't enough checks and balances. The Metropolitan Sanitary District will have an $800,-000,000 budget this year, and we will be spending another $600,-000,000 for construction. So we are now in excess of a billion dollars. You have nine trustees here, and there is no way that they can function the way we are politically structured, because the legislature has tied the hands of the commissioners here. The superintendent runs the day-to-day operation. The only thing we can do is to pay the bills or reject them; approve contracts or reject them; and they don't pay enough money over here in the higher echelon to attract the type of caliber that should be here. A corporation that is spending the kind of money that we're spending would be paying their commissioners $60,000 to $70,000 a year. The president would be paid a bonus of $70,000 to $80,000 a year. But here, it is $25,000 a year.

I am the head of the purchasing department and finance department. I'm getting the huge salary of $27,500 now. Up until now, I was getting $15,000. Every month I had a deficit for the six years I have been here. There is no way that I can live on $15,000, and if it wasn't for outside income that I have been able to generate throughout my life, I would have had to ask for food stamps.

Could you evaluate Mayor Daley for me?
Mayor Daley had the capacity of being able to take the labor tycoons, the so-called honest real estate combines, the pillars of our society, the Chamber of Commerce of Chicago, the extremely astute banking industry who sell the bonds of the city of Chicago and the Metropolitan Sanitary District, and the honest contractors who work together and take turns on who is going to get the next contract, and weld this honest group together, the pillars of our society, so that everybody got a piece of the pie. And then some trickled down to the ward committeemen, the aldermen, the precinct captains, and the good citizen of the community who wants his sidewalk for nothing, his garbage hauled for nothing, new curbs for nothing, lovely street lights for nothing, all the good things for nothing. This way, he was able to keep a city together. He was able to take the Poles and work them against the Greeks, the Greeks against the Italians, and the Italians against the blacks. Daley was a master at keeping all these factions divided and still working together, and the city functioned.

His weakness was that he surrounded himself with a very close-knit, uninformed group. He didn't want to hear any dissension or anybody who didn't agree with him or his clique. Forgive me for saying this, but anybody who can survive forty-five years in the suburbs must have a little bit of knowledge about politics, especially where the Republicans are always winning. At no time did he ever call me in and say, "Jim, how did you manage to stay in at the top of the heap all these years? What is the secret? What could you advise us?" If you went in there and said something, he wouldn't listen to you. He precluded the people who offered any dissension. And he had no more conception about how the suburbs operated than I have on how the League of Nations operated under Woodrow Wilson.

If you are a Democratic suburban committeeman in Cook County, you are like an ambassador without portfolio. They change the numbers on City Hall when they invite us down there so that we can't find the various offices. (That is being facetious.) If most of the ward committeemen in Chicago had to come to the suburbs and operate, they couldn't even get a job as a water collector out here. They're more sophisticated in the suburbs. They make Chicago politicians look like second raters. If you move into the Village of Elmwood Park, the first thing, a man would be at your home and would say to you, "Mr. Rakove, I represent the mayor of Elmwood Park. He asked me to come and extend his greetings to you. I would like to know if you would like to know a little about our politics out here. We don't operate like Chicago does. We are nonpartisan out here. We run on a nonpartisan ticket. We don't have any precinct captains. You are part of our group."

If you happen to be working on LaSalle Street, they will ask you if you will come to the Village Hall and meet the mayor on a given night, and after you meet the mayor (first time you ever met a mayor in your life), he will listen to you, you will tell him what you do, and he will say, "We'd like to put you on the mayor's staff." So they will give you a gold star. Now, you become a member of the mayor's staff. This will help you get passes, in case you get a ticket, and gives you prestige. If you happen to be a truck driver, they will put you on civil defense. They'll give you a little star. If you happen to be a Joe Doak, they'll put you on the fire department auxiliary and give you a little star. Before you know it the whole community has stars and you are somebody. It's the first time in your life that you have ever had any prestige. They'll put you on a commission of some sort. You finally arrived. Election time comes. There is no way that you are going to beat this mayor. He has it all tied up.

In a small town like Elmwood Park, there has to be approximately three hundred jobs. Three hundred jobs in thirty-one precincts is a lot of jobs. These are full-time jobs, not part-time jobs. I am not talking about the fellow who comes over and puts a cross on your tree when you have elm disease and gets several hundred dollars a month for that, or the fellow who marks the sidewalk and says, "We're going to replace this sidewalk for you," or the fellow who comes and takes care of your sewers. They sweep your streets and do great things for you. You are very happy.

Our Democratic committeemen can't do any of these things in any of these villages. They are nonentities. And we don't even have any patronage to speak of, because we can't produce votes in the suburbs as a Democratic committeeman in a Republican area. For a committeeman such as myself to get elected, it has to be strictly on my own personality and my own money. You have to be a man who has some means of his own and is willing to spend it.

You can't provide any services for constituents. You have to go to the local mayors and ask them for help. I can't get anything out of Schiller Park if I need it. Elmwood Park, nothing. Franklin Park, yes. We turned that Democratic. Northlake, they operate in a vacuum. I have very few captains who are holding jobs. Mostly the workers are volunteers, and volunteers is not a proper way to run an organization. They won't stay with you. Volunteers might stay with you for one election because they have a bull to gore, or an ax to grind, or they have a candidate they want to work for, and they only want to work for him. There is no way you can put any pressure on him to get out and work for the entire ticket.

If that is true, how do you see the future of suburban Democratic politics in Cook County?

If the organization will put up candidates with good credentials and run them for mayors in these villages, and help them financially, they then can become viable in the community. They have to elect Democratic mayors where they can do favors for people. People want everything for nothing. And there is no such thing. It is reflected on your tax bill.

The biggest problem we have facing the suburbs is metropolitan government. The newspapers, in the next ten years, after the tax crunch gets big, will try to sell the public on the idea of consolidating their police, fire, and garbage departments, do away with the boundaries, and make it one big metropolitan government. I think it is wrong to take this power away from the people.

Do you foresee a future in which Democratic suburban committeemen will coalesce, get together and form an internal power bloc of their own within the organization?

No, because most of your committeemen in the suburbs are on a payroll somewhere where pressure can be applied to them. They better not move. They won't take a chance. Their bread and butter comes first. The ward committeeman in the city, where he can do favors and get the vote out, will still be the power base in the Democratic Party. I don't really believe you are going to see too much of a visible change. I think that, like you said in your other book, they are all going to stay there, and as long as they get a piece of the pie, they are all going to be happy. Just the characters are going to change. It will be the same scenario.

Have you any regrets about the whole thing, or, as the priest says to Skeffington in The Last Hurrah, *"Would you do it again?"*

If I had my life to do over again, and I was to weigh my life against being in politics or not being in politics, in spite of the price I have had to pay, I think I would do exactly what I did.

NICHOLAS BLASE *Greek. About sixty years old. Committeeman of Northwest suburban Maine Township. Is also mayor of the Village of Niles. Vocal critic of the Chicago machine's policies and of Daley. Is also a lawyer.*

I was born and raised in Bridgeport, went to St. Jerome's Grammar School, DeLaSalle High School, Notre Dame, and to law school there. We moved to the North Side of Chicago and I got married. After I had my first child I moved out to Niles.

When I came out to Niles, I was the only lawyer in the area, so the people asked me to organize a home owners' association, which I did. Then a reform ticket popped up and they asked me to run for mayor, and I won.

What's it like to be mayor of a suburban community like Niles?
The major part of the job is to instigate programs, do things that are different than someone else is doing. That is where I spend most of my time. But I think that the thing that gets you immediately is the immediacy of you to the people. Anybody can reach me on the phone here or at home any time they want to, and they do. As soon as a department does not react to their problem, they immediately call the mayor. If there's a flood, everybody that gets water in their basement calls you on the phone personally. If there is a problem with too many accidents at a corner, in walks ten people with a petition, "We want a stop sign on our corner." If some act of violence occurs in a neighborhood, the next day you can expect to have ten or fifteen people sitting in your office.

The average person that lives in the suburbs is tied up completely in his home and the thirty or forty feet north, west, or east of him, and his family. As long as you don't disturb that existence, he is perfectly at ease and doesn't bother anybody. Do anything to disturb that, he gets upset. Talk about community problems, about other people, doesn't rattle him at all, as long as he is not bothered. It is a very selfish kind of a thing, but that's life out here.

I've been committeeman now for about twelve years, five years after I became mayor. I tried to get involved in our local Democratic organization out here, but they wouldn't let me in because they were afraid that as mayor of a community, I would be too strong. I licked the organization because there was no organization.

Democratic committeemen in the suburbs are probably the most useless entities in existence. I could not visualize myself as a committeeman without being mayor. Being committeeman services the mayor stewardship, because I maintain an organization that helps me be elected mayor. If I wasn't mayor, I would not be committeeman, because there is just nothing to it. All you do is set up judges for election day and maintain polling places. The Democratic Party has done an injustice to suburbia by never putting any authority in, giving recognition to, or giving substance to the position of Democratic committeeman out here. Committeemen who are nothing but committeemen get nothing done, and nobody pays any attention to them.

You have to go back to Daley's attitude about the suburbs. Daley actually hated the suburbs. Daley could not understand how any man in his right mind could move out of Chicago to these crazy areas. Everytime you said "suburb" to him, he got red in the face. He never did anything to espouse the suburban cause or to encourage it in any way, and always kept it demeaned and down to the bare essentials. He always kept a couple of token committeemen from the suburbs on the leash, people that he had control over, but really never gave anything out here. You might get five or ten jobs, but most of the jobholders you had, you couldn't even use, because the level of the job was so low that that same person couldn't run around the neighborhood trying to convince his own neighbors that he was talking for the party.

Most people out here do not like to identify either Democratic or Republican. They consider themselves Independents, and don't want to be tied to any organization as workers. It eliminates the big percentage of the good able bodies, and we end up, frankly, with bodies, but not necessarily people that can do the selling job. It's a volunteer thing. It's very difficult to man all our precincts properly. We lose them every three or four months. They come in and see us before an election because half of them want jobs that we are never able to get. As soon as the election is over, they disappear. So we are stuck most of the time with a basic core of nice, well-meaning people, but, generally, not many of them are effective.

You've been on the Democratic Central Committee for twelve years now. Could you evaluate that body for me?

Under Daley, it was eighty people moving into a room once every two or three months, being called to a meeting about which they knew nothing and didn't care, because in the minds of probably seventy-five of them, they had no function to perform that day, except to do what the lord told them to do. At the right moment, everybody, except maybe a few, stood up and said "Yes," or "No," whatever they were supposed to say. It was a big waste of time.

I remember when I first became committeeman, I stood up one time and said something that I didn't think was too strong. Matt Danaher took off on a half-hour diatribe about what kind of a person am I to get up and question the judgment of the leader, blah, blah, blah. I didn't believe what I was hearing! Then, at the end of the diatribe, everybody claps. I said, "What am I, the enemy?" This went on constantly. If anybody spoke up and said something contrary to what the leader said, you were immediately an outcast and some kind of a nut.

I remember a couple of occasions I was put on the slatemaking committee. The mayor and the inside three or four did everything. Then the slatemaking committee, which was for the public, just rubber-stamped the whole thing. The slatemaking committee, which involved some ten or twelve people, would sit there and interview different people, and then all of a sudden the word would come back from the chairman of the committee suggesting that these are the people that we wanted. No one would ever question it. That group involved Daley, Dunne, Dan Rostenkowski, Tom Keane, basically. Within the last five years, Dunne and Rostenkowski fell out of grace. Keane, of course, had his problems. It ended up with Daley, John Touhy, and Daley's kids. And then I think Daley started to listen less and less to anybody.

Can you evaluate Daley for me as a politician?

Strong points: He led his own life in a kind of fashion where nobody could point a finger to it. That was always a very important thing in Chicago politics. Good family man, religious, etc. The combination of party chairman and mayor of Chicago meant he absolutely controlled all patronage. If you had to get any kind of a job anyplace, you had to go through him. He knew how to use that well. Toward the last ten years of his chairmanship, he had so put himself in the position of God that everybody respected him. He didn't have to say anything. He was on such a high pedestal that just wiggling his finger created the kind of movement that he wanted. That meant the kind of charisma that you can't describe. And, although he couldn't articulate well, he always seemed to get to the nub of a problem, and in whatever way he phrased it, he got to the point that he wanted to make, and made it and got off. He rarely said the wrong thing. His mind functioned very well, even though what the mind was doing inside wasn't coming out exactly the way he wanted it to come out.

Weak points: Stubbornness and an inflexibility to see anything other than what he knew. For instance, the idea that there could be no good life outside of Chicago was absolutely insane. But he firmly believed that. Once you became his enemy he never forgot. His inflexibility on positions. His attitude toward suburbs. And once he determined that this was this, or that was that, he was not subject to change.

How do you see the future of Democratic politics in Cook County now in the post-Daley era?

I think that what is happening now is just to keep stability so that whoever is going to be taking on the show can get in position and start working on it. The young guys are going to start to move around and get themselves in position. I see a lot more fighting. That probably will be a generally good thing for the party. I see the suburban guys getting considerably stronger, if we can get together. The suburban guys will see that we are not going to be getting much different action, and they are going to get more rebellious, and we are going to mean a lot more. Right now it is all façade, peace for two years, and then look out.

Why has the Democratic organization in Cook County lasted so long?

I think it is really habit. I look at it a lot like I do the Bohemians in Cicero. There is no reason in the world why all the Bohemians, Polish, or whatever in Cicero, are Republicans. The only reason they are Republicans is because through the course of time, the organization, the guy that lives on the block, the guy that works for the city, has taken care of the garbage, has taken care of this and that, so the average person who has been living in these neighborhoods for forty, fifty years is just so used to the idea of his precinct captain who works for the city taking care of his problems. That's the thing that has kept the organization going. If the guy living on the block ever starts to lose that patronage thing, we are going to lose this so-called strength. Strength is patronage and people being used to that service that they get from the precinct captain.

How do you see the evolution of suburban politics?

Patronage has never had much to do out here and it isn't going to. In suburban politics the job of committeeman is just trying to feed information into people who are independent, and they are going to make up their own minds. At certain levels, we can be effective, where people don't know who is running (in township government, or state representatives in some instances), but as soon as you get to the area where people are aware of the candidate by virtue of the media, we lose them. So we are becoming less important and less effective. All we can do is try to have people that will spread information, try to stay friendly, hope to influence five or ten votes a precinct.

I think it is going to get worse. The future is more independence and less importance of the two parties, unless we get ideologies again that we can identify with. But as long as we have none (and we have none right now), we are going to get weaker and weaker. Being a suburban committeeman is a useless, thankless job unless you can use it in some way.

Why do you do it? Why do you stay in politics?

One, by being a committeeman, I maintain an organization on a day-to-day basis that helps me as mayor of Niles. Every time I want to run, the organization is there. Two, there is a satisfaction to me to try to get more Democrats into different areas. We are now getting involved in local government in Des Plaines, Morton Grove, certain school boards, etc., so that although we are not able to influence a governor or a president, we are able to influence local government.

Politics is a game I play with people around me who work in the organization, and with people out there, that involves trying to inter-ject my will someplace along the line and cause things to happen that otherwise would not normally happen. Most people who seek public office have some kind of a problem—megalomania, inferiority complex, out to prove something. I don't find too many normal, stable people wanting to get into it. Most people come in here because they want a job. You find women getting into politics because they want to start fooling around a little bit. They're tired of the home life. I don't find too many straights coming in. Not that we are all perverts

or screwed up, but obviously there are other reasons for getting into
it than what should be the basic reason, because I want to help the
country, I want to help my party. We don't have that anymore. I
would never advise anybody to get into politics at the level I am in,
as a committeeman.

Do you have any higher political ambitions?
I have a fiefdom. I am very satisfied. My law practice, I do well at
that. The politics is working out here, so unless I had some spot that
really intrigued me (that's why I ran for Congress one time), I have
no interest in another position. I just am not that driven any more.
I think I have found my niche, and, at some point, I am either going
to be kicked out (which I have adjusted my thoughts to), or I'll walk
out.

LYNN WILLIAMS *White Protestant. Sixty-nine years old. Graduate of Yale and Harvard Law School. Wealthy, successful North Shore lawyer and businessman. Was vice-president of the University of Chicago and president of the Great Books Foundation. Ran for Congress in 1962; lost to Donald Rumsfeld. Was elected township committeeman of North Shore suburban New Trier Township in 1966. Has been a vocal critic and opponent of Daley and the Chicago machine as a member of the county central committee. Was an unsuccessful candidate for the Cook County Board in 1978.*

I was born in Evanston in 1909. My father was a successful patent lawyer. My mother was active in the women's suffrage movement. I went to North Shore Country Day School in Winnetka, to Yale, to Harvard Law School, and then took a year at MIT. I was vice-president of Stewart-Warner in Chicago at the age of thirty-two. I was the first president of the Great Books Foundation, and became vice-president of the University of Chicago in 1948. In 1951, I went into the private practice of law. I began to make some inventions in electrical and metal working processes, gradually discontinued the practice of law, and have engaged in other business activities.

What got a man like you into politics?
I was moved by the assassination of President Kennedy, and in 1964, I ran for Congress against Don Rumsfeld. During the campaign I saw the weaknesses and the inappropriateness of the Democratic organization in the townships. I'd go to meetings and there was a retinue of speakers. Coroner Toman would get on and say, "I think it's important to the people of this community that the coroner should be a medical doctor, which I am. Otherwise how would they know whether the victim died of an illiatic spasm or whether he had a lumbar dislocation? If he didn't know those things, how could he write his report? I know those things, and my opponent is a dentist." Then Joe McDonough, who was running for Clerk of the Circuit Court, would come on and say, "I'm not here because I am a candidate. I

Annual softball game between mayor's staff and city council: Daley throwing out first pitch *(photo by Chicago Fire Department)*

The city council softball team. Left to right, top row: Aldermen Kenner, Sawyer, Bilandic, Washington, Singer, Laskowski; Bob Buchanan (Finance Committee staff); Aldermen Kwak, Vrdolyak, Stone, Barnett, Burke, Cohen. Front row: Aldermen Wilinski, Pucinski, Frost, Hedlund, Adducci, Roti, Langford, Cousins; Mike Coletta (sergeant-at-arms)

Alderman Eloise Barden, attending a neighborhood meeting at
Paul Robeson High School

Alderman Marilou Hedlund and her family with Mayor Daley

Left to right: Alex Granakis, Trini Lopez, Commissioner Irene Hernandez, Mayor Daley

Mayoral Candidate Jane Byrne, campaigning *(photo by Martha Leonard)*

Trustee James Kirie displays giant pumpkins grown with Sanitary District sludge

Nicholas Blase, Mayor of Niles

Lynn Williams, New Trier Township Democratic Committeeman *(photo by Stuart-Rodgers Photographers)*

John Waner *(photo by Sylvester Szymczak)*

Richard Friedman, campaigning

Timothy Sheehan and Robert Merriam in 1959

Benjamin Adamowski, at podium; John Hoellen, seated

Senator and Mrs. Adlai Stevenson III, with Mayor Daley *(photo by Associated Press)*

State Supreme Court Justice William G. Clark

Congressman Abner Mikva

Illinois Appellate Court Justice Seymour Simon *(photo by Lawrence-Phillip Studio)*

Alderman William Singer, donating blood

Former Governor Dan Walker

Alderman Dick Simpson resisting attempts to reseat him, per Mayor Daley's order, during a city council meeting

Michael A. Bilandic, Richard J. Daley

come here because of an obligation to you, to thank you for putting me in the post where I've had the opportunity to preside over the installation of the largest and finest court system in the world. When I came to that job, I had to employ 3,300 people, and I had to depend on people like you to send to me good-quality workers. Now the court system will be expanded from 3,300 to 4,300. I will need 1,000 new workers and I will turn to you and your outstanding committeeman to send me people who you can select so much better than I."

Well, this brought cheers. "There's going to be a thousand new jobs, and McDonough is going to seek the advice and help of the committeeman to find people to fill them." He'd bring down the house. When he got through, I'd have to stand up and talk to these people about national problems and national issues. And, if it weren't for the fact that it was such a novelty talk, I couldn't have held their interest at all.

I had an experience that stuck in my mind. I received a telephone call from a woman who said she was interested in my campaign and in beating Goldwater. She was anxious to help. She lived in Wheeling. "That's a very fortunate thing," I said, "because, tomorrow night, there is a meeting of the Wheeling Democrats, and I'm sure, if you come to the meeting, they will put you to work." She had a friend and could she bring her? So these two ladies showed up and stood in the back of the room in the storefront office of the Democratic organization. The committeeman, Jim Stavros, who later went to jail, said, "Now, you guys, we've got a registration day coming up, and this time I want you guys in the precinct. I know you get a day off from work, and you're not getting a day off from work so that you can stay home and play. You're getting a day off so you can be in the precincts. The last time a lot of you weren't in the precincts, but this time you gotta be in the precincts, and this time, goddammit, you bastards, you gotta be sober." This is what the ladies heard, and when they came forward to see the committeeman (here are two ladies who want to help), his jaw dropped open. He had no idea of what in the world to do with them, didn't want them. This experience was somewhat similar in other places. So, in 1966, I ran for committeeman in New Trier Township and beat the organization candidate.

You've been a committeeman now for twelve years. Could you describe the operation of the Democratic county central committee?

The principal task of the committee is to slate candidates. The form of an election is preserved. The committeemen vote, but there is no substance to it at all. The candidate would come forward and make a speech, and answer some very perfunctory questions. Usually, there are two questions. One, "If you were not to be slated for the office you seek, would you accept slating for any other office?" And the right kind of a guy would be expected to say, "I'm a loyal Democrat, and if, in the wisdom of this committee, I'm chosen for some other post, I can assure you that every bit of energy and talent that I have will be devoted," and so on. Another question is, "If you are not slated, will you support the guy that is slated?" And you are supposed to say, "I will be disappointed if I were not chosen, but I am a loyal Democrat and I will support whomever you choose." And another question is, "Will you support the candidate of the party after the primary against the Republican opponent?" And you say, "Of course I will."

Then a subcommittee is appointed, and usually there is no publication of the names of the persons. You don't know who they are. There would be seven, or eight, or ten guys. They would meet with Mayor Daley and bring in a report to the full central committee, and say, "After interviewing and discussing we recommend the following slate." Someone would say, "I move adoption of the report and the endorsement of the slate," and ordinarily there was no discussion at all. I don't think I can remember a time when there was anyone but myself who spoke against anybody. When I did, the hostility was unbelievable.

There was about all of this a kind of religious fervor. It's as though a couple were getting married, and the preacher says, "Speak now or forever hold your peace." Well, you don't expect anybody to get up. If someone got up, you would sense a kind of hustle and bustle, and a groan and a little quiet booing. That takes a lot of nerve. The whole central committee is very churchy in a sense of what is appropriate. The whole idea of the teaching authority, of the leader, is like the teaching authority of a priest or a bishop, and the loyalty is more as if Daley were the bishop or the cardinal. Then you come down to the pastors. The pastors are expected to follow the lead of the bishop, and the flock is expected to accept the teachings of the pastors. This creates a certain mystical obeisance to the leaders. He is not only the leader. He is charismatic, in the literal sense. He has a kind of God-given right to rule, a God-given quality that takes him somewhere a little bit beyond the ordinary human.

Thus it was that when any speaker would rise, he'd always begin with five or ten sentences with praise for the lord and say, "I've traveled abroad, and I don't mean just to Ohio, or some place like that. I'm talking about a place like Athens, Greece. The last time I was in Athens, I was walking down the street. A man comes up to me, I'd never seen him, a stranger, a Greek, and he says to me, 'Hey, you come from Chicago?' I say, 'Yeah, I'm from Chicago.' He says, 'Oh, how lucky you are. You got the great Mayor Daley!' And I tell him 'Yeah, God gave me Mayor Daley and it's the greatest thing!' So I want you to know that it's not only Chicago, it's not only Ohio, but it's Athens, Greece, where they're telling us, even there, that we've got the greatest man in the world. And so it's a great pleasure to speak up to second the nomination." So this is a part of the religious quality.

The organization provides, for many of these people, their social connections. The people they see are the people associated with the organization. These people see each other all the time. These are people whose daughters marry somebody within the organization. The second and third generation organization members are Democrats. It is also their sustenance. This is where they earn their living, so there is also the commercial aspect of it, the money aspect within the organization.

Then there is this kind of religious business. Senator Adlai Stevenson spoke of this system as feudal, and he meant there was something wrong with this. And, of course, there is, because this is really demeaning to a lot of the best human qualities. It's called a machine. Usually, it's taken to mean it is orderly, reliable, and effective. This is less true than it was, but true to some degree. But, in another sense, this is a machine in that it makes robots, gears, cogs, out of the people who become workers in it. They don't do any thinking. They're not expected to exercise any judgment, and they surrender their minds to the control of someone else, as surely as a horse surrenders his body. The ability to think, to judge, to discriminate, is the peculiar human quality. Dogs can have babies. Dogs can eat. But dogs can't think. They can be taught to play the piano, to bark when they're hungry, and to bring the newspapers, and all that kind of thing, but, in the human sense, they don't think. This is what the committeemen and the precinct captains give up. They become automatons. If they're good, they do exactly what is expected of them as reliably as does the machine. In that sense, the name "machine" is appropriate.

The key to all of this is patronage. You have a system in which the flow of authority is entirely from the top. The whole system is organized by statute. If one would read it, you would think that in Cook

County the people elect the committeeman to be their representative in the councils of the party; to convey to his colleagues the sense of what his constituents want, and perhaps work out a compromise with the other committeemen who, in turn, report the response of their constituents, and that, in turn, goes to the leaders. But what one hears there is from the top. "This is our slate. You vote for it," and everybody votes "yes." Then the instruction is, "Now, you carry the word back to your neighborhood." So that the flow is just like when the Chicago River was reversed. It used to flow into Lake Michigan, and this was what nature intended, but they dug it out from the back end, and now it flows from Lake Michigan backwards, upstream.

Why do these people do these things, and how does the system survive and perpetuate itself?

The key to it is that the government is used to sustain the government in power by hiring (no one knows exactly how many) maybe 12,000 city employees all the way up to 25,000, who are all hired because of their political allegiance and willingness to work for the Democratic Party. The organization, traditionally, does not want precinct workers who are not employees of the city, because they can't be controlled. Jesse Jackson told me that when he came to Chicago, he was interested in politics. He was also a preacher and he went to someone high in the Democratic Party and said, "I'm anxious to become a precinct captain." He was told, "We are very interested and we'll see what we can do." They finally got back to him and said, "You're on. You're going to be a precinct captain and you have a job as a toll taker at the Calumet Bridge." He said, "Yeah, but I don't want to do that. I'm a preacher. I'm employed." They said, "So what! You want to be a precinct captain, you gotta take the job. If you don't want to be a precinct captain, don't take the job. We're not going to put you on if you don't take the job."

This ensures control. You have a whole bunch of people who want these jobs, who surrender their minds politically. Moreover, there again is a kind of church overtone about this. These people say, "I haven't surrendered my mind. I'm a Democrat. I believe in this. I also believe in leadership. Daley knows all these people. I don't know them. He picks them and I'm perfectly willing to rely on him."

In the same kind of way, if a person is a member of the church and accepts the teaching of the pastor, and you say to him, "Look, you've surrendered your mind to the mind of the pastor." "Not at all," he says, "I went into this with a free choice, I can get out on my own

instances, the families they call on have a cousin or someone on the payroll somewhere, so they're glad to see the precinct captains. Perhaps they are restaurateurs or bar owners, or small businessmen in the ward, and they've had trouble with inspection, or with parking in front of their place. It's a good thing for them to be in touch. When there's a dinner to raise money, there will be an ad book. In this book, all the merchants in the ward can contribute for half a page, and if they're bigger outfits, a full page, "Best wishes to Jerry Huppert from Acne Furniture Company, Red Star Restaurant," and so on. They raise from $50,000 to $75,000 in a single whack, most of it coming from people who think that it isn't such a bad thing to have paid, so that they will have someone to go to if there's a violation, or an alleged violation, or if they want to close an alley, or they need something of one kind or another.

A lot of what's done isn't graft, except in a sense that people need something done about something. There are a whole lot of things they're entitled to from the government and, in the course of time, they might get them. But it might take too long. They want a license, they want to expand, they want to close the alley, they want to use the parking lot, or something of the kind, and they're entitled to do it. It won't happen just automatically. They go in and put their stuff in, and there'd be a long delay. If they can get to the committeeman, the committeeman will tell the alderman, "See what you can do for Henry Larson. He's got trouble with an alley. I don't know what it is, but his renewal hasn't come through, and he's worried." So, pretty soon, he comes back, gets a phone call, "I got it all fixed, it's in the mail, your renewal has gone through." "Oh, thank you very much." So when it comes around to have a dinner, "How about a hundred dollars for an ad? How about taking up to a full page? It's two hundred and fifty dollars." "Oh, yeah, yeah!" So this is the way it works.

I suspect it's all unconstitutional. I think that people are entitled to equal protection of the laws and I think that means everybody is entitled to equal consideration for a job, a license, regardless of his party connections. If it is unlawful to discriminate because he's black or white, or because he's Italian or Polish, it seems to me that it's a stronger case that he's discriminated against because he's a Republican or a Democrat.

There's an adjunct to the Shakman case that's pending. It's already been decided that you can't fire people because of their political beliefs. There's another case which is on its way up, which argues that you may not discriminate in hiring. This is a time bomb, because the

Chicago organization is utterly dependent on the freedom to discriminate on political grounds. The favors of the government go to
the people who are politically on the right side. If that's cut off, then
you've severed the whole nexus of this whole operation.

*Then politics in this organization is primarily the use of informal
processes to expedite or bypass the formal processes of the governmental systems. Is that a fair statement?*

That is only one small aspect of it. The main thing that keeps this
operation in power is the ability to hand out jobs. Next is the ability
to hand out contracts, because so much money is likely to be involved. The honest politician in the organization calls for a payment
to be made to the organization, not to himself. (Daley wouldn't take
any bribes at all.) A real crook, in the eyes of Daley, was somebody
who'd take the $5,000 for himself. A fellow who would ask someone
to make a $5,000 contribution to the party was a loyal party worker.
Then there is this business of expediting formal procedures.

*But the machine could not exist in a city like Chicago, could it,
without the willing participation of a large percentage of the citizenry of the city?*

One doesn't know how willing people are. A lot of people are
resentful that they need to go through some kind of extralegal chan-
nels. They think they ought to be able to get their license renewed
by complying with the regulations, and the fact that they need to go
to somebody to whom they pay money isn't regarded as a convenience. They're not willing collaborators. The question is whether it
is extortion. A whole lot of people are extorted for the things that
they need. They're held up, and finally they say, "Well, I guess
there's nothing left but to pay off."

Could you evaluate the committeemen for me?

There are a few who are quite bright, able, and energetic.
Some of them are lawyers, and many of that group are officeholders. They may also be aldermen or legislators. I'd say that that
group constitutes somewhere from ten to twenty percent of the
committeemen, and that may range on down to the place where
their competence is really in question. Many of them are not
bright. They frequently blundered in trying to ascertain what
Daley wanted. Some of them were regarded as unreliable because they couldn't even follow directions. It wasn't that they

didn't want to. They just didn't understand. Many of them came up as city employees. They were loyal and effective precinct workers and were installed as committeemen. I suppose that eighty-five to ninety percent of the committeemen are controlled because they are holding jobs, or because they have a law business that depends on their connections, or because they even have elective jobs. The way these people are kept in line as legislators, somebody says to them, "Look, do you want to go back? You got to get yourself in line on your vote here. You're not sent here to get off base. You are sent here to stay in line." They put out a so-called idiot sheet every day during the legislative session when there are bills to be voted on or amendments. A mimeographed sheet is sent around to the Chicago delegations—House Bill 2351, dog muzzles, yes; House Bill 2500, change judiciary, no; House Bill 2961, divorce, no. There's no secret about it. You can go to the desk and see them sitting there with this sheet. Some of them are competent enough to be leaders, but, generally speaking, this is not a talented group at all.

Tom Keane was unquestionably a bright and able guy. Seymour Simon, Marshall Korshak, Tom Hynes, Ted Lechowicz, John Merlo, Dan Rostenkowski, and Ed Vrdolyak are bright, able guys. Marzullo? I wouldn't call him very bright, but I think he has a cunning about him in a certain intuitive sense and a very appealing personality. This is partly because he is an old man now, and he's quaint.

A lot of these guys, their political horizons extend all the way to the end of the ward. They don't care what's going on in the state or the country. They don't care whether a bill passes or fails. They want the jobs. They want to run their wards. They don't care who is president or senator. How many jobs has a senator got? They're not interested in representatives in the House, except as a reward. You get someone who has been good for the party, you put him in there. Or give him a judgeship. These are the baits that are held out over and beyond just the daily job. If you are especially good, you can get one of the really good jobs. The guy they want to have elected is clerk of the circuit court, because there are more than 4,300 jobs. They don't care about state treasurer very much, but it's some jobs. They really don't care about Adlai Stevenson. Like him or don't like him, they want a guy at the top of the ticket who attracts votes. Stevenson does, so Stevenson is their guy. But how many jobs has he got? He can get two people into Annapolis or West Point. And, as far as doing personal favors for them, he doesn't do them.

Can you evaluate Daley for me, both as a politician and as a mayor?

He built and maintained his power by using the patronage power, which was ninety percent of it. He personally controlled the distribution of patronage, even at very low levels. People who wanted favors that were a little out of the ordinary went to him. He dispensed those favors and he expected the kind of loyalty that a dog gives to his master who feeds him. He was very strong on loyalty. It went both ways, in all fairness. But, once he had done a few favors for somebody, he fully expected that those favors would tie that person to him forever and in everything. And it worked. While he controlled all these things personally, it was also true that this was systematized and it is still systematized. He used to say, "Here's the formula. You get so many jobs when it's your turn, you get so many good jobs, and you get so many lousy jobs." This is not a person-by-person contest at all. You can't administer something with 12,000 to 15,000 people on a person-to-person basis. It isn't something personal. It's institutionalized.

Next, there are the favors of contracts, the favors of zoning, the favors of vacating alleys, and the very important favors in tax treatment. This is why the assessor's office is so important, because the good assessors, in the past, divided those things and asked the recipients to contribute to the party. The assessor's office has been a very important source of funds. A great many of the people who buy tables at the dinners are real estate people, who are doing it for zoning and on account of the tax.

How did Daley get his power? The ability to give or not to give the breaks of government, whether the breaks are wholly deserved or whether they're not quite deserved, the ability to give or withhold was an important consideration. Another first was his accommodation with big labor, giving big labor everything they wanted in respect to scale and in government employment. His accommodation to business. He believed in helping business, so if people wanted alleys vacated, or they wanted a parade, or any of these kinds of things, they got them. But, mostly, the power came from having this army of patronage workers which assured, at one time, that anybody nominated, anybody selected, would win the primary, and probably win in the fall through the existence of this army of patronage workers. He got their votes, their wives' or husbands' votes, their relatives' votes. He got a built-in 200,000 votes just from employees, their families, and not just their immediate families, but also the cousins, uncles, aunts and the rest. This meant that selection by Daley as a nominee was tantamount to election. When you get out into the county, as the suburbs grow, this isn't as much assured as it was, but patronage was really the source of Daley's power.

Daley subverted the city council. It's not a legislative body. They did what Daley told them. Within the county judiciary, not every judge would do what Daley wanted, but enough of them would, and Daley, by having the chief judges, was able to secure the assignment of any sensitive case to a judge that was friendly, frequently with an Irish name. The Irish controlled the top spots. He's had the executive branch, the legislative, and the judiciary when needed. All these, again, he held because he had gotten people elected, when he wanted to, by his selection through patronage. This is how he got his power.

His strengths lay in his being a very energetic, orderly administrator. Daley would have been a good success in running a big corporation, particularly one that was running on a steady track and didn't need to be realigned in direction. He was very efficient and ran a tight, hard schedule all day. When you went to see him, his desk was clear. He kept pretty close to his schedule. If you had an appointment at 11:55, you probably would get in within five minutes of that time. He went directly to business. He'd do his business with most people in five minutes and call the next person. His desk had nothing on it excepting a pen set and a little box about six inches long and four inches wide in which he had some individual pieces of paper a little smaller than the box, and if you had some kind of a question, or some kind of a matter to be taken care of, he would say, "Yes, I'll do that," and pick up one of these papers and write something on it, and put it in the top right-hand drawer.

He had good assistants, like Ray Simon, who was a bright, able guy, and who was very much disliked by the pols, because the pols thought that these fellows had influence with Daley beyond their own, which they had not earned by working for the party. Very frequently some alderman or committeeman would ask for a favor and was referred to Ray Simon, and Simon would say, "No, we shouldn't do that," and it wouldn't get done. These people were bright, capable assistants. They'd arrive early, get a lot of work done, come in Saturday mornings.

Of course Daley really loved Chicago. He knew Chicago. He traveled in every part of it, visited in every part of it, knew the city by the parishes. He was bright. People who have analyzed him in financial situations know it. He was the beneficiary of some restrictions put on him by the state legislature. Chicago couldn't borrow money. Daley couldn't have put the city in debt. He was knowledgeable about knowing which person influenced other persons. He was a great technician and a great implementarian. He knew how to get a plan executed.

His weakness was that he had very little vision of what Chicago needed. He had a kind of worship for the pouring of concrete. He liked physical things. He was not interested in ideas, but in getting skyscrapers into the Loop he was effective. In trying to harmonize relations between whites and blacks, in knowing what to do to have a decent school system, in housing, he was ineffectual. But in housekeeping chores—keeping water running, keeping curbs fixed, getting zoning adjusted, working out what was practical for people to put all the buildings over the IC tracks, getting McCormick Place put on the lakefront, he was effective. But as to the value or wisdom of his decisions, ought there to be a McCormick Place on the lakefront? One had to ask whether that was really the way to use Chicago's lakefront, or whether there were other places where they could have put it which would have permitted using slum-cleared land and improving that land instead of taking improved land and depreciating it. Or the opening up of the air rights over the IC tracks so that we now have a block of buildings putting up a wall extending east and west of Michigan Avenue, that will go all the way out into the lake, so that the sweep of lakefront, which was once a glory of Chicago, is lost in favor of a bunch of skyscrapers that would be lived in by rich people. I think that shows a lack of vision. Daley was a great doer. But, in the sense of what ought to be done, he was not nearly as great as in the sense of how to do anything that anybody put to him.

When somebody says, "The city that works," what does it mean? They pick up the garbage, but they don't fix the potholes or the curbs too well anymore. What can you say of a city in which the rank scores of the children in the schools are down about 14th among the big cities? I would suppose that one of the tests of the city that works is the ability to educate its children, and the mere fact that you can get in a taxi and go east and west faster than you can in New York, it may be because of the way the streets were laid out in the first place.

Was Daley a great political leader? He was not a great political leader because the ends in view were so dim, and so easy, and so modest, that he wasn't engaging his talents for leading others to what was needed for the future or even for a good present. At a quite different level, he's called an astute politician, and some of this came from his selection of candidates, on which he had a very poor record.

That he kept the party in power was without any question. But it was not because his judgments, politically, were so wise. It came from a kind of ruthlessness and a push for power. Daley was astute in acquiring power, but his judgment in the use of power was something else again. It was rather that with the patronage army that he institutionalized, mobilized, and organized, until the growth of the suburbs was sufficient, he was able to elect anybody he named. But he elected a lot of bad people and gave a lot of bad people power. It was almost, you know, like a football halfback playing behind an offensive line that's extremely strong, that could wipe everybody out. All the halfback has to do is to walk in behind these guys. He's going to go five yards.

He never understood the suburbs. He thought the suburbs were like the city. He frequently said that the principles that apply in the city apply in the suburbs. But he was wrong. In Chicago, the ability to do favors for people from the city government was a very important factor in the power of the committeemen. But nobody is going to go to a precinct captain in the suburbs. I go to the Village Hall. The effectiveness of precinct captains and committeemen is minimal.

Another thing is the increasingly pervasive influence of television and the press on how people form their attitudes about candidates. In the suburban area there is what pollsters call a high information area. The degree to which a house-to-house worker can equal people's judgment about the important offices, which is so much the subject of television and newspaper comments, is meager. When you get down to the lower level, many people would prefer to take the recommendation that the newspaper prints out at the end. They've got fifty judges to vote for. Which precinct captain could go and tell people which judges to vote for? They'd rather go to the Bar Association, or the Independent Voters of Illinois, or the newspapers, and say, "These people know more about it than I do."

How do you see the future of the machine, and the future of politics in Chicago and the suburbs?

First, I would think that there's a good likelihood for a period of time that there will be more graft and more boodle than you've ever seen. Daley didn't condone personal gain beyond certain reasonable limits. I'm very skeptical that there's anybody who will keep the lid on to the degree that Daley did. As for the machine itself, the division of power between the mayor and the county chairman will very much weaken the position of county chairman. I think you will see that for county candidates, suburban people may have a kind of veto power and reject candidates who won't do well in the suburbs. I think that ethnicity as a basis for slating will diminish. I think a great many of the committeemen, when they lose the ability to control the ward through the award of jobs, will find themselves utterly ineffectual. In short, it's very likely that, lacking the kind of power leadership that Daley put together through a combination of fear and love, when that's gone, I think the only thing that can control is democracy.

EIGHT

The Losers

ROBERT MERRIAM / TIMOTHY P. SHEEHAN / BENJAMIN ADAMOWSKI / JOHN WANER / RICHARD FRIEDMAN / JOHN HOELLEN

ROBERT MERRIAM *The son of Charles Merriam, dean of twentieth-century political scientists, a University of Chicago graduate, and a liberal, reform alderman from the 5th ward, he ran against Daley in 1955 and came close. Merriam then served in the White House under Eisenhower and is now a successful businessman.*

I was born and raised in Chicago, the son of Charles Merriam, a professor at the University of Chicago who was elected to the city council in 1909. Two years later he ran for mayor on the Republican ticket against Carter Harrison, the younger, who won by 18,000 votes. My father went back to the council, ran again for mayor in 1919 in the Republican primary against Big Bill Thompson, and was roundly defeated. That was the end of his elective political career.

I was elected alderman from the 5th ward in 1947. I was supported by the Democratic ward committeeman, Barnett Hodes, and the Republican ward committeeman, Bunnie East. East never really worked hard to get an alderman, and he didn't really have a candidate to run that year. I guess he just felt it would be to his advantage to join in a race that might be successful, and I presume he felt that Hodes would end up owing him a few favors in the process. I am sure he collected them.

What was the city council like in those days?

Kennelly was mayor. We really had a significant minority group of young aldermen, both Democrats and Republicans, that ranged anywhere from thirteen to nineteen members of the city council. Kennelly was a passive mayor and did not attempt to run the city council. Some say he really didn't attempt to run the city. The cast of characters was not too unsimilar, although some of the names changed. Tom Keane, who was emerging as a party leader in those days, was not the leader of the council but probably had the reins of the leadership. There were other people involved in controlling it—Clarence Wagner, who was a protégé of Pat Nash; John Duffy, who was from the South Side Irish group; Parky Cullerton, who was their West Side rival counterpart; George Kells, who was the state chairman of the Democratic Party; and Harry Sain of the 27th ward. The problems of the city were not being met well, nor are they now. The Democratic Party leadership in this city (and this really goes back to the New Deal days) has always been very conservative on social issues. I used to refer to the Democratic leadership as the Southern Democratic Party of the Northern Democrats. They're very conservative on racial policies, on modern public policies, on social policy, on providing those services that better human lives as opposed to cleaning streets and picking up garbage.

This was an almost totally white leadership. The black leaders were still few in number and not all that influential. The big one, of course, was Bill Dawson. We had, in the city council when I was first elected, not more than three black aldermen out of fifty. Black participation in Democratic Party politics was very limited. There were those who were Uncle Toms who took what favors they could get, and didn't do much for their people, partly because of Dawson. The white leadership of the Democratic Party used to throw them some crumbs to control those South and West Side wards—jobs and favors.

Mayor Edward J. Kelly practiced the old rough and tumble politics. If an alderman didn't go along, he suddenly found that garbage wasn't collected in his ward. This never happened under Kennelly and I don't think it has happened since. I think that was an era that ended with Kelly. Services were rendered—I wouldn't say they were good, but you could get something done. But there was absolutely no interest in housing programs.

We formed what was called "the economy bloc," because we had a series of fights about budget. We were not interested solely in saving money. We were also interested in social services. And there was no interest in those things from the machine. Support came from a variety of sources—from the Jewish community, the so-called lakefront liberals, and the rather significant Bishop Sheil liberal Catholic group, some of the ethnic leaders who didn't play machine politics —a number of the Czech leaders, and some of the German intellectual leaders.

The labor movement leadership has always been intimately connected with the machine for many years, with some significant exceptions—the Sleeping Car Porters' Union, the packing house workers, the jewelry workers, and the garment workers.

The newspapers, by and large, tended to play, I would say, a more independent, active role than they do today. They were still, in the

1940s, supportive of someone trying to propose things for the improvement of the city. They all made their peace with Mr. Daley. They sally forth now and then, and get very indignant, but by and large they don't seem to want to rock the boat.

How did you come to run for mayor as a Republican?
I was a registered Democrat, have always been an independent, and considered myself a liberal. The local organization can tolerate a lot of dissidence and independent thinking if they're not close to home. When you are in the city council and directly involved in city government, that's another story. They wanted conformity; they wanted somebody they knew they could control, and who would really do what they wanted to have done.

My second term—a number of very key things happened. We formed an emergency committee on crime as a result of the murder of Tom Keane's Republican counterpart in the 31st ward, a fellow named Gross. There was a great public hue and cry for once and we got this committee formed (and actually had a majority of it) to look into the tie-up between the police department and organized crime and politicians. As with any legislative investigation of that kind, particularly when you have a strong majority who don't favor it, we ran into a lot of roadblocks along the way. But the committee did exist for two or three years and did some very significant investigative work which got exposed. It gave me, as the leader in that fight, a great deal of attention.

There were some other things that occurred. In 1954 a group of people said, "Let's take a shot at trying to elect a mayor," and were kind enough to think that I could be the person to lead this coalition of liberal, independent, non-machine forces. We wanted a fusion concept. We dropped the independent idea because we felt that, with the machine control of the election board, even if we got all the signatures, we would be thrown off the ballot. We were prepared to run against Kennelly in the Democratic primary, then Daley decided to run, and Adamowski joined the picture. It looked to us like a four-way race would be a very difficult situation. I would be drawing votes from Kennelly and Adamowski, or they from me. It would just enhance the organization's chances. That left one alternative, the Republican primary. The Republican Party was really in poor condition, but Republican Governor Bill Stratton told me he was prepared to urge the county committee to accept me as the nominee, and ask nothing in return. The whole idea was to have a fusion ticket of independent Democrats, independents, and what there was of the Republican Party, which wasn't very much. I once said to Ed Moore, who was the Republican county chairman, "Ed, my guess was that 26 of the 50 Republican ward committeemen openly, and the rest covertly, supported Daley." He said, "Well, you were a little low." Stratton did some things, but not as much as he indicated.

We raised about $300,000, which was, in those days, a good sum of money. It was nothing compared to what the organization was able to do. They had over a million. We know that, but we don't know how much more. The newspapers divided three to one in my favor. The *Sun-Times,* the *Daily News,* and the *Tribune* supported me. The *Herald American* was in very bad financial condition, and the story, which has been told many times, was that the Democratic precinct captains agreed to go out and take subscriptions for the *Herald American* in return for their support, and a deal was made. The *Sun-Times* ran a poll, their straw poll, which they don't ordinarily do in a mayoralty election, and, two weeks before the election, it showed me running ahead of Daley. That poll has probably been the most accurate poll in Chicago. The organization really pushed the panic button and they played every stop that there was to play on the organ in those last two weeks. On election day, $1,500 or $2,000 was put in major key precincts. I had $30 to $40 per precinct.

Tom Duggan, the television personality, who had been a good friend of mine, really clobbered me on his program. Five years after the election, I was in California where Tom then went, and I turned on a late-night talk show that he had on television. He got started on the subject of Daley, whom he subsequently fell out with, because Daley promised to do some things for him if he clobbered me. All the chips they had collected were sent out for repayment.

I had hoped that I could get Kennelly and Adamowski to support me after the primary. I went to see them both. Adamowski said, "I have been a Democrat all my life and I really can't support somebody running on the Republican ticket." The next year he ran as a Republican for state's attorney. The night of the primary Kennelly wanted to come out for me. His campaign manager, the Democratic ward committeeman of the 49th ward, Frank Keenan, said, "Let's just wait a few days until the dust settles down." Subsequently, Keenan decided to support me, so I had one Democratic ward committeeman on my side. But he couldn't get Kennelly to do so. He sat out the election. Keenan went to jail, not because of that, precisely, but, I think, in part it was. He became county assessor. There was no longer any desire to protect him on the part of the organization. He was indicted for income tax evasion. They play a very hard game.

I lost by a little over 100,000. We carried twenty-two of the fifty wards. We knew that Republicans were a minority in the city and had no organization. The only way that running as a Republican made any sense was to have important and visible Democratic support, and the failure to get either Kennelly or Adamowski to actively participate in the campaign was a very major fact. There were then two million registered voters in Chicago. We figured that Daley would get 700,000 votes, or just a little over a third. If you look at his license plate today, which is still the number of votes he got against me in 1955, it's 708,222. We felt that a turnout of over 1,400,000 out of two million meant we were in.

Election day was the day of Colonel McCormick's funeral at the Fourth Presbyterian Church, across the street from where we now sit. The funeral was at 2 o'clock. I pulled up in front of this building, the Water Tower Place building, which was then a vacant lot, and heard the election commissioner's returns saying it looks like the turnout will be 1,500,000. I spent the whole hour, when I should have been thinking about the soul of Colonel McCormick, thinking about who I was going to appoint to my cabinet. As we went out, Mayor Kennelly was there, and he said, "How does it look?" I said, "Very excellent, Mr. Mayor, the turnout is good, and I think we're going to make it." But, instead of it being 1,500,000, the turnout was 1,300,000 and there was the difference. We were fighting the lethargy that comes in a city that has never had a reform movement. I got 600,000, approximately, and Daley got 700,000. I carried the white vote of Chicago, and what carried Daley was the black vote.

The black community has always puzzled me because they have settled for almost nothing in the way of city programs and services, and the betterment of their condition, and all that has come through the federal government, basically. We had a chance in Chicago to become an unsegregated city, which really is the only solution. We could have done a lot more than we did in improving race relations in this city through leadership by the city government, but Daley has never come to terms with the racial situation because this just isn't Bridgeport. The answer that Bridgeport has made to the racial question is that you keep them out with baseball bats, if necessary, and that's where the mayor lives. And, while Bridgeport is a charming little bungalow neighborhood, what they did, when the blacks shoved as hard as they did, was to make a shambles of Hyde Park and

South Shore by pushing black migration eastward and away from themselves.

Has Daley been a good mayor?

Milt, I have to answer that by the old canard about one fellow saying to the other, "How's your wife?" And the other saying, "Compared to what?" Compared to his Chicago predecessors, I would certainly say, in terms of his own personal conduct, of his ability to hold together an organization, this polyglot group that we mentioned, he's done a great job. In terms of the potential of city government to make life in the city better, there are a lot of other things that can be done. It is unfortunate that the comparison then gets made to, "Compared to what?" I hear, so many times, the Lindsay comparison. Those are not the only alternatives that exist. There are mayors in large cities in this country who have taken a much more active role in leadership, using government as a means to improve everyone's life. There has been some good things done, but they're done usually under pressure.

Obviously, the man is a master craftsman and tactician in the art of political manipulation. You can't help but admire a skilled craftsman, and he was that. He has held together what is really a very motley crew, and has somehow managed to keep himself out of the muck and seemingly above the battle, even though those of us who watch him know what's going on and realize that he is involved in every major decision that has to be made. He tends to be a reactor rather than an innovator in government services, programs, and organization.

You are a man who almost became mayor of the second largest city in this country. What did it do to your life, when you lost?

If I said I was not disappointed, I would not be telling the truth. But I went into the whole thing rather philosophically, as one must, with full intention of winning, but with an understanding that the world wasn't going to come to an end if I lost. I returned to Chicago after a tour of duty in Washington, and I am very happy that I did. I very much love the city and think it is a very dynamic city. My relations with the mayor are good. In 1958, I came out here to make a speech, and on the plane with me was the then Senator from Massachusetts, John Kennedy. I hadn't seen him until I was just getting out, and there, at the bottom of the stairway, were the mayor, Tom Keane, and the whole retinue, to greet Kennedy, who was

coming to make a Jefferson Day speech. I couldn't resist the temptation. I ran up and grabbed the mayor's hand as the cameras were
turning, and said, "Mr. Mayor, it's nice of you to be out here welcoming me back to Chicago." He was so startled, he didn't know what
to say, and I went down the line and shook hands with all my former
colleagues.

Politics is a very fascinating business. One meets a variety of people that people in many walks of life just never do. I have friends,
from Paddy Bauler to Dwight Eisenhower. You do get to know different types of people, and why they think the way they do, how they
live, and what their customs are, from a Polish wedding to a bar
mitzvah, or what have you. These are things the guy in business just
never does, that many people never do. I enjoyed getting to know
every neighborhood, as I did in the campaign.

There is another side of it. It isn't just whether you win or lose. You
do see the playing for interest, in someone, not for who he is or what
he thinks, but because of what he can do for you. I remember a lady
calling me up for some group that wanted me to speak. Finally, in
desperation one day, she said, "I got to know right away, because if
we can't get you to do it, we'll have to pay somebody." People use
you, but I think the participation in public decision-making, and the
ability, hopefully, to have achieved something in that process, is a
very rewarding and satisfying thing, aside from anything else.

TIMOTHY P. SHEEHAN
Wealthy, successful businessman and life-long Republican politician. Ran against Daley in 1959. Served eight years in Congress. Was Republican county chairman. Has been 41st ward committeeman for many years— the best Republican ward committeeman in the city.

My father and mother were both born in Ireland in the 1880s, came to this country when they were young people, around 1900, got married in 1908, and, like a lot of Irish people, came to Chicago because a lot of their relatives from County Kerry lived here. My father started out in politics rather early and was a precinct captain. My earliest memory of him was of him always writing home to his uncles or to his brothers and sisters in Ireland, telling them about America, and telling them how important he was because he felt that as a precinct captain, that he was doing a great service. As you know, the Irish people, under the domination of England, were never allowed to participate in politics and didn't even have a vote in Ireland. So he felt that this was a great country with great opportunities, that politics was a great thing, and he carried this on to me.

I was born right across the street from the stockyards. (I won a bet from Mayor Daley once about who lived closest to Back of the Yards. He lived a mile away.) We moved to the West Side of Chicago, to 15th and Ashland, and lived there until I got married. It was a typical ethnic neighborhood. The gangs we belonged to were German, Polish, Irish, Jewish, and you name it. No one nationality predominated. We all sort of mixed together in the proverbial melting pot of Chicago—various religions and nationalities hanging around together.

My father was a Republican precinct captain and got me to help him. In those days, a great number of the Irish were Republicans. In the early 1920s, we had no social security system, and when people who were out of work wanted help, they usually went to the local political person. The ward committeemen and the precinct captains would distribute baskets at Christmas and Easter, taking care of the poor. Everybody in the neighborhood burned coal, and you would see to it that people had coal. Therefore, I got started very early helping my father, and just grew into politics from that.

Our ward was the so-called bloody 20th ward. It was called the bloody 20th because more political people were killed in that ward than all the rest of the city together. They played their politics hard in those days. When the blacks started to move into the West Side, a black named Octavius Grandy ran for ward committeeman against Alderman Bill Pacelli. On the day of election, he was gunned down and killed in typical gangland fashion because he was the first black on the West Side who attempted to run for office. Once, in a polling place that I was in on Washburne Avenue at two o'clock one morning, they were counting votes. A group of five people came in and said they needed 75 votes for a certain judicial candidate. They were armed and the judges of the election wanted no trouble, so they re-marked the ballots and gave that particular candidate about 150 more votes. Milt, you didn't want to be a hero, because of the shootings by the gangsters and the tough guys, so you said nothing and went along with them.

During those years I worked my way through Northwestern University, graduated in 1931, got married in 1936, and we moved out to the Northwest Side into the 41st ward. The first thing I did was to go to the ward committeeman and tell him I wanted to be a precinct captain. He made me an assistant precinct captain and after the regular precinct captain died, I was named the precinct captain. I became very active in the 41st ward, became chairman of the picnics, dance chairman, gradually became an officer of the organization, and in the early 1940s, became president of the organization. I ran for alderman in 1943 and lost. I then ran for Congress in 1950, was elected, and served for four terms until I was defeated in 1958. They redistricted the area and put more Democrats in, which made it difficult for me to win. The migration from the inner city was already taking place. The blacks were moving strongly into the inner city of Chicago from the South Side and the West Side, and the Italians, Poles, and ethnic groups, who were staunch Democrats in the inner city, were moving out to the outskirts of the city into wards like the 41st, the 38th, and the 45th, which were the backbone of the 11th congressional district. Every time five German or Scandinavian Republican voters moved out of this area to the suburbs, five inner-city people would be moving in, and four out of those five would be Democrats. So gradually, our particular area was weakening. I was the last Republican congressman elected from within the city of Chicago.

I left Congress in January 1959. The Republicans were looking for a candidate for mayor and I consented to run. They had talked to some of the businessmen and told them if they ran a good race, they'd run them for the Senate in 1960, because Paul Douglas' term came up. I asked to be given the same consideration, and they promised they would give it to me. So I made the sacrifice and ran, realizing that Mr. Daley would be unbeatable. When 1960 came along, and they were looking for a candidate for the Senate, they forgot about Sheehan and picked someone else.

I knew there was no chance of beating Daley. The best we hoped to do was to present a good campaign, and we ran a good, clean campaign. The machine functioned the same way it has since Daley was first elected. Daley got the support of the newspapers because he was in office. The news media are always conscious of the power of City Hall, and many things such as realty assessments and favors can be done. They seldom take out too much after an incumbent mayor, unless the guy is absolutely no good. The business community supported Daley. Chicago is a great labor town. The head of the AFL–CIO, Bill Lee, and the president of the Plumber's Union are staunch Democrats, and lent money and the power of the unions to supporting Daley and his people. In Chicago, the Democrats have the labor vote locked up.

What do they get in return?
Look at the school system and the union jobs that are around. In the sanitary district and the County Hospital, when union jobs come up, the Democrats are involved in it. If there are five electricians to be appointed, they work out a sweetheart deal. The union names two and the Democrats name three. The Democrats have an agreement with them. The unions have jobs in the city and the county, and can place people who are active in the union movement into good jobs. I'm sure every electrician would like to be an electrician for the city of Chicago where he gets vacation time, days off, pension rights, and is sure of working 365 days a year. There is no other power structure left, so the net result is that even the news media doesn't want to beat the incumbent mayor over the head. Even if they were staunch Republicans, they would know that there is no chance, so they don't antagonize anyone. What was the name of the book you wrote, "Don't Make No Waves"? That's exactly right! The business community,

the social community, and the neighborhood community don't want to make waves and they go along with the people in power.

Daley had his political organization, and this is what wins votes. In politics, you build organizations with political workers. Volunteers come and go, but precinct captains who have jobs know, if they want to be promoted, if they want more pay, if they want more recognition, they have to work for the organization that's in control. In our own 41st ward, I would guess that the Democratic ward committeeman has somewhere between four and five hundred jobholders who report to him. Election day the Democrats have ten to twelve jobholders in every precinct getting out their friends and their families to vote. Many Republican workers and even Republican ward committeemen were and still are obligated to the Democrats. They get jobs from the city, or have jobs in their organization. Many of them feel that it is a hopeless task, and why kill themselves trying to get somebody elected when they know they can't elect him. The Republican Party depends upon volunteers, and is not able to get every precinct filled. We have very few sources of jobs in the Republican Party. In our 41st ward (which, incidentally, is the best Republican ward in Chicago), we have eighty-four precincts. At the present time, we only have about fifty precinct captains. Of those fifty precinct captains, only about eight of them have jobs. The other forty-two are volunteers, and yet, I am expected, as a Republican committeeman, to hold down an organization like the Democrats, which has 450 jobholders. It just can't be done in realistic politics.

Most of the Democrat precinct captains are jobholders who have to get out the vote. Many who are not jobholders are lawyers who get work out of the city, free offices and things like that, and they make sure that they contribute to the organization and they help get out the vote. Daley has enormous power. He is mayor of Chicago, he controls the sanitary district, the county board, County Hospital, and has a tremendous amount of patronage jobs available. When he runs an affair, they have six to eight thousand people at $100 a plate, so they have all the money they want. They get out all their jobholders, all the lawyers who are obligated because they get money out of the city, and businessmen who have their names on the page endorsing Daley. When the local ward committeemen come to see them, it's good politics to buy ten tickets from the people who are in power, because you never know when you need favors.

Is there a difference in the way Republican officeholders handle patronage compared to the Democrats?

This is one of the reasons why the Republicans have not been successful. When the Democrats get in they have a central organization in Cook County, and even at the state level, when they elect a governor, they let him name his top people, but all of the jobs are put under the control of the county central committee. Democrats who are elected to high office, even if they are not regular politicians, let the Democratic organization control the jobs. When we elect people to high office, they don't do this. They build personal organizations, not the party. And they wind up getting defeated.

Could you analyze Daley for me?

Daley is a party guy, first, last, and always. He got his eyeteeth cut in politics at the best of all levels. He knew what politics was all about. He saw how it operated. He also rose through the ranks in his own 11th ward organization, started out as a precinct captain, and rose up through the party. He knows the strength of the party. He knows how to use it. When somebody arises who might want to disrupt the party, he is usually against him. Sometimes he has to live with him, but basically, if an alderman, or a ward committeeman, or somebody comes along and shows too much independence in the sense that he wants to fight the organization, Daley is against those guys. Daley builds the organization. His home life and his political life are exemplary. They have never found anything dishonest or shady about him. From a leadership standpoint, he has been a paragon of virtue. The Democrats allow their precinct captains to make money when they can. I am not talking about dishonest money, but for favors. They allow the smaller guy to participate. Yet Daley has had a very strict code of conduct. When a guy gets caught doing something wrong, Daley just walks away from him. When you do something wrong, you are on your own. He doesn't try to protect them and he doesn't try to help them make illegal money.

Daley is a good mayor who has built a tremendous organization. If you are to operate a proper political system, you have to have a machine or an organization. It could be a good machine or a bad machine. Take Russia. Those guys don't stay in power because the people want them in power. They have a machine. They have X number of people who are members of the Communist Party and they subdue all opposition. Hitler had a machine. Mussolini had a machine. Pretty near any political guy who is going to be successful has to have a machine. The machine can serve a good purpose, or it can serve a bad purpose, but whether you are a Franco, a Mussolini, a Hitler, a Stalin, or a Mayor Daley, you've got to have people who will follow you. That's the essence of all machines.

Independent movements are nice for people who want to rationalize a code of conduct, who don't want to belong to a machine, but when has an independent party ever been successful? They may defeat candidates or elect candidates, but this is only for one or two terms and then they all disappear. Usually, independents are against somebody. They want to get somebody out of office. But once they get them out of office, they don't know what the hell to do with it. And they either disappear from the scene or they get sore at the people they got into office because they didn't do what they wanted them to do.

You've spent a lifetime in politics. Have you made a living in politics?

No. As a Republican, I realized very early that there is no way a Republican can make a living in politics in Chicago. I very early came to the conclusion that I wanted to stay in politics, but that I had better have my own business and my own means of livelihood so I can always keep bread on the table for my family. But I have always felt that I had more ability than the average person and I feel that anyone who has those God-given gifts ought to devote part of his life to helping his fellow man, and I thought politics was the way to do it and I hope to continue in it until I die. I have gotten a lot out of it, too. How could a poor kid from the West Side of Chicago, raised in a poor ethnic neighborhood, get to know presidents of the United States—Mr. Eisenhower, Mr. Truman, Mr. Nixon, Mr. Ford, Mr. Kennedy—all of whom I knew personally on a first-name basis? How could I associate with guys like Senator Ev Dirksen, guys who have made great names in history? Last Tuesday, I was invited to Washington to attend a seminar. Three people from Chicago were there—Mr. Clem Stone, one of the wealthiest men in the country; Mr. Gaylord Freeman, the chairman of the board of the First National Bank; and me. And then we all went over to the White House. How else could a guy like me, coming from the neighborhood I come from, associate with people who have made their marks in the business world, the professional world, and in history, if you please? Politics does have a lot to offer.

What's the other side of it, Tim? What kind of a price do you pay for being in politics?

Oh, you pay a price for being in politics! Too many people think of politicians as crooks. When people know you are a politician, and they don't know you, they assume there is something wrong with you, that you make money illegally, and you don't have the best reputation. It has drawbacks on the family. Politicians are away from home, especially evenings, a lot of the time. You're going to meetings, you're traveling, and a guy like myself, who was in Congress for eight years, you have a family of five kids growing up, they lose some of the things by not having you close to them. By the same token, my kids will all tell you that they enjoyed the relationship, the people their father knew, the affairs they went to, and things like that. Like everything else in life, everything has advantages and drawbacks, and politics is no different.

Was it hard to readjust to private life again, after being in Congress?

I didn't have that problem. Many politicians do. That's why they talk in Washington about Potomac Fever. People who are there ten or fifteen years cannot go back to the small town because they have tasted the big town, so they stay in Washington. They don't go back home.

I had a different situation. I have always had two businesses of my own. I never moved my family to Washington. I'd come home every weekend and always kept my hand in the business, and was never divorced from regular, ordinary life. I kept my own friends in business; I kept my own friends in the neighborhood, unlike many congressmen who were elected for twenty or thirty years, and don't know anybody from their home town, who cut all their strings. They cannot come home because there is nothing to come home to. They've sold their homes, which many guys do. Oh, sure, they keep a voting address, but they don't come home. Many congressmen and senators, when there is a recess in Washington, junket all over the world. They don't come back home, except when they have to make speeches or something like that. Especially those coming from the smaller towns. So they will stay in Washington or go to a big city. They've tasted the big life and they'll stay in the big city.

But the real strength of any politician, big or small, is to know his own limitations. You and I know that anytime Daley wanted to run for senator or governor, he could have run. He was the boss and he

called the shots. But he knows his own limitations. He can stay as long
as he wants as mayor of Chicago, but he had to know in his own heart
that if he ran for governor, senator, he would be blackened by all the
news media, everybody all over the state. And a guy like Marzullo,
a very astute and successful politician, knows his limitations in his
ward and his area, and he doesn't want to be the governor, senator,
or president, because he knows that that is not in the realm of possibility. So if you live within your own capabilities and your own limitations, you'll never be disappointed or heartbroken. But we all work
on ego trips in the sense that we like to be known or we like to
accomplish something. One of the great attractions for a politician is
that he gets to be known by his fellow men, by people in ways which
people in other professions don't. You may be the best doctor in Cook
County, but the only people who know about it are the people in the
hospital or the people you operate on. Or you may be the best
political science professor, like Milt Rakove, in the city, but very few
people get to know about that. But a politician can walk down a
street alongside the president of General Motors, and the people will
all know the politician, but they don't know who the president of
General Motors is. This is one of the things that feeds the political
ego. And politics does give you this distinguishment, if it is a distinguishment.

BENJAMIN ADAMOWSKI

Polish. Seventy-two years old. Active for many years in Chicago in both the Democratic and Republican parties. Ran against Daley in the 1955 Democratic mayoral primary and lost. Was elected state's attorney of Cook County in 1956, as a Republican. Was defeated for the same office in 1960. Ran against Daley as the Republican candidate for mayor in 1963 and lost. Came back to the Democratic Party in the early 1970s. Is also an attorney.

Ben, can you describe the major political figures in Chicago you knew?

Mayor Edward J. Kelly was a cold, calculating type, whose promise came easy, but his performance came tough. Kelly would promise you something, and, two minutes later, pick up the phone [and go back on it]. I've seen him do it. The committeemen were mad at Kelly.

Pat Nash was revered by the committeemen. They adored him. If you could get him to make a commitment, which was difficult, you could walk over to the First National Bank and put it on deposit. He'd never break his word. Had it not been for Pat Nash, Kelly would have been in trouble nine times out of ten. The old man, as they used to refer to him (and I do affectionately), was the greatest man I've met in both parties. His word was his bond. Some of the stories about him may or may not be true, but I found him to be a man of his word, a man you could go to, a man who would listen to you, a man who would counsel with you.

Mayor Martin Kennelly was just a nice guy. He never should have been mayor of Chicago. He should have been a cardinal or a monseigneur. He was that kind of a person. I told Kennelly, "Dollarwise, you're honest, but morally you're dishonest. Letting some of the things go on that you know are going on makes you as dishonest as though you were participating, because you can stop some of it. I'm not telling you to become a partner or become involved, but you're delinquent by virtue of the fact that you don't stop it."

Daley is a lot like Pat Nash, except that he's shrewder, more knowledgeable. He's made politics and government his life. You can't get his word easily, to get him to make commitments or promises. Eddie Barrett had a candidate for judge in his ward, and they had thirteen committeemen on the slatemaking committee. I met Eddie, and I said, "You know, your guy got twelve, and the other guy got one." And Eddie said, "Well, if my guy got twelve and the other guy got one, how come the other guy got it?" I said, "You didn't ask who the one guy was—Dick Daley." That's a true story.

Politically, I don't think Daley is above the normal political animal. I think he has the instinctiveness of his ethnic group, a natural aptitude for meeting people, visiting with people, pulling people out, getting them to do things. He learned early what Kelly and Kennelly had problems with. He realized that to be an effective mayor, you have to have power, and so he became chairman of the county central committee.

It was never money with Daley. It was apparently power. As Tom Keane used to say, "Daley wanted power and I wanted money, and we both got what we want." I think Tom Keane was right. I think Daley set his goal—he went after the mayoralty, that was the seat of the power.

I think he has been a reasonably good mayor, in most respects. There are several things that I've been critical of, that others have been critical of, that he had the power to change. Some of these "uncoverings," he could have nipped them in the bud.

Because of the organizational strength, Chicago has had the least problems, ethnicwise, racewise. When they had the Martin Luther King riots, Daley didn't say, "Why did they do this to Chicago?" He was quoted as saying, "Why did they do this to me?" To Daley, Chicago is "Me." I don't think he's got a prejudiced bone in his body. He's gone out of his way, and continues to go out of his way, as far as the blacks are concerned, but he's also smart enough to know that you've got to take one step at a time. He has given the blacks recognition that, if they had fought to get it, they wouldn't have had it. In that sense, he has been a particularly effective political animal because he has kept the lid on.

Now, you go down the other side of the coin. The labor leaders—he has worked with them day and night. This is why I think that the business community, fearful that even Ben Adamowski might not have that same approach, are so in favor of Dick Daley. They know what they've got. They know how he works. They know he has kept his finger on the pulse. I've said to people, if I were elected mayor tomorrow, with all of my background, with all of my knowledge, and with all of my governmental experience, it would take me a year to find out what the buttons on his desk mean. And then if I pushed one of them, I'm not so sure I would get a response. But he could push any one of those buttons and have twenty people inside the door in ten seconds. Because of their organizational setup, I'll bet you that Daley knows if something happens on Madison and Pulaski before Police Superintendent Jim Rochford does. They've got it set up in such a way that they can start to contain it. That's important in the City of Chicago.

When Len O'Connor called me in 1975, and said, "How could you possibly endorse this man after the way you fought him?" I said, "You can't be serious, Len, that you want John Hoellen to be the mayor of this city. For your information, if by chance (God forbid it should happen), he was elected mayor, I'm gonna sell my home and get out of Chicago." I said, "Another thing, Len, let's quit kidding ourselves. We're sitting on a keg of dynamite if we don't work like this man has been working, with the black and the white communities, and now the Latin community." The people out in the community know that there is conversation going on, efforts are being made to solve their problems, and there is an input on their behalf. That's where Daley has his strength.

The only man I think who has hurt himself with Daley, in my time, is Ed Hanrahan. John Boyle is a good example of how they forgive and forget. John ran against them, fought the organization hard, fairly. He's now the Chief Judge of the Circuit Court of Cook County. A top job. Daley could have prevented that, but he knew that John, basically, wasn't going to try to tip over the organization.

Daley has always been a family man. One of the things they tell me he will never forgive, with anyone around him, whether they're close or far, is if he knows that they're not true to their family and their vows.

If he has a weakness, it's that he does keep things to himself. He doesn't have any confidants. He doesn't have anybody that he really trusts outside of Sis [Mrs. Eleanor Daley]. It's a different kind of trust. It's like Vito Marzullo says, "When I play cards with my wife, I want to beat the hell out of her, but I still sleep with her." Daley is the same way. He lives, eats, and sleeps [politics and government]. He really believes the things he talks about. As far as Chicago is concerned, he made that his whole life. He's probably the last of his kind in the United States.

JOHN WANER *Ran against Daley in 1967. Polish. High school dropout. Was a journeyman plumber and successful businessman. Republican ward committeeman for many years of Southwest Side 23rd ward. Was regional director for HUD under Eisenhower and again under Nixon.*

My mother and father came from Poland at the turn of the century, settled in Chicago, and were married here. I was born in 1914, at 18th Street and Paulina. I attended parochial elementary school. In those days it was quite common for Polish children to attend parochial schools. The teachers were volunteer nuns who also came from the old country, and invariably we learned to speak English with the accent of our teachers. I was able to speak Polish long before I was able to speak English, with the "deses, dems, and doses." In fact, if I get a little excited, I still have a tendency to go back to that once in a while. The same thing happened in Italian neighborhoods, German neighborhoods, Irish neighborhoods. For a lot of kids their parents' language at home was primarily the language of their ancestors. I never spoke a word of English at home. We always spoke the mother tongue, said our prayers in the mother tongue, and studied the grammar of our ancestors. Many of our parents had an idea that they were going to make it here in this country, and then go back to the old country and live a life of luxury. But most of our parents became accustomed to the American way of life, there was nobody breathing down their backs, and there was a lot of employment here. Chicago wasn't built by people with big academic backgrounds. This city was built by the blood and sweat of immigrants who couldn't even laugh in English.

I worked while I was a youngster from fourteen on. During the depression of 1919, I went to work as an apprentice plumber to help keep the family going, so I dropped out of high school. In those days you worked on the two-flats and three-flats [apartments], and, as you were down below cutting some threads or pipes, the craftsmen would urinate and say, "At least you'll smell like a plumber." I carried their equipment, I worked with them, and, Milton, they were great teachers. If you didn't do your work properly, they would make you take it apart. I became one of the finest craftsmen in the business, and am still a card-carrying member of Local 130, Chicago Journeymen Plumbers Union, and then started my own heating and air-conditioning business, which was very successful.

We talk about the gangs of today that are scattered around the city. We also had gangs, but they were ethnic gangs—Polish boys, Italian boys, and Jewish boys. We'd play together, and, once in a while, we'd fight like hell. But we didn't resort to knives and guns. If one of the young people would reach for something other than his own fisticuffs, everybody would look upon him with disgust. But we were friends, and would visit each other. I can remember when I would have some of my Jewish friends over, and I would have them sit on the porch, because my mother (Lord have mercy on her soul, she was a very religious woman), couldn't understand how we could get along because of the difference in faiths. By the same token, some of my Jewish friends would say, "You better not come into the house because the old lady won't understand." We'd use an expression, "This guy is my friend with no discount," which means that he is a hundred percent. You take a kid like myself, who was born Jan Ludvig Wojnarowski, coming up in what was then a white, Anglo-Saxon society —it was difficult. My brother, Joseph, was a musician and went around trying to get a job as Joseph Wojnarowski. They wouldn't even interview him, so he changed it to Joey Waner, and wound up with some of the top name bands. So, after I got married as John Wojnarowski, I went to the courts and put a petition in to change the name of my family to Waner.

How did you get into politics?
I started to vote in 1935. Everybody was a Democrat in those days. My family was rabid Democrats. I hadn't particularly made up my mind who to vote for, but I had always had a strong sense of independence. I walked into the polling place, and the Democratic precinct captain met me and said, "John, I know you're going to vote like your parents." Something triggered inside me. I didn't like that. I said, "What gives you that idea?" He said, "You wouldn't do anything else." I said, "The hell I wouldn't." I turned around and said to one of the judges, "Give me a Republican ballot." When I came out, he called me every kind of a name. I took exception to this effrontery. I went to the Republican headquarters and said, "Who have you got in that neighborhood?" He said, "Nobody." I said, "You should." He

said, "You're absolutely right. How about helping us?" I said, "Fine. What do I do?" They told me, and I went around and started to talk to the people in the neighborhood, telling people, "Look, you don't have to follow the dictates of one party. Vote for the man, not the party." I found a lot of resistance. I remember one case when I knocked on a door and the fellow who answered the door said, "Who is it?" I said, "The Republican precinct captain." He said, "Wait a minute." He went back into the building and his wife opened the second floor window and poured a bucket of water on me. That shows you that the Republicans weren't too popular in the Polish community. But we formed a little club and worked on our parents, and within six years, a precinct that was solid Democrat turned over and became solid Republican. I think the Democrats received five or six votes in the precinct. Subsequently, Milton, I was able, as the Republican committeeman, to deliver the 23rd ward with huge pluralities for Republican candidates and gain recognition within the Republican Party. I was looked upon as the spokesman for my community, and I took a lot of pride in that. I was also very successful in my heating and air-conditioning business. I employed a lot of young people in the neighborhood and helped them get their union cards. I was able to devote time and more money in organizing the community. In 1955, Bob Merriam was selected as the Republican mayoral candidate, and I was selected as his running mate for treasurer, but Mayor Daley and his ticket won.

How did you happen to run for mayor against Daley in 1967?
That was somewhat of a mistake. I was not meant to be the candidate. Ben Adamowski ran for mayor against Daley in 1963 on the Republican ticket. I was a ward committeeman in 1967 and met with Dick Ogilvie, who was president of the Cook County board and a very powerful individual who looked like he was going to be the candidate for governor and subsequently was; Chuck Percy, who was just elected United States senator in 1966; and others. We decided that we really wanted to go after the City Hall administration this time for keeps. Ogilvie, Percy, and other political leaders, in a series of conferences with prospective candidates, were looking for someone with the charisma of a Mayor John Lindsay of New York—a very effective speaker who made a fine television appearance. They were talking to Norman Ross, a vice-president of the First National Bank in Chicago, a very fine young man—good looking, handsome, articulate. In the meantime, someone had to do the work at the central

committee to box out some of the prospective candidates, and, of course, Ben Adamowski was again chomping at the bit. He had a running feud with the mayor and wanted to go after him. Well, I did a pretty effective job there and knocked him, Bob Podesta, and Jack Sperling out of the box in the so-called smoke-filled room, the caucuses.

I said to Dick Ogilvie and a number of political leaders in his office, "Well, we knocked out all the aspirants. Now we can pave the way for this young progressive that you have in mind." They said, "Waner, it looks like we're out of luck. He just changed his mind." I said, "What the hell are we going to do now?" They said, "You knocked everybody out. There's nobody left. You better go." I said, "I don't have the background, or the charisma. I'm a guy from the other side of the tracks." They said, "Waner, go. We'll help you."

I got the hell beat out of me. I tried to put on an effective campaign. I couldn't raise any money. God, when I think of what took place in those days! Everybody went for Daley. I got hold of James C. Worthy, who was one of the pillars of our community and chairman of the Republican Fund, the fund-raising arm of the Republican Party, and said, "Jim, I gotta get a committee together to raise some money. Will you be chairman?" He said, "Of course I will." Every top name Republican was already on Daley's list as supporters. But he said, "I'll find someone." He called me, quite excited, and said, "C'mon, you and I are going over to see John T. Pirie of Carson Pirie and Scott." Pirie said, "Mr. Waner, I'm a strong believer in the two-party system. One of my vice-presidents, Virgil Martin, is with the mayor. I am going to do everything I can to help you in your campaign against Mayor Daley." I said, "That's great." We called our public relations people together and made a press release on it, "Waner's new committee formed by James Worthy, the head of Carson Pirie, and a few others." I got a call from Jim Worthy the next day. He said, "I've got bad news for you." I said, "What happened?" He said, "Pirie withdrew." I said, "Why?" He said, "I don't know. They must have gotten hold of him. Suddenly, he's taking a vacation to Jamaica." That was the end of that.

We had a difficult time raising any money. I went for a considerable amount of money myself, perhaps a little more than I should have. Candidates get carried away. It was a clean fight. I attacked the issues. But I got beat bad. You know why? Most of the Republican committeemen that we have in Chicago are committeemen in name only. Most of them couldn't hold a meeting in a telephone booth.

They're self-serving to the "ins" in Chicago. They live on the hand-outs that they receive from the machine. Look down the list of committeemen that we have in Chicago. They're paper organizations. There is really no Republican Party in Chicago.

What kind of help did you get from people like Ogilvie, Percy, and Republican leaders outside of the organization?

From a monetary point, very little. They made their own private donations, sold a few tickets for a banquet, a few appearances, sort of generally, "He's a good guy sort of thing." It's a helluva note when you run for office and your own leaders feel that you haven't got a chance. You feel like an orphan. The local media supported the administration one hundred percent. The press will attack something all year long, talk about the system doing this and that, yet, when the election comes around, they support the incumbent. A lot of them also received handouts from the Democratic Party. I know many a reporter that had a brother-in-law, or a cousin, or somebody, on the Democratic payroll. By the same token, you have to remember all the taxable assets that these newspapers own.

What kind of a campaign did Daley run?

In Chicago, Daley doesn't have to come up with any new formulas for winning elections. When Dick Daley runs for office, he follows a stereotype campaign which is very effective. The first thing he does, he wraps up all the men of prominence within the community. Most of them don't live in Chicago, but they practice their various professions in the city. So he has this big executive committee which virtually locks up anybody who will challenge him. They are very effective in raising money. It was very simple for Daley to raise millions of dollars by many favors that are handed out through an established, entrenched political machine. There are a lot of goofs out there. Here's a guy that maybe is cum laude from some college and has a very successful business, but he is obsessed with the idea that he has got to have a three-letter license number, which is a very simple thing for a politician to do. He sends him a three-letter license number. Then someone will come around and say, "So and so is running for office. Would you care to make a little contribution?" He takes out a checkbook and sends a few thousand dollars. There are a lot of nuts, and the more money they got, the goofier they are. A guy may get a little sticker for his car where he could park in some place, something that will say, "Official business." It means a lot to him. Milt, you can't begin to believe how some of the so-called leaders of our community respond to politicians!

You know what makes bad politicians? A lot of good people that love that fanfare. Queen Wilhelmina comes to Chicago. Daley will send out a list of invitations to some of the pillars of our business community, "You're cordially invited to attend a reception in honor of Queen Wilhelmina." Everyone will come because they want to be part of the "in-crowd." Then if somebody taps them for a contribution to the party, you can bet your bottom dollar they'll take the checkbook and write a check because someone invited them somewhere. Many of these fellows, when they ride back to the suburbs in their high-powered limousines, if they heard of one of the Democratic ward committeemen or precinct captains being in their neighborhood, they'd say, "What's he doing out here?" He's beneath them. But when they are in Chicago, they just enjoy playing that up. They go to lunches in places where they can meet some of these people. They turn around to the others around them and say, "I know that guy. That's Senator Schmaltz." When one of the fellas is having breakfast out because he's too busy and his wife didn't cook for him, and he's sitting at Maxim's Restaurant, and the mayor waved to him, this guy gets his jelly sauce. The mayor waved to him. Big thing! But, Milton, it's there.

The strength in the Democratic Party lies in just that. They're able to deliver services within the city, even if it means delivering a garbage can, a 55-gallon oil drum with the head cut out of it that somebody was glad to dispose of. They deliver it to Joe Schmo, and Joe Schmo says, "Jeez, I got a garbage can from the city." Or when a precinct captain or one of the politicians come around and says, "Haven't we been good to you?", he reaches into his checkbook and writes out a check for $500. He could have picked up a brand new galvanized garbage can over at Goldblatt's for a buck and a half!

What about the labor unions and the Democratic organization in Chicago?

Labor unions in Chicago are part of the Democratic Party entourage. Again, it's because Richard Daley and his party play a very smart political game. The business agent of the Plumbers Union, where I'm still a card-carrying member, was just appointed a member of the school board. You'll find Bill Lee of the American Federation on the park district. The Democratic Party continuously works at making friends. They follow the old maxim that you make friends by addi-

tion. The Republicans are not smart. If someone takes issue with
something within the party platform, the party line, they immediately ostracize them. They want no part of them. He's too reaction-
ary, too liberal, or too progressive. A party has to consist of every type
of an individual. That's what makes a strong party.

*John, what did Daley do for the labor unions in return for this
support?*

The labor unions have always received everything that they have
asked for from City Hall. All of the municipal services that are rendered by the city of Chicago are under union contract. People who
work at the building trades receive substantially more money than
in the private sector. A plumber, a sheet metal worker, a steam fitter,
an iron worker, an electrician in the private sector receives well in
excess of $15 an hour today, with all the fringe benefits. That's predi-
cated on the fact his work is seasonal. He may work six, seven, eight
months out of a year. When they enter into contract negotiations
with the city of Chicago, these labor organizations demand the same
wage scales as they get in the private sector. Daley gives it to them.
We are paying through the nose for services that should be coming
to the people of Chicago for substantially less money, because working for the municipal government, you should work for substantially
less per hour because you're working twelve months a year.

*How can they work twelve months a year, if they can't do it in the
private sector?*

That is something we will wait for posterity to determine. You
never see any layoffs, Milt, in municipal government. If they got two
hundred electricians working in the summertime, there will be two
hundred electricians working in the wintertime, unless there is an
election in November of that year. In cold weather the building
trades on the outside are all out of work, but most of them will get
jobs with the city. The taxpayers pay through the nose for that. This
is one of the reasons that labor is so closely allied with the City Hall
administration. There has never been one single instance of the City
Hall administration getting up and saying, "Enough already! This is
it. For goodness sakes, what do you want?" I hope in the years ahead
that Chicago doesn't get into the same position that New York is in
today, because they give these huge pension funds and welfare
funds, and obligating people to the future for something that could
be eliminated today. Every person should have job security, but we

have no right to obligate future generations for the payment of these huge pensions. Daley is strong enough not to be euchred in some positions. Chicago bonds still have a top credit rating. I hope this continues, but if we continue to give away the store, we're going to be in serious trouble.

Can you evaluate Daley for me, John?

Mayor Daley's strength lies in the organization itself. The organization in Chicago is all-powerful. Daley is a creature of a machine that he created. Yet Daley is probably a lot stronger than other political leaders in the past. Daley exercises very strong authority within that political system. At the same time, he's smart enough to bring in high-grade talent. He also has aligned himself with many of the leaders of the business community by having an open-door policy to them. He makes up his mind on the advice of his planners, but he won't move ahead with his program without first consulting many of these people, in order not to draw flak. Once in a while he will go off the deep end on some program, like he talked about an airport in the middle of Lake Michigan, or a new stadium on the IC Railroad tracks. He does this without consulting these people, and the media and everybody else gets after him and he'll drop it, sometimes reluctantly. But very seldom will he move into an area where there is or may be strong opposition without first calling in particular individuals or groups and trying to convince them that the program he is contemplating was something that was necessary.

On a personal basis, the guy is a beautiful guy, a very human individual. I pick up the phone and, invariably, he will give me an appointment. Many times, I've seen many of his strong political leaders waiting in the anteroom and he will say, "C'mon in, John." One thing about Mayor Daley. You can go to him and say, "Dick, I'm interested in so and so," and he'll say, "I'll look into it." If he doesn't make a note of it, you can forget it. If he opens his drawer, takes out a pencil and starts making notes and asks a few questions, it's just as good as done.

Once, I had to auction a lot of properties, and I found strong opposition from his head of development, his planners, and the members of his housing authority. I called the mayor. I came in and said, "Dick, I've got a problem. I've got to put these buildings back on the road. There's a helluva big housing shortage out there. I think that the programs that you fellas are planning are unworkable. I don't think that you are fully aware of what I am trying to do, and I don't think you are getting it as you should." He said, "John, are you sure of what you are doing?" I said, "Dick, I never lied to you." He took his pencil out and made a note. My people had to meet with his planners that afternoon. They didn't even have to open up their briefcases. The head of city planning took a complete flip-flop. He said, "We've been thinking it over. I think we are going to go along with the program suggested by Mr. Waner." I then knew that Mayor Daley must have picked up the phone and said, "We go with Waner's program."

I got the hell beat out of me by Daley. There's nothing so lonesome as a politician that gets beat. John Lindsay said, after he lost, "After the count comes in, I walk the street and nobody wants to talk to me." That happens every time in politics. I'm sitting in my office the next day after I got beat by Daley. I get a phone call, "Mayor Daley's on the phone." I thought somebody was pulling my leg. Anyway, I said, "I'll take it." He said, "John, this is Dick." I said, "Congratulations, Mr. Mayor. You won." He said, "I know how you feel, John. I got beaten when I ran against Walsh and I just want you to know I respect you." I thought it was so nice. I waited for calls from Dick Ogilvie, Chuck Percy, Ed Kucharski—all Republican leaders. Hell, they were afraid to call me because maybe I would want to borrow money from them. This is one of the tragedies of politics. It's a lonesome day after you get beat. You feel real bad and your family feels sorry for you. They kind of look at you. Every daughter, every son, every wife, feels her husband is the greatest and he should win. "What's the matter with the public? They're crazy!"

Does Daley have any weaknesses?
I don't know. The press says he favors members of his own family, members of his own political party, members in business, and this is nepotism. But who isn't interested in the well-being of their children? I hate like hell to say he has weaknesses, other than that. He knows when he makes this type of a decision that he is going to have to stand a barrage of public criticism in the media. The fact that he stands up to it denotes that he has got a lot of strength. Daley is a strong-willed individual. If he makes up his mind that he is going to do something, he'll take on anybody to achieve that, even though it may not be a popular thing, until he finally strikes out because there is a lack of support to achieve that.

John, you have been in politics or government most of your life. Why did you get into it, and why did you stay in it?

That's a tough question. I'm a successful businessman. I've been able to make it through blood, sweat, guts, and perhaps a lot of con and baloney. There's a certain thing about politics that intrigues me and intrigues others. It's the fanfare. You can see people on the street and give them a nod. But when you meet them at a political meeting, or a wake, or a wedding, you greet each other like long-lost friends. We all love that hurrah in politics. In the private sector, you don't get that. You lack something. So you made a lot of money! Your wife knows you made money. Your employees hate you because you made money. In the political arena, if you're successful, they look up to you. John Lasinski (and John was a Democrat) would tell me, "John, never let anybody know how rough it is, even if you haven't got a quarter. Shine your shoes, put on your best suit, put a cigar in your mouth, take off the label so that nobody knows it's a cheap one, and if somebody comes up to you and asks you, 'How's things?' tell him how good it is." If you tell him how great it is, he'll want to follow you. If you start complaining, if you tell him, "I just got laid off, I haven't got a job, things are bad," they walk away from you, figuring you're going to make a touch. I can remember times when I didn't have a contract in the office and things looked tough. A guy would come in and say, "I'd like you to look at it." I'd take my time and I'd say, "I don't know whether I can fit it in or not." I'd cross my fingers under the desk and hope that the guy wouldn't walk out. But if I jumped at it and showed a lot of enthusiasm, he'd figure, "This guy needs the job. Maybe he won't be able to finish it." The same thing in politics. If you went ahead and went in with that gung ho, that "We're the greatest," you rally people around you.

Milt, if I wasn't HUD area director for the state of Illinois, and I called a press conference, I could hold it in a john. On the other hand, when I tell my public relations guy to call a press conference, "Waner is going to make a statement," he goes out there and puts it on the wires. The newspaper reporters come and you got six cameras up in a hurry. "What are you going to talk about?" I am not going to tell them until they're all ready. Newspaper reporters are a lazy lot. They like to get it the first time, shoot it into the newsroom, and then duck for a ball game. It gives you a forum.

At the same time, you get a lot of flak. The city groups come in and complain. Many a time, I would like to join them, and go down to Washington and say, "What the hell you doing out there?" Invariably, people who come from the neighborhood know what the neighborhood needs, and I know what the neighborhoods need because I am part of a neighborhood. The guy I'm always leery of in Washington is the guy who says, "Waner, I want you to know that I want to 'hep' you." They are the most negative bastards I have ever met. I hope, in the years ahead, they clean that bureaucracy out. The worst thing that ever happened in Washington was when all these people were put under civil service and have that security. Government in Washington isn't run by GS18s, the GS17s, and the '16s, and all that high-grade talent that moves into Washington. It's the guys in the line that are afraid to make a move. They want job security. They couldn't care less if Rome is burning or Chicago is falling apart. Congress passes legislation, and then the bill is turned over to some agency to administer, to some bureaucrat to write the regulations. After the regulations are written, any similarity to the law is purely coincidental. He took all of the meat out of it.

Here in Illinois we have twenty-four congressmen today, half of which are Republicans, half Democrats, but in Chicago, we have only five congressmen who are in the so-called areas of deprivation, where they know what's happening. The ones up Northwest or on the lakeshore, it doesn't affect them. The same thing in Detroit, and in Philadelphia, and New York. In Washington, they represent a very small body out of the total amount of congressmen. The fella who is from Salt Lake City is a congressman who, when he hears the Chicago congressman complain about the problems of the inner city, what in the hell does he know? "I don't believe it because it doesn't happen in Salt Lake City, or Keokuk, Iowa, Podunk, or Lame Duck, Mississippi." The result is that they don't really get the backing they should. Our people are deprived of good legislation because it don't affect the particular individual in a remote area, where here, it is a matter of life and death.

I think that big government has actually gotten away from little people. We think that we can settle the problems of our society in Washington by legislation. Milt, we can't do it. We have to do it on a local level. That is something that Daley attempted to do. I read your book and I thought it was great, and you said that Daley couldn't care less what happens in Washington. He's more interested in what happens at 42nd and Meadow, what happens at State and Madison, what happens up north. That is what he wants to know. He wants to know what we can do to help these people. He doesn't want to go beyond that. When I talk to Daley and I say, "Dick, I've got a prob-

lem with Washington," he'd say to call Frank Annunzio who is on the
housing committee in Washington, and he'll have one of his people
explain to him that there is a problem there that should be corrected,
inasmuch as it affects Chicago. Not that it affects Lower Slobbovia,
but that it affects Chicago.

I feel the same way. I'm interested in what affects Chicago. What
are we going to be doing with those thousands and thousands of black
kids who have struck out? There's no place for them to go. These kids
don't have a chance to get into gainful trades and professions. We've
got to catch these kids before they become dropouts. Once they're
dropouts, they're gone. Somewhere in our academic field, they're
going to have to look at this and say, "This kid looks like a potential
dropout and he doesn't look like he wants to study. Let's channel him
into some useful trade or profession. Let's indenture him to an uphol-
sterer or let's indenture him somewhere so at least he won't be out
there ripping off something, and he can have a little self-respect."

I don't know what your ethnic background is, but you were able
to become a professor, and I became a federal official and successful
in business, because we had a chance. Some way, we've locked these
kids out. When our ancestors came from Europe, they didn't have an
opportunity to go into a bank and get a mortgage, anymore than
these young blacks today have a chance to get a mortgage. Can you
imagine Ludvig Wojnarowski, my father, being able to go to the First
National Bank and say, "I want mortgage," in his broken English?
Why, they'd laugh at him! But you know what they did. They formed
a little thrift association, a savings and loan, the forerunner of the
massive institutions that you see today. First Federal, Bell Savings.
Look at the programs we got today. Nowhere in government have
we got a program that will instill home ownership in Chicago along
the lines our ancestors were able to buy homes. All of the Poles and
Bohemians and Germans, first thing they wanted, they wanted a
two-flat, or three-flat, and when they were able to get one, they
exercised social pressure on their tenants. As soon as the tenants
came in, immigrants, they told them, "Now look, keep the stairs
clean and keep your kids from writing graffiti on the walls, etc."

What we do today, we build one big building with federal insurance and federal subsidies, one landlord, 650 families. The kids hate
it. They come home and they put graffiti on the wall because they
think that represents Uncle, "It's not ours." Where, on the other
hand, that three-flat, that two-flat, that belonged to an individual.
Doesn't it make a lot more sense to have three hundred owners or

buildings and each one with a sense of ownership, a sense of pride, a sense of unity, than one big building?

What's in the hearts of people? Pride of ownership. The ability to own a piece of land. The ability to be able to point to something and say that this is mine, every bit of it. These are the things everybody looks forward to. I think the giveaway programs have done nothing but destroy the incentives for people to go out and work to achieve some of these things.

John, I won't even ask you what someone asked Curley of Boston at the end, "Would you do it again?" I know you'd do it again.

Of course, I'd do it again. One of my regrets is that life is so short, and we have so few productive years to carry out the things we stand for, the things we are dedicated to accomplish. If I had a little more academic background, but the same pragmatic approach, I think there would have been a lot more changes that I could have played a part in. Most people would say they had some disappointments. I haven't. I've been married over forty years. I've had a good life. I haven't been the greatest husband in the world, but I've raised a fine family. I'm proud of my kids. They may not all agree with me politically. I have a very conservative daughter, I've got a liberal daughter. I've got a kind of duke's mixture at home. At times I have to plead with them, "Look, this guy's a friend of mine, give him a vote." One thing they all agree on is that the old man is dedicated. I'm proud of that. If I come home, they say, "Dad, we saw what you said, or read what you said. Keep it up." I haven't missed anything. If someone would say, "Did you regret losing the mayoralty?" I'd say, "Hell, no!" I wish I had a little more academic experience. Perhaps it would have helped me say the things that I like to say. I don't like to lie about anything, Milt. I may duck an issue, but I say the things I believe in. If you don't like something, say it! And if you say it and something isn't done about it, then get into the battle and fight for it. I think if you do that, you got one helluva satisfaction. You look back and say, "I've done it. That's the important thing."

RICHARD FRIEDMAN
Jewish. Bright, able Democratic lawyer who served in state government and as Executive Director of the Better Government Association, a reform, civic watchdog group. Ran against Daley in 1971. Was HEW regional director under Nixon and Ford.

I was born in 1929 in Chicago, grew up on the South Side in the Hyde Park area, went to public grammar school, graduated from the Harvard School for Boys. I graduated from Grinnell College in 1951 with a degree in economics with honors, and from Northwestern University Law School in 1955. I was with a private law firm in Chicago, then served in the office of the Attorney General of Illinois until 1969, when I became the executive director of the Better Government Association. I ran for mayor in the spring of 1971, then became regional director of HEW in July 1971.

By inclination, in my formative years, I was a Democrat. Throughout all of my voting life I took particular pains to regard myself as an independent, as well. I voted for people on both sides. I worked for Bob Merriam in his mayoral campaign in 1955. I worked both for Attorney Generals Bill Clark, who was a Democrat, and Bill Scott, who was a Republican.

How did you come to run for mayor of Chicago as a Republican in 1971?

A group of citizens who were concerned about the well-being of Chicago met from time to time in advance of that 1971 election in hopes that they could develop some interest in a credible candidate. I consulted with that group and agreed to step forward. I had no illusions about the possibilities of winning. But my candidacy would provide an opportunity for someone who had a pretty good knowledge of the city to present a campaign based on issues. I raised something like a dozen major issues, some seven or eight of which, in subsequent years, were affirmatively acted upon by Mayor Daley. I withdrew $2,500 from my personal savings account. I had a nucleus of one-half-dozen people who had been interested in the campaign.

I used them as my initial source, formed various committees, finance, publicity, and the like, raised some initial monies, and hired a core staff of about fifteen people on a two-week by two-week basis. We had, ultimately, between 6,000 and 8,000 people who were actively involved.

The total amount of money that was raised was approximately $200,000. I solicited those funds by breakfasts, lunches, and dinners with groups of people, imploring them to contribute to the welfare of the city. I received zero support from the labor unions, but I received what I felt was good support from the Republican business community. Typically, the Republican business community has been Republican in national and state affairs, but Democratic in Chicago affairs. Help from the Republican ward organizations was spotty. There were perhaps a dozen organizations that were viable. The balance were either marginal, or adjuncts to the Democratic Party in their wards. I felt that the only way that I could equalize the tremendous array of power of the machine was to utilize the facilities of the media. I was treated very fairly by the media.

How much money did Mayor Daley raise in that campaign?
I have no way of knowing. My guess is that on election day, in terms of cash to the precinct captains, he spent on the range of $400,000 to $500,000, which almost doubled my total campaign. He also received a lot of services in kind—billboards, free advertising, and the like, things which I had no opportunity to get close to. I would estimate the total value of goods and services, cash contributions, and the like at close to a million and a half dollars. Daley ran a very low-level, non-issue-oriented campaign. There was virtually nothing of substance that was said by the mayor in terms of the future direction of the city. It was run wholly through the organization. The mayor spent all of his time at the organizational level. He propounded sheer platitudes and generalities. They based the campaign wholly on the ward organizations, the precinct captains, and turning out a predictable number of people on election day. We did a poll (and I am told the Democratic Party also did a poll), which showed that some five or six weeks away from election day, forty percent of the voters polled had not yet made up their minds. Probably ninety percent of that group ended up voting for Mayor Daley. I think that in large measure the reason for that was that they wanted something different, they wanted something better, but they were very apprehensive about any change. Even in 1971, he was more than an insti-

tution. He was regarded as something of a deity. He was above politics. He was above many, many other things and there was just a curious feeling of his being a ubiquitous father figure, and the usual give and take of politics did not apply in his case.

In 1955 he had begun a very intelligent political program to coopt virtually every group in the city. He successfully did that with the business community, the academic community, and the ethnic groups, even though there should have been tension between competing groups. He had a marvelous knack of promising a great deal and giving very little, but the illusion of effort was there. The matrix which bound this together was the fact that he had something like 40,000 patronage jobs. When you multiply that by immediate family, you have a very large segment of the total population in the city of Chicago who were either directly or indirectly dependent on the paycheck from the city. And their ticket towards that was participation in politics.

The mayor loved the city. There just was no question about that. But he loved power more. He was interested in power for power's sake. The secondary element was to do good things for the city. But if it were a choice of doing the right thing by the city or retaining power, there was no question of where his decision would be made. He was not an ideologue. He accepted new ideas and good ideas which were nonthreatening in any way, but he totally rejected those kinds of things which would tend to dilute his power base. The prioritization was—maintain the power base. Regenerate yourself in power and all other consequences flow from that. There is widespread corruption that has been tacitly accepted by the people of Chicago. Maybe it's the fact that we are heir to the tradition of Al Capone within our heart of hearts, proud of that tough image. That's an iniquitous thing, to accept corruption as a way of life, but we have it here in Chicago. One can then go on from that and say that by having that kind of corruption we tolerate other kinds of non-venal corruption in our neighborhoods—the willingness to pay off political debts to real estate developers at the expense of neighborhoods.

I have the highest respect for the mayor as a public administrator. He knew the operation of his key departments. He knew the needs of the city. He was well versed in budgetary matters. He moved things along rapidly. He knew when to make a decision. He knew when not to make a decision. His sense of timing was superb. He was just a very, very able administrator. I have worked very closely with the mayor and key members of his staff in an interrelationship between the federal government and the city of Chicago, and they always did their homework. They were very professional, very competent in the things that they did, and it was very easy for us to relate to Chicago on complex matters.

He did not deal well with state government. There are traditional tensions and problems that accrue there. But in terms of the federal government, both during the time when there was a Democratic administration which owed him a debt of gratitude or a Republican administration, he did very, very well. The Republican administration handled Mayor Daley very gingerly. My strong sense is that he was not regarded as an enemy. On the contrary, he was handled very deferentially throughout Washington during the period of 1970–1976. In part, it was a reaction to a consummately good politician. The people in Washington are public administrators part-time and they are politicians part-time, and that part of them that was involved in politics made them very respectful of Mayor Daley's talents.

How do you see the political future of this city now, after Daley's death?

I don't know. It would be an error to say that there is no opposition, that there is a political naivete on the part of the power structure of Chicago that would preclude our maturation as a politically sophisticated city, one with a real two-party system. I see a possibility of various forces coalescing, at least having the beginning of an opposition to typical machine politics in Chicago. There are many problems within the city that have not been attended to, and, if they are not attended to, there will be a sufficient number of people who recognize that the way to change things is through the political process, and that they would be sufficiently energized to organize and do something about it.

Chicago is essentially a workingman's city, remains so to a much lesser degree now than in the days when I was growing up, when it was a first-generation immigrant city. That's much less of a factor now. It's a city which is increasingly becoming constituted of poor people. The inner city is expanding, the younger middle-class white people are leaving the city to go out to the suburbs. The essential character of the city is changing toward a lower-income, predominantly poor, less educated citizenry.

Its strengths are the diversity of its industry, talking of Chicago as metropolitan Chicago. In increasing ways, the strength of the city is now in Gary, East Chicago, and Elk Grove Village, as opposed to the South Side, the West Side, the North Side of Chicago. The diversity of industry has been able to serve us well in periods of economic recession. There is a growth factor, when we talk about cumulative employment. We have enormous potential as a major international city, in terms of exports. The amenities are marvelous, the lakefront and the like. But we have a very thin veneer of beauty in the city along the lakefront, and then you go inland, and you get some areas of great squalor.

The glaring weakness is a very inferior educational system. The Chicago public schools are not adequately preparing young people for lives in modern America. We have an uneducated group of young people who are moving through our public schools. Funding is a problem, but I don't think that this is the common factor. There is an unwieldy, overly centralized bureaucracy. There is a great absence of tradition of respect for learning. A very high proportion of the children who are in the Chicago public schools come from families which our sociologists would say are culturally deprived. They have no real role models that enable them to place education and learning as a high priority item. Until we are able to craft that kind of cycle, it is going to be very difficult for anyone to change the face of education in Chicago.

What about the racial problem in Chicago? How do you see that evolving?

The city is a great deal less tense now from a racial standpoint than it was five or six years ago. The percentage of blacks ranges from thirty-five to forty-three percent. You factor into that ten to fifteen percent of Latinos, and you get a very uneasy racial balance. Chicago is the most segregated city in the country. The compartmentalization of the city has been drawn in a way so that it is going to be very hard to change. Neighborhoods have been carved up and created by bisecting them with highways and the like. Traditional barriers have been erected which are not only historical and sociological in nature, but they are physical boundaries as well. There is a prospect that it will remain a highly segregated city unless someone recognizes that there is a need to actively support change. But on balance, Chicago is a conservative town.

How do you see the economic future of Chicago?

I think it is rather bleak for several reasons. One, the labor pool is not the kind of pool that is needed. You've got young people who are uneducated, who do not present a very good cadre of workers to attract industry. Two, the crime rate is very high. Three, the tax climate in the city is not particularly good. Four, someone who wants to locate a business or factory in Chicago must deal with the fact of life of corruption, of building inspectors and the like, who can hassle a businessman in many, many ways. Cumulatively, those four factors all militate against locating in the city. It's a great deal more attractive to locate not only in suburbia, but exurbia, where you've got a good labor pool, you don't have transportation problems, and you are not hassled by corruption and the like. When you balance those two together, the growth factor of Chicago has been negligible, and the growth factor of the suburban ring around the city has been quite different.

Would you run for public office again?
No, I would not do it again, but I have no regrets for having done it. It was a great growth experience for me. I learned a great deal about myself, the city, and the political process. But being a candidate is a very subjective thing, and when you run and do the good fight once with some style, you're fortunate. If you do it many times, you become quixotic, and all the luster soon disappears. So I would not be tempted to participate in the future. I cannot foresee a set of circumstances that would make me change that consideration.

JOHN HOELLEN *German. About sixty-five. Long-time Republican alderman and committeeman from Northwest Side's 47th ward. Vocal critic of Daley in city council for twenty years. Lost his aldermanic seat in 1975, when he ran against Daley for mayor, and is now practicing law.*

I was born in 1914, and lived my entire life in the same house that I still live in now, at 1842 Larchmont Avenue, about a block from my office here at 1940 Irving Park Road. There was a certain security in the old neighborhood. I had grown up in it. I like the people. I feel I know the trees, the children, and the people that have been here. The neighborhood has been somewhat resistant to change, and hopefully the three decades that I put into politics, and the decade or two before me put in by my father, contributed somewhat to the stability of the old Ravenswood community. I am proud of Ravenswood and hope to keep my roots deep in Ravenswood.

My father was born of German-born parents in Chicago. He served in the city council from 1925 until 1933 and was crucified by the machine. He had a coronary shortly after that and died in 1936. He was just forty-nine years old. I have always felt that the machine was evil because of all the evil they wreaked upon my father.

I went to public school, Lakeview High School, Northwestern University, and Northwestern Law School. I was trained for a career in public administration at Northwestern, where I majored in political science, and dedicated my life to politics.

I was elected to the city council as a Republican in 1947, served twenty-eight years, and was reelected six times in spite of all the hooting and name calling through some seven turbulent terms. I served with Paddy Bauler, Tom Keane, Vito Marzullo, Harry Sain, Jim Bowler, and some of the famous names of yesteryear. The council during that period was a heady group. Almost totally corrupt and easily corruptible. On one occasion, the general counsel of the Pennsylvania railroad came to me quite seriously, wondering what the going rate for a switch-back [vote] would be involving one of the prominent industries in Chicago. Apparently $27,000 was asked to lay a track across there. They used to think that I was something of a queer or boy-scout when I wouldn't take $8,000 for a driveway during the period when all the driveways were going in.

It was a sickening and terrifying experience to be involved in the city council during that period. Graft was rampant. I was shot at on January 21, 1947, by a hoodlum. He had been told that if he killed Hoellen, he would be able to take over gambling in the 47th ward. I was spared death on that occasion. It was a rough and tough experience to be a part of a situation where you had gambling joints going, and trying to be a crusader against some of the problems that were incipient in gambling. Each gambling joint (there were three of them operating when I first became alderman), had a daily gross of $45,000, of which $15,000 was net profit. If you tried to cut in on $15,000 per day, you were dealing with some very big numbers, and the syndicate in Chicago was a very rough and tough organization, but I stayed in it and tried to change the system.

Has the council changed since Mayor Daley took office in 1955?
It has changed enormously. Martin Kennelly, when he was mayor, looked at the independents and the opposition as kind of benign. Even Ed Kelly, when he was mayor, and Tony Cermak, during the 1930s, always wanted to have opposition for opposition's sake, at least to color the cloth so that it wasn't all black. Mayor Daley always looked at it as a kind of a cancer and he struggled to eliminate all of his opposition to stifle it. He brooked no quarter.

Chicago has always been a tough town to be in politics, but I think the graft is more sophisticated now. I don't know that they are paying $8,000 for driveways, but I am certain that there are payoffs, where people get prior knowledge of important things like public land acquisition. Obviously, there is an awful lot of that going on in Chicago. There is graft and ripoffs that deal with parking lots, big franchises, big building permits, pieces of deals, and things of that sort. It's difficult for me to believe that Sandburg Village can get through the city council without stains of impropriety, Chicago being what it is.

Chicago is a breed unto itself. I was privileged to talk with some of the New York Republicans way back in 1952, when I was given the job of leading the moderate Republicans for Eisenhower. Tom Stevens, who was part of the Tom Dewey/Herb Brownell group, told me that only in Chicago could you find that the wards and precincts are partitioned into military ranks, so that by going to county headquarters you can find the political person responsible for Suzie Schmaltz living in her cottage on Cuyler Avenue. It is only in Chicago that they have that kind of discipline and it has been that way through the years. And it is more disciplined today than it has ever been.

Chicago has always been kind of a frontier town. We have always had much of the wild west in Chicago. The syndicate, Al Capone and some of those people gave Chicago a temper and a mark. We maintained a heady bunch of politicians in City Hall—the Paddy Baulers, Jim Bowlers, the Vito Marzullos. They realize that politics is a business and it's a business that pays very well when you are in it. They may well be representative of the city, but I hope they are not.

I see the city machine as a sinful operation, denying most of the kids of Chicago their birthright—decent quality public education. Perhaps it is because so many of the leaders in Chicago have been involved in parochial education, but they just don't give a damn about public education. For years (and I have traced the school budget going back for thirty years), we have been committing some 40 percent of our tax dollar for public education, where most of the suburban communities throughout America commit somewhere around 60 to 75 percent of public funds to education. More than that, the funds that are committed to education have been prostituted. For years we have been denying teachers, while hiring more janitors, because the janitors are precinct captains and are part of the political structure. Big school contracts are given to people because they contribute to the funds that politicians need in order to win elections or steal elections.

Today, we have been reaping the wrath of the citizenry because the people have been leaving Chicago. There are few neighborhoods that are really stable. Today we have less than 25 percent of the school population in the Chicago public schools that is white. Twenty years ago it was over 50 percent, and you can see what happened to the middle class. They are leaving Chicago in order to find better educational opportunities for their kids. But it is even worse than that. What the machine has done to public education in Chicago, you find in the cemeteries of Vietnam, because many of the kids who might have been able to go on to college were denied a college education because they simply couldn't graduate from a college or get anything other than being draft fodder in the armies when they graduated from Lakeview High School, reading at the 23rd percentile. It's a curse. It's an outrage. They just don't give a damn.

Why does the citizenry tolerate these schools?

Because, through the years Daley has been permitting the people to shift from independence to dependence in playing the game of the *pater noster.* The precinct captain is the person who does everything for people. He fixes the tickets for the parents. He gets transfers for the kids. They are becoming more and more dependent upon the precinct captains. Today, the greatest dependency of all is to have a precinct captain shovel the snow for people. Each captain is supposed to buy a snowplow in order to make the people in the precinct dependent upon the precinct captain in order to get out of their homes.

The quality of people in Chicago has been shifting enormously. The young, energetic people who graduated from college want something better for their kids. They leave Chicago, and go to the suburbs. That crescendo has been increasing year by year. We have been having a total decline in population. From 1950 to 1960, we lost about 4 percent of the population in Chicago, and from 1960 to 1970, we lost almost 8 percent of the population. More than that, there has been a shifting of dependent people into Chicago, people that need their precinct captain to get their welfare checks, to get their jobs, to get the kids out of jail, to get the old man a fix for a drunken driving charge. And people pay the due bills at the time of election.

Every year, more and more of my friends are moving up to Morton Grove, Skokie, and the northwest suburbs. They are not content to leave their kids in Lakeview High School or Amundsen. They want their children to enter college, and the opportunities for a college education for one graduating from Lakeview or Amundsen are microscopic today. When I graduated from Lakeview High School, everybody who wanted to go to college could go.

You ought to realize what has happened to Chicago. When I first became alderman, I used to fight against some of the building violations. In those early years, there were many conversions where they tried to make a two-flat into a four-flat, the thing that has gone on so much in Uptown and in other communities. Everytime I fight that, I find a Democratic precinct captain trying to fix it, because the Democratic precinct captain thrives on the transients, the people who just don't give a damn, people who have no roots in the community, people who don't care if there is a sausage factory next door, because they have no commitment to the community. Their commitment is to a job, or the corner tavern, or a place where they find the

machine precinct captain helpful to them. The downward trend of
the city is so evident when you let a sausage factory in the middle
of the block, and, gradually, people who do care get tired of fighting
City Hall. Then others start going, and, gradually, more people don't
care about attending a PTA meeting. The quality of life just sinks and
sinks until you have a quagmire of people and buildings that rot
away. In Chicago today, we have thirty-five square miles of desola-
tion, dead blocks, dead property that is close to the center of the city.
That's the outrage of Chicago.

*How do people like you, who are a permanent minority (you were
once the only Republican alderman in the council), get anything
done for your wards?*

When you are number two, you have to work an awful lot harder
in order to get something done. I had no trouble getting anything
done up until the last four or five years of my career, when Daley
gave the call to Ed Kelly, the Democratic committeeman in my
ward, to get Hoellen. Kelly put Tom Allen, one of his roughest and
toughest precinct captains, in as the ward superintendent, and after
that, I just couldn't get anything done. It was hopeless and total
frustration. Until that time, for twenty-three years, my relations with
the ward superintendent were extremely cordial. We would fight
like the dickens during election time, but would always be able to
maintain a respect for each other and get things done. I was able to
get decent city services for the ward.

I had to be a local alderman, to have my office in the neighborhood,
to work at it all the time, to make almost a total commitment to it.
But I was able to get services for a wide variety of things. You have
to play many games to get things done, and maintain an intense role
of activity to be successful in a Democratic city.

*Was it worth it? Wouldn't you have been better off just to practice
law?*

I can't answer that. Obviously my salary as an alderman, $5,000 in
the very beginning, $8,000 when I ended a career of twenty-eight
years, is insufficient to maintain a political presence against the overwhelming odds of the Democratic machine where they spend almost
a thousand dollars a precinct and have ten to twelve payrollers in
every precinct. They probably have more patronage assigned to the
Kelly organization in my ward, the 47th ward, than anywhere else
in Chicago. I know other Democratic committeemen, friends of

mine that frequently comment on the inordinate power that Kelly has been getting to crucify me.

What about Mayor Daley's role in Chicago?

Mayor Daley has developed. He has always been a good student of government, he knows municipal finance, he is able, he certainly is industrious, and he is dedicated to Chicago. I think that his methods are all wrong in building one of the most corrupt political machines in the history of the world. He has been able to govern the way Hitler governed, where you are able to govern because you have total control, thought control, personal control, and mostly financial control over the entire machine. When the history of the Daley years are written, they will have to describe the days of despair of the Chicago public school system, the stealing of the birthright of kids in Chicago, the generation that must succeed Daley denied a decent chance to have an education or job training because of the lousy quality of the schools.

Maybe Mayor Daley was the right person at the right time. He always prides himself on saying that he makes the city work. He has been able to avoid the worst riots, and probably kept the lid on the city from exploding. However, I think that had Daley been more sensitive to the needs of people, and the needs of communities who want a decent place to live, he would have been able to keep the lid on the city without repression by providing job opportunities and through education. He would have been able to rebuild the center of the city where people are tearing out their plants at an increasing number, simply because they can't get quality employees in the city.

On the basic things in Chicago, Daley has been an abject failure. He has been a failure in maintaining stability in Chicago, and in maintaining the quality of life in the neighborhoods of Chicago. Most of the neighborhoods are a shambles. The ethnic leaders are uprooting themselves and leaving Chicago for suburban locations. I think that they are wrong. Chicago, the center of all the cultural greatness that is ours—the universities, the museums, the libraries, the theaters—shouldn't be a vast vacuum. When I go down to the Loop at night, I cry. The College Inn is gone, the great theaters are not there anymore, Randolph Street is a shambles. You can shoot a cannon down the street. In order to avoid State Street, we are building the new Miracle Mile on Michigan Avenue. A mayor ought to create stability. Chicago is a city in turmoil, in convulsions, and where it will end I just don't know.

What about Daley, the politician?

Daley as a politician is as smart as an alley rat. He is vindictive, knows nothing but raw power, and the sharp fang, and he will use it wherever he can in order to obtain his goals. The amount of patronage he puts on the public payroll, people that work little or don't work! Their payroll dollar is obscene. It is a disgrace. It is overkill. Why should they have to put eleven or twelve patronage workers in every precinct in the 47th ward? It's just outrageous! He could have beaten me with just one or two, but he had to put all of these people on the payroll, just in order to have a precinct captain for every block. It is just disgraceful because it not only denies education a piece of the action, but it just ruins Chicago.

I think Daley is intensely loyal. All the members of the syndicate have their own basic loyalties. Daley (although not a member of the syndicate that I know of), certainly has his basic loyalties—Alderman Vito Marzullo and the first ward bosses, and people of that kind. And loyalty begets loyalty. I think that he would have gone under a long time ago had he not maintained the power. He grabbed the marshal's baton the same way that Hitler grabbed it during 1933, and by maintaining raw power, total power, he has been able to keep that marshal's baton in his hand. But one day he is going to meet his bunker at the time his chancellery caves in.

Everybody has the idea that Daley is unbeatable. I could have beaten Daley in 1975. When you show these power statistics that Daley has, you have to realize how illusory that power really is. In 1975, when I was a candidate against Daley, there were 1,537,000 registered voters. Daley's strength has been pyramided to 537,000 primary votes. Those were his election votes when he ran against me. But I don't know how the Tribune Corporation, or Proctor and Gamble, or any of the big corporations, if they went into a shareholders' meeting holding about 35 percent of the proxies, could possibly survive in a proxy battle. I was defeated because I got no support from my party. Most of the Republicans that have money are beholden to Mayor Daley, because Daley has been either scaring them half out of their wits if they have a plant in Chicago, or taking care of the State Street advertisers in the major metropolitan newspapers.

Jim Thompson could have beat Daley, because Jim Thompson could have had the respect of the Republican business officials who might well have contributed the $2,000,000 which is necessary in order to have a war chest to beat Daley. But, in 1975, because everybody thought I was a loser, I was only able to collect $29,000 as a campaign fund, and I had committed upwards of $75,000. I'm paying off, at the rate of $750 a month for the rest of my life, a total of $50,000 that I had borrowed. It is outrageous and disgraceful. I was told it was not going to cost me anything.

Daley had upwards of a million dollars. He had so much money, he was hiring a private airplane to take him back and forth and to his Florida fishing retreat, an expenditure which strikes me as being rather questionable.

Why did you run for mayor in such a situation?
I didn't want to run. I was talked into it by the party leadership, when I failed to get Jim Thompson to run. I tried very, very hard to get somebody of strong personal magnetism, where we could have mounted a winning campaign. You know, professor, we say there are a million and a half registered voters in Chicago—but there is probably another half million that should be registered in Chicago, the Latins and the blacks that Daley has successfully been able to exclude from the electorate, simply because the precinct captains don't register the people who should be registered. Then they are out of the political process. But Chicago is ready for reform. Make no mistake about that. One day, soon, we will have it.

NINE

Some Dissidents

ADLAI STEVENSON III / ABNER
MIKVA / SEYMOUR SIMON / WILLIAM
G. CLARK

ADLAI STEVENSON III *White Protestant. Forty-eight years old. Son of the former governor of Illinois and two-time Democratic presidential candidate. Is now United States senator from Illinois. Was state treasurer and state representative. Is also an attorney. Has differed from time to time with Daley and has been an occasional critic of the machine's policies.*

I was born in Chicago, but my family moved in my infancy from the North Side to Libertyville. We traveled a lot, and lived in Washington and London with my father. When my father was elected governor of Illinois in 1948, I was away in the east at college, but spent a good deal of time with him at the mansion in Springfield during vacations.

What got you into politics?

I suspect heredity had something to do with it. But there was more to it than that. I can never remember being interested in any other line of work. I studied government and theory in college, went into the Marine Corps, and went to law school, but every action in my life was aimed at a political career.

I had my first opportunity to run for public office in 1962 when Sidney Yates, the congressman from the 9th district, was running for the Senate. I heard, many years later, that Dick Daley called up my father, who was then Ambassador to the United Nations, to see if he had any objections to my running for Congress. If I had known about it at the time, I might have gone off to Congress in 1962. My father said to Dick Daley what he always said to me—"Young man, practice law, build up a reputation in the community, make some money, and some day enter politics," the way he did it.

In 1964, the legislature failed to apportion. All the candidates for the Illinois House of Representatives ran at large, and each party slated 118 candidates. The Republicans had slated Earl Eisenhower, the brother of Dwight Eisenhower, which apparently had caused some consternation in the ranks of the regular Democrats. Mayor Daley asked if I would run for the legislature on the Democratic ticket. This time he decided not to consult my father. I consulted my father and we agreed that this would be a good way to get some political experience without giving up my law practice. I told the mayor that I would be willing to run. In those days that was about all that it took. Our ticket won and I led all 236. It was some kind of a record in American politics. We even beat Eisenhower.

I approached the campaign with some diffidence. I wasn't unaware of the physical and emotional ordeal. I wasn't very good on my feet. I really felt very uncomfortable in that job of campaigning. It didn't come naturally. The political contact with people was enjoyable and fairly easy, but public speaking did not come naturally to me, and, of course, in those days and the days which followed, I was possibly held up to comparison with my father. Since no public figure of our time measured up to his standards, especially his eloquence and humor, I didn't come off and never have come off too well by that kind of comparison. It took awhile to learn to live with that and be philosophical about it, to be my own self, and try to establish my own identity in other ways.

The Illinois legislature was hardly a model, either in ritual or efficiency. Those of us who had been brought in to dress up the ticket had been known in the campaign as the blue-ribbon candidates. In Springfield we were known as the blue-nosed candidates, and were excluded from the power structure, from the world of the special interests and the political leaders. We put together some beautiful bills, but we didn't, by any means, get all of them enacted. I learned about the mysterious ways in which bills die without any trace of violence. It was a great experience for me and I have always been glad that I could say and feel that I had started at the bottom. I loved it. I learned more about politics and government in those two years than in any other two years. It was a humbling experience, and I acquired a great deal of respect out of it for people in politics.

The United States Senate is, by comparison, a model of efficiency, virtue, and wisdom. Any legislative body in a state or nation is faced with a difficult job. It has to reconcile conflicting interests. With events moving as rapidly as they do nowadays, just staying on top of the most routine workload is a task. The Senate is, by state standards, a very efficient legislative body, and without discipline. That's one of the principal differences. In the Illinois legislature, we were given our idiot cards—instructions—just told how to vote. That would be unthinkable in the Senate. Senators are individuals, powers, each in their own right. There's no party discipline. It's difficult to coordinate

activities, to divide responsibilities in the Senate, but because of
highly qualified staff and extremely skillful political leadership,
wheels turn. We're slow to take new initiatives but there are a myr-
iad of bills that are required to be approved, just to keep this enormous government functioning. It's an impressive performance. The
men themselves are intelligent. You never know how skillful they are
as debaters and politicians until you've crossed them on the Senate
floor. You have to be careful. Before you know it, your head is just
gone, and you haven't even felt it. They are a remarkable group of
men—tough, shrewd, principled, and, with some exceptions, a very
high order of intelligence.

What do you do as a Senator, Adlai?
You work all the time. You never get the job done. It's not as bad
now as it was because we have better staff assistance. In this Congress
we reorganized and we reduced our committee assignments, the
most sweeping reorganization and reform since the committee system was formed in the early nineteenth century. We had, on the
average, in the last Congress, eighteen committee and subcommittee
assignments. That's been reduced by almost forty percent. But still,
when you serve, as I do, on four committees, as chairman of one, and
chairman of three major subcommittees, you're always expected to
be in at least three places at the same time. I receive maybe 12,000
letters a month, all of which have to be answered. I have to get the
funds for the projects in a state of 12,000,000 people. I have to meet
with constituents. I have to be on the floor. I have to be in committees. I am under pressure to make political appearances in the state
and around the nation. I am under increasing pressure to be involved
in the Congress on foreign political and economic questions for information and action. You work as hard as you can and you never catch
up. That's what really makes it so difficult. You're just driving yourself
to the limit. Every day. The stories you hear are just not true. We
don't go to embassy parties. We go home at night and work. When
the Congress is in recess, we don't go and sit under a palm tree
somewhere. We hold our hearings and we keep working. We go back
to our states and finally get back to the people, which is what this is
supposed to be all about.

I enjoy it, I suppose. It's hard to feel at times that I enjoy it when
I can barely drag myself to the next session. There will be two or
three breakfast meetings every morning. You drag yourself out of
bed at dawn to go meet with a labor delegation over the same old

tired scrambled eggs and bacon, and that's just the beginning of another day. It really makes you wonder at times whether it is all worth while. And the members are dropping out. Every Congress, now, in recent years, senators, before their time, are voluntarily dropping out for a variety of reasons. Public attitudes toward Congress, as toward other government bodies, have soured. They have been reacting toward scandal with more and more regulation. It's probably good for us. We've begun to understand what it is like to be regulated.

It's very expensive financially. There isn't a member of the Senate who couldn't do much better on the outside. I had a friend in the last Congress who was a member of the House. He had been a teacher. He was much better off financially as a teacher than as a member of Congress. We've increased our salaries to $57,000 and that's adequate, but what the public doesn't realize is that we also have tremendous personal expenses. Two homes, for example, to maintain, and official expenses which are not all reimbursed. That's changing and improving too. But the travel in your state is not compensated. When I come back to Chicago, I have to spend the night at my expense, unless I stay with somebody. The expenses are large and that's what causes the financial sacrifice for the members.

You have to have a saintly wife. She has to be willing to be tolerant. There's not much time for family, and you usually feel guilty about that. But I think it is probably more difficult in other political offices. I do get home at night and see my kids over dinner before I go back to work when we're in Washington. Governors spend more time on the banquet trail than we do. It's very hard on family, but so are all elective offices.

Let me turn you to Chicago politics. What kind of relationship did your father have with Dick Daley?

I think it was a very cordial relationship. I don't remember very well what the business and professional relationship was. When Daley was in the cabinet when my father was governor, I certainly never heard anything critical. I think he was regarded as a good member of the cabinet. They weren't intimate friends. Daley was Cook County regular organization, and my father was not. But I always saw strong indications of friendship—not intimacy—and mutual respect. My father in later years, after the governorship, when he was back here, would frequently call up Dick Daley to find out what was going on. He was interested in keeping abreast of local political affairs. He always counseled me to stay close to Dick Daley. In 1960, my father was asked to run for the presidency, after having failed twice. He didn't feel he should, resisted all the overtures, and encouraged Daley to go out and support someone else, which he did. Toward the end, I think my father's attitude changed. He came under tremendous pressure at the convention and then, apparently, overtures were made to the mayor who, by then, had made other commitments. My father understood that. He never resented it at all. I think Daley resented it. The signals had changed. The signals had been that he go out and make a commitment to Kennedy. Many years later, when I was being urged to run for the presidency, Daley said to me, "If you do it, I hope that nothing happens to me like what happened to me in Los Angeles." He was saying, "If you want my support, you've got it, and I expect you to go all the way. Don't say 'No' now and expect it later." He was urging me at that point to run.

What about your own personal relations with Daley?

I had very little contact with him in the legislature or after I was elected state treasurer in 1966. He never asked anything of me that I can recall. In 1968 we had some difficulty. He didn't ask me to run for the Senate but he indirectly indicated that he hoped I would run for the Senate against Dirksen. I indicated that I would prefer to run for governor, that one of the reasons that I didn't want to run for the Senate was my feeling about the policy in Southeast Asia, and that I could not support President Johnson's Vietnam policy. The roof fell in. The mayor was really quite upset. He was very respectful of my strong feelings on Vietnam, and he made the suggestion that if I could just qualify my position a little on Vietnam, everything would be forgotten and I would be slated for the Senate. I just kept repeating to him that I just could not support the policy in Vietnam, and that any trimming of my position would not be smart politics. He became quite imploring before it was all over. I was convinced that he really wanted me to run for the Senate. But that was an act of disloyalty that it was very difficult for the members of the organization to accept. I was dumped from the slate.

I don't think he cared at all about Vietnam, or had any strong feelings about it. What did matter to him, and probably more so to others, was discipline. Discipline is another word for loyalty. Party loyalty down the line, and he recognized only one leader at that point, the president of the United States. The obedience is blind, particularly on a subject that is as symbolically important as that. To a party in Chicago that lives by ironclad discipline, they could foresee from their own experience what might happen nationally. And it did happen nationally when the candidates started getting out of line. Johnson himself fell. I don't think they had any strong feeling about policy. It was party discipline. It was ingratitude and disloyalty on my part.

After that experience, I began putting my own troops together. We tried to build our forces around reform. In the fall of 1969, I was holding a large rally, at which we were going to raise money for reform, at my father's farm in Libertyville. Fifteen thousand people came to celebrate reform. Jesse Jackson came with a black chorus. Senator George McGovern and Senator Harold Hughes came. The liberals and reformers were there. It was an extraordinary scene, a lovely sight, a beautiful day on the banks of the Des Plaines River. In the middle of this the mayor arrived. He saw something building up in the party that needed to be reckoned with. In the course of the rally that afternoon, Senator Everett Dirksen died. I held back the news until most of the speeches were over, and then asked Senator McGovern to announce the death of Senator Dirksen, which he did with feeling. Then I asked Jesse Jackson to pray for the dead senator. And Jesse Jackson prayed. He prayed and he prayed with his beautiful black chorus chanting "The Battle Hymn of the Republic" as a background. It was a dramatic moment. At that point, George McGovern, Dick Daley, and the others all joined hands, and before it was over, they were all singing "We Shall Overcome."

Dick Daley was singing "We Shall Overcome?"
At the end somebody said, "Now, Adlai, why don't you just walk down to the banks of the Des Plaines River and see if the water will part?" There wasn't a moment's doubt from that minute about who would be the candidate for the United States Senate.

Could you evaluate Daley for me?
I don't think that the public appearances conform to the reality at all. My wife really doted on Dick Daley. He was funny, humorous. He would call up at the most ungodly hours. He never got up later than 5:30 in the morning. He was on the phone starting at 5:30 A.M. He'd get her on the phone. I knew who was on the phone, and I would be sitting around waiting to get a chance to talk to the mayor, and they were talking about ERA. Or, he'd call me regularly, especially toward the end. He always wanted to know what was going on.

He wanted to talk about housing. He wanted to talk about the issues. We rarely got down to the nuts and bolts of running a political machine. It was on issues and on the family, and he could be warm and entertaining. He was quite voluble. He wasn't the Buddha he was pictured as. He used to call me, when I was living in the 43rd ward, and say, "What are we going to do about Paddy Bauler? He's about to endorse somebody for some office who's no damn good." I'd say, "What are you asking me for? There's not a damn thing I can do about Paddy Bauler, but certainly you can." I could see him visually wringing his hands at the phone, saying, "These decisions get made in the ward. I can't tell Paddy Bauler what to do. Don't you have any advice?" Daley went with the power. His genius, I think, was to be able to perceive it. He knew where it was and he always accommodated to it. And he did the bidding.

I developed, over the years, a great affection for him, and so did my wife. It was partly because he took an awful paternal interest. He was not free and forthcoming with his advice, but he did, at times, volunteer it. He took a great interest in my career and I undertook, from time to time, to ask his advice, which pleased him. I think it was partly because of his feelings toward my father. Maybe because he was Irish. Maybe it goes back to the feeling for loyalty. He talked often about his own children. He almost implied that he hoped I would develop a close relationship with them. I think he made a little promise to himself, after my father died, that he was going to keep an eye on the old boy's son. He owed my father a lot. This was an indebtedness of loyalty. My father supported him in that bitter internal fight with Kennelly, and that's the sort of thing you don't forget. Not in this business.

He was loyal to the end, and it was a weakness. He was loyal to some who let him down. I don't think he was the omnipotent, infallible leader that he tended to be portrayed as. Nobody could live up to the reputation that he had acquired as a boss. He was a legend in his lifetime. He was supposedly pulling every string in the country before it was over, but he wasn't, and we knew that. There were people in positions of authority, close to him, who were giving instructions in the legislature without any knowledge on his part, sometimes making mistakes. He was isolated from a lot of the realities. He did not adapt to changing circumstances easily. He never could, for example, understand the changing demographics, the shift of power out of the city and into the suburbs and downstate. I tried to suggest, from time to time, that he had to broaden the base, that he had to make a greater effort to win votes down there. He responded a couple of times, "They can't get as many votes out in those counties as in the 11th ward." It was changing, some of it. It would be hard for any human to accept. I'm not sure he could accept the reason why Mike Howlett was in difficulty. He was the reason. Jimmy Carter never understood that it wasn't Mike Howlett. The basis was Daley. But he kept some distance between himself and Mike Howlett. Daley had become a symbol of bossism in Chicago and Cook County, and it was too late by then for him to shake it. There were some things that could have been done. Why the slatemaking sessions had to always take place in Cook County. All those fellows filing out of the private room, announcing the statewide candidates. It was unnecessary but he couldn't quite see it.

Are you saying, Adlai, that he was parochial in many ways, and unable to come to terms with change?

Yes, I think so. Even on the issues. He was a doctrinaire New Deal liberal. He'd make some of the liberals look like reactionaries. I remember talking to him once about the railroad industry. He said, "Nationalize the railroad industry. Make it a public service." Talk about big spenders! When it came to the cities, particularly housing, he wanted to spend money to improve the condition of the cities. Of course, he stood to gain personally from federal expenditures for urban problems. The organization here benefitted. On the changing of politics, on the changes overtaking the schools, on race, his vision was opaque.

It was partly the fault of many of us. We'd complain and barely make the effort to go and talk to him. Others did. He wasn't exposed to as many viewpoints as he should have been. At times you'd talk to him, he just wouldn't hear. He wouldn't listen. He shut it out. At other times he would be very animated, searching for a way, or for an answer. But not many people knew that. They'd complain bitterly. They'd vilify him. Rarely would they make an effort to talk to him. One of the great failings of his critics, particularly the so-called liberals and reformers, was that they rarely got in there and tried to talk to him. It would have been a revelation to some of them.

He was tough as nails. He just let criticism roll off him. His advice was "Don't read those newspapers. Just make sure they spell your name right." He never let it bother him. I'm not saying he was very amenable to criticism, but unless he had made up his mind (in which case he would stonewall), he was very receptive to ideas. The unfortunate part about it was that the circle was pretty small and, in fact, there really never was anybody that I could really identify as being intimate, really close. There were a few who talked to him. Nobody that was close. I always had the feeling that he was quite conscious of that. He really wanted to talk to me. He'd call and he would talk. He'd say, "Why don't you come by?" I always felt that it was a little presumptuous. I felt a little diffident about it. There was a generation between us. It got less so in later years. As a senator, I began calling him Dick. It took me about ten years to work myself up to that. I'd cross him up, and because of that diffidence, I'd do him the courtesy of calling him in advance if I could.

Did he try to tell you what to do in the Senate?
No. Never. He would call occasionally and discuss, in a very general way, politics in the city. He would ask for help a couple of times. That usually came from his subordinates. We had some discussions on the Crosstown. It wasn't to ask for anything really, except for my advice on that, because he wanted to break the impasse with the state and hoped that I could be of some help with Governor Walker, which I tried to be.

I was the senator, and we talked about party affairs from time to time. We talked about issues. I remember him saying a couple of times, "Why don't you fellows get that act together down there? Why don't you tell them how we do it in the Illinois legislature?" I tried to explain that we do it a little different in the Senate.

He was a great mayor. He had his blind spots, but he knew how to exercise power. He exercised it by getting along with it. Right or wrong, he got things done. There are times when I think just doing something is a whole lot better than doing nothing. This city was on the move under the mayor. When you look across the country at the other cities and consider their resources, this city has great resources. Not that that explains the difference. I think it has a great deal to do with the way that man ran the city, which is not to say that his time hadn't come.

ABNER MIKVA *Jewish. About fifty years old. Is now United States congressman from a North Shore suburban district. Very liberal. Was congressman from a district on Chicago's South Side and was euchred out of his seat by a congressional redistricting. Was a state representative, elected in opposition to the machine, for a number of years. Has always been on the outside or on the fringe of the machine.*

I was born and raised in Milwaukee, attended public school there, did my undergraduate work at Wisconsin, and came to the University of Chicago Law School.

I guess I had always had an interest in politics. The year I started law school, 1948, was the year that Douglas and Stevenson were heading up the Democratic ticket in Illinois. I was all fired up from the Students for Douglas and Stevenson and passed this storefront, the 8th Ward Regular Democratic Organization. I came in and said I wanted to help. Dead silence. "Who sent you?" the committeeman said. I said, "Nobody." He said, "We don't want nobody nobody sent." Then he said, "We ain't got no jobs." I said, "I don't want a job." He said, "We don't want nobody that don't want a job. Where are you from, anyway?" I said, "University of Chicago." He said, "We don't want nobody from the University of Chicago in this organization." That gave me my first taste both of machine politics and how you have to find other ways to be a part of the political apparatus if you don't want a patronage job, and if you don't want to march to the regular organization drummer. Shortly thereafter, I joined the Independent Voters of Illinois and became moderately active in that organization.

When I finished law school, I was given the assignment as law clerk to Supreme Court Justice Sherman Minton. I spent days sitting in the gallery watching the nitty gritty of congressional business, becoming fascinated with it. When I finished the clerkship, I came back to work for Arthur Goldberg's law firm here. I was involved in minor political causes, but nothing spectacular. In 1956, we had our first legislative reapportionment in many years, and the district of Hyde Park and

South Shore, where I lived, ended up with no incumbents. I was the freshest face on the scene, and the IVI and the others decided that they would go with somebody who wasn't already old hat as far as independent politics was concerned, and I was elected to the Illinois House of Representatives.

What was it like being in the Illinois legislature as a liberal independent representative from Chicago?

A good part of the time I spent persuading people I really was independent. My difficulties with Daley were never as great as people thought they were. As far as Daley was concerned, I never was his favorite, but I shot my way into the organization, and while he owed me nothing, I wasn't like some of those people that he used to get very angry at who turned on him. I was just a dumb kid who had gotten into politics through the wrong door. I was absolutely lonely as far as any other Chicago Democrats were concerned. They couldn't vote with me, they had to avoid me like the plague because I was a misfit, the first independent that had ever been elected in the city. The first couple of terms, my performance record was not good. I made good use of the forum, but I didn't pass a lot of bills. I was not an effective legislator. About my third term, I began to be accepted by some of the powers, and by my fifth term, Jack Touhy made me chairman of the House Judiciary Committee. By that time I was able to get some bills passed.

There was an interesting mix of people in the legislature. There were some people down there who were ideologues. They were there because they believed that the legislature would make a change and looked on that as an end in itself. There were some down there who used it as a stepping stone, as a kind of apprenticeship. I must say, in retrospect, it was an apprenticeship. There were others who were there because it was a credential to have in terms of their law practice or their business. It gave them clout, it gave them an entree. And there were some who just were there to pass the time away. There were perhaps thirty or forty legislators who really were interested in the process; maybe another thirty or forty who were willing to abide the process. The rest of the 177 fell into other categories and, as a result, if you were interested in the process and you did want to make it work, you could have great influence.

I like to think of myself as a legislator by training, by temperament. I like the legislative process. But if I ever were to put aside my ombudsman role, I couldn't survive. A person who's got a problem

with the Veteran's Administration or Social Security or the Secretary
of State in Springfield doesn't care how many bills you've passed, and
how great you have been on the issues of war and peace. "Why didn't
you get their uncle in the Veteran's Administration hospital when
they asked you to?" Most people need help in dealing with the
bureaucracy, but not at the expense of taking the legislator out of
that role. It is a marvelous way of oversighting, of supervising how
programs are working. It makes you aware that you can legislate up
here on some high plane, but those programs that you are legislating
get administered down below, and if you aren't aware of what tran-
spires between the word and the deed, as carried out by the governmental official, you'll never be a good legislator. The best of laws
don't work if they don't deliver benefits to the people, or solve
people's problems.

*If that's true, Ab, there is validity to the Democratic machine's
concept of politics. But the big difference between people like you in
politics, and people like Marzullo, Neistein, and Daley, the machine
guys, is that, while you all understand the need to touch the bases
at home and take care of those personal needs on which their whole
system is based, you differ on the purpose of politics.*
Absolutely. They have been successful. My quarrel is that they
never had any ideology. They would deliver services—good, bad, or
indifferent, and use them to elect an Adolf Hitler if he was on the
Democratic ticket. They'd use that ombudsman function to elect
him, no matter who he was or how contrary he was to those policies.
It used to be a cause of great dismay to me that the Democratic Party
performed an awful lot of service to people in the precincts, but
when it came to the ideology of the legislators that were elected as
a result of those services, most of them either had no ideology or
ended up with a much more conservative ideology than those services represented, and were Democrats for convenience's sake.
We both use different kinds of people to carry out those functions.
To them, patronage is a perfectly logical way of doing all that. You
have this guy, he wants a job, you want him to do something besides
the job, you mesh the two, and pretty soon you've got an effective
political apparatus. I feel that the price you pay is the ideology, the
content of the party. The patronage party of Illinois stands for nothing except jobs and winning. I think you can accomplish those results
that the political system wants to accomplish by volunteers, particularly in an area like this one where you have a lot of young people,

a lot of people who are interested in politics, not because they want jobs, but because they believe in certain causes. You can accomplish those same results that the Marzullos accomplish on a volunteer basis. I've never touched a patronage job, even on those rare occasions where some have been dangled in front of me. I've eschewed them because there is a price. There is no free lunch.

What is the price then, Ab, if you take the deal?
You've got to go along with the program. Those were the people that Daley used to be angry with, who wanted to be held as independents by the IVI and newspaper editorials, but who wanted some jobs for a few deserving constituents besides. Nothing would make him angrier than those who supped at his table and then didn't want to pay the price. I think I had much better relations with him than a lot of people who were considered good party regulars.

Did the representatives of the machine in the legislature always have to subordinate their own personal ideology and their own ideas to the overall interest of the machine?
Absolutely and completely in Springfield. In Washington it has not been the same, but in Springfield it was total commitment to the party line. Daley kept an absolute close watch on everything that happened in Springfield. He knew the league. He served down there. He knew how it functioned. The party leaders in both houses were in daily contact with him and held weekly meetings. He knew every major piece of legislation. He had his finger on it. There was a party line. There were very, very few free votes. I remember once, there was a credit bill that I was debating on the floor. One of Daley's key guys used to sit next to me and he was slipping me notes on what to say. He's a very bright guy and they were good points. Meanwhile, he was not taking part in the debate at all, which isn't that surprising. Not everybody gets up on every bill. But when it came time to vote, he voted the other way. I was irritated because it was a close vote. I turned around and said, "You know, your notes are very helpful, but it would be nice to get your vote every once in a while." He looked at me kind of sadly and said, "Ab, if I could have voted with you, I would have. You know the way the game is played." I realized that there was just no way that he could vote independently of what the party or the organization voted and get returned to office. There was case after case of people who tried that and were just never heard of again politically.

Many of their programs were very good. They were concerned about seeing that the schools had sufficient funding for Chicago, that there be a decent public health appropriation, that there be welfare legislation. There is the traditional fight between downstate and the city about aid to dependent children, and the machine was interested in preserving and protecting the ADC programs. On a lot of other things, they were neutral. If you used the forum right, the forum of newspapers, the legislature and the business community, you could get them supporting things like credit reform. That was an issue where there wasn't any direct interest that the machine had, but it was an issue that clearly hurt a lot of poor people in the city. The newspapers were editorializing that the legislature ought to do something. The church got very active for credit reform. Some of the decent businessmen in the community got very active, and by orchestrating all these different groups to support it, notwithstanding that I was the chief sponsor, at a magic moment in time, the Daley organization threw all their support to the program and it went sailing through. Mental health was not something they had any direct interest in, but when the right set of circumstances came about, they supported it.

There were some issues that were their bread and butter issues, that they either were solidly for or solidly against, and nothing could shake them. One of the committees they always made sure was very carefully stacked with solid supporters (I was able to get through and get on the committee one time only) was the election committee. That committee is always headed up by one of the stalwarts, and it was peopled by people that were totally loyal. If you told them to pass a law repealing the elections, they would vote for it. Those are the kinds of issues on which the machine brooked no interference. Ed Derwinski and I still hold the record for a bill that got the least number of votes in the state legislature. Derwinski and I cosponsored a bill to repeal the party circle for the Democrats and Republicans. They thought it was so funny that we would be serious about this that they let it go out of the committee. It got two affirmative votes, mine and his. I used to put in a bill eliminating temporary employees in the civil service system. I had a bill to prevent double dipping (double dipping is where someone is in the legislature and also has a job for the county or city back home). We would lose on that every time. Adlai Stevenson and I put in the first code of ethics that had any teeth to it in the state legislature that would have applied to all government employees, and that was shot out of the water so fast that it didn't even get a decent burial. Those are kinds of things that they consider important.

How did you get elected to Congress?

Along about my fourth term, I was beginning to find that I was coming around the second time on many of the issues. There were many frustrations connected with being a legislator. One is that, it being a part-time job, you had to try to maintain a law practice. Early in my legal career that was fairly easy, but as I became more important to my law firm, I also was getting more and more involved in the legislative process, and trying to carry water on both shoulders was getting harder and harder. My partners were unhappy. I was unhappy. I was robbing Peter to pay Paul. At that time we had absolutely no legislative staff. We had a secretary who was a part of a pool so that we had one-sixth of a secretary. Part of being a legislator is being available at the state level. I found myself using my lawyers, volunteers, secretaries of the law office, to do all of this ombudsman work for my constituents. I was always carrying around little tasks on the backs of envelopes that somebody wanted me to perform, and I just didn't have the time or the resources to get it done. That was as big a frustration as anything else. It's not a good way to run a railroad.

In 1963, I announced I wasn't going to run for the legislature again, and started to make noises about how I was going to run for Congress. The legislature couldn't agree on reapportionment of the legislative seats, and we ended up with the at-large election. It was the one and only time that Daley ever asked me to do anything politically. He asked me to run again for the legislature. They were putting together that blue-ribbon slate headed up by Stevenson, and I enjoyed a certain reputation. He called me in and said, "You really ought to run again, Senator. You've been a good legislator, we need you, the party needs you, and I know that you are interested in that congressional seat. We'll work it out next time, but this time you'll run for the legislature." That was about as firm a commitment as I could get. So I ran for the legislature again and won.

In 1966, I decided that I was definitely going to run for Congress. The same syndrome started all over again. I think the mayor sensed that I was going to run and that there was nothing he could say or do. Marshall Korshak and Jim Ronan, my two committeemen, kept trying to woo me out of running. First, they wanted me to go back to the legislature. I told them, no, that was out of the question. Then they said that they would make me a judge. I said, "I don't want to be a judge." Korshak said, "We'll make you a circuit court judge!" Ronan said, "Wait a minute, that's mine." I said, "I don't want to be a circuit court judge." Marshall became more and more angry because the last thing in the world he wanted was a fight with me, and he said to me, "You mean there is no judgeship that you're interested in? That's ridiculous. Everyone is interested in a judgeship." So I ran in 1966 and I lost to an eighty-two-year old man who beat the pants off me. The organization had much more strength left than I thought they did. I went back and practiced law for two years.

But there are marvelous things that happen when you are dealing with machine politics. There is a time gap between what they perceive and what is fact. They just can't stay current. They're always operating on information several years old. Their information trickles up. It's a filter-up process to committeemen, to downtown, and then it finally penetrates to the real movers and shakers downtown. In 1968, I was not in good shape, because of my own independent political resources, as I was in 1966. The district was starting to change, a lot of the most enthusiastic, dynamic young supporters I had were already moving out of the district, I had been out of politics for two years, and it is very hard to keep your name alive when you don't have a forum. I think that if they had taken me on in an all-out fight, it would probably have been easier to beat me in 1968 than it was in 1966. But their information was to the contrary, that I had come close in 1966, and therefore the machine and Korshak and Ronan were worried. Better they should make peace. That was the only time that I had an affirmative support from Daley. He announced that the party was going to support me for Congress. I won the primary very handily with that kind of support.

What is the machine's policy toward its representatives in Congress?

From the time that I have been there, and a period predating that even, there has been almost no effort to really control what the congressional delegation does. Part of it is that Daley wasn't that unhappy about my going. Better Washington than Springfield. I'm farther away. And none of the problems that we deal with in Washington deal with those kinds of bread and butter issues that can wipe out the machine, get rid of temporary employees, or promote a code of ethics. On most of the issues that affect Chicago, the Democrats in the delegation respond naturally. He doesn't need to call me or

crack the whip to get me to be for transportation for Chicago; I'm
for it. Part of the ideology that I used to complain about is nonexistent
in Washington. There really wasn't that kind of heavy-handedness.
I don't think there were more than two or three votes where anybody even said that the machine had a position. I had better relations
with Daley in the Congress than I had in the legislature because I was
not in his way. To quote that famous author, "Just don't make any
unnecessary waves."

Could you evaluate Daley for me, Ab?
Well, he was the last of his kind. There probably had been others
like him. There certainly are no others around any more, and I doubt
that there will be any others. He almost was a political anachronism
in terms of the monolithic power he had as party leader and as
mayor. He had to clear with nobody. He had the absolute power to
make decisions. With a lot of the people in Chicago, a lot of the
business community, a lot of the unions, with a lot of others, that's
a big plus. If you wanted to get a project approved, all you needed
was one person's approval, and away it went. It went sailing through.
The council would endorse it, the zoning board would give it varia-
tions, the agencies would give the money, and the people would go
out and get it done. In New York, on the other hand, when Lindsay
was a good reform mayor, he could be all for something, and that and
a dime, sometime, would get you a cup of coffee. So Daley was an
effective mayor in that sense. That's the plus part.
    The minus part is that he was very much a human being with lots
of faults and flaws, and nobody to tell him when the emperor didn't
have his clothes on. There were lots of things that weren't done right
in Chicago, or weren't done, that we will pay a high price for in the
future. Nobody could ever say, "Mr. Mayor, you're wrong." That was
a no-no. When we ended up putting in the super-highways, the
Kennedy and the Ryan, and his almost fanatical zeal for the Crosstown, there was no one who had the courage to say, "Mr. Mayor,
those expressways are part of what caused Chicago to have the
problems it has." They broke up communities. They destroyed the
ethnicity of the city. They uprooted whole peoples, as well as neighborhoods, and he's got to stop building them. Nobody would ever say
him nay.
    The same thing was true about the party. He was a very effective
party leader, when he was right. When he said something, it happened. But, when he was wrong, there was nobody to bring in the

pluralism that I think is absolutely the essence of a political party. That's the price we paid for Daley's one-man leadership. You look at the Democratic Party of Illinois. What's wrong with it is that we have very few young people in the Democratic Party; we don't have a statewide party; we have it in name, but in fact, it is considered a Cook County party as opposed to the downstate party. We don't have a party that is based on issues, on ideology. It's based on jobs. We don't have a party structure that can survive beyond patronage. Patronage is a wasting asset, if it ever was an asset, and you put all that together, and I think that the Democratic Party of Illinois has a massive rebuilding job. If you talk about monuments to Daley, the Illinois Democratic Party is not going to be one.

As far as the city is concerned, I feel sorry for whoever wins the mayoral election because he is going to be blamed for a lot of things that are not of his doing. The fleeing of industry, the breakdown of the public school system, the decline of the housing supply, the unwillingness of capital to stay in the city and reenter the city, the crime in the streets—those didn't happen on the day that Daley died. It was a long time building. It was swept under carpets of a new State Street, a new lighting system, a new Crosstown, and a few other things that Daley was for. They came down from Mount Sinai, but may or may not have been the top-priority items in Chicago that we should have had or needed in order to remain a great city. It's a very mixed bag and I have enough bumps on my head to assure you that he was a very effective political leader. So I take nothing away from his effectiveness. But because, like other strong leaders, he could not delegate, he could not share power, we paid a price for the nature of the decisional process, when Daley was party leader and mayor.

What about your personal relationships with Daley?
They were always pleasant. When we were in the midst of that shooting war on reapportionment, they weren't very good. There were a couple of cases when he would come into a room and I would be there, when the re-map was going on, when he would literally sail right on by without saying hello or shaking hands. But most of the time it was a very civil relationship. I had a few saving graces as far as he was concerned. One of them was that I was a good family man, and somehow it was incongruous to him that a Jewish Hyde Park liberal could be a good family man. We used to both have summer places out in the Dunes which weren't too far away from each other, and when he would see me on the golf course, and my kids were

along and he would be with the boys, his whole face would light up, and he would hustle over, and say, "Hello Ab, Hello Senator, good to see you. You got the girls out, huh?" And he would beam at me and my wife. He was delighted to see that even I could enjoy family life and family values.

Every once in a while, he would pleasantly surprise me. He took his antecedents very seriously. He had a great feel for the average person. He felt very strongly about things like immigration and helping people get jobs. Whenever I was on anything that involved job security or immigration, I would end up getting strong support from him. He was the number one proponent as far as big-city mayors were concerned for effective gun control. That was one of my major issues, so whenever we could talk about guns, or jobs, or immigration, we'd get along famously.

What's it like to be in Congress?

It's the most exciting job I have ever had. I commute every weekend. My family lives here in Evanston and I catch a 6:40 A.M. plane to Washington every Monday morning. The alarm goes off about 4:30 A.M. Like most people, I am not that wild about getting up at 4:30 in the morning, and when the alarm goes off and I'm lying there trying to get my head together, and I'm thinking, "Should I get up or shouldn't I get up?" But I find that with all the problems that Congress entails, professionally and personally, it's exciting to get up and contemplate the week ahead. I find that after a minute or two I really jump out of bed and I start to think about what is going to face me when I get to Washington, what battles I'm going to be involved in, what kind of legislative problems are going to be coming up.

Part of it is the great variety of things. I like to be a generalist. I find it hardest of all to discipline myself to sit down and do a particular task. Congress allows you to be a generalist. It encourages it. It demands it. You can't just know something about health care. You've got to know something about Crosstown, about war and peace, about jobs, and about energy. So you have a chance to dabble in an awful lot of things, in the House particularly. I don't think I would enjoy the Senate as much. The House gives you a great sense of challenge and drama, because there really are very few issues that are cut and dried in the House of Representatives, and on almost any one of them there will be tensions and questions of how it will come out.

You can have great input. I was amazed that by my second term

in Congress, I found myself being much more effective as a Congressman than I was as a state legislator, even though the league is
tougher. But, because it is so evenly balanced, because the process
itself is so much more finely tuned, you can be an effective legislator
early on. I think some of the freshmen last year were amazed to find
that they could come in and really help, they could pass an amendment, they could pass a bill. It wasn't a case of their having to sit there
and wait until their beards grew long to be an effective congressman.
So it's those parts that turn me on.

For all the faults and flaws of individual members of Congress (and
we have our share), it probably is the highest caliber group of men
that I have associated with. I've practiced law, I've taught, and I have
been in business, but overall, there are more bright, attractive, interesting, involved, dedicated people in the Congress than I think in any
other milieu that I have been in. I want to add the word "honest"
too, because perhaps that's what makes the ones who are dishonest
show up with such clarity, because most of them are honest. So that
the ones who do cheat, the ones that do put their hands in the cookie
jar become very, very visible.

The other part that turns me on is that it really is a very effective
forum. If you have something to say and you feel very strongly about
it, if your kids are small enough, maybe you can get them to listen
to you. Other than letters to the editor, that's it. The average person,
when they are mad about something, they can kick the dog or go out
and talk to themselves, but that's about it. As a congressman you have
a forum. If I didn't like what General Brown said to that group of
officers (and I didn't), I can get up on the floor of the House and tell
him he ought to resign, and, because I made that speech on the floor
of the House of Representatives, the newspapers picked it up, television picked it up, letters are coming in to me denouncing me, even
one or two supporting me, but I forced the issue into the public arena
and I have been able to have an input into that issue.

The downside? The downside is that I put in more hours than any
job I have ever had or ever will have other than this one. I work for
less money than certainly I would as a private lawyer. I end up with
complications to my personal life that would be avoidable in any
other career. I am not a good bachelor and Daley was right—I do
enjoy my family and it's no fun seeing them two days a week, if then.
There are great complications of trying to maintain your freedom to
be a legislator and a good one, or at least what you think is a good
one, and take care of those other political responsibilities as well. Not

so much as ombudsman, but in a close district like this, just paying close personal attention to the district, to making sure that the mail goes out on time, to making sure that I am visible at the various kinds of political events and other things that I ought to be at, of trying to walk that narrow line of being a presence in the community and not trying to dictate from Washington who the people ought to vote for for the mayor of Skokie. Those are complicated problems. I'm not sure I always resolve them right, and sometimes I get discouraged.

Are those also the rewards and penalties of any life in politics, or is it special in Congress? You certainly can make a lot more money in private life and live an easier life.

Yes, but I am sure I would not have enjoyed it as much, when it comes down to it. I suppose that, at least for me, Congress is the epitome of everything that is good and bad about politics. Insecurity. Here I am, 51 years old, and the next election I can be out of a job. I have no backlog of capital that I can fall back on. I have a profession, and I used to think I was pretty good at it, but even so, 51- or 52-year-old lawyers are not that attractive a commodity, and this concerns me some. But the ups are up. The excitement of winning a hard-fought legislative battle, of carrying an important issue.

Maybe I can demonstrate it best with a non-sexy issue. At the beginning of the session, for years, I've been unhappy about the fact that our rules tolerate using quorum calls in the House as a way of delaying the process, just expressing hostility to the process. You get mad at somebody, you call a quorum call. Everybody has to stop what they are doing, leave their committees, and come over to signify their presence. It stems from the fact that the Constitution says that in order to do business, a quorum must be present. I did research and I found that that clause was intended to mean "business" in its most substantive sense, that is, when the House is approving a matter. We can't pass a bill if a quorum isn't present, if someone challenges the absence of a quorum. I was able to put through a rule change, after a great fight with all kinds of constitutional lawyers, which said that from here on in, the Speaker could refuse to recognize a quorum call. In the first three months of this session, I have cut the quorum calls down by two-thirds. I felt very good about it. I did it.

You're impacting the history of the country, if that's the right way to say it. I don't know what any one else's nightmare is. My nightmare would be working on an assembly line, eight hours a day, forty hours a week, fifty weeks a year, for all my productive years, applying a wrench to a nut, making sure that it went three times around before I passed it on. Obviously, that has to be done. I don't demean the work and I am glad that somebody is doing it, and I hope that when they do it, they do it well. But that would drive me up the wall. It seems to me that a life in politics has been for me exactly the opposite of that. I have had variety. I have had the excitement of feeling that I really have been involved in the stuff of history, of what the country is about, of how the system works. Every once in a while I even have had a meaningful impact on that system. That's got to be a very large reward.

SEYMOUR SIMON *Jewish. In his early sixties. Very tough, bright, and an extremely able attorney. Was an alderman from the North Side 40th ward, and then also became the committeeman. As a fair-haired boy, was elected president of the Cook County board of commissioners in 1962. Had a run-in with Alderman Tom Keane, the number-two man in the machine, and was dumped in 1966. Ran for the city council again and was reelected, since he was still the committeeman in his ward, and became a persistent and vocal critic of Daley and the machine. Was slated by the organization in 1974 for the Appellate Court and is now a judge on that court. Gave up his aldermanic seat and committeemanship when he went on the bench.*

I was born in Chicago in 1915. My folks lived in the Lawndale area and moved to the Albany Park area in 1924. I went to Haugan Grammar School, Roosevelt High School, Northwestern University, and Northwestern University School of Law. I liked debating, my father had been a lawyer and, listen, what was a Jewish boy going to do if he wants to be a professional man, and he doesn't want to be a doctor. Being a lawyer was a little more prestigious than being an accountant. I was number one in my class, and I was elected to the Order of the Coif, and was one of the editors of the Law Review. In college I was Phi Beta Kappa.

I'd always liked politics. The first campaign I fooled around with was the Al Smith campaign in 1928. I remember going around putting up posters when I was thirteen years old. When I got out of law school, I went to Washington to work for the Anti-Trust Division of the Justice Department. After the war, I came back here to Chicago, and started to work for a law firm. I got to know my precinct captain, Al Hoffman. I used to go with Al in the precinct to see voters, to help them out, then we'd end up drinking a little beer. You had to be goofy to like that kind of life, but I liked it. I was giving the organization contributions, although I wasn't getting anything from it. In 1948, I got active in my own precinct in the Truman campaign.

Politics gives you a tremendous ego satisfaction. There wasn't any place else where you could stand up before large groups of people and make speeches, get the applause, get the recognition, get the hoopla. Lots of fellows get into politics simply because there's a tremendous amount of excitement and color in it. I stayed in for the excitement. I'm positive that I would have been tremendously better off financially and professionally in the law, had I never run for office. But once you get that bug of running for office, you get into all that excitement, and then have the misfortune of getting elected.

Being in politics never attracted any substantial amount of business to me. I'm not saying that I didn't get some, because people knew me from politics, but it was a very minor amount.

There was a time, right after I was elected president of the county board, in 1963, when I was asked to become general counsel of National General Corporation, which would have necessitated my moving to Los Angeles. It was an intriguing opportunity, but it would have meant having to resign from office, so I passed that up. The man who was picked in my place as general counsel did very well, with stock options and all the other goodies, and today he is a much richer man than I am.

In 1952, in the Stevenson campaign, I became a precinct captain on my own in the 40th ward. I was around the organization and I used to be at meetings. Ben Becker said to me, "What are you hanging around here for, Seymour?" I said, "Frankly, I'd love to be able to run for office someday." He said, "You'll never be able to do it unless you're a precinct captain, and you're not a precinct captain." I took a precinct, and I started ringing doorbells. I thought I wouldn't like it, but I found that it was really fun doing it, getting to know the people, and sitting with the people.

In December 1954, the Democratic Party selected Daley to run for mayor in the primary against Kennelly, and Daley asked Ben Becker to run for city clerk. Becker wanted me to run for alderman. Chris Jensen had been committeeman for twenty-six years, and he said he would support me for alderman, too. Jensen had heard me speak, knew I had enough money by that time so I wouldn't be coming to him for money to run the campaign, and he knew my background and record. Becker [incidentally] was caught up in this charge that he had been receiving money for zoning changes in the ward, and then was dropped from the ticket after the primary.

What was the city council like in 1955, when you first came in with Daley?

I had never got to City Hall before I became an alderman, but it was exciting. I used to love to go to those meetings. You'd go down that back hallway. I used to feel this was like a baseball player must feel going out through the tunnel to the dugout to get in the ball game. The council had a lot more arguments and differences of opinion and debates in those first six years than it had when I came back to it in 1967. It was a much more open body. Daley did not like being opposed in any way. He would show his dislike, particularly for Democrats who opposed him. I did, on several occasions, but he made no effort to cut down speeches and clamp down on the debate the way he did later on. There was infighting between Parky Cullerton and Tom Keane. Cullerton was the chairman of the finance committee, and Keane really didn't respect Cullerton's ability. Keane felt that Cullerton would fall down if he didn't have him to lean on as a crutch, that he was the man who supplied the brains for everything that was going on in the council. That was an interesting thing to watch. There was jockeying for position, of being on Parky's team or on Keane's team. If you'd ask them if they had teams, they'd say, "Of course not! We were on Daley's team." But they each had followers and there was rivalry between them.

And that was resolved by making Cullerton the county assessor, and Keane became head of the finance committee?
I don't know that Cullerton's becoming county assessor resolved that exactly. That was quite an elevation for Cullerton.

How did you become a committeeman?
In 1959, after I got elected alderman, Jensen told me that he wanted to run for committeeman again. He had been in office then about twenty-six or twenty-seven years as committeeman. He was eighty or over. He used to go away all winter and he had a home in Kenosha where he'd go all the time, although his legal residence was on Kimball and Catalpa. Four of us—Nate Kaplan, Louie Liberman, who was the best precinct captain in the ward, Leroy Weiner, who was president of our organization then, and myself—went to him and told him he could not run, that he would be beat if he ran. He was angry for a few days, but finally called me and said he decided that he should not run again, and it should be me. I thanked him very much for his confidence, and I had a big retirement dinner for him.

Why did you want to be committeeman, too, Seymour?
Because, if you're in politics, the power is supposedly in the hands

of the committeeman. I'm not sure that committeemen are all that powerful, but if you're an alderman, and if a different person is committeeman, there are always little irritations between you. Between the time that the alderman is elected and the next year, when the committeeman is elected, the committeeman is always very nice to the alderman. But, as soon as that committeeman gets elected in the primary, and the alderman has three more years to wait to get elected, an alderman leads a pretty rough life, because the committeeman does not have to be so nice to him anymore. So I figured the best thing was to be both.

What is it like to be a committeeman in an upper-middle-class ward like this up here on the North Side?

What's it like? It's a different thing for every man. It's a different thing for me than it is for the present committeeman, different for me than it is for the neighboring committeeman. I didn't want to run an organization with a lot of jobholders in it. I made a lot of members of the organization judges. I didn't get jobs on garbage trucks; I didn't get jobs on street gangs; but I really was happy not to get them, because if you had lots of jobs like that, you're building up strength that makes you a captive of the organization. I was glad to build an organization of volunteers. I never earned my living by being a committeeman. Some committeemen take the jobs. They're like employment agencies; they hand them out to people, and in turn the workers support the organization. I supported the organization primarily with my own funds. We had no dues. The organization lived on a very low and modest budget. I delivered my ward.

How were you selected as county board president in 1962?

You had something in your book *Don't Make No Waves—Don't Back No Losers* about that, and you were inaccurate. I wish you'd talked to me about that before. But, I'll tell you how I got to be selected. There had been a Jew on the county board, traditionally. Arthur X. Elrod, father of the present sheriff, had been on the county board when he was the committeeman of the 24th ward. When he died, Sidney Deutsch, who'd been an alderman and city treasurer, succeeded him on the county board. Sidney was then the committeeman of the 24th ward. Deutsch died suddenly. I was at a dinner the night he died. Colonel Arvey was there and talked about how terrible it was that Sid had died. Then he said, "Seymour, who do you think ought to take his place?" I named a lot of names. At that point, I wasn't thinking of myself. But then I started thinking, "Maybe I'll be considered." But I didn't know whether I would be or not. I knew a Jew had to go in there. I knew at that time there weren't too many Jews in the Democratic Party, and there weren't too many of us in the city council who were Democrats. The most articulate Jew in the council at that time was Leon Despres, alderman of the 5th ward who, I think, was the finest councilman in all the United States. Jack Sperling was in the council, but Jack was a Republican, so he wasn't going there. I thought I'd have a pretty good chance, because when I went to Deutsch's wake and funeral, I got more attention from the politicians there than they usually gave me. So I was wondering what was going on.

There was a city council meeting a few days later. Keane used to meet with the mayor before a city council meeting, and then he'd come down to the council. I always used to walk up to him and say, "What's new, Tom?" So, this morning when he came in I said, "What's new, Tom?" He said, "Plenty new. You're going bye-bye. You're going to take Deutsch's place." I said, "How do you know that?" He said, "Daley just told me and he's going to call you up to his office after the meeting to tell you, but don't let on that you know." I said, "Is that good or bad?" He said, "It's wonderful!" I said, "Gee, I don't know if I want that." He said, "You're nuts!"

The meeting started (and Daley had really never done this to me), when all of a sudden, I saw him beckoning me to come up to the rostrum. I came up there and he said, "It's too bad about poor Sidney, isn't it?" I said, "Yes, it is." He said, "I was sitting home last night thinking about who should become his successor and do you know who I decided should be his successor?" I said, "No, who?" He said, "You!" I said, "Me? I'm very surprised to hear that, Mr. Mayor." He said, "It will be a fine opportunity for you." So I said, "Mr. Mayor, I just don't know what I should do." He said, "You call Roz (that's my wife) and see what she thinks, and then let me know this afternoon." (I have a beautiful, brilliant wife who has put up with the difficulties of being the wife of a politician, and she's been very helpful to me.)

Well, the council meeting broke up early, and there was a lunch and some kind of a political affair. I was at it, and Daley was there. Daley takes me in the corner and he starts hitting me on why I've got to take this, what a good thing it is for me.

Once Charlie Weber got hold of me, and he said he wanted me to go in and ask Daley to make me a judge. I said, "I don't want to ask him to make me a judge. I don't want to be a judge." He said, "Yes, but I want to see what plans he says he has for you." I said, "I don't want to do it." Well, Charlie made me promise I'd do it, and the next day I called Daley for an appointment. I didn't get it for a few days and by the time I got the appointment, Charlie Weber was dead of asphyxiation. I didn't know whether I should go in to see Daley or not because Charlie Weber is dead, but I decided, I had the appointment, I'll go in. I went in to see Daley at the Sherman Hotel. I came in and he said, "Gee, isn't it terrible about poor old Charlie?" I said, "Oh, terrible, Mr. Mayor, about poor old Charlie." So we talked about Charlie a little bit. Then I asked him if he could make me a judge, and he said if I wanted to be considered, I'd receive serious consideration. "But," he said, "Seymour, you're an active fellow. You wouldn't be happy there. I think you'd be foolish, and once you're there, you can't come to me and say you're not happy, you want to do something else. You're there and that's it! But," he said, "you have ability. There's any number of things you can do. There are many offices that you can hold."

Well, at this luncheon now (this is now a couple of years later), Daley is reminding me that when I asked him to be a judge, he told me that there were other opportunities that would open up, and here it is! Here is the opportunity and I'd be foolish not to take it. So, I said, "Well, I want to talk to Roz." I figured I had it, so I'd hold 'em off a little bit, and, finally, the next morning, I told him O.K., I'd go there. The nice thing about it was, I was being made not only a member of the board to succeed Deutsch, but he also told me that I would be made chairman of the finance committee of the county board. That is how I got on the board.

Right after I got on the board, I realized this was an unusual situation, that John Duffy, the president, was a sick man. He started missing meetings. As chairman of the finance committee, I would preside at meetings in place of Duffy. Eventually Duffy died, in July 1962, and there was a lot of speculation about who would succeed him. My name wasn't mentioned, incidentally. But I figured I had a pretty good chance because, after all, Daley had selected me to get on the board. He'd made me chairman of the finance committee, and if he didn't have me continue as president, it would be like going back on his own judgment and saying he'd made an error. That's what I thought about when Duffy died.

Duffy died and Daley, called me to the Sherman Hotel very early that morning after he died and told me I was his choice for president. After that there was a lot of speculation, and my name didn't figure in the speculation. But that didn't bother me, because I knew that Daley had said that I was there, and that he couldn't very well get away from supporting me without casting doubt on his own judgment of just a few months before. So I kept still. Tom Keane had started calling me to ask what I'd heard that was new. I'd tell him that I hadn't heard anything new.

The last night of Duffy's wake (Duffy had a tremendous wake, a tremendous number of people, a magnificent wake), Tom Keane was at Duffy's wake and he said, "Seymour, would you and Roz stop by my house on your way home? I want to talk to you about something." We went to his house and he said he wanted to tell me how much he liked me and appreciated the support I'd given him in the council. "But," he said, "Seymour, I want you to know that Don O'Brien (who was a state senator then, and who is now a judge of the circuit court), "is my lifelong friend, and we're very close. You know that." I said, "I know that, Tom." He said, "Don O'Brien wants to be president of the county board and I want you to know that I'm supporting him and I'm not supporting you." I said, "Tom, I thank you for your honesty. It really is decent of you to let me know." But frankly, I wasn't scared or worried because I had Daley telling me that he was supporting me, not O'Brien. I still felt that the logic of the situation compelled Daley to support me rather than O'Brien. I didn't tell Keane that Daley was supporting me. I just thanked Keane and went home, and a couple of days later the meeting was held, and Daley came out with my name, and I was chosen. (So that is why, in your book, when you said that Keane was the one who made me president of the county board, that was absolutely inaccurate. These canards get going and then people have a way of repeating them. Some writer in the *Daily News,* some years ago, wrote that Keane was responsible for my career and that he was the one who had made me president of the county board, that he was my sponsor, then everyone kept repeating it.)

I don't know whether Daley figured this or not, but his logic was great. If he had not chosen me, I think there would have been some resentment among Jews that he had put me on the county board and then jumped over me. Certainly I wouldn't have been happy, because what would I want to be on the county board for as second there if someone else had jumped over me? The next year, in 1963, Daley had his toughest mayoralty contest with Adamowski. Daley was saved in large measure by the Jewish vote. You look at the Jewish wards. They gave Daley tremendous support, and I think one of the reasons they supported Daley was in appreciation of his having made a Jew a county board president. I didn't represent solid support of the Jewish vote. There is no such thing as solid support of the Jewish vote, but at least the fact that he had made a Jew president of the county board would not put him on bad paper with the Jewish voters. It would put him on very good paper.

What kind of a record did you have as county board president?
I thought I had a sensational record. I had too good of a record. That's why I couldn't get selected a second time. I went after waste, nursing home operators that were giving terrible care and decrepit facilities to welfare patients, veterans who were making a racket of getting county funds to help indigent veterans and lining their own pockets. I went after Karl Meyer at County Hospital. I told them that we couldn't go on with the kind of County Hospital that we'd had in the past. I helped develop the Botanical Gardens. I passed ordinances that were really good. I enforced the laws against pinball machines, B-girls, and bars in the unincorporated areas. I enforced the county liquor laws with a vigor they had never been enforced with before. I was active. I was vigorous. I never ducked anything. I always was ready to lead.

My relationships with the party leaders were good, except that George Dunne and I were both on the county board, and we were really in there fighting most of the time. I think ambition motivated it. George and I came from different backgrounds, had different philosophies, and took different positions on matters because our backgrounds, our philosophies, our education, our experiences were so different. I got along well with the party leaders until the time came when I was not able to go along with the idea of the zoning change for a garbage dump up in Techny. That was the beginning of the end for me as county board president.

Keane had come to me, and said that he wanted to do a favor for a pal of his named Murphy, a lawyer who'd been on the harness racing commission. Murphy was the attorney for the religious order that owned this land up in Techny, and they wanted to use it for a garbage dump. People think that a gold mine is good, some people think that an oil well is even better, but a garbage dump has both the gold mine and the oil well beat because you're dumping real gold into the ground. You're getting paid for dumping. There is a great need for garbage dumps and if you have a place where you can dump, you can charge a lot of money. It's probably more profitable to put it back in the ground than to take it out of the ground.

Keane said he wanted to help Murphy. I said I'd see what I could do. This was to be put up in an area of very expensive homes next to Glenview, Northfield, and Northbrook, and there was tremendous opposition. The only ones who favored it were Keane and Murphy, and the villages along the North Shore on the lake, like Wilmette, Winnetka, and Glencoe. They wanted to have this, so they'd have a place to take and dump their garbage out among the people of Northfield and Glenview. It's like the old Marine slogan. They say "Semper Fidelis" means, "Pull up the ladder, Jake, I'm aboard."

I told Keane that the zoning board was going to vote against it, and that I wouldn't try to change it. He said, "Just have the county board overrule the zoning board." I said, "Tom, in all the history of the county zoning, there's never been a case where the zoning board has voted against the zoning and the county board has reversed the zoning board, and I'm not going to break that precedent. Even if I try to break it, it wouldn't pass, because there are five Republican members. We need twelve votes to pass it over the negative vote of the zoning board, and I couldn't get twelve." He said, "I don't care about that. All I want is for the Democrats to vote for it. That's my only commitment to my friend, Murphy. If it's defeated because Republicans don't vote for it, I have nothing to do with that." I said, "I'm not going to do it." He said, "Okay, that ends our friendship. I'll never ask you for anything again, because I know the way we stand." I said, "Why?" He said, "Because I know I can't depend on you. Also, I will never recommend anyone for a county position." I said, "Why is that?" He said, "Because if they got in trouble and I needed your help to help one of my precinct captains out, I know I couldn't depend on you to do that." He said, "I'm going to speak to the county board members myself about voting for this." He did, and some of the county board members did vote in favor of the garbage dump.

I thought Tom would change, because other times he had gotten mad at me and changed. But the next day, I knew it was really for real this time, because the county personnel officer came to me and said, "Boy, something's going to happen!" I said, "What is it?" He said, "I called Matt Bieszczat (Tom's great close personal friend), and I offered him a job in the Forest Preserve that he could fill, and he told me to shove it." I said, "He turned down a job?" When he told me that Bieszczat had told him to shove the job, I knew that my relations with Tom Keane were at an end. And they were.

How did you get dumped in 1966, after you had that record for four years in that office?

I think up to then Daley had never done anything like that, but I believe that Keane had to be vindicated. Everyone knew he wanted the zoning change and he couldn't get it, so Caesar had to be served. I believe that Keane and Dunne importuned Daley not to reslate me. Something happened that was a tipoff. Daley replaced Frank Bobrytzke, a Polish county commissioner, a wonderful, able man, [with] Bieszczat, [who was] Keane's delegate to the county board. In my disputes with Dunne, Bobrytzke had always supported me and influenced the other commissioners. I thought, Oh, what a terrible experience this is going to be. What do I need it for? My mother didn't send me to law school for this! The other commissioners are going to say, "Look what happened to Bobrytzke, the guy that went along with Simon. He got thrown off the board." In the afternoon I got called up by the subcommittee and they gave me the news that they didn't want to support me for president of the county board, but I could run for county treasurer. People have often asked me, "Why didn't you make a primary fight?" But I was really relieved to get out of that damn place at that time. Without Bobrytzke there, with Bieszczat, it would have been four years of hell.

But Seymour, what about the Jewish vote? Didn't Daley have to worry about that in the 1967 mayoral election a few months later?

Let's think about that. Who ran against Daley? John Waner. He didn't need any votes in 1967 when he ran against John Waner. That was no campaign. It was a nothing. I believe that is what happened. Daley was a man who looked ahead and who was motivated a lot by emotion, by hatred, by love, by resentment, but still he was a logical man and he plotted his moves out long in advance, and logically. John Waner was put there by Richard Ogilvie. I always suspected that Daley, great politician that he was, was leading Tom Keane, who thought he was a greater politician than Daley. But he wasn't as great a politician as Daley. So, while Daley was letting Keane and Dunne think that he was giving them their pound of flesh and getting Simon's head, he was really making Ogilvie president of the county board. Ogilvie might not have been elected if I had been running. Harry Semrow ran in place of me. I told Harry all along, "You can never win. If you criticize me, I'm going to put my foot right in your mouth, because you'd be attacking me without justification. So, you are in an absolutely impossible situation. You've got to lose this election. Ogilvie will win." Ogilvie won, and I think Ogilvie showed his appreciation to Daley by throwing up a very soft pitch to him in the 1967 mayoral election in the form of John Waner. Then Ogilvie went to Springfield to replace Sam Shapiro [as governor]. That made Dunne the president of the county board without any election. Ogilvie and Dunne were very comfortable together. I was not nearly as comfortable with those guys as Dunne and Ogilvie were with each other.

What about the other Jewish committeemen? Didn't you get any support from them in this thing?

No. Marshall Korshak and Bernie Neistein were appointed to the subcommittee that dropped me from the ticket. They were in on it. For years I chided Marshall. I used to tell him, "Marshall, you made a terrible mistake. What happened to you? I was pushed out as president of the county board. I survived it. You ran for county treasurer, the office I could have run for but didn't want to run for, because your eyes were big and you got beat. You never had an office after that that really amounted to anything. But if you had stood up in that subcommittee and said, 'I'm a Jew, and I'm not going to see Seymour Simon treated this way,' you would have been the greatest Jewish political leader in the United States, not in Chicago, but in the United States. You had that opportunity for leadership and you blew it!"

Seymour, that raises a question about the role of the Jews in Chicago and Cook County in the Democratic organization. What role have they played and how have they been treated by this organization?

They played a very important role at one time, but Jews are not as interested in being workers in the vineyards in politics as they used to be, because the Jewish community has prospered without politics —in business, in teaching, and the arts. They don't need politics as a stepping stone to accomplishment any longer. Another reason is that Jews no longer live in one place. They've dispersed, so there isn't the cohesive political force that could be brought to bear like when the Jews lived in the 24th ward and the 24th ward was 95 percent Jewish. The only area you have that maybe resembles that is Skokie. There's never been a time when we had more than one major county office where there was a Jewish office holder.

Another thing, it is very difficult to control the Jewish vote or to

get the Jew to vote cohesively or think cohesively, and that's good!
That's probably part of our strength. It's impossible for anyone to get
up and say, "I'm the Jewish leader." The last person here who was
a Jewish leader, Colonel Arvey, was a man of magnificent talents,
perception, and understanding, but that was in a different time.

*Let me take you back to your political career. What motivated you
to go back to the council?*

I wasn't happy with the way I'd been treated. Daley tried to tell
me everything would be the same, that we'd be close friends. But it's
like when you get a divorce—it's tough to go back again. There's
recriminations and resentments. Daley became more tyrannical as
time went on. If anyone, no matter how high he was, dared to say
no to anything, or about how things were being run, off went his
head!

I was still a committeeman in the 40th ward, so I ran for alderman
and was elected twice. Then came the years of my greatest fun in
politics. I realized I wasn't going to become governor or United
States senator. I didn't have to watch my number and I figured I'd
just have a good time in the council. I'd say what I had to say, I'd do
what I wanted to do, and I just would be my own man completely.
When I look back at those years, when I think of times when I was
up there shaking my fists at this great and mighty leader, and the
great and mighty leader was screaming back at me through the
microphone, and the tussles I had with him, the numbers of times I
stood up to him, belly to belly, and several of those times he backed
away. I enjoyed it. Not many people had the opportunity or the
courage to stand belly to belly with him. It was a frightening thing,
particularly when he'd start yelling up there from the microphone.

Why did you leave the council to go on the Appellate Court?

I'd been in there a long time, and it starts getting to the point
where you feel you're getting a little bit too old for the yelling. You
make decisions in life. You think the time has come to switch and
change. In a way my timing was wrong, in retrospect. Had I known
what was going to happen, I think I would have liked to have stayed
in the council. But Daley at that time seemed just indestructible. He
seemed strong physically, emotionally, and mentally. He was at the
height of his power and I decided that the time had come for me to
go on.

Daley was tough. He had a lot of guts. He had a lot of courage. He'd go flying into an issue. He wouldn't back away from it, and he'd scare people off. People would duck under the desks when Daley was coming. The newspapers did it; citizens' organizations did it; and when enough people ducked, pretty soon there was this myth that he was a great leader who was invincible and everyone had to follow him.

As an administrator, Daley was really quite poor. The city has deteriorated a lot. Daley was terrible at giving city services. The streets were full of holes, curbs were breaking up all over the city, even in the 11th ward. When we had Dutch elm disease a few years ago, it took three years to get the forestry department to cut the trees. This thing about him being a great city administrator was a myth.

There were so many myths that grew up around Daley. I remember the myth that no one around Daley dared drink, no one around Daley dared gamble, no one around Daley dared cheat on his wife. Just think of how many people that were close to Daley who died of alcoholism and had families that were broken up because there were other gals on the line. He was a flesh and blood man who had a powerful position. He wasn't a myth himself. There were a lot of myths around Daley, and a lot of things he got credit for doing as mayor really were not so. He got credit for building all the privately financed buildings in Chicago. In New York, in Los Angeles, in San Francisco, and in Houston, there has been much more building than there was in Chicago in that period that Daley was mayor here. Mayors there weren't getting credit for it. The people who were financing it and creating the development were getting the credit. In Chicago the mayor gets it.

He had tremendous ability to exploit these things. He had a tremendous memory, tremendous recall, good understanding of the way government worked, good logic, and a good way of expressing himself. He wasn't articulate or eloquent, but when Daley got through saying something, people usually knew what he had said. He didn't beat around the bush.

I respected him tremendously as an adversary. I never underestimated him. I respected him in another way. Although he was rough and tough in many ways, he was still a very decent man, a compassionate man. I remember the day Leon Despres got shot by a couple of kids on the street near his home. We had a council meeting the day after he was shot. Daley came to the meeting and said he had called Mrs. Despres to express his sorrow and the sorrow of the council. He had a nice talk with her, and that was very nice of him to call Mrs. Despres. That showed his decency. But before the meeting was over, it ended up with an attack by Keane and Daley on the liberals, the do-gooders, and the "perfessors," who were always trying to have free speech for everyone, and always have bleeding hearts. I got up and said, "If this is a tribute to Leon Despres, this is the kind of tribute he'd like to have least, because you're attacking the very things he always stood for."

Could you evaluate Tom Keane?

Keane was a strong debater, had a quick mind, and was not a very emotional man. Not as tough as Daley, but icier. Very capable. Maybe not as capable as he claimed to be, because Keane claimed to be the greatest debater that ever existed, the greatest lawyer that ever hit LaSalle Street, the greatest trial advocate. He wasn't that good, but he was plenty good. Daley ran the organization, and Keane, when the showdown came, had to follow Daley. Keane did not sit at Daley's level. He was number two.

One final personal question, Seymour. As a political activist, how do you like being a judge on the Appellate Court?

It's sometimes distressing, because it's so anonymous. No one seems to pay any attention to what you're like. You work on an opinion, you rewrite it, you draft it a fifth and sixth time, and you want it to read good when it comes out. I'd be happy if someone said, "Seymour, that opinion stunk," because I'd know someone was reading it. It's a quiet life and it's bothersome to me. I didn't think it would be that quiet. There are some interesting challenges that come to you in cases. Intellectually, it's quite stimulating, but it's different for me. In practicing law I was alone. In politics, in a way, I was alone. I made my decisions, I didn't have any board of directors or committees, I used to consult a lot of people and get their opinions, but I was alone. Here, I sit on a three panel bench. I'm not alone any longer.

I like politics. You're in issues that are important, you're in this excitement, you have the opportunity to express yourself, and you're not expressing yourself over something that is unimportant. A lot of the things you're dealing with are very important to people. You're helping to decide them and you're articulating a point of view. I also like the maneuvering in politics, the uncertainty of it. The thing I disliked about politics the most (I don't think this is true of politics all over), was the discipline we have here, the tightness of control, particularly in the last ten years of the Daley administration. And I don't see any sign of it abating too much.

Seymour, you've spent a good part of your life in politics as well as in law. Would you do it again?
I think if I was doing it again, I would stick to the law practice. Yeah, that's what I think I'd do.

WILLIAM G. CLARK

Irish. About sixty years old. His father was Cook County assessor and a Democratic powerhouse in the pre-Daley era. He served in the state legislature, was attorney general of Illinois for eight years, elected by heavy majorities. He was slated for the United States Senate in 1968 against Senator Everett Dirksen. Broke with President Johnson on Vietnam and criticized Daley and the organization during the campaign. After he lost, he was ostracized for years and practiced law with Jacob Arvey's law firm. Ran against the organization in 1976 in the primary and defeated its candidate for the Illinois State Supreme Court. Is now a State Supreme Court Justice.

I was born on the West Side of Chicago, in Austin. My father, John S. Clark, was the 30th ward Democratic alderman and committeeman, as his father had been before him. In our family, it was all politics. That's all we talked about at home. Aldermen, committeemen, state legislators, and precinct captains were at our house all the time at the dinner table.

My father never liked politics. He always wanted to be a farmer. My grandfather died in 1914 and was succeeded in his aldermanic seat by my father two years later. My father was an alderman for eighteen years, eight years of which he was chairman of the finance committee of the city council. In 1934, he was elected Cook County assessor, and held that job for twenty years.

In the pre-Daley era, my dad was one of the most important ward committeemen in Chicago. The position of ward committeeman was much more important in those days than it was under Daley. Thomas O'Brien, one of the most powerful congressmen in Washington, was from our ward. Next to Speaker Sam Rayburn, he was the second most important man in Congress, and he and Rayburn were very close. Nobody would go to Washington without calling on Tom O'Brien to pay their respects. But, at home in the 30th ward, he was nothing. Every two years he'd come to see my dad, the committeeman, and say, "Mr. Clark, I'd like to run for just one more time, if you can support me." And my dad would say, "Well, Thomas, you've done a fine job and the organization will support you. I hear good things about you in Congress." He ran in a district encompassing our ward and some other wards, but he lived in the 30th ward. He was a Pat Nash man. Nash had made him sheriff of Cook County at one time. They used to call him "Blind Tom" because he couldn't see the gambling in Cook County. He had moved to the West Side and my dad ran him for Congress. If my dad had said, "Thomas, we're not going to support you," none of the other ward committeemen would have supported him, and he just could not have gone back to Washington.

In those days, the ward committeemen were the key figures in Chicago. The executive committee of the Democratic Party, at that time, was very important. Mayor Ed Kelly wasn't able to make all the decisions. You had John S. Clark, the McDermotts, Tom Nash, Jim Bowler, Joe Gill, and Al Horan (when he got rich he started calling himself HorAN). No one man could dictate everything that was going to happen. They all had to be consulted.

The election of Mayor Daley changed all that. When Daley ran for mayor in 1955 and beat Kennelly, he made it clear that if he was elected he would resign as chairman of the Democratic Party of Cook County. After he was elected, he decided that that would weaken both the office of the mayor and his role as chairman of the party. He felt he would be more powerful if he held both, and he was correct. He remained on as mayor and chairman, giving to those two positions power that they had not had before. He strengthened the office of mayor, did away with the aldermen's rights to give driveway permits (it was a means of income to local aldermen), and took the right to prepare the budget away from the council. (The aldermen had been like priests in the Catholic Church, where the pastor ran his parish.) Daley had the support of the press and the people. He had all the power himself, and, for a period of years, he reigned supreme.

I knew Daley well. I recall when the party determined that they were not going to reslate Martin Kennelly for mayor. Daley was chairman of the party and county clerk of Cook County, but had not yet been able to get all of his power. In 1955, Daley went around and asked the important committeemen for their support to run for mayor. He didn't call them in. He came out to my father's house. It had been rumored that my father, who was very close to Martin Kennelly, was going to back Kennelly. That was what Daley wanted to determine.

I'll never forget it. Daley came out with Billy Lynch. I sat there and listened. I heard Daley say to my father, "I'd like your support. I know that you and Martin are good friends. I'm going to run. However, if you decided to run for mayor, I would support you. But, if you don't run, then I'm going to run to beat Kennelly." My dad told him that he had no intention of running, that he had no interest in being mayor, although he had given it a lot of thought. He said that while Martin Kennelly was his good and dear friend, the Clarks were always organization people, and that if Daley got the support of the organization, he would back him. And he did.

My dad should have been mayor of Chicago in 1933, when Cermak was killed. He was chairman of the finance committee of the city council (like Bilandic in 1976). My dad had been a very independent alderman and had always supported the people against the utilities. When Cermak was killed I believe the law said that if the mayor died or became incapacitated, the chairman of the finance committee of the city council would succeed him. The finance committee chairman ran the council and was like a lieutenant governor.

Pat Nash was the chairman of the party and my dad wasn't favored by Nash. Nash went to Springfield. Senator Richie Graham, a Democrat, was president pro tem of the state senate and was able to pass legislation very quickly during this emergency saying that the aldermen shall, in the event of the death of the mayor, elect a fellow alderman to succeed the mayor. As a result, it had to go to a vote of the city council. The organization had considerable control over aldermen like Jacob Arvey and Barnett Hodes (both of whom are law partners of mine at the present time). They were against my dad and for an alderman named Frank Corr. Pat Nash had Corr's resignation as mayor in his pocket. Nash wanted a young engineer from the sanitary district named Ed Kelly. Corr was elected temporarily, then resigned, and Nash and the Democratic Party made Kelly mayor.

Kelly had a tough time in his first session because my dad was chairman of the finance committee in the city council. The council was not a rubber stamp council. My dad had a number of fights with Kelly. I remember him saying that Kelly was in the arms of Morpheus.

What accounted for Daley's rise to power?

Daley's strengths developed after he was elected mayor of Chicago. He was very lucky in that each job he wanted, it so happened that whoever had it died. He moved ahead steadily. He had been secretary of the Democratic Party. I never thought of him as being brilliant. I don't think in those days he was a great strategist. He also had some loyal friends and he was from the right part of Chicago. Along the way he learned a great deal. He was director of revenue under Governor Adlai Stevenson, although I don't think he had an outstanding administration in that office. I don't think he was the greatest county clerk we ever had. My cousin, Mike Flynn, was a better county clerk.

But, all the time, Daley was looking, he was hard working, he was there. He got up early, he planned everything, and was able to be at the right place at the right time. When others would be in Florida or someplace, he was there, getting the job that maybe they could have gotten. He had good advice from people like Billy Lynch, who was a great asset to him. In later years, he ignored the advice of many. He wouldn't appreciate it if someone would make a suggestion to him, and you would be in difficulty with him because of it. He didn't look for any advice, except from his family and maybe a few friends that used to sit in his basement on Thursday nights and talk politics. Those were his real friends—Matt Danaher; Billy Lynch, in the earlier days; Daley's father; Bill Cahill; a few more, probably, that I don't know. He didn't trust anybody else. The longer his career matured, the less he trusted anybody at all. It had to be just Daley and his family. He would see you and he would listen to you for a little while. But you could always tell he was suspicious. Rather than looking around at all the talent that was available, before he'd ask a question, he knew where he was going, and it didn't matter what you said.

He's probably been the best mayor we have ever had. He was successful, as far as the city of Chicago is concerned. As far as Daley being a political genius, I think that's a myth. I think that he made a lot of mistakes because he didn't listen to others in the county and the state on who would be the best person to slate for what particular position. I don't think he was a good political leader. I think he was a great mayor. We had many unnecessary fights while he was the chairman. In 1956, he dumped Herb Paschen as the candidate for governor and slated Dick Austin, who was probably one of the few men who couldn't beat Governor Bill Stratton. Stratton only beat Austin by 38,000 votes. Daley could have slated somebody who could have beaten Stratton. I've never really been sure that he wanted to beat Stratton. Maybe that's why he did it the way he did it.

*Why would he not want to beat a Republican governor like Strat-
ton?*

A mayor of Chicago is always much better off in his legislative
program if he has a Republican governor in Springfield. I am not
talking about anything for Daley personally, but for the city he loved
—bond issues, home rule, whatever it was, some things that he
wanted to pass, others that he wanted to beat, for whatever reason.
If he had a Republican governor, he was always in a position to make
a deal. When I use the term "deal," I don't mean it in any sense that
it wasn't necessarily good government. It's politics. They were able
to log-roll. That's how Stratton got his sales tax increase one time.
Part of it went to Chicago. "I'll give you this and this and this, and
you give me this, this, and this, and a deal can be made." You had
to have eighty-nine votes in the House in those days, and thirty in
the Senate to be able to pass anything. If the mayor of Chicago has
a Democratic governor, and if they're in the minority, they can't get
anyone else to switch. But if you've got a Democratic mayor in
Chicago and a Republican governor in Springfield, and the governor
wants toll roads, or roads downstate, or needs more money, or wants
to pass a sales tax, he can reach out to the Chicago Democrats,
because he needs the votes. And the Chicago Democrats, under
Daley, would wait to see what they should do. They would do, for the
most part, anything that he said through his legislative leaders in
Springfield. When Billy Lynch was in the Senate, and I was in the
House, and Bill Pollack was the Republican leader, we would sit
down and work things out for the best interests of the state and the
best interests of Chicago. That's politics.

That's why I often wondered whether Daley ever wanted Dick
Austin to be governor in 1956. But, in doing this, he didn't meet with
downstate, he didn't confer with Paul Powell, and a few others that
should have been talked to—Kenny Gray, Mel Price, Al Fields. They
didn't even know that Paschen was being dumped, they didn't even
know who Austin was, and, all of a sudden, they were supposed to
go out and work for a lawyer from Chicago they never heard of who
was running for governor. Their feelings were hurt. They wanted to
be consulted, and, being consulted, of course, they'd say, "We want
Secretary of State," or whatever it was for downstate. But there was
no contact with downstate. They refused to work for Austin. I believe
that was bad politics, unless of course Daley wanted to defeat Austin.
In which case, it might have been good for him, but it wasn't good
for the Democratic Party.

There were other instances where he made serious political mistakes. When he decided he would not support Seymour Simon for reelection as president of the Cook County Board, that was a serious mistake, because Dick Ogilvie was then elected president of the Cook County Board. When Daley summarily dumped Seymour Simon a few days after putting his arms around him, this was not making a slate. This was dumping an incumbent president of the Cook County Board. Then he ran my good friend, Harry Semrow. Semrow didn't have a chance. Daley, I think, outraged a large segment of the Jewish community. He also got a president of the county board [Dick Ogilvie] who had some power and patronage. It started a war in the Democratic Party that we didn't need. I don't know why he dumped Simon. Tom Keane was disenchanted with Seymour Simon. He wanted something and Simon wouldn't go along. But, if he placated Tom Keane, I think he seriously damaged the Democratic Party in not reslating Seymour Simon. He didn't confer with other leaders. Many of the committeemen who were in that meeting that day will tell you how surprised they were when he introduced the new candidate, Harry Semrow. Simon didn't even know he was being dumped. It happened in the inner office.

He also succeeded, in those years, in alienating the Democrats in the suburbs. Rather than trying to bring them into the party, he built a Chinese wall around Chicago. The suburban committeemen would go in and say, "Mr. Mayor, I know we can do much better in this coming election in our township, but we've got to have some patronage. All we have is five or six political jobs, and we don't have workers, we don't have people to go out and distribute literature." And he would say, "Well, you come in with the vote, and then we'll give you the jobs." "But we can't get the votes without the jobs," they'd say. So he alienated all of the Democrats in the suburbs, he alienated the downstate Democrats, and there was always this downstate/Chicago rift.

There's such a difference between downstaters and Chicagoans. Part of Illinois is below the Mason–Dixon line. Memphis, Tennessee is closer than Chicago. Chicagoans don't even know that the downstaters exist. The downstaters are suspicious of you, if you're from Chicago, until you prove yourself. They're either farmers or miners, and some of them are still fighting the Civil War. You get the Southern approach. In central Illinois, you've got a much different group. You've also got the northern part. Some of the counties that they call "downstate" are north of Chicago. Some of the fellows in Lake

County call Cook County "downstate." But actually, it's Cook County against the rest of the world. There's more rapport between somebody from Rockford and someone from Union County than there is between Rockford and Chicago. It's an old, old fight that was there before Daley. I thought it was diminishing, during the years when I was active in Springfield. I think it is starting to come back again. It's just a natural thing. Chicagoans don't realize it. Downstaters do, and you've got to prove yourself.

How did you come to run for the United States Senate in 1968?

I was the attorney general of Illinois at the time. I was down at the state fair, sitting next to the mayor. He said, "Could you come and visit with me in the car for a minute?" He told me he wanted me to run for the U.S. Senate against Everett McKinley Dirksen. I said no. I didn't want to run against Dirksen. He asked me to come and see him. There was a series of meetings covering three or four weeks, and finally he persuaded me that the party needed me, that I could win, that he thought I'd be an outstanding candidate, and even if I lost, we would elect a Democratic county ticket if I could hold Dirksen down. That was the name of the game. I finally reluctantly did agree. There were commitments made—$1 million for the campaign, I would be the standardbearer, I would develop the issues in running for the U. S. Senate, and he would back me up. All this was agreed. That's how I got on the ticket.

The commitments were broken. I took independent positions and found that not only was Daley not supporting me, but he was talking against me. I heard of instances when my literature, instead of being delivered by ward headquarters, was ordered burned. Dirksen had a lot of friends. It was never intended that I win. I didn't realize it at the time. I was the last to know. I got the endorsement of labor on paper, but with a very few exceptions, even labor wouldn't support me. A lot of international labor union money was available. Paul Douglas had received it, and it was available if the mayor would write a letter, saying that he was for me. He wouldn't write the letter. They probably thought I wouldn't win anyway, and they'd use the money elsewhere, I suppose.

I took a position against the war in Vietnam. Daley felt that I was being disloyal to a Democratic president, Lyndon Johnson. He believed in great loyalty. So did I. It was a question of where did your loyalties lie? I thought I was being loyal to myself and my country in every position I took, and I just have never been a rubber stamp. This irritated Daley.

I also was asked who I supported for president after Johnson decided he wouldn't run again. I couldn't get a position from my party. I talked with Daley about it many times. He was waiting to see if it was going to be Ted Kennedy and he wasn't sure. I had come out for Bobby Kennedy. The party didn't like that at all. County Assessor Parky Cullerton took me to task for coming out for anybody before the party had decided who it would be, especially Bobby Kennedy, who didn't like the leadership in Chicago very much. Then Kennedy died, leaving me with all those new enemies. Then I came out for George McGovern, and it just deteriorated. I was just being myself, but you were not supposed to do that, at least in those days, if you got the endorsement of the party, no matter how you got it.

Did that lead to a severance of your relationships with Mayor Daley or anyone else?

Just with Mayor Daley. The other committeemen were sensitive to it and knew what was going on. They still remained my good friends, but publicly, of course, they didn't do anything for me, even though they were for me privately in a subsequent election.

I had a heart attack right after that. I was greatly in debt. All the promises were broken and I had to pay my campaign debt off out of my own money. For eight years I was just practicing law, in political oblivion. During those years, I'd go in to see the mayor at least once a year, and say, "Well, Mr. Mayor, how are you?" He'd say, "Fine. How are you? How's your wife?" I'd say, "She's fine, and how's Sis?" He'd say, "How's your mother?" "She's fine, Mr. Mayor." I'd say, "I'd like to be considered for an appellate judgeship." He'd say, "Well, you'd make a fine judge. I have a lot of fine men and women in the Democratic Party who would make fine judges. Certainly, you know the party will consider you." Well, I don't know if I was ever considered, but nothing ever happened. I'd see in the paper where somebody else would get it for eight years. Finally, one day, I realized that there were two vacancies for the Illinois State Supreme Court, and I said to my wife, "I'm going to run." She said, "Are you going to go see the mayor?" I said, "I'm not going to go see him, I'm just going to run." I hadn't seen him in three years. I did run, and I won.

Why do you think you won in that situation, Bill, with the mayor against you, supporting his old law partner for the vacancy?

There were a lot of reasons. Again, I don't think the mayor was that great a political leader. I could see that in Cook County there was a large division at this time between the factions of the party and the mayor. He had alienated Congressman Ralph Metcalfe and his people. I felt that I could end up on a team with Ralph in the black community on the South Side. Also, Bernie Neistein apparently was for a particular committeeman, who he felt should take his spot in the 29th ward with the West Side bloc. The mayor, for some reason, wouldn't go along with the local people out there. He picked his own black out there to support, and I knew that there would be no sample ballots in Neistein's ward on the West Side of Chicago for Daley's candidate. I knew I would do very well in the suburbs on my background and record, and just running against an organization candidate. That and many other things just fell into place.

Bill, you've spent your whole life in politics, and I know that the law means a great deal to you, too. What does it mean to be a politician in Chicago in this milieu?

I never thought it meant anything until I got out of it in 1968. I was out for eight years and I found I missed it very much. I can't describe it. I don't want to use terms like "It gets in your blood." Certainly, it cost me a great deal of money and a great deal of time, which, if devoted elsewhere, would have been much more financially rewarding. I really don't know. Maybe it's an ego trip, a feeling of importance, to be known in the community, a sense of family pride, trying to do something that's important. I think that the big thing is that it's important.

TEN

The Loyal
Opposition

DAN WALKER / WILLIAM SINGER /
DICK SIMPSON

DAN WALKER *White Protestant. About fifty-six years old. Successful attorney and long active in reform Democratic politics. Wrote the Walker Report criticizing the Chicago police in 1968 for their handling of the demonstrators at the Democratic convention. Ran against the organization candidate for governor in 1972 in the Democratic primary and defeated him, an almost unheard-of feat in Illinois. As governor, had a rocky time with the legislature and a running fight with Daley. Walker was anathema to the machine. In 1976, Daley's candidate, Michael Howlett, defeated Walker in the gubernatorial primary. Walker is now practicing law and awaiting another political opportunity.*

I grew up near San Diego, California, in the back country, and went to a variety of schools out there because we moved around a lot. We didn't have very much and never could buy a house. I went to San Diego High School, graduated valedictorian of my class. In 1940, I joined the navy as an enlisted man for two years, took the competitive exams, and went to the Naval Academy at Annapolis, served two years after graduation from the Naval Academy, and left the navy to go to law school. I spent my early stint in governmental service in Springfield and in Washington. I then went into the private practice of law.

I became more and more upset at the machine's control of statewide politics in the Democratic Party and the closed nature of the system. Regardless of what one may say (and you have articulated it very well) about how that kind of a system is important to keep the big city running, I don't think there is any excuse for it on a statewide basis in terms of control of the party. I worked every two years for a candidate of my choice and I continued to practice law. I finally came to the conclusion that the only way it could be done was to beat them in a statewide primary. When I acquired enough money so that my family could afford to take the risk, and when we couldn't get anybody else to do it, I went out there and did it.

Governor, you were the first man that I can remember since Henry Horner in 1936, to beat the machine in a primary like that. How did you do it?

We knew, from very careful surveying, that Paul Simon's popularity was not what everybody assumed that it was. It was a surface kind of popularity. A good guy, but no real deep attachment to him, and, therefore, that could be broken through with the right kind of campaign. Number two, we didn't think that Daley would take me seriously, and I don't believe he did. Number three, we figured out that if the primary vote was substantially under 1,500,000 we would lose; if it was over 1,500,000, we would win; and if it was right at 1,500,000, it would be a horse race. That's exactly the way it turned out. One million and four odd came out and I won by about 30,000. The walk played a very large part in that victory. The Republican crossover did not. People who do not ordinarily vote in either primary came out and voted for me. Working people related to me. The waitress who was on her feet all day; the scrub woman whose feet hurt her; the farmer; all kinds of people related to me because I was out there. I was working hard. I was sweating, and they knew I was sweating. Many people told me, "Any man who wants to be governor bad enough to go out there and walk 1,200 miles has got my respect."

What was it like to try to govern a state like Illinois?

It was a fascinating exercise. Fortunately, I did know a little more about state government than people attributed to me because I had served in it, and I had done a lot of reading. I surrounded myself with some people who had good backgrounds in government and in politics, and I gave them head room and listened to them. It was very difficult to take over a government as big as the one in the State of Illinois. Most of my problems, Milt, were political rather than governmental. I'm not a natural politician in terms of thinking the way that they think. I don't count myself as one of them. They sense that, and that hurts in my relationship with them. I had problems with politics in terms of reacting the way I should have reacted instinctively to interpersonal political relationships. Government is a management problem, and I like management. I think I know something about management and that part of it, and I enjoyed it from the day that I sat down in that chair until the day I left.

If you look around the country, the situation is very rare where sooner or later the chief executive doesn't have problems with his legislature, whether they are the same party or the opposite party.

It's the separation of powers and it's a turf problem. The executive, by the nature of the beast, is always trying to encroach on the legislature's turf, and the legislature is resisting that and trying to reach out and get some of the executive's turf in terms of control of policy, administration, programs, etc. It's a natural kind of thing and will always go on. I did not spend enough time on legislative relationships. I delegated that to my deputy and his staff. That was a mistake on my part. I think if I had worked harder at that, I could have done somewhat better. It was confrontation politics from the day I sat down in that chair. The Chicago machine legislators and Republicans confronted me. At that point, you have a choice, Milt (those people play hard ball politics, as you know), you either lie down or you fight. There is no middle course in that kind of a situation. If it is the opposite party that is doing it to you, there is a middle course. But when it is a combination of your own party and the opposite party, you have a tough situation on your hands.

The only major resource that I had was people. I knew that the only way that I could make any progress with the legislature at all was to let them know that if they didn't stop it at least every now and then, and go along with me on something, that I was going to let the public know about it in a dramatic way. From that came the flya-rounds, the frequency with which I was on television and on the media throughout the state. I didn't have the power base in the media, in the legislature, in the regular organization in my own party. What is left? People.

What resources did they have available in dealing with a governor like you?

All of the traditional power bases and the ability to cut interparty deals in the legislature which caused me all kinds of problems— Democrats working with Republicans to defeat me, instead of supporting their own party governor. There is always the ability to make life difficult for you by putting bills on your desk that they know you are going to have to veto and hurt yourself. Forcing you to spend when you don't want to spend. Overriding your vetoes. My successor accuses me of spending the state into bankruptcy. The legislature overruled my vetoes to the extent that it has cost the state $250,000,000. If we had that $250,000,000, he would have had no problems at all. It was his party that joined with glee in overriding the vetoes. They had all the traditional power bases, including the media.

There are three areas [in Illinois]—Chicago, suburbs, and downstate. It's not Cook County, suburbs, and downstate. It is Chicago,
Cook County suburbs plus collar counties, and downstate. The other
important division is Chicago metropolitan area television market
and downstate. You have to analyze it from each of those perspec-
tives. A very important thing that is happening in the legislature is
that, increasingly, suburban legislators and collar county legislators
are finding that they have much in common with some of the downstaters, and you see some alliances growing up there that were not
present in prior years. The other factor is the downstate feeling about
Chicago.

*How does a Democratic governor in Springfield normally deal
with the Democratic machine in Chicago?*
Accommodation. Accommodation means, again—yielding turf.
Daley and the Chicago machine have their turf. It's called Chicago,
and you keep your hands off, and you let them know that you won't
encroach on their turf. That's the way you reach an accommodation.
You can also do it by symbolic things, or by picking a couple of things
that are of very great importance to them. If I had given Daley the
Crosstown Expressway and remap, I could have had the Democratic
nomination in 1976 on a silver platter. Both of those involved important matters of principle to me that I was not about to turn around
on. I believe that I probably would still be governor today if I had
given him those two things. I was in Indiana campaigning for the
Democratic candidate for governor in the summer of 1976, after I
lost the primary. Mayor Daley called me. He said, "Governor, I just
wanted to ask you a question. Would you be willing to change your
position on the Crosstown Expressway?" I said, "Gee, Your Honor,
I'm kind of strung out on that issue. I've been very vocal on it. I don't
see how I can change my mind." He said, "Well, I think you have a
great future in the Democratic Party, Dan, and we've got several
months remaining in your administration. We could go ahead on that
Crosstown." I said, "Sorry, Your Honor, no deal."
In the legislature, issues in politics, statewide, are of interest and
importance to the Chicago legislators only to the extent to which it
has present or future impact on their power base, their turf, which
is Chicago. But they are very careful of that. They don't let the
slightest little thing go by. If it is going to have any effect on Chicago,
on goes that Home Rule Amendment! They do their homework,
many of those guys, and you have to respect them for that. They

work hard for their power base. A Republican governor doesn't have to worry about making that kind of an accommodation because he is of the opposite party and he looks for his power base elsewhere. One of the truisms about Illinois politics and government is that being governor of Illinois is easier for a Republican than it is for a Democrat, in part because Illinois leaned Republican, in great part because the media is so overwhelmingly Republican.

What was your relationship with Mayor Daley like in your four years as governor?

I don't think he took me all that seriously politically. I was what he called, "One of those independents," and he never had much respect for the independents in politics. They didn't win elections and he was in the business of winning elections. He didn't think they were practical. He embraced me, once I won the primary, because he was that kind of Democrat. I always respected him for that. We got along well on a personal basis. It has been suggested to me that if I had taken the time to spend more time with him, it might have been a little different. I don't believe that. There was such a sharp division between us in our approach to politics and government that I don't think having dinner, lunch, breakfast talks would have made that kind of difference. We didn't communicate very much. He didn't call me with any frequency. I didn't call him with any frequency. I must have had, outside of affairs of state, maybe four or five meetings with him when I was governor.

I have, and always have had, a tremendous amount of respect for Mayor Daley. He was obviously a very canny politician, and a good manager who grasped detail and spent his time working. He knew how to work. He knew what things to spend his time on. He knew what details to leave to others and what details to work on. He didn't pass on all details. That is an important thing about managing that some people never grasp. He also loved Chicago. He had this amazing ability to work together with the political community, the religious community, the labor community, and the business community.

I think one of the problems that the mayor had was that he grew up in a time, and a milieu, and a way of life where he didn't really come into contact with and understand some things that were not a part of his life. He doesn't understand Californians, and I am originally a Californian. He doesn't understand independents. He doesn't really understand neighborhoods, except his neighborhood. He understands downtown Chicago, he understands his neighborhood, but I don't think he understands what is happening out there on the Northwest Side. He never understood the suburbs. He never understood the legal profession. What he understood, he knew and practiced with expertise. What he did not understand, what he had not grown up with, what was not a part of his body and his mind, he did not learn about. That was one of his defects—his unwillingness to reach out, intellectually and personally, into areas that he was not comfortable with.

Was Daley the epitome of the old politician, and is there a new politics evolving in this country which people like you, Senator Dick Clark, Governor Michael Dukakis, Governor Jerry Brown, and President Jimmy Carter are representative of?

That is too much of a generalization, because Daley succeeded very well in his latter days, as in his early days, in being an old school politician. Sure that's a part of it, but you just can't put it down that way—old and new. Milt, a lot of the things that I did are old in politics and are old politics. They just haven't been done for a while. There really isn't much difference. Look at Daley and the media, and me and the media. In many respects, not too much difference. We have a different style, and I used television more than he did. But his continual problem (and he succeeded in doing it) was getting through the media out there to people. We had the same basic approach.

Politics has a purpose only insofar as it involves government. Once politics gets separated from government, then the system isn't working right. Some people enjoy politics for the sake of politics, and some people in government are in government for political ins and political reasons, rather than being in government for governmental reasons and purposes. I wish that everybody who was in politics would get out of politics every now and then, so that it would not become ingrained in you. I wish I could remember the words that Senator John Stennis used when he retired from the Senate. It has something to do with being around marble too long—the columns of the Capitol. He said that you became so much a part of that system that you reacted as a part of the system, and for the sake of the system, rather than relating to the public. That's very true.

In Illinois, I call it a club system of politics. That's what I have been trying to break up. I don't believe in a club system in politics. Most of the people in the state are on the outside looking in. I was a governor and I was on the outside looking into those club windows. Some people love the club. Every time I see individual X in state office go to individual Y state office's fundraising dinner and pat him on the back, I have to say to myself, "There's the club operating."

The system needs to be changed to be more open. I recognize that politics is inevitably intertwined with government. Adlai Stevenson was a great governor, a great man, but didn't like politics, didn't want any part of it, and shoved it aside and gave it to others. I think you've got to practice politics, but you have got to practice politics with government in mind, not with politics in mind.

What is it you like about politics, and what don't you like about politics?

I like the one on one with people. I love to campaign one on one. To be out there with people, and to talk with them and kid with them, is, to me, just a tremendous amount of fun, whether you are campaigning or in office. The big speeches, the dinners, everybody says the applause is great, and you are up there on the podium. I do not get turned on by that. (Some people won't believe me when I say this.) Neither do I get turned on by power. Power for the sake of power interests me not at all. I know some people in my own administration who were concerned about it, who enjoyed power for the sake of power. I don't enjoy pushing that lever down just to see something pop up over there and to know that it came about because I pushed that lever. I don't get my jollies out of that, as the kids say.

There is a price to be paid, not only for a life in politics, but for four years in politics, as I had. Travail. What it does to you inside. What it takes out of you. The necessity of constantly making decisions that are not black-and-white decisions. Let me give you an example, Milt. It doesn't bother a certain kind of a politician if legislator X comes into his office and says, "Hey, you want my vote? Well, Uncle Charley goes on the payroll, okay?" It doesn't bother him. That's a way of life. That's how the system is supposed to work. It bothered the devil out of me, Milt. It really did. I never got used to that, and those kinds of decisions which you have to make constantly. I just wonder whether it's worth it, although I recognize that it's a part of the practical life of government. You gotta do it. You gotta stay with it. And you gotta hope that most of your decisions are on the right side and not giving in to that temptation that, "Gee, we gotta have that great big program through the legislature. It's so important to the people that I can make this little compromise over here to get that through." How far do you go?

You give up your personal life. You really don't have any, I would say, starting at the level of governor, senator, and on up. You can still keep some of your personal life, at lower office levels. But not as governor, senator, and certainly, president. As far as your family is concerned, that's the bad part of it. Very few wives enjoy it. Very few kids enjoy it. There is a lot of travail involved for an individual and his family in this business of governing. There's some fun, there's some challenges, but a devil of a lot of travail.

I am giving consideration to the possibility of running for the Senate, although I can't get excited about it, really. I don't think I am a legislator, and that doesn't denigrate the legislative role. It's just that some people are cut out for one role and some people for another. If I run again for anything, most likely it will be for governor, and I don't know whether I will run or not. I am enjoying building this law firm. I am enjoying being a father and a husband again, and I am enjoying the absence of that travail.

It's as simple as this, Milt, this schedule right here. That's my handwriting. I made that schedule out. I decide what I am going to do next Monday. I don't have a scheduler doing it for me. I don't have fifteen staff people saying "Dan's got to go here, and Dan's got to go there" and having meetings to decide what's best for Dan to do. *I* decide. It's great to be back in control, at least of the little things of your life that you can have some control over. I don't know if that makes any sense to you.

WILLIAM SINGER *Jewish. About forty years old. A liberal, he is an attorney who was elected as an independent to the city council in 1969 in a special election and reelected in 1971. In 1972, combined with Rev. Jesse Jackson and led a slate of delegates to the Democratic national convention, and had Daley and the Chicago machine delegates thrown out, the worst defeat Daley suffered in his career. In 1975, he gave up his aldermanic seat and ran against Daley for mayor in the Democratic primary and was solidly defeated. Appeared before the machine slatemakers in 1978 for the U.S. Senate nomination, but didn't get it. Is still politically ambitious, and may have a future.*

I grew up on the South Side, went to Horace Mann Grammar School and South Shore High School, Brandeis University, and then to law school at Columbia University. I was fortunate to get a clerkship in Chicago with a great federal judge, Hubert Will, who was probably the best federal judge in this district. Judge Will was a spectacular teacher, and that made a lot of difference in my life. I joined a law firm in 1967, but took a leave of absence in 1968 to work for Robert Kennedy. I was in charge of his Chicago office. I was pretty shook up when Bobby was killed.

In 1968, there was a vacancy for alderman in the 43rd ward. An independent group in the neighborhood was looking for a candidate to run. I was invited to a meeting to discuss the aldermanic race with a group of people. They went around the table asking if anyone was interested in running. I said I might be interested, and that was it.

It was the coming together of a number of things that made it possible to beat the machine in that ward. Eddie Barrett, the Democratic boss in the ward, was committed to running a candidate who was an inarticulate stooge. A lot of young people had been moving in, and a lot of the old rooming houses had been converted to single family houses. There was this enormous reservoir of people who wanted to do something after 1968, and this was their first opportunity. Since it was a special election with no other race going on at the same time, we were able to pull together all sorts of resources in the ward, and so did the machine. They sent captains in from other wards and it became a test. We wound up winning 12,100 to 11,700. When I ran for reelection for my second term as alderman, I carried the ward with seventy percent of the vote.

I loved being an alderman. I loved both parts of the job. You do two different things if you are a full-time, conscientious alderman. One of them is being a legislator. I don't want to be overly critical of my colleagues, but most of them are not legislators. They vote, but they don't draft legislation. They don't think of bills to introduce. They'll put in an order to commend a church for a hundredth anniversary or something, but not real legislation or in spending time on the budget. I made that my special area of interest. I spent hours with Tom Keane learning about that. There weren't more than four or five major pieces of legislation that I eventually got through. But there were a number of pieces of legislation that I did sponsor that were defeated when I sponsored them, but later picked up by the machine. I voted with the machine, or the majority, ninety-five percent of the time, because most of the matters are routine, things that you want to support—motor fuel tax appropriations for street cleaning and snow removal, the sidewalk appropriation increased, things like that. I really liked being a legislator. I liked knowing how to run the city. It was a great learning experience.

Another part of the job was, in some ways, more satisfying. Nothing would ever happen in that ward without a public meeting. If anybody was going to be effective in a governmental decision, they were entitled to know what was going to happen. I'd come home at nights, all charged up because we were able to pull people together. We were able to say, "All right, if you want your zoning ordinance, you are going to have to give up something, you're going to have to put up a fence, you're going to have to reroute your traffic patterns." And sometimes we defeated things that were bad.

Being an alderman and having a full-time office means getting hundreds of requests every week, all the way from mundane matters like someone getting their garbage picked up to broader issues—getting a park for the neighborhood, getting a park or vacant lot cleaned up, a zoning matter, or a school situation. You dealt with everything. I really loved it.

How did an independent liberal like you, who was in the minority in the city council, get decent city services for your ward?

It is interesting that you use the term "independent liberal." Independent is one thing; liberal is another. The issue of whether you are a liberal or a conservative has no bearing on this. In terms of someone calling you and saying, "Hey, my street lights are burned out," there is no liberal or conservative way of fixing it, or picking up the garbage. Of all the fifty wards in the city, we probably had the best services. I was a full-time alderman. We had a staff and I was on top of all service requests. We developed systems whereby we would make sure that if we phoned in a complaint, it was followed up. If they weren't, we made it clear that we were entitled to it.

There really are three major things here. One is just being full time and doing it. Two, most city servants are not bad people, they're not evil, they're not out to deny city services to anybody. In fact, quite the opposite. They want to do a good job and they want people to know that they are not hacks. They want people to know that they can perform. I think it is important to give them that recognition. The 43rd ward had the best ward superintendent in the city, Pete Schivarelli. He's terrific. We had great garbage collection. If there was something we needed, he took care of it. He wasn't my appointee; he came through the ward committeeman. But he was a professional who knew how to do his job, and still does.

Treating city employees with respect is very important. I called up a police officer one day and I said, "You know we have a lot of abandoned automobiles in certain parts of the ward, and I would like to talk to you about it." He said, "Fine." I said, "Let's have lunch." I think he was shocked. We had lunch. He said, "You know, no alderman has ever invited me to lunch." I said, "What can I do to make it better for you and how can we achieve the goal that we want?" He said, "I've been in this business for a long time. Most aldermen have just called me up and said, 'Hey, do this, get that car out, I need it out in 24 hours.' " We worked out a system where every Monday he would come into the office and we would give him a geographical list. He loved that. He thought we were great. It was a simple matter of being respectful of him and his position, and him knowing it. I think that's an important part of the job.

The other weapon we had was the fear of embarrassment if something wasn't done. I made it clear that I wasn't going to accept the absence of service. I wasn't going to let them take advantage of me. That's a stick approach, I suppose, but on the carrot approach, I also made it clear that I was very respectful of city workers. I wanted them to do a good job, and I let them know that they did a good job, and let the people know that they did a good job. That's why guys

like Schivarelli were terrific. They did a good job. And Joe from the
police department did a great job with towing vehicles. We sent out
newsletters and we let people know. By and large, the city bureaucracy is responsive, yes. The only complaint I would have is that I
think there was a good deal of waste in that process. That is, they
could deliver, but there was waste on a city basis.

Did you have access to the media for help?

You'd have to build it, but I could do it. You had to build up
contacts. Obviously those of us in the city council who spoke were
something of a novelty for them. They had live bodies. There were
times when the media were important to work with. There was a
land deal in the Old Town area which was an absolute rip-off. It was
terrible and the city council passed it over my vigorous objection to
rezoning. It would have given this guy the right to build a huge
building, to acquire the land from Urban Renewal at a virtual steal.
He was going to build a thirty-three-story building, and buy the land
for roughly $10 a square foot when the land in that area was going
for $30 a square foot. I opposed it and I was pretty upset about it. I
called the city editor of the *Sun-Times* and said that this was disgraceful, and they said, "Come on over." The next morning they made it
a front-page story. They reconsidered that zoning change. There was
no automatic thing. You had to be right. It had to be something that
was grabby. The media doesn't get involved for any story, and it
doesn't get involved even if you are right. It has to be something that
they feel you're right, that the issue is important, and that it is going
to be attractive as an issue as well.

What kind of a body was the city council?

You could hardly call it a legislative body, as you and I would
describe a legislature. It didn't really meet the standards. When I first
went there, there were three or four guys in the city council who just
snored. Keane used to put one of the sergeant of arms next to Brandt,
who would fall asleep. There were times when they called his number and he said, "Aye," and went back to sleep. It was really a riot.
There wasn't much give and take. In Springfield, the legislators, even
the machine guys, have a lot more flexibility to vote for and against.
Not every issue was an article of faith. I remember once, when I was
in my first year in the council, the issue was framed in the negative.
That is, if you wanted to vote with the machine, you had to vote
"No." That was a difficult concept to understand and the first couple

of guys voted "Yes," because you know, when you vote with the machine, you vote "Yes." What else is there? As I remember, it came to about the seventh or eighth alderman, Keane finally got to them and said the vote is "No," the vote is "No." They weren't voting against anything, but it was framed with a double negative. It was really weird. The votes then went, "No, no, no, no, no." At the end of the roll call, six or seven of the first guys who had voted "Yes" stood up and dutifully said, "I wish to change my vote from 'Yes' to 'No' on this issue."

The mayor determined all the legislation. Everything had to come from him. Some guys in the council were smart, the younger guys in particular. Paul Wigoda was not a dummy by any means, and some other guys had some brains, but they all were preempted. If they had an idea, they had to give it to the mayor. If they wanted to introduce it, it wouldn't go any further than if I introduced it. I was a constructive opponent of a lot of things and a constructive supporter of a number of things. I tried to vote with the organization and the mayor when I thought he was right. That meant that I sometimes voted against some of the independents.

You couldn't get any of your own legislation through, not directly, but you could get things done indirectly by introducing something and trying to build a constituency for it, knowing that when you introduce it, it will lose. It's the classic case of Len Despres' lead-base paint ban which he fought for for years (before I got into the council). Then he took a vacation to Europe. The mayor introduced the ordinance and they passed it in one session while he was away because they thought it was a good idea. There were a number of issues like that. I led the fight for a strong air pollution code in the city. The mayor had a standard that said you couldn't burn fuel with more than three percent sulphur. I introduced an ordinance that we should have a standard that you can't burn fuel with more than 1¼ sulphur. When they came back in with the revised ordinance to make it effective six months later, after there had been some serious air pollution problems, they had the one percent standard. So you know that if you can't get it in your way, it doesn't mean you quit. You fight losing battles because, ultimately, you know you are going to win. I was the first to introduce the disclosure ordinances that are now law in Chicago, conflict of interest provisions that are now law, labeling of packaging, and lots of other things. Len Despres has a whole catalog of those as well.

There is a mistake in the assumption that the machine operates in the city council. The machine doesn't operate in the city council. Daley operated in the city council. Daley controlled the city council. When he was mayor, he made the decisions, not the machine, not the council. When he decided to do something, it was done. You know Daley well enough to know that over the years he adopted lots of other people's ideas, that he was a very conservative politician, that he wasn't an aggressive leader charting new paths all the time, but was capable of picking up a lot of good ideas. His great genius was being able to put them all together and make them work. There are lots of people who have ideas who sometimes couldn't make them work. To his credit, he did make a lot of them work, and he created the conditions where some of them would be able to work, like a good financial base and all the rest. But you can't mistake the council for a legislative body. You should not have any illusions that, in the back room, ten or fifteen guys got together and planned. It didn't exist that way. There was Daley and there was Keane. Keane controlled the finances, and Daley made the decisions essentially on what was going to happen and what wasn't going to happen.

Did the aldermen who were powerful ward committeemen have a great deal of influence in the city council in terms of public policy for the city?

They didn't care to. You take a guy like Vito Marzullo, who is a powerful ward committeeman and an alderman. Vito was quite content to be just like any other alderman and vote the way he was asked to vote or told to vote. His happiness stemmed from the fact that he was boss of his ward, he controlled patronage in his ward, he controlled jobs, and he had a committee chairmanship which was a valuable patronage job for him, and that was it. It was a trade-off. Daley got the broader legislative things, and the aldermen are taken care of in their wards. It didn't really matter who was sitting there, whether it was the committeeman himself, or his tool or his stand-in. Whoever was there was there for that same purpose, except for the few of us who weren't.

What about Tom Keane's role in the Daley years in Chicago?

I don't know anything about how he operated in his own ward. I've heard negative stories about his being high-handed, things like that. I didn't observe that. I observed him in the city council. He is and was brilliant. I've never met anybody like Tom Keane. Daley had his genius in terms of being able to manipulate things and pull things together, but Keane was the brains in many ways. Not that he usurped Daley's function, but in terms of the finances and keeping all that together, no one came close to Keane. He knew where everything was, and that the dollars and cents were what made the city go. I didn't agree with the way he ran the council, but there was nobody like Keane in terms of running the council. Keane could quote votes, ordinances, issues from twenty or thirty years previously. I spent a lot of time learning from Tom Keane. I'm not ashamed to say that. I disagreed with him, but I had enormous respect for Tom Keane, and found him a very charming man, too.

I think he and Daley had an agreement between them. I think Daley said to Keane, "Okay, I'm going to trust you to run the council. You run it. It's your ball game. You watch the finance committee. You make sure. I'll worry about urban renewal and the broad legislation, and I'll bring things to you from my department heads, and I'll attend the ground breakings." Keane was a partner in many ways in running the city, unlike any other relationship after Keane was sent to jail. Keane was as important a figure as anyone else, much more important than anyone else in the city. In some ways, I think Keane and Daley had jealousies of each other. I think Keane wanted to be mayor, but knew he couldn't be, and he and Daley made their peace. Daley was going to be the guy who slated candidates, although Keane had a role in that, too, and he was powerful enough to say, "I want someone slated for judge." Daley had more pervasive powers than Keane. Daley was not as heavy-handed as Keane. He was more the master politician in some ways. But Keane was and is brilliant, and Daley needed him very badly. Daley was much better than Keane in working with the bankers and people like that. Keane was much more of a behind the scenes guy who had enormous power. He controlled the council with an iron fist.

Most of the council wasn't on the floor. Once it got to the floor that was just for show. There wasn't anything that you didn't know the result. There were one or two issues where it needed a two-thirds or three-fourths vote, where, occasionally, there would be some battle about what was going to happen. It was only a matter of how soon they wanted to cut off debate, how authoritarian they wanted to be, and how little they wanted to show on television. Keane was a master. There were lots of things he could do. He could set the matter over to the end of the agenda and hope the television cameras would go home. He could set a meeting for late in the day. He could not give enough notice. He was great at that. The issue was only how

Keane was going to get it through, of what procedures they were going to adopt, because they had the votes. Keane's role generally was just to get them through with the least amount of objection.

What led you to run for mayor in 1975?

It became clear to me that what I really liked was not just the city, but running it, and the idea of service. I can't think of any greater challenge than proving that a large city can work for a large number of people. The common assumption is that big old cities aren't going to work anymore. I don't believe that. What made me run was simply a desire to participate politically in what was, I thought, the most important thing in government, making a city work. I was exhilarated by doing it in one ward and being an alderman.

When I announced in October of 1973 for February of 1975, it wasn't clear that Daley was going to be the candidate. There had been a lot of talk, when he ran in 1971, that he wasn't going to run again, although you had to figure that the only way he was going to leave was in fact the way he did. But no one knew that. In the middle of my campaign, he had a stroke, which even made it more likely that he wouldn't run. Yet, he came back. He was a very strong-willed and strong man.

I really felt that Daley did not understand the school problem, and the schools were going to hell. You had an exodus of families; anybody who was middle class and who could not afford to send their kid to a private school would move out to the suburbs. I also felt that he didn't understand what was going on in the job market. Daley took everything so personally. If a company left Chicago, it was like they were doing it to him. When someone would say to him, "Why don't we have a business incentive program and offer the kind of competitive incentive that other places are?" he would think, "We shouldn't have to offer an incentive. They should want to be here." His love for the city actually got in the way of some sound public policy decisions that he should have been making. The city did not respond to these problems. As strong and as effective as he was in many ways, there was the need for the things that he was not doing. I felt that I could be a strong, effective, and more sensitive leader in terms of the things that needed to be done right now, particularly in the jobs and school areas, and the need to rebuild the neighborhoods.

I came close to beating the machine, but not beating Daley. Daley won that election himself. He transcended the machine in that election by 100,000 votes. People consciously went out, not because the precinct captain forced or cajoled them, but because they made a decision that they were for Daley. They felt a greater sense of stability in the knowledge of what they had. We said, "Who did you agree with on schools, Singer or Daley?" "Singer." "Who did you agree with on jobs?" "Singer." "Who did you agree with?" "Singer." "Who did you vote for?" "Daley!" It was an incredible thing. There was an enormous stability factor, and some people simply felt they couldn't vote against him, a man who had given up so much of his life for his city.

Daley clearly loved the city. That love sometimes got in the way of sound public policy and judgments. He probably loved Bridgeport even more than he loved the city. He was a very fundamental man. He believed in some very fundamental values like loyalty. He was a tough man. He never gave an inch. He fought for everything he believed in, and I respected him for that. But he also had his blind side, especially in his later years.

I think there were two Daleys. There was the Daley of the late 1950s and early 1960s who was much more innovative and open to new ideas and change, and to other people. Beginning with the convention of 1968, and maybe slightly before that, you had a much more conservative Daley, as he grew older, who didn't trust many people in those later years, who became a little bit more authoritarian, and placed a premium on those things like loyalty. There was that open, great compromiser, the guy that brought all kinds of people into the party, who knew how to move and work with his opponents, and who knew early that the city needed redevelopment, particularly in the downtown area, but who couldn't see that same need for industry ten years later in the neighborhoods as they deteriorated. I am not as much a student of Daley as you and others have been, but he is the only mayor I really ever knew. I have always been struck by what I thought were the differences as he grew older.

In the earlier years his strengths far outweighed his weaknesses. He was always able to compensate for his weaknesses. If one of his weaknesses was the machine and the way it operated, and he couldn't see a need to change it, he could still take in a candidate and open up the party, and wanted to do that all that time. In later years there were these strengths and weaknesses which were both good and bad for the city. As the later years went on, his weaknesses began to catch up.

When I was first elected, Daley was surprised that he couldn't get me into the organization. There were attempts to say, "Why don't you be one of us?" Keane had talked to me about it. I thought it was necessary for the party to be more of an open party and not to demand that kind of loyalty in the council. But Daley didn't always want to fight with me, or a lot of other people. In 1971, when I ran for reelection, he was running, too, and he was not interested in having me as an opponent. But he was persuaded to run an opponent against me for alderman because some of the other committeemen in nearby wards were fearful that if I didn't have an opponent my workers would go into their wards.

He was very angry with the 1972 convention, obviously. He never forgot that. There were any number of attempts to compromise the situation. Senator McGovern, who was the nominee, called and said, "Look, we don't want to divide the party. Will you support a compromise with both delegations seated with half of them?" I said that the selection was not perfect, and all we wanted to see was that the rules were enforced. He said, "Fine. If you support that we'll get Daley to support it." But they couldn't get Daley to support it. Daley and his people all voted against it. He never forgave me for that.

After the campaign for mayor in 1975, we had a long talk one day, and he said to me (he was being magnanimous, of course, because he won and felt that maybe he had settled the score), "You ran a good race and I'll never forget that you were a gentleman throughout the race. You never said a thing about my family and you never attacked me personally, and I respect that." Tom Donovan told me several weeks after Daley died that Daley told him that I had given him the toughest fight of his life, that he had been worried about that race.

Why didn't you run against Bilandic in 1977, after Daley died?
My dream, as I told you, is to be mayor. But you really can't impose that in a situation where it isn't right. The timing just wasn't right. I thought the public was worried and felt that the best course for the city was to let things go on with Daley, in effect, being allowed to finish his term, even though he was not alive—"Let Daley's team finish the term."

I think the time will perhaps be more appropriate in 1979. There is now beginning to be a realization that the mayor, Mayor Daley (you notice I keep saying "Mayor Daley" as if he is the only one who was), is dead. I am not sure he believes he's dead. He may still believe he is alive, for all I know. I don't meant to be irreverent, because I respect him, but there is almost a feeling you have that this man was so much larger than life that he can't be dead. And even if he seems to be dead, he really isn't, he's still running things. In many ways he is, and what he set in motion still is. But that's going to come to an end. There is going to be an inevitable change and the question is when it's right to present that to the public. At a point in time when they are very worried and not sure of the future, it is probably best not to present what will inevitably be a new direction for the city. Yet I believe that that will happen.

The things that Daley did that held Chicago together were not so firm that they can withstand all the modern pressures that hit a city —the boom in the suburbs, modern transportation, the educational system falling down, and things like that. There are pluses. There are some very good neighborhoods which have not reached the point of deterioration that they need to be torn down. They need shopping centers, new sidewalks, new streets, and tearing down those buildings which are beyond repair. We have neighborhoods that are good and that work. But that is going to require a kind of thinking that hasn't been here for a while. It's going to require that the city get involved in rehabilitation, land banks, home banks for rehabilitation of homes, the creation of industrial parks. No one is going to locate a modern factory by itself anymore. Loft buildings don't serve industry anymore. We have to clear some of those loft buildings. The city needs modern thinking, modern industrial know-how, a school system which is attractive to parents of school-age children. One of the great frustrations I had in my ward when I was alderman was to watch the young families move in before they even had children, watch them have their children and even send them to some of the elementary schools, but leave in the 5th, 6th, and 8th grades for the suburbs because they didn't have confidence in the schools.

We've got a job pool, good rail, water, and road transportation. We can build on our strengths. The strengths are a solid base for delivery of services. In most areas some of the services are good. We have to continue to build downtown. But more important is an effort to rebuild some of the older neighborhoods without clearing them, to help the people who live there now to stay and improve their property, and to have that job base back in the city. It will never be what it was, but there are still plenty of resources here.

What about race relations—the black, white, Latin thing in Chicago?

I think those tensions are decreased to the extent that you have a stable job market, a good educational system, and neighborhoods which are strong. I think those tensions will decrease. The pressures in black communities to get out are not necessarily pressures to take over Latin or white communities. The pressures are to find those things which they want for their families and children—a job, a good education. If the neighborhood is stable, you'll see them coexist. Building the base of the city is responding to someone's basic needs.

How do you see the future of the independent movement in Chicago, and your own role in the city?

You will see more and more people run for and win offices. They may be national Democrats, but unless and until the local party opens up to be a more embracive organization, they will run opposed to the party and beat them in primaries. You will see a lot more of that. The public's interest is in people like that. The hardest thing is to get them to run. You know how tough it is. You'll see more independents and more women. The real effort will come when and if a major office is won. The most likely one is mayor, the most likely time is 1979, and, to be immodest, the most likely person is me.

So that's where you see your future in Chicago, again going back after the mayoralty. You still have that dream.

I am going to make that dream happen.

DICK SIMPSON *White Protestant. About forty years old. Professor of political science at the University of Illinois, Chicago Circle. Genuine liberal reformer. Elected to the city council as an independent in 1971 and reelected in 1975, from the North Side's 44th ward. Persistent and vocal critic of Daley and the machine in the council. Staunch supporter and spokesman for neighborhood and community organizations, and for all good reform causes in Chicago. Donated his aldermanic salary to his ward office to provide funds for services. Did not run for reelection in 1979.*

I guess mine is an unusual background for a Chicago politician. I was born in Houston, Texas, was involved in things like the scouting movement, and got three Eagle Scout awards. I went to college at Texas A&M, transferred to the University of Texas, became part of the Christian faith and community there, joined the sit-in movement, and became involved in student politics. My parents are several-generation American. They perceived no ethnic group identity except white. My father is a conservative businessman. My mother is much more liberal. She comes from a church family. My grandfather was a Nazarene minister from the Oklahoma–Arkansas area. After the University of Texas, I went to Indiana University for graduate work, and to Africa to do my dissertation. My wife and I had been active in the civil rights movement, and decided that we were going to try to have some impact on politics and life in the major cities. We had a social obligation to try to do that. So we moved to Chicago to take a teaching job here.

I became involved in community affairs, and in 1968, I became campaign manager of the 9th Congressional District for Eugene McCarthy and state campaign manager in the summer before the national convention. All of us were dissatisfied afterwards, and we decided that we would learn on the basis of the McCarthy experience and we created the Independent Precinct Organization, based on principles which are quite contrary to most Chicago politics.

How did you come to run for alderman?

I worked on a variety of campaigns and we elected a number of
fairly good people. We built a base for political participation in the
electoral process, but we had not built a base for the governmental
process. I am not the normal candidate or officeholder type, but I
wanted to try the spokesman role. I would then have a base for trying
to transform the governmental process into a participatory one.

How did you find being a candidate for office in Chicago?

The good aspects are when you stand up at a big rally, make a
speech and everyone claps, and also the small coffee gatherings. The
debates can be fun. The hard part is dealing with the high-strung
personalities that are involved in a campaign, doing things like standing at a bus stop and shaking hands. After a few hundred people, the
voters aren't really paying any attention, and it's very hard to actually have meaningful communication, or to make that consistently
rewarding, because you do it every morning at 6 o'clock. It becomes
a very hectic style of life. Most people think it is only during the
campaign. It lasts as a continuous process thereafter. There's a lot of
ceremonial functions that has to be done. It keeps the voter knowing
that you exist and it makes them feel like the government is there.
You have to have a lot of stamina, to be able to work from 6 o'clock
in the morning to 6 o'clock at night for months on end, and to
compete with what may be fairly unfamiliar kinds of processes.

Being an alderman has been a huge educational experience for me.
I've learned a great deal about how budgets are made, how laws are
passed, how the administration works, how people interact, how the
whole process of vote politics in government operates. It has also
been one in which I have had a chance to develop skills like public
speaking in a way that I would never learn in the classroom, of how
to put together a successful pressure or electoral campaign. I am
much different than when I started this process a decade ago.

There are really several levels of experience. Outside the council
chamber there is a sort of hail-fellow-well-met atmosphere. I get
along all right with most of the aldermen on a one-to-one basis. On
the floor we each have our duties, and sometimes their duty is to
attack whatever we are proposing. I see that as part of the total
confrontation going on here about the future of the city—whether
it is going to have a participatory base, whether it is going to continue
on a machine base over the long haul, and, as such, we are kind of

warriors in a larger battle. We have a role to play, and we play it as a public role. When you may be the only one on an issue and there are forty or fifty people and a packed gallery of a couple of hundred who are shouting on the other side, that is a lot of pressure. I've learned things like it's worth it to stand six and a half, seven, eight hours like a statue in protest in the council. If there really are issues of principle at stake, you sometimes have to find dramatic means to do it. People frequently confuse politics with words, because words sometimes seem to be what politics is about. Politics is often a matter of finding the right action to be able to demonstrate what is at stake. In other words, you have to translate ideas into actual actions. Sometimes it is so simple as standing up to ask a question. I've frequently gotten further by asking questions than giving speeches. Labeling is often important—words like "nepotism," or "honest graft." The machine, in its tyrannical aspect, is a monolith. It cannot tolerate any attempt to say that it isn't in total control. So you stand up and ask a question: "Isn't this nepotism? Isn't this bad to make this particular appointment? Isn't this honest graft and isn't this cheating the citizens? Isn't there a matter of race at stake here?" Any of those things really undercut the machine very badly, and that's one point where they get flustered, shout and scream and carry on, because they feel it imperative that that kind of protest be put down. One of my best allies is genuine outrage. In the first year or two (it was still new enough to me that I could be outraged fairly easily), I would stand up and say, "This is an outrage!" and they would all go bananas about that. After you've seen a hundred of these events, corruption of various sorts, it's hard to still feel as outraged about it. I've had situations where they set the police to try and seat me. They had very small policemen and it didn't do any good. I'm 6'2" and weighed about 210 pounds at the time, so they were sort of hanging on my arms.

What resources do you have available to you as an independent alderman to try to buck the machine in Chicago?

The biggest resources are that we're able to raise enough volunteers and enough money to beat them in elections. Since we have sort of stood the system on its head, since I make personal sacrifices of money and time, we have no hesitancy to ask a lot of other people to make sacrifices of money and time, whereas the average public official has to pay people for everything. In my office, even after I turn over my salary of the city money, we have to raise $25,000 a year. We have a ward assembly which has as many as two hundred people participating once a month. That's a lot of people, money, talent, skill, and concern which the machine can't match. You can't have a patronage precinct worker do the same thing. Normally, if you have good volunteers, you can beat them at precinct work and you can beat them in terms of knowing the issues. Their strength is that they are based on an economic reward system, so that they are not going to go away. They are constant and they already have such an overwhelming number on their side, whether it's votes, or precinct workers, or whatever. But on a one-to-one basis, if you can mobilize enough volunteers, you can beat them at every level.

The media can be helpful, can really make an issue dramatic, can lend credibility to the movement. I like the way they treat most politicians. They figure they're crooked. The problem with the media is that they will cover action more than words. It is very hard to get the media to pay attention to a lengthy explanation. They will cover a crisis in the city council, if there's an action. Thirty-second clips on television don't do much for the big issues in the town, so you either have to find some very dramatic action or you have to find a few words like "nepotism" or "honest graft" that the media can communicate. The media tends to be cynical in this town, so we have to try to combat the cynicism. The media has specific limitations, which limits democracy in a real sense. I can sometimes point the media to information that they wouldn't dig up on their own. The media will cover the press conference and take down the words given in a press release approach. Good reporting in the city is pretty rare, and is more likely to be the scandal news sort and less likely to be positive news. Analysis is almost always missing in any significant depth on the part of the media.

Dick, how did Daley and Keane run the council?
They apparently met in advance of the actual council meeting and worked out what they thought would happen. I don't think they had to have terribly long or complicated discussions about it. Keane was experienced in what he was doing. Essentially, Keane ran the council for Daley. He knew enough about what was going on to be able to control the floor. He knew what the party wanted out of a situation. He knew what the likely tactics of the opposition were going to be and he enjoyed personal combat. He wasn't going to back off if an argument started on the floor. He would usually take it upon himself to give the last answer to the opposition and would reserve the right

to close debate on most of the important things, if he thought that that was necessary. He had, after all, forty-some votes at different times. He had a stacked deck. All he had to do was to handle the problems of the parliamentary tactic and the rest, and he knew parliamentary procedure well enough and the rules of the council (he wrote the rules of the council).

All Daley had to say was, "Remember that we need to be sure that we get such and such action today because we have to go on the bond issue tomorrow, so we've got a timetable problem." I have a feeling that Keane probably briefed Daley more often on that because of his position as finance chairman. He knew when most of the things were going to come up. If it wasn't on a financial matter, if it wasn't on something that went through Keane's committee, the rest of it couldn't matter all that much to the machine. If it was a resolution on the Vietnam War, on racism, or something, the machine would, in the end, win because of the votes, and so what if the minority got to state the case on the floor? Keane was confident of what his strengths were and Daley was confident that Keane could be counted on in most situations to bring the will of the machine to bear. They had, after all, a twenty-year working experience together. It was not a new team. They knew exactly what the strengths and weaknesses of each were. It's clear that Daley was in charge within that framework. It was Keane's job to run the council. In the early days, Daley used to stay in the council the full time, and chaired the entire meeting himself. In the latter period, partly because of health, he started staying in the chair only through the ceremonial functions. His behavior changed and by the time Bilandic was floor leader, Daley really left the council alone and ran it from behind the scenes. One of the consequences of that was that Daley was not there to personally understand what was actually going on. It was a more tight control and also a more remote control. One of the problems is that Bilandic has copied the pattern of the mayor in his late years without the same reasons. He doesn't have a health problem and he doesn't have to worry about his blood pressure. Bilandic's mistake is copying the late Daley, rather than the early Daley.

If Keane and Daley were running the council, what did the aldermen do?

The aldermen did what they were told to do. A motion would be put and we would take a vote. Fred Roti, who is the 1st ward alderman, would stand up and vote. Everyone would copy Fred's vote.

Keane would either signal thumbs up or thumbs down across the chamber, if he really felt they didn't know what was going on. Sometimes, on a procedural vote, it was not clear if it was all right for the minority aldermen to have the floor on the issue, and Keane would signal to Fred what the right solution was, or the first several aldermen who were voting.

The aldermen were not there to offer legislation. For instance, in 1971, about three hundred pieces of major legislation were introduced. Daley introduced about one hundred and five pieces of legislation, the minority aldermen introduced about one hundred and thirty major pieces of legislation, and the entire bloc of machine aldermen introduced about fifty pieces of legislation, about the average of one piece of legislation each. This included Keane, Wigoda, and aldermen who knew what they were doing, not just the dummies who introduce none. The others came through committee or special process. The minority aldermen were introducing, on the average, something to the tune of twelve pieces of legislation apiece. The minority aldermen only got eight percent of their legislation passed that year, but the machine aldermen only got twenty-nine percent of their legislation passed. The machine aldermen were not expected to introduce legislation, and if they introduced it, unless they had gotten leave from the mayor to do so (leave to do so just like the Pope gives dispensation to do extraordinary things), they would not have legislation passed. So they were not to do legislation and they weren't really to consider too much their votes. They were there to perform their ritual duty of voting correctly, and correctly was determined simply by paying attention to what Fred Roti did.

Then Daley and Keane were virtually free to run the city in any way that they saw necessary?

The power was a little bit more broadly spread than that. Essentially the chairmen of committees were free, to some extent. There were about six or seven committees of the eighteen in the council that functioned. The others didn't function. Four of them didn't meet at all in the year 1971; four of them met once or twice; thirty percent of the legislation went through Keane's own finance committee; and the others apportioned out the rest. Building and zoning handled a lot of it and the rest did almost nothing. Those six or seven key committees were where their committee chairmen had some role. I am talking about people like Paul Wigoda who had traffic and public safety, Bilandic who had environmental control, and so forth.

There were five, or six, or seven aldermen who even knew what was going on, had leave occasionally to introduce legislation, could decide whether or not to give it a hearing, and were required only to notify Keane and Daley. They had some latitude. So you had a situation of a group of powerful aldermen, maybe six or seven in number in the best days, and not all of those really knew what the hell was happening, but they tended to.

Were there, in the city council, in the Daley era, active ethnic and racial blocs, in contrast to their membership in the machine?

Generally speaking, no. For example: in 1971, the first day the council met after it had adopted its rules on April 22nd, Bill Cousins introduced a resolution that the city council stand four square against fire-bombing homes. (There had just been a black family who moved into a white neighborhood, and they had been fire-bombed out, on the Southwest Side.) All of the black aldermen, except the independent aldermen, Cousins and Langford (and I think Cliff Kelley), and two white aldermen (I think Marilou Hedlund, and one other), voted that it was all right, in essence, to fire-bomb homes. That clearly did not represent the view of their constituents. There was such pressure that at the next meeting they came back and Claude Holman and the machine blacks offered a resolution saying that the city council was opposed to fire-bombing homes, and that passed unanimously. How can one not be concerned about fire-bombing homes on April 22nd, but by May 4th, think that fire-bombing homes is a bad thing? The machine tended to have such control that they could absolutely control their votes against ethnic interests and against the constituency the aldermen represented. Only when political pressure got dramatic enough, the machine then completely reversed the process, accepted the proposal, and it changed *en masse*. It was like a tank battalion that all switch and go the other direction. As long as Daley was in control, the ethnic group vote was kept in check, and the aldermen would vote absolutely against either their constituent interest or their ethnic group interest.

What was the role of the independent minority bloc of aldermen in the city council?

We had a series of roles. Since the breakdown of the economy bloc in the early 1950s, there had been no unity. In 1971, we formed, for the first time, the minority aldermen under the leadership of Despres. We would raise issues that would try and display what the problems with machine government were. Our most general stance was probably to propose democracy for Chicago versus machine control. There is no way to convince the aldermen who are sitting in the council chamber that they should have a democratic legislative body which would consider issues on the basis of merit. We addressed our comments to the city of Chicago. In addition to that we would work on individual projects and issues that particularly happened to interest us.

Could you evaluate Alderman Keane for me as a politician and as a parliamentarian?

Keane was the brightest man in the council, with possibly the exception of Despres. In some ways, he was brighter, particularly in financial matters, parliamentary matters. Arrogant, terribly arrogant. Unfortunately, he made the mistake of knowing he was bright, and, if anything, overestimating. Keane was not always right. He did make parliamentary rulings that were clearly incorrect, and simply bulled his way through because he was usually right. If Despres offered a correction, normally, Keane was willing to sustain it. Keane had respect for Despres, and even, over time, sometimes for Bill Singer and myself. We sometimes convinced Keane to switch ground. Keane ran things in the council with a lot of intelligence in the planning. He had a sharp tongue and hated even members of his own bloc when they were too damn lazy. He had much more respect for the minority than he did for aldermen that were supposed to be bright young rising upstarts who didn't do their homework.

Keane was a man who wanted some precision. He wanted you to be able to say, if you were saying that this was too big a cost, why is that true, what is the right way, and what's the legal basis on which we let bonds, and when must we do it. And you had better be right on all those things or Keane would rip you up, in terms of the intellectual debate. It was a fair challenge to argue with Keane.

Keane also was a man, who, if he gave his word, would probably keep it, or at least make every effort. Once he gave his word to me and it wasn't kept. He actually almost went back and undid the whole process to keep his word. With Keane it was a fetish of the old-time politician on that score. The problem is, of course, that Keane would rarely give his word, but you were in fine shape if Keane promised you that you would get that ordinance passed; it would be passed.

Keane was more of an intellect than Daley by a long shot, and tended to think of matters in the way that intellectuals do. He was very bright and he was also a lawyer, not so much in the spirit of the law, since he understood why the law was written, but he was really a master mechanic, a master chess player. Within his own scope he was an honorable man, meaning things like keeping his word. As a parliamentarian, he was first rate. He was sometimes wrong, but when he was wrong he had enough finesse to usually carry it, unless he was against an awfully good opponent. Keane would just over-whelm his opponent. He'd bludgeon him to death with facts and figures. He's different from Mike Bilandic.* Mike Bilandic may be the chess player and just as good, but Keane was a master who had so much confidence and intellectual capacity that he enjoyed the battle and liked to do it with flair. Keane used to let the aldermen ask questions at budget hearings. What did he care if Simpson or Singer or Despres ask questions? Keane would get the answer done and he would control it. He had forty-five votes, he's no dummy, he knows forty-five votes is more than five or ten, and he was going to win. The combat would be almost enjoyable. Keane would be glad to let us ask questions. He didn't show us up for what fools we were, and how much more he knew than we did, and he was up for battle.

Mike orchestrates the budget hearings. He will not let the other aldermen ask questions, as a general rule. He will not even brief them. Mike forces the independent aldermen to have to ask all the questions, maintain all the burden of carrying on the conversation, not put the commissioner on the spot, and do that sequentially. In other words, we have altogether fifty heads of departments come in before budget hearings. That means, if I am going to handle the budget battle on the independent side, I have to be prepared in advance for all fifty, handle them sequentially, and handle every battle, and I don't have the latitude of the kind of interplay with Keane. And, also, I am in a different position now because I don't have as many allies with as many skills. I don't have a Despres, a Singer, a Hoellen, and a Seymour Simon—all of whom brought differ-ent backgrounds and skills. So, essentially, the burden in the current city council is reduced to myself having to fend off the whole other side on all fifty sets of questions.

Now, Bilandic is smart. He knows that that way he's got it. But he's got it without any joy of battle. Keane wanted to fight and win a victory that was worth while. Mike Bilandic wants to keep the lid on

*Bilandic succeeded Keane as chairman of the finance committee and floor leader of the city council.

everything. He wants order. He has a penchant for things. He is insecure enough that he's got to not only have the deck stacked, he has to then restack the deck so that he has got the ultimate advantage and is going to win the battle. In fact, when Bilandic rewrote the rules of the city council after Keane, he tended to take away some of the few advantages the minority aldermen had in parliamentary procedure. Bilandic is smart enough to do it. There is an intelligence there—it's kind of slow, methodical, careful, overwhelming, that is different from Keane. Keane was a man of battle. Keane was willing to fight. He thought he could win. He thought he could beat anybody. Bilandic isn't really sure, so Bilandic is going to so overmobilize his side so that it is impossible to lose, and in doing that he's willing to make some mistakes that Keane did not intend to make. Mike wants to overkill. He doesn't understand the advantages of opposition. Keane could understand that, occasionally, you get some ideas out of all this and they would improve things, and that they would have a more viable operation.

Dick, could you evaluate Mayor Daley for me?
As a politician, he is usually equated with some of the great savvy politicians of the century. He was extremely good in organizing the support on his side so that he most often won, and when he couldn't win, he was very good at delaying the decision until circumstances would change so that he would win. If none of those could be brought about, he would capitulate as little as possible. At the end of the process, he would always remain the one in power. He was, in a very special sense, a conservative. That is, he had built up, out of the Cermak traditions and the rest, the machine. He had assembled it, and once having assembled it, he spent most of the time preserving it and using it to do certain kinds of things in the city. Maybe he did it the other way. I'm not sure whether he thought about doing things in the city as a means of conserving the machine. Probably both.

He was not terribly innovative, in the usual sense. He was quite willing to pick up other ideas, particularly if they fit in the liberal Democratic tradition. If it was things like more welfare for senior citizens or whatever, he was very quick to see that, if it fit in his framework. If it was a major problem of resolving social conflict, like the pressure from the black community, he was unable to see it, and, therefore, that turned into a major deficiency. So, as a politician, he was able to first of all build a very strong machine and then to preserve its power for twenty years in the face of all kinds of changes. He was very masterful.

In terms of shaping a city or a nation, he didn't start the same kinds of waves rippling that, say, a Kennedy did when he came into office, that resonate down for decades afterward. I don't think we will be saying thirty, forty, fifty years away, "Remember, Daley wanted to have more of the arts and now we have finally gotten around to having more of the arts, or whatever, and that really traces back somehow to a germ of an idea that started in his administration decades ago." What he did for Chicago did not have such immediate significance over the nation in the same way. He might have a role in making presidents, but he was not inventing a new system which was going to be adopted widely. He was not anxious to proselytize Peoria into taking his system, or any place else in the country. He thought all systems would naturally be like this, that he ran a good one and that was enough.

It's really hard to evaluate him as a politician because once you do it straight within the terms of the machine, it's hard to get a fix. What standard do you compare him to? If you compare him to machine bosses, he comes out at the very top of the list. If you use some other measuring stick, he doesn't come out as well; particularly, did he come up with modern solutions to the great social tensions of our time? The answer to that is almost uniformly no.

He was an excellent administrator in the sense that he was able to have everyone anticipate what he wanted, but they didn't always anticipate correctly. They sometimes made mistakes because they would do it in too narrow a frame. But most of the departments and the rest operated the way they thought the mayor wanted them to. They conveyed information to him most of the time and he was able to adjudicate decisions. The right kinds of questions got taken to his desk in the early period. There was a burst of strong, good adminis- tration when he was doing the expressways and all the new projects, and they would do McCormick Place, one big huge project after another. In the late period, this wasn't really true. He was unable to do his great projects like Crosstown, and, also, the administrative machinery was mostly keeping the government going rather than being innovative, or first in the nation, or best in the nation. So it breaks down in his last years of his life. But up till then, he would be accounted as a good administrator. He knew what was happening, knew how to hire fairly capable people. As an administrator he would probably get fairly good marks.

He was good for Chicago in the 'fifties and even into the 'sixties. In one sense he overstayed his usefulness. He should have taken off at the crest of his career before any of the negative things happened. He was good for Chicago in that he did build the machine, obviously did keep the city fairly solvent, had a good fiscal base for the city, did major projects, rebuilt the Loop and so forth, and those physical features will, of course, be with us for many decades to come because there will never be the resources in the foreseeable future to change them. So, the mayor's physical imprint on the city will be here for many decades. That was sort of good for Chicago in the early period. He pulled it together, gave it economic strength, revitalized the Loop.

But the administration really became more and more out of touch. The economic plans of the city got to be P-R fluff. They really were saying, "Well, everyone should move businesses to Chicago, and we'll make Chicago well known." And the business people were saying, "The reason businesses leave Chicago, or don't come to Chicago, is that they don't understand what a good city it is." Well, of course, that's nonsense. Business makes its decision on much harder criteria than that. The criteria were that Chicago was no longer viable for industrial purposes. The really major kinds of transformation to modern industry were never undertaken by the Daley administration. They don't know what a calculator or an electronic computer is, or space technology. It's an alien world to them, which they never adjusted to. They don't understand artists and the communications industry. They understood the stock market and banks pretty well. But they were never really able to capitalize on putting together the financial center of the country here because, I guess, the businesses weren't able to come up with the answer, and the administration was in the position of mainly helping out businesses on those kinds of things. And, for some reason, we didn't have the leadership in the financial arena to quite pull that off for future decades.

We will have an answer in a couple of decades from now, because the real test of whether Daley was good for Chicago is something like how you would view a developing country. We had a tyranny in Chicago, and the tyranny produced a certain kind of economic development and a certain kind of physical stability which would be the appropriate point in which to develop a better democracy. But Daley wasn't able to take the second step. Daley could not develop a democracy. He couldn't go to a neighborhood government forum, he couldn't go to more participation, because the party's interests were such that the party could only work as a closed shop, as a guild, almost in the old feudal ways. So Daley couldn't go to political development in the real sense. He could only do the economic stage. When you view it decades from now, Daley will have been said to have been good for Chicago only on the assumption that Chicago has had a good future, and that didn't lie with Daley.

One of the things that may turn out, which would be a very strange, ironic twist, is that the tyranny under Daley sponsored such creative forms of participatory democracy in opposition that they might someday flourish, overcome the machine and replace it. If Daley's tyranny turns out not to have spawned an opposition strong enough to break through, if the city continues the machine and a sort of Mike Bilandic retread of Mayor Daley, and you get continually worse and worse, less confident, Mayor Daleys on down the line, the city will end up in shambles. The city needs more than one thing and Daley was very good at giving it one kind of thing that it needed. It needed strength and cohesiveness, it needed to develop some economic understructures, it probably did need a Loop in those days, it probably did need an expressway system, but those aren't the needs now. If we hang too tightly to what things were good in the 'fifties for the city, the whole game will be lost.

Was there a Daley style?

Sure. The mayor was something like a petty tyrant or an old monarch of the feudal days, in many ways a kind of throwback. He had very strong support from people. They thought of him as a benevolent despot. They wouldn't use those kinds of terms, but they thought he was taking care of things and they were willing to surrender to him the power necessary to do so. Those who weren't willing to surrender faced an implacable foe. Daley was not someone with whom you could have disputes and then go out to cocktails afterward. Daley was egocentric enough that you were either for or against him. That was the same as being for or against the city or for or against the party. There was not any place to stand except completely for him, which meant essentially being a ward committeeman or precinct captain or worker in the administration, or a businessman who supported the party, or something of that sort. Those who stood on that side were good, and everyone else was bad. It was not drawn in an ideological way. The rule became personalized. A lot of it is very reminiscent of the kind of advice Machiavelli gave the Prince, though I don't have any reason to think that Daley ever read

Machiavelli. He ruled like a prince or ruler in that feudal period. Daley thought he was ruling for the best interest of Chicago, he thought the party was best for Chicago, he thought what he did was important, and he had the support of the people which reaffirmed at elections that he was doing the right thing from his perspective.

It was an odd style, in the sense that you don't normally think of a law school graduate mumbling incoherent sentences. As a public speaker Daley was atrocious. Reporters spent whole careers learning to make fun of his malapropisms, the lack of logic, the incoherency of style, parroting the Daley style of discussion. It *was* a style which communicated. I think Daley probably had a political skill, the skill of action. His speech skills were never very good. He never made speeches. He either was just mumbling completely inane niceties about, "It's good all you senior citizens are here today for the good of Chicago," that kind of garbage, or he was having a tirade. Sometimes he would wax terribly emotional, be set off by an odd kind of sentimentalism, which obviously clouded the thinking.

He was not a man of words. He was a man of action, primarily. In his action he had what seemed to be several kinds of norms, as I think back on it. One of them was that there was no need to pussyfoot around. You do what you have the clout to do, to use a Chicago phrase. If you have the power, if you've got the votes in the council, then you carry your policy one hundred percent. Why should you carry your policy eighty percent and compromise with your opponents? If you don't have the power, then you compromise. Therefore, in the city council it always became the question—could we threaten Daley's power by appealing to civic groups or others that would look like they might defect from the party and vote some other way in upcoming elections? If you could do that, we could get anything we wanted. If we couldn't do that, we couldn't get anything. The social niceties were really cut out. We never had a discussion with Daley, never intended to, never had any purpose from our point or from his.

How do you see the future of Chicago, Dick?

I guess the future of Chicago right at this juncture looks much worse than it did at other periods. As a city, we have been, to some degree, losing our will. Chicago has always been a city which looked to the future and which planned for a better future. It wanted to be the first in the nation, the best city, the biggest city, the richest city, everything it could think of. This is a place where you could make a buck, where you could move ahead, where something of importance was going to happen. Individually, for most workers in the city, there was a sense that they would get ahead. This was the way to the American dream, no matter which level of society they'd come in at and what they were trying to improve to. Currently, there is a much greater disillusion in the liberal community. It has been now more than a decade of fairly intense activity of trying to transform the city, and the city has not transformed itself very much.

On the other hand, the machine is undergoing a process of disintegration. It is losing more elections than it used to lose. It is unable to accommodate the racial and ethnic components any more. The black and Polish blocs are breaking away from the machine, and others are unhappy with the machine and would break away if they saw a place to go. I think, right at this particular point, Chicago is at a curious crossroads, where it is beginning to doubt its own ability to make the future. There is a sense of decay about the machine, but there is not a sense of some other alternative that is so well in place that others can say, "Well, we'll just join the independent movement, the reform movement, the black movement, or whatever movement." I don't know how long that phase will last. It's lasted now since before Daley died. In the liberal community, things have been on the downhill slide since 1972, and in 1976 picked up and started turning in the other direction with the accumulation of more state legislative seats and those kinds of things. But it is a very slow process. I don't think there is an easy answer. My guess is that we aren't going to find an easy answer over the next several years. We're talking about a period of readjustment which is going to take several years, partly because it will take longer for the machine to disintegrate than many have thought, and the shape of exactly what is going to replace the machine is not as clear cut.

EPILOGUE BY
MICHAEL A. BILANDIC *Croatian. Fifty-five years*
old. Was elected alderman from Daley's 11th ward in 1969.
Served as Democratic floor leader and chairman of the finance
committee of the Chicago city council from 1974–1976. Was
elected mayor of Chicago in 1976 after Daley's death, and was
defeated by Jane Byrne for the mayoralty in 1979. Is now prac-
ticing law in Chicago.

Mayor Daley did so many great things.

Years ago, when I was practicing law and traveling around the
country, people would ask me where I was from. When I replied,
"Bridgeport," they'd say, "I didn't know you were from Connecti-
cut." Since Daley, Bridgeport has become quite famous. When you
mention Bridgeport to anyone they immediately identify it with the
city of Chicago, and a particular area in Chicago.

Just as Mayor Daley had a great pride in his own neighborhood, he
had the same great pride in his city, his church, his religion, his
family, his friends, and anything that he had touched or anything that
he had become involved with. That was one of the great hallmarks
of Mayor Daley's success—the pride that he had in his origins, his
surroundings, his friends, and the people that he dealt with.

He had admiration and respect for other people's personal affairs.
He was one of the first people to pay tribute in a very personal way
to the ethnicity of our city. People used to say we had too many
parades. But every parade that we had celebrated another ethnic
group. It gave them an opportunity to show their best. One of the
places where we always had a great time, when I accompanied him
so many years, was at the folk fairs we had at Navy Pier, where all
the different ethnic groups came in and showed their cooking and
their own various wares, and displayed their own personal pride. The
affection that passed between the mayor and all the individuals there
was heartwarming and genuine. There was a deep emotional feeling

Excerpted from remarks made by Mayor Bilandic at a conference sponsored by the
University of Illinois, Chicago Circle, at the Chicago Historical Society on October 14,
1977.

that went from him to each and every one of these people, and related back from them to him. There may have been a language barrier, but when you saw the looks in the eyes of both parties, you knew that they communicated, that they understood, and that they responded.

The same attitude was carried out in the office of the mayor. The office of mayor and the name, Richard J. Daley, became synonymous in the city of Chicago. I learned that very quickly. I hadn't been in this position more than a week when I stopped to visit the McClellan School, as I did every year with Mayor Daley. He attended kindergarten at McClellan, only a few blocks from his home. Every year we used to go there to visit during the science fair, or some other special event. I felt somewhat different and a little bit empty this time, because I was going there alone, without my usual companion. The children were the same—bright-eyed, neat, well-scrubbed, alert, and intelligent. The faculty appeared to be the same. They had long tenure in that school. The facilities were still very nice—a red schoolhouse, probably one of the oldest in the city—immaculate, well-maintained, orderly. As we started going through the various specifics, the children still gave us the same response and attention. Some of the media that had come along asked some of the youngsters in the second or third grade, "Do you know who that is?" The children answered, "Yes, that's the new Mayor Daley." So you can see, even with these children, starting school at the earliest age, they associate the office of mayor with the name "Daley." They believed that the name and the office are one and the same. And if anyone ever attempted to flatter me, they couldn't have flattered me more than by saying, "That's the new Mayor Daley," because throughout the country, the office of mayor and the name of Daley were synonymous. They were, so to speak, the Medal of Honor, the Nobel Prize, the Pulitzer Prize, the Super Bowl, or the World Series of the office of mayor. That's what the name of Richard J. Daley symbolized.

When I would attend the National Conference of Mayors with him (which I had done for five or six years), and he would arrive, every mayor from every small town would come to him. They wanted to see him, to touch him, to speak with him, to have their pictures taken with him. You could say, "That's exactly what you expect from a small town mayor." When the big city mayors did exactly the same thing, you'd know that this was something special, something different, somebody that really counts. After he had served his term as president of that great organization, he didn't interfere or meddle with

later administrations. Many great mayors followed him—Henry
Maier of Milwaukee, Mayor Alioto of San Francisco, Mayor Moon
Landrieu of New Orleans, and many others. He let them handle
matters in their own way, but whenever they got into difficulty,
whenever the hard decisions had to be made, they always came
looking for him. Many times, during the course of the convention,
they'd start to stray, take on issues that were going to wind up being
counterproductive to the mayors. I recall very clearly when the cities
were strapped for money and needed it very badly, when revenue
sharing was one of the hot subjects being discussed. They had a hot
line set up in the lobby so that every mayor of every city could call
his congressman directly and lobby for support, so that they would
vote for what was going to provide resources for the cities in the
United States. President Nixon had been in office and he sent his
representatives to the convention, and they weren't too eager about
the issue. The thing had to be carried so that the funds to meet the
financial crisis of the cities could be met. It was a very tough issue.
Someone had imprudently included a resolution that was very derog-
atory and downright hostile to President Nixon personally. (This was
pre-Watergate and before the election, when all the polls showed
him winning.) It was Mayor Daley who stopped that unwarranted
attack on President Nixon, because he never liked to engage in
personalities and personal attacks in any political campaign, and
because he saw how imprudent it would be, on the one hand to ask
for financial relief, and, the next moment, adopt a resolution blasting
the hand from which you expected to get the funds. Had he not
intervened and stopped that imprudent resolution, we wouldn't
have those funds and many of those cities would have been in great
difficulty. So he proved himself to be a diplomat. He was the elder
statesman, the senior citizen, and a wise counselor. He was always
available and ready to direct you on the right course.

I don't think that there has ever been a time in history that a man
showed greater talent than Mayor Daley did in 1972, when we never
made it to the [Democratic National] Convention, although we were
elected. When we came home from our ill-fated session with the
credentials committee in Washington, and when we came back
home again from Miami Beach without having had the opportunity
to participate in the nomination of our party's presidential candidate,
he showed the true measure of his loyalty to his party by supporting
the very forces that engineered our not being seated at the convention. I might add personally, wrongfully, in not being seated. Most

people regard that as having been one of the great political mistakes of our time, not seating the Chicago delegation. But when we came back, he suggested (and I want you to carefully note that word, "suggested," because he never ordered anyone to do anything) that we support the candidate of our party. Many people began to feel quite unhappy. I had difficulty with my own mother. She said, "What a terrible thing they did to Mayor Daley! He wasn't even there!" She was one of his staunchest fans and supporters, and he was a great fan of hers. Later, a few months from that day in July or August, when we came home, I told my mother that she should vote for Senator George McGovern. My mother was very respectful of every elected official. She always addressed them by their title and by their proper name. She said, "Michael, please don't ask me to vote for that George!" But she did, only because her son pleaded with her to do it, and because I assured her that that was exactly what Mayor Daley wanted her to do, and after she got a call from him saying that it was all right. I think he showed his true measure as a gentleman, and as a dedicated and loyal party leader.

I have probably had more good fortune than most people. The good fortune that I had was that early in my life I had the opportunity to become acquainted with a man named Richard J. Daley. I remember him, when I was a little boy in the neighborhood, as a man whose name we used to see on the posters in people's windows, when he was a candidate for office. There really never was what you would measure as an important office, but, as a little boy, if you saw anybody's picture in the window after he was elected, and if you saw him walking around the neighborhood, he was your neighborhood hero. He was the person with whom you could identify, that you knew, not a remote mystery or myth, like maybe some of the other people whose picture you'd see in the paper, but never see in person. So we used to see him quite a bit.

I really got to know him when I became active in the 11th ward organization in 1948. Many people don't realize this, but Mayor Daley (not mayor then, but Richard J. Daley), became the committeeman of the 11th ward in 1947. I spoke to many of the organizations during the course of my campaign, particularly committeemen, and I would tell them that I remembered those days when Richard Daley became a committeeman, that he did not even have an alderman from his own party in his own ward. People were shocked. "How could it be that such a thing could happen in the 11th ward? I always thought that the 11th ward was number one." Nobody could

have started lower than Richard J. Daley started in politics—a committeeman without an alderman from his own party! You can't be
any lower than that.

Nineteen fifty-one was the most exciting election that we were
involved in, because it was a test of the new committeeman. The test
was whether he could elect an alderman from his own ward. He
spoke with Mayor Kennelly at the time of this election. Mayor Kennelly told him that the incumbent alderman wasn't a bad fellow,
[and] maybe a candidate shouldn't be slated against him. Richard
Daley, being a staunch and solid party man, said that he didn't understand that. He thought that the first function of a party was to elect
its own people to office, and it was the wish of the mayor that the
incumbent of another party should remain? He was talking to the
wrong person. Against the wishes of the then mayor, he slated a
candidate for office. That was one of the most exciting elections I ever
participated in. We went from door to door, from corner to corner,
to every single area of the ward, whether it was down in the third
basement or up in an attic, any place where we could get a few
people together to talk about our candidate and the issues of the
election. I've never seen a neighborhood so brought together.
There's nothing as exciting as a local aldermanic election. Presidents
come and presidents go, but the people in the neighborhoods never
see their presidents. But their alderman, they see him every day.
They are vitally concerned about who their alderman is. This tore
families apart, pitted mother against son, father against daughter,
and it really was an exciting thing to see. We won that election by
only 500 votes. But it was a beginning. And since then, we kept
improving.

In 1955, Richard Daley won [the mayoralty]. Every little boy and
girl in the neighborhood had seen him. Everybody recognized him,
and recognized that this was no ordinary individual, because of the
way he acted—the quickness of his step, the twinkle of his eye, the
compassionate feeling that he had for his friends and neighbors, the
concern that he had for those in difficulty, for those who needed help,
the genuine sincerity that he brought to the tasks he was working on.
The spark was contagious. People followed him loyally, without any
concern for their personal future, for their personal gain. They did
it because they believed in the person, and they believed in the
righteousness of his cause. They believed that he was a man dedicated to try to improve, and they were right. And they elected him
mayor in 1955.

The excitement that that brought to our community was something that no one will ever forget. The torchlight parades that we had
on Halsted Street, starting off the campaign. The excitement of the
campaign, then the excitement of the victory, which was even
greater. But it hadn't changed him, and it hadn't affected him. He
was still the same fellow from 35th and Lowe—a fine family man, the
same person who walked down the street, tipped his hat to the ladies,
smiled at the youngsters, and always had a moment to stop and talk
to his friends and neighbors. That was the genius of Richard J. Daley.

When we were campaigning during that aldermanic election (and
you get very few people to get interested in what we were going to
do and say), he would be the very first man at a meeting. Whether
the meeting was at 6 o'clock in the morning, or 10 o'clock at night,
he always looked like he just came out of the shower—neat, fresh,
eager to go, always well groomed and immaculate, always interested,
always vibrant, always exciting, introducing everyone to everyone
else. He was the last man to leave the hall when the meeting was
over. This is what inspired the people of the community, inspired
those who followed him. He wasn't concerned about who you were.
Whether you were Polish, or Lithuanian, or German, or Irish, or
Croatian, or anything else, he was concerned about the individual.

I'll never forget, after I had been involved for a number of years,
people started noticing me speaking at the meetings, involved in the
affairs of the organization of our ward. They would come to our ward
from the other wards to seek our help in county, statewide, and
presidential elections. Some of them (and I daresay many of them),
would tell me, "What are you wasting your time for in the 11th ward?
You know that a Croatian could never go anywhere there." Many of
the people who said that to me are still alive and still remember,
although I never call it to their attention. What a shock and surprise
when, one day, a Croatian became the alderman. And the Croatians
represented, throughout the history of the ward, almost the smallest
minority. But it was no concern to Mayor Daley whether I was
Croatian or anything else. He was concerned with my interests and
concern. It didn't matter to me that he was Irish or whether he was
anything else. I was impressed with his dedication, his compassion,
and his feeling. I think that brought the two of us together.

The only disagreement we had in those early years was that he
wanted to bring me into government, take a job and work with him.
I kept saying no. He kept urging me. I kept saying no. I always had
a good excuse. I had to continue to be very creative with my excuses.

In 1969, I ran out of excuses. He finally got me to be the candidate for alderman. We talked about it on three separate occasions. The first time, he called me to the office to talk about searching for a candidate to fill a vacancy. I gave him a list of names that I thought would be appropriate candidates, with the benefits and detriments of each as a candidate, and how I thought we could handle it. When we concluded the session, he said, "How about you?" I laughed and disposed of the matter. A few days later we talked about it again, and the same thing happened. A few days later (it was close to filing time), we talked about it again. He proposed the same thing, "How about you?" This time I could see a different look in his eye. I knew I either had to say yes or leave town. I decided to stay in Chicago.

It was interesting, because, from the first moment, as I look back, he knew exactly what he wanted. I wasn't aware of it. He wasn't going to quit before he was able to make the sale. Even to the end, I was reluctant and had to check with a few people. There were major cases pending that I had to finish up and make some arrangements which these people could consider. They were concerned about the future of their government and their city, and they cooperated in releasing me from some of my private obligations to permit me to do this.

I must say it was one of the good decisions that I made. I am very happy that I lost that argument, because, in losing that argument, I began to find out and to learn more about my friend of many years. I had known him reasonably well, probably better than most people had known him, but I really got to know him then. During the campaign we talked every day, first thing in the morning, before I started out, and the last thing at night, when I finished, and a few times in between during the day, when any problem arose. He was eager to give me direction and help. I learned more than I dreamed I would ever learn.

Then, after I was elected (the first Sunday), he told me to drop over to the house on Sunday afternoon so I could go over the rules of the council with him. I brought the book along, *Robert's Rules of Order*, and the tutoring session started in the basement. I don't think many people saw Richard Daley without his prize-winning clothes, just dressed in his undershirt and suspenders, relaxed completely. I felt like I was back in a class in the early Greek days, one of Aristotle's students, sitting with a conversation and a dialogue. The dialogue would go on for many hours. We'd forget what time it was. That was the best tutoring I ever received. During the whole winter, we spent every one of those cold Sunday afternoons together down in the basement. You could talk about Oxford, Cambridge, Harvard, Princeton, Yale, any one of the great universities of the world. I don't think any one of them taught what I learned in the basement at 35th and Lowe. I not only learned about the rules, about parliamentary procedures. We got over that in very short order. The dialogue would remind me of the dialogues of the great teachers of ancient times, because, during those dialogues, we covered every subject— national, international, local—you name it, we talked about it. In that way, he was able to indoctrinate in me the important principles and philosophies of an orderly government, of where the pieces fit in our society, of the nuts and bolts, how to get things done, and the timing of getting them done.

I was impressed with the great depth and knowledge that this man had about world history, international affairs, the operations of government in many obscure and remote places of the world. I had never recognized or realized that he had been such a great student of so many important subjects, down into our local affairs. The breadth and the capacity of this man for facts and knowledge and information was just overwhelming. How he crammed it all in, and was able to do it with the busy schedule that he had, was something that was certainly incomprehensible. So I was the beneficiary of an education that very few people received, and, for that, I will be eternally grateful.

Then we worked together in the council. [I was] his leader in the city council. We were always able to talk things over, to counsel and to suggest. Contrary to public opinion, he was not autocratic, he was not dictatorial. He listened to more people than any one I knew. He always got all sides of every argument, and he would make a calculated and intelligent decision. We very seldom had any differences on the conclusions.

There was only one occasion where we had some differences. I told him that I felt rather strongly that we would be making a mistake in following a certain course. He didn't think so. He thought we should do it another way. I said, "Well, I yield to your superior experience and knowledge, and now I'll go and do it the way you want it done. I just don't think that it is the right time." I started to work on the matter, and, as I got into it further, I became more convinced that we probably were making a mistake. I went back and saw him again, and we talked about it again. I still was unable to persuade him the other way. It was late on a Friday afternoon. The hearing was going to be held on Monday. He said, "No, we'll go ahead with the way I proposed it." I said, "Fine, I'll do the best I can." And I did. At 10 o'clock Friday night, there was a call at the house. I got home a little later. He left a number for me to call the following day. He was out of the city. I called him at 8 o'clock in the morning. He said, "You are right. You can change it."

The man was always willing to listen, always willing to recognize and understand there would be another way. We did it the way we had agreed upon formerly, and everything worked out well, and he thanked me. This was nothing unusual. Because this very same thing happened on other occasions, with other people, I'm sure.

He would always do what he perceived to be right. As circumstances changed, [if] it was pointed out to him that there was a better way, he was very quick to adopt the better way. And he never hesitated to tell you that you were right. He didn't like yes-men around him. He didn't care for people who were just professional cohorts or camp followers. He wanted people to give him some meaningful input, who could be constructive, who could be helpful to him. He was one of the great champions of giving opportunities to the minorities, people from every ethnic origin.

The record shows that Richard J. Daley is one of the few people that really was a legend in his lifetime. There was no way that he could walk down the street without attracting a crowd. There was no way that he could be in a public place without being noticed, whether it was in the city of Chicago, or anywhere in the United States, or even if it was abroad. He was a local boy from Bridgeport, but kings, queens, princes, and paupers were people who could communicate with him, who understood him. Foreign-speaking people who couldn't speak English too well could communicate with him.

I have improved immeasurably professionally by having worked with him. I have become a better human being by having been touched by this bit of greatness. My life has been enriched for having known him.

GLOSSARY OF NAMES

Bauler, Mathias (Paddy). Longtime alderman and Democratic committeeman of the 43rd ward.

Bowler, James. Alderman and Democratic committeeman of the 25th ward before Vito Marzullo. Was elected to Congress in 1953 at the age of seventy-eight.

Campbell, Kenneth. One of Congressman William L. Dawson's key lieutenants, and alderman and Democratic committeeman of the 20th ward.

Cermak, Anton J. Mayor of Chicago, 1931–1933. Was president of the Cook County Board of Commissioners. Was assassinated in 1933.

Connors, William J. Democratic state senator and committeeman of the 42nd ward before George Dunne.

Corr, Frank J. Mayor of Chicago for one month, after Mayor Cermak's assassination. Resigned so that Edward J. Kelly could take his place, and became a circuit court judge.

Courtney, Thomas. Cook County State's Attorney and candidate against Mayor Edward J. Kelly in 1939 Democratic mayoral primary. Lost to Kelly and was elected a circuit court judge.

Cullerton, P. J. Democratic committeeman of the 38th ward and county assessor of Cook County.

Dawson, William L. Democratic boss of the black South Side. Was alderman and Democratic committeeman of the 2nd ward, and was elected to Congress. Controlled five or six South Side black wards.

Despres, Leon. Liberal, independent Democratic reform alderman of the 5th ward. Longtime opponent of Daley in the city council.

Dever, William E. Democratic mayor of Chicago from 1923–1927.

Douglas, Paul. Liberal, independent Democratic alderman from the 5th ward. Was elected to the United States Senate in 1948 and served eighteen years.

Evans, Timothy. Alderman and Democratic committeeman of the 4th ward.

Frost, Wilson. Alderman and Democratic committeeman of the 34th ward. Was president pro tem of the city council and succeeded Michael Bilandic as chairman of the finance committee when Bilandic was elected mayor.

Gill, Joseph. Democratic committeeman of the 46th ward and chairman of the Cook County Democratic Central Committee from 1950–1953.

Holman, Claude. One of Congressman William L. Dawson's key lieutenants and Democratic committeeman of the 4th ward.

Horan, Albert. Democratic committeeman of the 29th ward.

Horner, Henry. Democratic governor of Illinois from 1932–1940.

Howlett, Michael. Democratic secretary of state of Illinois. Was Democratic organization candidate in 1976 gubernatorial primary against Governor Dan Walker. Defeated Walker, but lost to Republican James R. Thompson in the general election.

Jackson, Jesse. Black civil rights leader and head of Operation PUSH (People United to Save Humanity).

Kelly, Edmund. Democratic committeeman of the 47th ward.

Kelly, Edward J. Mayor of Chicago from 1933–1947, and co-leader of the Democratic machine with Patrick A. Nash in that period.

Kenna, Michael (Hinky Dink). Alderman and Democratic boss of the 1st ward with John (Bathhouse John) Coughlin.

Kennelly, Martin H. Mayor of Chicago 1947–1955. Was slated as a reform Democratic candidate in 1947 to replace Mayor Kelly. Was beaten by Richard J. Daley for the Democratic nomination for mayor in 1955.

Kerner, Otto. Democratic governor of Illinois from 1961–1968. Resigned to accept appointment to United States Court of Appeals. Was convicted of mail fraud and sent to prison.

Marcin, John. Democratic committeeman of the 35th ward and city clerk under Mayor Daley.

Metcalfe, Ralph. One of Congressman William L. Dawson's key lieutenants. Was alderman and Democratic committeeman of the 3rd ward. After Dawson's death, was elected to Congress to replace him. Broke with Daley over civil rights.

Nash, Patrick A. Democratic committeeman of the 28th ward. Was founder of the contemporary Democratic machine with Mayor Anton J. Cermak in 1931 and was chairman of the Democratic Cook County Central Committee until his death in 1943.

Ogilvie, Richard B. Republican governor of Illinois from 1969–1973.

Percy, Charles H. Republican United States senator from Illinois from 1967 until the present.

Romano, Sam. Key figure in Alderman Vito Marzullo's 25th ward and a Democratic state senator.

Rostenkowski, Daniel. Democratic committeeman of the 32nd ward. Is also a congressman and head of the Illinois Democratic congressional delegation.

Sain, Harry. Alderman of the 27th ward.

Shapiro, Samuel. Was Democratic lieutenant governor of Illinois and succeeded to the governorship in 1968, when Governor Otto Kerner resigned. Lost to Republican Richard B. Ogilvie in the 1968 gubernatorial race.

Stevenson, Adlai II. Democratic governor of Illinois from 1949–1953. Ran for president of the United States as the Democratic candidate in 1952 and 1956, but lost to Eisenhower both times. Served as ambassador to the United Nations under President John F. Kennedy.

Stratton, William G. Republican governor of Illinois from 1953–1961.

Thompson, James R. Republican governor of Illinois from 1977 to the present.

Thompson, William Hale (Big Bill). Republican mayor of Chicago from 1915–1923 and 1927–1931.

Touhy, John. Democratic committeeman of the 27th ward.